The author as a young man.

EDWARDIAN CHISLEHURST

Memories of the Village Baker

Arthur Battle

MERESBOROUGH BOOKS

Published by Meresborough Books, 17 Station Road, Rainham, Kent. ME8 7RS.

Meresborough Books is a specialist publisher of books on Kent and the monthly magazine 'Bygone Kent', founded in 1979. They also own the Rainham Bookshop, Kent's largest independent bookshop, 17-25 Station Road, Rainham, Kent. For more information visit their website www.rainhambookshop.co.uk.

ISBN 0948193 433

Printed by Lanes Limited, Broadstairs, Kent.

CONTENTS

Prior to his death the author repeatedly stated that Rosemary, his daughter, had not received due recognition for her contribution in writing and illustrating the book. He added that should there be a reprint the omission should be rectified. In this reprint his wishes are being fulfilled.

FOREWORD

In the writing of this book my wish has always been to give others a glimpse of the local past which has now taken a legitimate place in our social history. Important events and the famous are already well documented, but we seldom take into account how the ordinary citizen fits into the larger picture. Each small village and town makes a contribution indirectly to world events and Chislehurst is no exception. By illuminating our village during the Edwardian era I hope to bring alive some of the spirit of that age. Hardworking, industrious, thrifty, patriotic, insular and parochial are some of the adjectives to describe the villagers of that time. Far, far removed from how I would comment on life here today. I do not infer we were in any way superior in those days, only different. It is that difference which proves to be so interesting.

I would like to thank so many people for their kind help and encouragement which made this book possible. I shall always cherish the goodwill which this project has engendered and would particularly like to show my appreciation of Lord Willis, Messrs John Bone, Reg Browning, Michael Cooling, George Cully, Geoff Goemans, Robert Head, Rex Pierce, Gordon Hodsdon, Brendon McGurran, Mrs W. Hall and Mrs Sheila Twigg.

I have also drawn on 'The History of Chislehurst' by Beckwith, Webb and Miller, 'Imperial Chislehurst' by Mr T.A. Bushell, 'Patchwork of the History of Chislehurst' by Dorothy McCall and 'In Trust for Chislehurst' by Mr Clifford L. Platt, MBE MA.

The shop and bakery where I was born at Deptford. My elder brother and sister-in-law at the door.

THE BEGINNING

Wandering the common daily with my dog at the sedate pace of an early nonagenarian, and surrounded by numerous reminders of the past, memories and ghosts enter my mind unbidden and engulf my thoughts. It occurred to me that I had lived through the reigns of six monarchs and witnessed more rapid changes than the world had hitherto seen. From the interest of social history it could be worthwhile committing my day dreams to paper. I am confining my memories to the Edwardian era in an attempt to create a picture of Chislehurst in a specific period of time.

I was born in Deptford in 1898, the place where once our ancient naval ships were built in sturdy English oak. The Pett family were known for generations as ship builders and naval commissioners from the time of Henry VIII until Charles II. They leased locally a 'sappy oak wood' for this purpose. Petts Wood is named from this family and it is only recently the apostrophe was dropped from the Petts.

At this time the docks both sides of the river were teeming with activity. Cranes with drooped heads like medieval dragons lined the waterfront waiting to unload cargoes from all over the world. In one day it was recorded that 121 ships arrived in the Pool manned by 1,387 seamen with a registered tonnage of 29,699 tons. Stacked warehouses and ships bordered the river displaying overwhelming wonders of wealth which reflected the stimulus and reward of men who made London the jewel of world trade and commerce. Clippers from the East and brigs from the West disgorged cargoes of tea, rice, rubber, sugar, tobacco and wheat for the adjacent factories and mills. It was across the river the East Indiamen came and where the Great Eastern, the first ironclad, was built. Even in my time dreadnoughts were constructed and launched into the Thames.

Deptford was often shrouded in fog and heavily polluted with industrial waste. Endless smoke spiralled upwards from a multitude of soot blackened factory stacks bearing grime which fell to earth insinuating its filth into every crack and crevice. Row upon row of houses, back to back, gave forth their share of coal produced soot through an army of squat terracotta chimneys. Here lived the working class amid the bustling docks and factories.

Grey cobbled streets echoed to the sound of clopping horses hooves, the rattle of iron bound wheels and the cries of playing children. Away to the main road the clang and drone of trams could be faintly heard. Poverty abounded, but in the main people did their best to maintain 'cleanliness and respectability', two great Victorian ideals. Starched lace curtains hung at the windows filtering the light into the crowded rooms behind. Steps and

My father, James Abraham Battle

My mother, Isabel Battle

window sills whitened with hearthstone contrasted with the unattractive yellow-grey London bricks. Pale women, abundant hair imprisoned with ferocious hairpins, stood in doorways chatting with neighbours and passers-by. Sleeves rolled up in a business like manner betrayed the fact they had only stopped for a moment during the daily round of chores. Dark dresses were worn long, covered with an equally long white apron. It was the aim of every family to be independent, with all that word implies, but in times of stress neighbours could be relied upon to rally round and lend support where needed.

The night watchman filled the dusk with the familiar chant 'Parrst nine o'clock' and waited for a lighterman to ask for a call in the morning. Placards told of the war in South Africa and pawn shops were as numerous as taverns. Along the road the music hall gave some colour and glamour to lives otherwise filled with long hours of work and thankful nights of sleep. 'Soldiers of the Queen' and 'Goodbye Dolly I must leave you' aroused patriotism and wild cheering. Woe betide anyone who put in a good word for President Kruger. Marie Lloyd swayed her ample hips across the brightly lit stage to the latest tunes and outrageous lyrics, taking the audience with her. Harry Champion singing 'Any Old Iron' and Sir Harry Lauder were other favourites of whom the crowd never tired. Any lack of talent by some of the artistes was amply compensated by an excess of humour, vitality and general goodwill all round.

My father, James, was brought up by his grandmother on a small farm in Suffolk and did not come to London to join his mother and stepfather until he was six years old. Grandpa Wright worked on the cranes in the victualling yards and brought home a modest wage. Young James attended the elementary school at Clifton Road where he proved to be a conscientious and diligent pupil, collecting many prizes for good progress, punctuality and attendance. He rose early in the mornings to clean the steps of some big houses in Jerningham Road before school, for which he received the princely sum of 6d per week. He knew from an early age that rewards were only to be achieved by effort and hard work. Leaving school at the age of fourteen he found a job as a delivery man for Nevils, the bakers. Loaded with carefully packed bread and bushels of flour he set off daily for Peckham, Brockley, New Cross and Lewisham with a horse drawn van. Having a good appearance, pleasant manner and a great determination to improve his position, he soon became very popular with his customers. One in particular, a Miss Isabella Johnson, who was housemaid to a family in Lewisham, was impressed with this gentlemanly, attentive young man. Fresh rolls, still warm from the oven, were delivered to her each morning before 7 am. Other delicacies soon followed.

She also had endured a hard childhood. Her mother died of tuberculosis at the early age of thirty-five leaving seven children, two by a previous marriage. Isabella's father, a short stocky very bald man, was given to periodic bouts of drinking. They lived in the military town of Aldershot and he maintained his family by buying and selling anything that came his way — an orchard of fruit, the contents of a house or a few tons of coke, the deal to be celebrated to excess in the local tavern and followed by days of remorse and reparation. Tired of this life of continual turmoil and uncertainty, Isabella left the Dame's school at the age of twelve, made her way to London and found a housemaid situation in Lewisham with an excellent master and mistress with five children. Tiny by any standards, she made up for her diminutive stature by boundless spirit and energy. She also had ambitions for the future so it was not long before the young couple were married at the age of twenty on twenty-three shillings per week. They lived for a while in furnished rooms at Herne Hill and made many wonderful plans for the future.

Old Mr Hawkins, who owned a bakery in Pagnell Street, New Cross, had no family and took kindly to young James who often came at weekends and evenings to help him in the business. The extra money was a wonderful boost to their modest income and with care and thrift managed, even with the arrival of their first child, Stanley. After a few years the couple were allowed to take over the business for a small sum on mortgage, when Mr Hawkins retired.

The accommodation was small, especially for a fast growing family. The shop sold bread, flour, broken biscuits and Peak Frean's cakes. Peak's

Myself and my two sisters, Dorothy and Tessa

factory was a short distance away in Bermondsey and kept the shop supplied with biscuits stacked in large square tins from which they were weighed when needed. An enormous set of scales with a gilded wheatsheaf at the centre was used to weigh each loaf at two or four pounds. Any discrepancy was made up with 'make weight', a slice from another loaf. A set of brass weights from ¼ oz to 7 lb gleamed brightly in military precision on the marble topped counter. From time to time an official called from the Weights and Measures Department to test the authenticity of the weights. Small pieces of lead were added on the underside of the weight if found to be lighter than was indicated. The date of the check was stamped underneath to prove you were within the law. For customers who wanted a chat there were two bentwood chairs for their convenience. The black and white tiled linoleum was clean but worn and curling at the edges. This completed the furnishings. Above was a lamp on a brass bracket. Gas hissed through a white mantle illuminating the highly polished till containing farthings, half-pennies, pennies, silver 3d pieces, shillings, florins and half crowns. Occasionally there was a crown piece but a sovereign was seldom seen with bread at 2¼d per loaf and cakes seven for 6d.

Over the front window proud outlined print proclaimed 'James Battle and Son'. Adorning the brick wall was an advertisement for the health giving properties of Daren bread, one of the many varieties of brown bread available. If a company was allowed to advertise their particular commodity, the delivery vans, carts and barrows were painted by them at a discount. These solid vehicles stood in the road packed with cottage loaves, coburgs and bloomers, all oven bottomed bread, waiting for delivery to the surrounding area.

There was a small general store next door. It sold everything and had a wonderful smell: a conglomeration of soap, bacon, rope, paraffin and tobacco. I loved being sent on errands to this Aladdin's cave and gazed with yearning at the humbugs and sticks of liquorice. Behind the counter in a mahogany cabinet were earthenware jars of tobacco labelled with gilt and black letters. It was not the run-of-the-mill packets of tobacco but tobacco for the connoisseur to be savoured and enjoyed by the favoured few. Periodicals were neatly arranged to show their titles and were scattered with coins of payment when the shopkeeper was temporarily absent. There were the Family Herald, Bow Bells, Jack Harkaway and the Boys Own Paper. Cassels Popular Educator and some controversial literature were pushed to the rear, together with a pile of Penny Poets. Displayed in the window was a dish of Nankin ware which contained an assortment of carved teeth of sperm whales, each etched with a different ship. I envied the boy who rushed in, sure of what he wanted, took Ally Slopers Half Holiday and left his penny, whilst I stood, still hesitating at the counter.

Sulphurous fumes from the bakery furnace often filtered through to our parlour causing my sister, Dorothy, to cough incessantly. Sydney, the second child, died in infancy and Hilda, Dorothy and I had arrived within two and a half years of each other. It was inevitable that Hilda, the eldest girl, was involved with helping my mother in the home so it was Dorothy, fourteen months older than myself, who was my constant companion. After work was done we were allowed to climb into the van and play 'Beat Your Neighbour'. Sitting on a pile of flour sacks with the doors pulled almost closed we were in a world of our own. Behind the oven in the back yard thousands of black beetles fought for a place of warmth and comfort on the bricks and mortar of the oven, undeterred by the rattle and roar of the steam engines as they crossed the bridge behind the house.

Each day we visited Granny Wright who lived in a nearby street. I now realise she would be considered to be an agoraphobic as she never left the house, viewing the world over the aspidistra, behind lace curtains. The terrace cottage in which she lived was humble but immaculate. My sister and I were sent with our household scraps for her chickens, which scratched about happily in the back garden. She was a strange old lady, appearing to be much older than her years. I was rather nervous of her with her quaint ways and sayings. 'Smell your cheese and eat your bread' she would intone when giving us a morsel. I probably missed the twinkle in her eye as she said it. Life was confined to basics and nothing was ever wasted.

To reach Granny's house we passed a soap factory and tannery. The smell was indescribable. I never accustomed myself to the stench, running past as fast as possible holding my nose with one hand and the chicken pieces in the other. Here we often encountered the cats-meat man calling out his wares and holding long strings on which unidentifiable morsels were impaled. Hopeful strays trailed behind at a respectable distance eyeing the swinging meat which swished tantalisingly close to their sensitive nostrils.

On Sundays the muffin man rang his bell around the streets to announce his presence and to advertise his goods. He carried on his head a tray piled high with muffins and crumpets and covered with a green baize cloth. Sunday was also the day for the ladies who sold watercress. With aprons pinned up from their skirts they called from house to house offering the fresh watercress from deep wicker baskets. Sunday tea was never complete without the prior visit of the fish man with winkles, whelks, shrimps and prawns which were sold by the pint.

Belle and James had been repeatedly warned by the doctor that they would be unlikely to raise Dorothy, with the disadvantage of a weak chest, in the existing environment. The horror of her mother's early death and that of her own little Sydney filled Belle with dismay. Not for the first time the couple considered moving into the country.

A representative from the yeast company happened to mention a small business for sale in Chislehurst. It had long been neglected, being run by a very old lady and her daughter. The living was small but in his opinion it had potential and the property was large enough for the growing brood.

Already we had happy memories of Chislehurst, having made exciting excursions to the commons on fine Bank Holidays. For such a day the horse was saddled and, with a substantial picnic packed in a baker's basket, we set off in the van. We played cricket, fished in the ponds, looked for scarlet toadstools and identified birds, returning home healthily tired after a day in the country. How wonderful, we thought, to live there permanently. Plans were immediately put into action to make this a reality.

My eldest brother, Stanley, attended the Roan School where he had won a scholarship. He was overjoyed to leave school at the age of fourteen and be left in charge of the shop and bakery at New Cross. He was responsible for the production and delivery of bread, employing three bakers, delivery-men and numerous part-time shop staff. The weekly takings were brought to Chislehurst every Sunday when he came to dinner, and for his mother to check if his neck and ears were clean!

The goodwill of the Chislehurst shop was purchased in the spring of 1904 but the family did not move in until September of that year. A horse drawn brake from Peppercorns of Peckham conveyed us lock, stock and barrel from Deptford to Chislehurst. It was a mellow, golden afternoon in early autumn when we arrived at our new home on Royal Parade, opposite the Bull's Head. Our excitement was uncontrollable as we spilled out from the loaded brake and ran across Bull Lane (then Church Lane) to the wide grass verge in front of St Meddens. This was an ancient house which was later destroyed by fire. Here was an immense hollow elm with a prodigious girth in which to play and hide and behind a magnificent row of chestnut trees. The hollow elm, although dead many years, is still to be seen today.

Some years before the village stocks had stood upon this green. Perhaps the imprisoned victims were grateful for the shade of that great elm when the sun's rays would have shone unmercifully on their unprotected heads. St Meddens claimed some memorable residents, amongst them Lord George Lennox.

Exploring and staking out our claim to the green we were rudely inter-rupted by some other children of a similar age. They were the children of the butcher across the road who firmly put us in our place as they had played there for years. A compromise was reached and we all used this green near our homes as a safe place for games.

Alas, it took longer to establish the business. Father had his own high standards of quality and morality and would in no way compromise with his conscience. The local traders had to deal with cooks, housekeepers and bailiffs of the big houses and estates. They often demanded remuneration in return for the favour of their custom and dealt with the highest bidder. Also pride prevented a cook from buying that which she considered she could better produce. Expansion was slow and the goodwill only increased with infinite service and care. It was not unusual to deliver four ¼d buns, to be paid for at the end of the month. During my school dinner hour I often

The cottage, Abury, with shop on the left

MY HOME ON ROYAL PARADE

My home on Royal Parade

delivered hot jam tarts to Northwood in Manor Park Road. One fateful day I tripped, smashing the pastry to pieces. I deposited the mangled remains on the kitchen table when the cook's back was turned and fled. My parents duly received a complaint and I had to return and apologise. Sometimes I took hot meat pies to the old ladies who lived in the Governesses Institute, also in Manor Park Road. They supplied their own dishes for the pies to be made and baked in the bakery and conveyed to them ready for lunch.

In 1908 my sister Hilda died of cerebral meningitis and whilst at the funeral our house was burgled. My youngest sister, Tessa, was born the previous year and my mother developed peritonitis from which she nearly died. She was very ill for many weeks in Cray Valley Hospital in Sandy Lane, Foots Cray. My father cycled some sixteen miles to visit her twice a day for eight weeks. One wonders why the Cottage Hospital for Chislehurst was sited in such an inaccessible area. It was a bad year but public sympathy was aroused and from that unhappy time the business steadily grew. Four years later another sister arrived, a Mongol child. This caused even more strain on the family although we loved her dearly.

Our house was timber framed infilled with brick, wattle and daub and could well have witnessed Queen Elizabeth I as she rode by to be entertained at Scadbury by Sir Thomas Walsingham. The remainder of the house and shop were pre-Victorian but the bakery oven was of much older origin, the house having been constructed around it. The 16th century house consisted of the cottage known as Abury and part of the building behind the shop where we lived in my childhood. The cottage was let to bring in extra income. Some bricks recently uncovered revealed the dates 1825 and 1832 together with the initials of the builder, so it is a fair assumption that part of the house is from that date. The thin red Tudor bricks of the cottage could possibly have been made in the brickyards on White Horse Hill. The yard is known to have supplied bricks for the building of the famous tennis court at Hampton Court in the reign of Henry VIII. Abury is reputed to be the oldest complete inhabited cottage in Chislehurst. Unfortunately at some earlier date the timber frame was faced with brick and subsequently covered with rendering and stones. The interior beams, some of massive proportions, were also plastered over at some time but were unexpectedly revealed when a bomb fell in 1940. An enormous lead water tank saved the house from more extensive damage. It was full of water at the time and absorbed much of the blast, although everywhere was drenched.

It was probably built originally as a hall house, one big room with a hole in the roof to let out the smoke from a fire in the middle of the room. Later flooring and stairs were added and separate rooms were formed. During part of its chequered life the plot contained a farm and later a small-holding. Evidence of this was discovered when animal bones and teeth were found in the garden and boars tusks under some floor boards. There were several very ancient apple trees and old cattle stalls and stables.

17

The cottage interior

The walk-in pantry had marble topped shelves and a brick floor angled towards a soak away in the corner. Due to its size it probably did service as a dairy. The old kitchen range provided the cooking facilities. These wonderful stoves were the mainstay of the house and although there was much hard work to burnish the surface with black lead, the uses and comfort derived were immense. There were two ovens fuelled by coal but banked up with cinders and small coal and with the damper shut down the fire would stay in for hours. There was a rack above for heating plates and airing clothes and beneath was a brass tap from which water could be drawn. The hot plate could accommodate six or seven saucepans and also provided a point for heating flat irons when not in use for cooking. The whole family gravitated to the kitchen for that was where mother could be found and it was a natural progression to the stove to warm our chilled fingers and toes. Impossible as it may now seem these stoves cost from £5 15s to £23 10s and were supplied by Messrs Richard and John Slack, 336 Strand, London.

Toast tasted wonderful when cooked before the solid red coals. It was an accomplished technique to impale a slice of bread on the brass prongs of a toasting fork and hold it steady until it browned to perfection. There was always the danger it would fall from the fork into the fire or a sudden chance flame shooting up to cause a soot blackened patch to appear. Our faces became progressively redder as the toast became browner and shone with expectation of the feast to come.

Each room had an open brick fireplace and the windows were fitted with special shutters which pulled up from beneath the window rather than the more usual side to side variety. Fires were not lit in the bedrooms unless there was illness as this was considered unnecessary extravagance.

Access to the bedrooms was by a narrow winding staircase of rough hewn black oak. An even narrower stairway led to the attic bedrooms, the heavy beams of the roof forming the ceiling. Floorboards were at least a foot in width whilst those comprising the ground floor were laid directly on the earth. There were no foundations, the house being built on clay. Damp was endemic as there was no damp course and the draughts were atrocious. Nevertheless the house was cool in summer but correspondingly freezing in the winter.

At night rats and mice and other free boarding residents could be heard scuttling across the ceilings and under floorboards. As children we took no exception to this as it had always been thus. Comforting sounds emanated from the bakery and the forge next door, where farm machinery and other repair jobs were executed as well as the shoeing of horses. A few noisy rodents or hibernating bees buzzing in the walls, therefore, were of no consequence. From these windows we witnessed the sinister approach of Zeppelins during the First World War. Following the River Thames as they navigated their way to London they were sometimes shot down with gunfire. A burning tomb slowly descending with men on board, albeit our enemy, was a dreadful sight.

The cottage garden was confined behind a well shaped and clipped holly hedge. In summer the garden glowed with scarlet geraniums, blue lobelia and white marguerites, always a popular combination for a patriotic generation.

As I mentioned previously, we lived above and behind the shop and bakery. The house was named from the milestone which stood outside. It recorded eleven miles to London Bridge, the next stone being at the apex of Red Hill and White Horse Hill. This measured mile was frequently used during the last war to record a mile of pennies when collecting from the public for War Weapons Weeks.

A heavy oak door led to the kitchen from the garden. As in all homes this room was the hub of the home and was warmed by another kitchen range. A built-in dresser carried blue and white china and occupied one wall. On the top shelf stood Uncle Sam, a metal money box. There was also a deep cupboard which obscured part of the Tudor house. This has since proved to be correct as grand timbers, in perfect condition, have now been exposed. There was a deep stone sink with cold water and a wooden plate rack above.

The visit of the Duchess of Albany in 1913. The milestone outside our house is visible on the right. The Atkins family are watching the progress from the window above the shop.

Hot water was obtained by the kettle constantly simmering on the hob, or a big boil up in the copper on a Monday. The only modern concession was a gas stove which heated water for teas which were served to the public in the shop or outside in the garden.

In these days of automatic washing machines and modern detergents the amount of effort required to accomplish an average family wash is incomprehensible. Water had to be heated by lighting a fire under the copper and most cotton and linen articles were boiled and starched. At Christmastime a copperful of puddings bobbed about in the boiling cauldron exuding the spicy aroma of rich Christmas fare. Hard wearing materials were scrubbed with a stiff brush on a scrubbing board whilst many articles were washed by hand until knuckles became red and sore.

Sheets and pillowcases of cotton or linen were of more generous proportions than their modern counterparts and were mangled through a cast iron contraption with heavy wooden rollers. Hand embroidered pillowcases were part of every bride's trousseau and all linen was marked in Indian ink with the owner's name and date of purchase. Some marked 1921 are still in regular use in my home and bearing the original linen buttons which were used to eliminate breakages during the mangling operations.

Much washing-up was done in our old stone sink, the crockery stacked to drain in the plate rack or on the scrubbed wooden draining board. Bowls were of enamel and easily chipped causing rusty patches. Zinc baths and buckets gleamed with a dull lustre. Stained steel knives were inserted into a knife machine, a powder was added, a handle turned and the cutlery regained its former shine. These old steel knives were much sharper and more efficient than those of stainless steel which came later for general use. The deal kitchen table was scrubbed daily to whiteness, together with the bread board.

Thrift was encouraged, indeed insisted upon. Cocoa tins were polished to silver brightness with Bluebell metal polish and used for a multitude of purposes. Twice a week we children were put to rolling tight spills from newspaper. Another regular job was cutting up squares of newspaper and threading them on a string to use as toilet paper. What a blessing printer's ink was superior and more permanent than that of today! Egg shells were crushed and dug into the garden whilst soapy water from the weekly wash was sprayed on the roses to kill the greenfly.

Beneath the kitchen was a cellar reached by brick steps from outside. Very useful as an air raid shelter during the last war, but in my young days it housed many of the ingredients needed in the bakery. Wooden barrels contained Siberian butter; only butter was used in the confectionery. White wood casks from Patras were full of currants and sultanas, ripened by the Mediterranean sun. Eggs from Holland and Poland were supplied in 'long hundreds' in baskets and packed with straw. Each egg was broken separately and sniffed before being added to a mixing. This was a measure of insurance as a musky egg could ruin an expensive recipe. Jam was bought in 7 lb stone jars and these made excellent utensils for cooking. Steak and kidney, beef tea or oxtail stew slowly simmered in the jars at the entrance to the oven were cooked to perfection. The jars were also useful for preserving runner beans in salt for winter use.

There were almonds from Spain, sugar and treacle from the West Indies and the finest Bigareaux cherries and walnuts from France. A horse drawn van delivered these raw materials once a week from a wholesaler in Peckham. The cellar was cool in all weathers, the temperature remaining constant. At night the moss covered steps leading to the unlit cellar beneath looked dark and foreboding to a young child contrasting sharply with the friendly bustle of the working day. Mother kept her perishable foods there in a 'safe' with perforated holes in the zinc sheets to allow the air to circulate. None of we children cared to visit there at night with a flickering candle. Shadows were menacing and the flame could easily be extinguished by a puff of wind. Occasionally we were enchanted by the brave light of a solitary glow worm but we were more often frightened by huge spiders or a hibernating toad.

The room behind the shop was known as the shop parlour. Here we ate our meals so that Father could keep an eye on the shop at the same time. We were the proud owners of one of the early telephones which was connected to the Bromley exchange of Ravensbourne. Sir Alfred Bowers lived at The

The shop parlour during renovation in 1985

The tea rooms in the garden

Grange, now known as Chesil House, in St Paul's Cray Road, and for one year served as Lord Mayor of London. He refused to have one of these 'new fangled instruments' installed in his own house but made free use of ours. Several times a day we received messages from the Mansion House which were relayed to His Worship and replies taken and transmitted back to the Mansion House. There was another 'phone in the shop and a blue and white enamel notice informed the public 'You may 'phone here'. Chislehurst did not have an exchange of its own until after the Great War and this became the Imperial exchange after the Second World War. Later came the all number codes with which we are now all familiar.

The shop was doubled fronted with a black and white tiled step. I always suspected this was connected with the fact my father was a Freemason but it was never mentioned at home.

The counter of marble topped mahogany ran along one side of the shop. The fittings were of solid brass and plate glass and the walls were panelled. The cost to fit out a shop on that scale at the present time would be astro-nomical. A row of tall glass jars with heavy lids contained a variety of homemade biscuits — Langues du chat, African fingers, butter, wine and almond biscuits, ginger nuts, brandy snaps and long finger meringues. Cakes were displayed on glass dishes and on an attractive set of green hazel leaved plates with lacy paper d'oyleys. All types of bread, brown, white and fancy shapes, were arranged on wooden racks. Rolls in the shape of mini-ature loaves gave a variety, as did croissants, brioche and finger rolls glistening with butter. Here again were the large scales and brass weights. There was also a small scale with a pear shaped scoop for sweets. Large metal boxes, to contain and keep moist sponge cakes and fingers, were housed under the counter, together with a bin for stale or damaged cakes to be sold cheaply or returned to the bakehouse for use as cake crumbs. Toffees and butterscotch were displayed in shallow glass containers as were pastel fondants and chocolate violet creams.

Buns were popular and cheap, many varieties being produced daily: Bath buns bursting with sultanas and covered with crunchy sugar; Chelsea buns curled round with sugar and spice; currant buns for ¼d, ½d or 1d and Swiss buns heavily coated with water icing; rice buns dipped in jam and sugar nibs and piles of fresh doughy scones; Sally Lunns for toasting and special gateaux for parties. Hot cross buns were made fresh on Good Friday and delivered to customers on the same day.

Fresh cream goods such as eclairs, meringues, French cream horns, cherry cream rolls and sandwiches were only produced for weekend trade and were sold on Saturday. Countless other cakes were carefully produced and finished off with fondant or marzipan. Pure ground almonds produced a variety of macaroons. Synthetics or substitutes were never used. In 1911 our cooks won first prize for morning goods (buns, etc) at an exhibition in Islington.

The shop in 1950

My youngest sister, Tessa. Tea rooms on the left

The Drag Hunt passing my home on Royal Parade

Teas were served in the shop and tea garden and tables were in the shop for customers requiring service indoors. Outside in the garden were covered tea rooms. Roses and clematis rambled over the wooden trellis as customers enjoyed their tea in a rural setting. The bicycle had become very popular and groups of cyclists, eager to escape for a short spell from the confines of London, called for refreshment in our garden.

Our sitting room was above the shop and looked across to the Bull's Head and down Royal Parade. From this window my sister and I watched the world go by. Punctually at 8 am each morning the steam wagon from Chislehurst Mineral Waters in Park Road rattled its way to their Sevenoaks depot. It was heavily laden with crates and bottles and made about eight miles per hour. It was the only one of its kind in the area and never failed to turn heads when it puffed and grunted along the dusty road. The homeward speed was somewhat more jaunty returning empty at 4 o'clock in the afternoon.

Occasionally we saw the colourful sight of a drag hunt as it passed through Royal Parade. Uniformed officers from the Royal Military Academy at Woolwich and others mounted on spirited hunters shouted encouragement to each other as they galloped after an energetic pack of hounds. The dogs bayed and barked gaily waving white tipped tails, damp noses following the scent, close to the ground.

The early hours of the morning were punctuated with the creaking carts of the small-holders making their way to the London markets with their

My parents in the garden at the rear of the shop

produce. They came mostly from the St Mary Cray area. All kinds of fruit and vegetables were loaded on the wooden carts in baskets and boxes for transportation. Later in the day they returned, reins held limply in their hands with heads drooped in sleep whilst the horses slowly plodded homewards knowing every step of the way. Licencing hours in the markets were more liberal than the regulated opening times locally and many were sleeping off the soporific effects of the beer and spirits.

In September came the hop pickers en route for the hop gardens further down in the county. All who could took advantage of the extra work, combined with a trip to the country. Even the workhouses emptied as the inmates went hop picking. To most it was a holiday, the only opportunity they had to get away from the grime of London. Although it took a woman and her children six weeks to earn £6 to £8 it provided the families with clothes for the winter. Many passed by our window, the carts overflowing with mattresses, blankets and all manner of cooking gear. They came particularly from the East End; Stepney, Mile End, Stratford, Commercial Road and Whitechapel. The women often wore men's hats and caps and wore thick sacking round their waists as aprons. Some, of course, travelled by special trains put on for the pickers, often hiding the children in sacks or under their skirts to avoid paying the fare. The country folk were appalled at the dirtiness of the Londoners but the extra labour was essential and their presence was endured. Cleanliness was a matter of pride in the country which endowed them with an air of superiority. Despite the Londoners' ability for hard work, their sociability and sense of fun, their language, drunkenness and nits condemned them before the locals.

Beside our living room was a bedroom situated over the bakery oven. It was a delight in the winter as the floor was always warm from the furnace beneath. Conversely, it was most uncomfortable during warm spells. This room was usually designated to the live-in maid whom my parents employed despite their meagre income. She was paid 8s per week plus board and lodging with one half day off per week. There were three other bedrooms and we also boasted an upstairs lavatory. The downstairs bathroom was a misnomer as it had no bath.

Saturday nights were set aside for bathing which took place in the bakehouse, it being the only night of the week when it was not in use. Water was drawn in buckets and put into the oven to warm, eventually being tipped into a white enamel bath. Towels were stacked in the entrance to the oven (the stock) to warm and one by one we were washed. I remember the soft glow of the lamp and the feeling of security and warmth which permeated the old building. Cheeky chirping of discordant crickets resident in the warm bricks punctuated the atmosphere whilst the aroma of baked bread lingered and the smell of primrose soap smarted my nose. Soap was purchased in 18″ long bars which were cut into manageable pieces and stored until hard and dry. New soap was soft and wasteful, too extravagant for

St George's Hall in our garden

My father outside St George's Hall

Another picture of St George's Hall

Robert Brett Smith (back row, left) and the Camden Ringers

careless children to use. Our hair was washed in rain water as it was soft and lathered easily with green soft soap. Copious quantities of water cascaded over our heads until clean and shining. Heads spun and ears tingled with rubbing until the hair was dry. My sister Dorothy had a wealth of deep brown curly hair which tumbled to her waist. After this treatment the hair would snap and fly in all directions, defying the discipline of a brush and comb. My mother heated bricks in the oven and wrapped them in flannel to warm our beds. These were the delightful forebears of the stone and rubber hot water bottles.

At the rear of the garden stood St George's Hall, a small building of wood and used mainly for Primrose League meetings. This organisation was founded by Benjamin Disraeli for the younger members of the Conservative party. My father hired out the hall for meetings, for small catering functions and as committee rooms during elections. Many of our Christmas parties were held there when we entertained large family gatherings. Trestle tables were put up for meals to be removed afterwards for games and dancing, blind man's bluff, oranges and lemons and charades being but a few of the entertainments. Mattresses were hired from Dunns of Bromley and put on the floor for the men whilst the women and children slept indoors.

During the Christmas season ringers gave performances with hand bells in the hall, playing all the favourite carols and tunes. The hall also supplied storage space for apples harvested from the surviving trees from the old farm which still produced a healthy crop from the gnarled and twisted branches. In late autumn the apples were gathered and laid out in rows to test for soundness. If found to be so they were wrapped individually in

Coronation Day, June 22nd 1911. A procession through the village.

Coronation Day, June 22nd 1911. My sister on the horsedrawn float with Rosie and Sybil Atkins.

The famous primrose and green van with Ivan. Note the Bromley 'phone number.

newspaper and stored in wooden boxes until needed. Much to my mother's annoyance an inquisitive mouse would sometimes invade the crates and cause havoc. St George's Hall was destroyed during the last war and never rebuilt.

The stables situated at the rear of the garden housed our horse Ivan. He was ex-military with all the appropriate training. He had been used for tent pegging during his army career and had plenty of spirit. He pulled our four wheeled box cart. It was a magnificent equipage, coach-built by Robinsons of Croydon, in the finest mahogany and painted primrose and green. My father had seen one at a Bakers Exhibition in Islington and would not be satisfied until he owned one himself. Although I was afraid of Ivan, lashing out with his hind legs when I tried to leave the stable, I was inordinately proud of him and the van when I went out on deliveries.

Above the stables was a pigeon loft and below were my Blue Dutch rabbits. These were my hobby. Imagine my sorrow on returning home from the Great War to find them gone. They had fulfilled a useful purpose in view of the food shortages, as the war progressed.

Unlike today, when patriotism seems to be out of fashion, my father would fly a Union Flag in the garden on special occasions like Empire Day, St George's Day and royal birthdays. Everyone owned some bunting which would be strung across Royal Parade and the High Street for coronations, jubilees and other special celebrations.

CORONATION DAY AT CHISLEHURST, JUNE 22⁻ 1911.

Coronation Day, 1911

Father was most particular to protect his cakes from the sun. Too much sun and light melted chocolate and turned perishable goods stale, causing wastage. The afternoon sun was obscured by a striped blind and side blinds which were moved from side to side as the sun moved across the heavens.

A passageway which led from the shop towards the bakery was lined with shelves stacked with plain and self raising flour. Baking powder was sieved three times before being added to the plain flour to make it self raising. The tedious job of filling these bags was usually accomplished in quiet periods. At the end of the passage was a stable door which led into the bakery.

THE BAKERY

The bakehouse was a whitewashed building with a stone floor. When this was recently dismantled the oven and furnace were found to be made up of some thirty thousand bricks. It is more than probable that the present building was built around the oven, it being considerably older than the house itself. A thick metal door opened to reveal a square oven capable of baking two hundred and fifty loaves at one time. It was illuminated by a gas jet on a movable metal arm. The oval topped roof, perhaps two feet deep in the centre sloping to one foot at the sides, comprised seven thousand small red bricks. At the time of construction the crown brick in the centre was the last to be placed in position. The floor of the oven was made of foot square stones on which the uncooked dough directly rested during baking. Over the roof of the oven were square slabs of York stone and the floor above was filled with masonry rubble to act as insulation.

There was a wooden bench for ordinary jobs such as greasing and cleaning tins or sorting and cleaning dried fruit. A marble topped bench for pastry making was under the window which overlooked the garden. The constant coolness of the marble made it ideal for this purpose. Then came the prover, a tall metal cabinet fitted with trays and heated by gas. A container of water placed inside provided steam for proving buns and other yeast goods. There was also a 'trough', a deep container of wood five feet long, three feet wide and three feet deep with a thick wooden lid. It was here 280 lb of flour (a sack) was turned into huge hand made doughs for bread. Flour was tipped through a calico hopper from the loft above into the trough below.

The flour was delivered from the millers each week. Contracts were often drawn up for a year's supply at a constant price, or could be ordered according to the fluctuating cost. It came from Keyes of Dartford, Mark Mayhew, Canon and Gaze of Erith or the Sunflower Mills at Deptford. A wagon drawn by three dray horses lumbered up to the back gate, a ladder was placed up to the flour loft and the men carried each 280 lb bag of flour resting on their backs up the ladder to the loft above. Their only protection was a split hessian sack worn on the head and hanging over the shoulders. One wonders what the trade union attitude would be now to this practice. Later Foden steam wagons fuelled by coal were employed in place of horses.

All our bread was made manually, we had no machines. At 8.30 pm the flour was tipped into the trough. A sack of flour took 1 lb of yeast and salt and fourteen to sixteen gallons of water according to the type of flour. The

The old oven during demolition, showing the door, furnace and prover below

Ground floor housed the bakery, the area above contained the flour loft. The oven was situated behind the iron staircase.

Back door of bakery

flour and salt were put at one end, the water and yeast at the other. Gradually the two were combined, the dough becoming stiffer and tighter. It was 'cut back' three times in order to clear the dough and to ensure that it was thoroughly mixed. A wooden wedge was fixed to keep the dough in position and left overnight until 4 am. By then the lid of the trough was pushed up with fermentation. The strength of the rising dough was sufficient to lift a sleeping man lying on the lid and tip him on to the floor. This was a most efficient method of rousing him. Potatoes were often used in bread making, giving it a delightful flavour and improving the keeping quality. The vegetables were washed and cooked in their skins and forced through a wooden sieve into a wooden tub, leaving the waste behind. A proportion was added to the flour when making the dough, ensuring a moist crumb and a crisp crust.

The air was then knocked out of the dough, which was turned again and left to recover. The weight to lift was considerable. At this time of waiting I made cocoa for myself and rum and milk for my father. After a short break the dough was cut up and scaled off at 4 lb 4 oz, 2 lb 2 oz and 1 lb 1 oz, the extra ounces allowed for moisture loss during baking. The 4 lb loaf was known as a quarten but it is not made these days. Each loaf was hand moulded into round balls of dough. This is called 'handing up'. Tins were greased and the dough moulded into various shapes.

My father and sister dressed for the Coronation Day Celebrations June 22nd 1911

Meanwhile the furnace had been lit with wood and paper and coal added to get a roaring fire. When this stage was reached the damper was shut down and twenty minutes later the oven would be ready for use. Only experience provided the necessary skill to obtain the best from the oven. A practised eye could at a glance judge what a thermometer now tells us. A piece of sacking on the end of a pole was dipped in water. This was quickly flashed around the oven to clear away any soot. If the atmosphere in the oven was clear it was hot; if very clear it was too hot and had to be left longer before use.

The early loaves first moulded would now be ready for baking and the oven was 'set'. This was done with three different sized peels; long poles with flat ends on which the dough was placed in position for baking. A large peel took four loaves at a time and the smallest set single loaves in place. Tin loaves were set all round the 'search' (the side of the oven) and the centre was used for floor baked bread. An iron block full of water provided the steam, the ashes from the furnace falling below into a pit.

The afterbake followed, the oven being filled with cottage loaves, coburgs, fancy bricks and milk bread. A little more coal on the furnace and more bread was baked, thirty-five minutes for each batch. This was followed by buns ready for the early morning. A few more shovels of coal to revive the oven for puff pastry goods, jam puffs, Banbury and Eccles cakes, apple turnovers, vol-au-vents and sausage rolls. Gradually the oven was allowed to cool and the production of cakes geared to its heat — cakes, macaroons and lastly the coolest oven for meringues.

The only concession to automation was a metal drum in which eggs and sugar were whisked for sponges. A handle at the side activated a whisk inside until the sponge thickened. Large eclair mixings were all done by hand. With Royal icing and meringues it could be difficult and time consuming to achieve the right consistency, cramping and crippling the muscles.

One of our cooks lived in Adelaide Road, Chislehurst. His wife, never knowing at what time her husband would return for his meal, sent their terrier Nip across the common to his master. The appropriate time was written on a piece of paper fixed to his collar and he came back with the relevant information. A novel method of communication before the general use of the telephone.

Wages were low, bakers earning 28s per week and cooks 32s. The bakers commenced work at 4 am and made the bread, later going out on delivery, perhaps getting home about 5 pm. They returned at 8.30 pm to make the doughs, finally finishing at 10 pm. Some of the cooks were extremely skilled and had served a long apprenticeship.

Quite a proportion of our business income was derived from outside catering and it is of some interest to note the content and costs of menus of seventy to eighty years ago. For example, an estimate for the Coronation Committee for George V is as follows:

Cold Roast Beef
Ham
Lamb or Boiled Mutton   2s 3d per
Hot Potatoes   head
Salad   Not less
Butter and Cheese   than 100
Fruit Tarts and Pastries
Custards and Blancmanges
Tea

These prices are inclusive of attendance, crocks, cutlery, linen, tables and chairs.

A tea on the common for Miss Sophie Tiarks —

White and brown bread and butter
Scones and buns buttered
Cakes, fancy biscuits of a good assortment
Genoa cake, Seed cake
Jam sandwiches and Swiss rolls
     Inclusive price of £7 10s for 200 persons (£7.50p)

A typical estimate for a dance —

Assorted sandwiches, ham, tongue, foie gras
Chicken and lobster patties, lobster croquettes
Veal and ham rissoles
Lemon jelly and Maraschino cream
Fruit jelly — Rose cream — Coffee cream
Charlotte Russe — Fruit salad
Homemade strawberry and vanilla ices
Still lemonade — Coffee
Fruit and fancy biscuits — Assorted fancy cakes
     2s 6d per head for 200 — 2s 9d for 150,
     inclusive of everything necessary for the table and service.

A Garden Party Tea —

Tea — Coffee — Still lemonade
Ham sandwiches — Sausage rolls
Assorted pastries — Fancy cakes — Genoa cake
Jam sandwiches — Fancy biscuits
     £3 for 50 guests
     1s per head for all over that number. All inclusive.

Win Browning (next to girl in dark dress) taking part in a skipping race on Church Row, Coronation Day, June 22nd 1911

We provided the teas for the Ladies Tennis Club at Camden House. Father cut the bread and butter so thin it rolled up as a swiss roll. Mother made the cucumber sandwiches of thin brown bread and packed the cakes. There was always a special gateau decorated with some reference to the game of tennis, in pale green and white icing. I carried these items, together with a can containing a quart of milk for the teas, every Saturday afternoon to Camden House.

Sometimes customers were reluctant to settle outstanding accounts, our patience and tact being stretched to the limit. One such example is as follows, a letter written to a titled lady by my father.

May 20th 1912

Dear Madam,

In answer to yours of this morning disputing the account of 2s (10p), the goods delivered were ordered by your ladyship, the order being taken by myself as at that time I had no assistant. The goods sent were 9d Sponge Cakes, 6d Rolls, 5d Biscuits on June 14th 1910. On June 6th, 7th and 9th a 1d loaf was sent on each day to your ladyship's order. This being the sixth application for the account I hope your ladyship will not allow the whole amount to be swallowed up in postage.

I am, Madam,

Yours faithfully,

James Battle.

This communication was sent to the London home of her Ladyship in Eaton Square after two years of fruitless application for payment.

I came across another interesting item in the form of a reference for a former employee.

19.3.1911

Dear Madam,

In reply to yours of 15th November Miss . . . was in my employ about 11 months.

We always found her honest but I am sorry to say she would not keep herself tidy enough for shop work.

I could not recommend her to take charge as we could not leave her in the shop without someone to superintend.

She makes a good maid for the house but she is not suitable for business.

I had to complain also that she would not get up in the mornings when called.

Yours faithfully,
James Battle

It was accepted practice for bakers to cook large joints on Sundays for customers who required the service. Rows of sizzling legs of pork and lamb, ribs and sirloins of beef gave off an exquisite aroma from the bakehouse oven when the door was opened.

At Christmas it was the turn of turkeys to be basted and the goose to be browned to a turn. The goose grease was saved as a linament to rub on the chest for colds and congestion. The bowls of dripping were superb, the thick layer of jellified gravy being eagerly sought after to spread generously on our bread.

As well as earning our living, the bakery was useful for drying and airing clothes, bathing, washing hair, cooking the joint, baking a pie for Sunday lunch and cooking kippers and bloaters for tea. As children we played in the flour loft amongst the flour laden cobwebs and watched the cooks at work, unconsciously learning the tricks of the trade. Time came for me to join my sisters at school.

CHILDHOOD

When I was five years old I was sent to the National School which is now St Nicholas Primary School. Mr and Mrs Greenfield were the headmaster and mistress and taught the boys and girls respectively until the age of fourteen. They had two children of their own, Jack and Sylvia, who also attended the school and the family lived in Pendine, the house adjoining. Miss Owen was responsible for the infants class where boys and girls were taught together. Although by that time schooling was compulsory no one seemed concerned if a particular child was needed at home to help with the younger children or to help with seasonal work which supplemented the family income.

There was no school uniform. Little boys wore sailor suits often with lace collars, Norfolk jackets and caps. Always caps, Eton collars affixed with studs, some celluloid, some linen starched and worn on Sundays. Jerseys were commonly worn with knickerbockers. Some had bands at the knee and were tucked into long socks. It was common to see bare chapped knees and chilblained ears in the winter. Black lace-up boots were the order of the day to be polished daily without fail. Copious applications of dubbin kept the weather out and prolonged the life of the leather. Boys, as now, scorned the use of an overcoat even if the family could afford it. They wore instead short thick grey or dark blue jackets commonly called 'bum freezers'. The girls wore longish skirts, very long as they progressed up the school, lots of petticoats of flannel in the winter, long woollen socks and button boots. I was fascinated at the rapidity my sisters could manipulate a buttonhook to fasten fifty buttons. White pinafores, laundered and starched, were worn to school to keep dark serge dresses clean. Lace collars and cuffs were changed regularly to freshen up dresses worn daily. Both sexes wore combinations, usually of cotton or pure wool according to your means. Linen buttons down the front and 'stable doors' at the rear facilitated natural functions. These articles were handed down from brother to sister. The quality was good and if carefully washed were extremely hard wearing.

Infants wrote with chalk on hinged slates but graduated to pencils and finally ink. Fearsome damage could be inflicted with a thwacky ruler and ink soaked pellets. Dire threats of punishment were delivered by parents and teachers alike. Basic subjects were taught, the three Rs, reading, writing and arithmetic complemented with recitations, history and geography with the British Empire well to the fore. Empire Day was commemorated with flag flying and the singing of patriotic songs. After all, were we not the head of the greatest empire the world had ever seen, an empire on which the sun

Empire Day 1909 at the Annunciation School. What a wonderful turnout in costume, particularly in view of much poverty in the area at the time.

never set? On this day we were assembled in the quadrangle and sang the National Anthem, the Old Hundredth and saluted the Union Jack. We were made aware of British action overseas by providing comforts for the wounded soldiers. On June 22nd 1911 the school celebrated the coronation of George V and we were presented with pictures of the King and Queen and a souvenir mug of real china. Each class had their own Union Flag.

The school marked armistice day on November 11th 1918 with due pomp and ceremony. Hardly a family had escaped some bereavement during the four year struggle and there was a mixture of gladness and sorrow as the flags were hoisted before the assembled children in the 'quad'. Here they sang the National Anthem and gave hearty cheers for the King and his ministers, soldiers, sailors and airmen, doctors, nurses, uniformed workers and all who had done their bit for the Great War.

Games were played in the 'pit' which was drained and levelled out in 1907 at the cost of £45. Parents and the school managers provided the money and the children helped with the work to keep the costs down. School feast day was a grand affair with a fête and fancy dress party with a tea provided. Toasts and cheers were raised for the King, the Rector, Princess Royal, etc.

The teaching of nature study was frequently assisted with walks around the common. On one side of the Overflow on rising ground at certain times of the year bumble bees could be observed coming and going to nests underground. If you kept quiet a low hum was clearly audible from these

Children and teacher National School Infants Class 1 1906. Arthur end of middle row right, seated on rocking horse. Fred Hussey middle row 2nd from right, Arthur Hussey middle row 4th from left (their father was coachman at Frognal House). Jack Greenfield front row 2nd from left (son of headmaster and mistress). Dolly Hope front row 5th from right. Douglas Say front row 6th from right. Sybil Atkins front row 5th from left. Nellie Phelps (teacher).

(R. Chapman)

industrious creatures. Before the present strain on the water supply in this area of Chislehurst the Overflow was a magnificent stretch of water. In common with the other ponds in the neighbourhood it was originally created by the excavation of gravel. Situated off Bromley Road it had an old road across the common from Prince Imperial Road to Bromley Road running along its eastern side. The water level rose with the onset of winter rain and overflowed this road to a sunken area of the common behind what is now the War Memorial. This in turn formed another stretch of water and earned the pond its name. At the end of Holbrook Lane there was a smooth flint stone. It was surrounded with the broken remains of snail shells and if you were lucky a hungry blackbird or thrush could be seen cracking open a succulent meal, glancing frequently around to see he was not observed.

Harebells grew in profusion around the Cockpit and there were plenty of delicate wild roses to take home for Mother. We eagerly awaited the ripening of the orange coloured wild raspberry which grew on the common near Webster's pond, and hunted avidly for the exquisitely flavoured wild strawberry.

Pupils and teachers of the National School, 1906. Mrs Greenfield, headmistress, on the left. Dorothy second from left front row and Hilda second from right front row (my sisters). Lily Pentlow middle row 2nd from left. Nell Pentlow front row middle. Olive Bristol middle row 5th from right. Maggie Bristol front row end right. E. Goddard front row 4th from left. Two Capel sisters. Violet Emmens. Maggie Beechy (student teacher) 2nd right. Mrs Greenfield (headmistress).

(R. Chapman)

Old hollow oaks supported animal life at all levels. We often heard the tawny owl hooting to the moonlit sky and wondered what tiny mouse or vole would provide his meal that night. Grey squirrels built dreys for protection from the cold winds and in which to rear their young. Tree sparrows were excellent parents, scolding their young beneath the cool canopy of leaves in the spring. Blue tits gorged on a multitude of caterpillars and migrating birds did not arrive until these grubs had developed, nature continually adapting to the prevailing conditions. Weevils in acorns burrowed into the earth for the winter. Oak apples full of insects, smooth and delicately coloured, decorated the sturdy oaks. Pear and wild cherry trees made a brave show of blossom in the spring, the crab apple causing many an aching tummy to those rash enough to risk their eating. Growing in huge round bunches the mistletoe thrived in the branches of the hospitable oak. Old decaying wood formed host to all kinds of weird shaped fungi.

What a wonderful sight is a buttercup field glowing in the June sunshine. Do children still hold one beneath the chin to see the reflected glory and say 'Do you like butter?'. Watercress flourished in the damp hollows with the marsh marigolds and kingcups. Masses of yellow furze or gorse (or whin) covered the common in gold every spring and early summer. Frequently it was set alight during the hot summer months by the sun heating a piece of broken glass and igniting the tinder dry grass. Most of the common was heathland and was much less wooded than it is today. Heather now no longer covers the soft peat mounds in the autumn, neither does the blue periwinkle twinkle beneath the trees. There are no ox-eyed daisies, purple foxgloves or flaming poppies decorating the hedgerows. Sweet smelling honeysuckle bloomed on many parts of the common whilst deadly night-shade twined its malignant way across brambles and nettles displaying tempting berries. Herbs thrived, the aromatic scent of wild thyme, sage, basil and the pungent smell of horseradish and wild garlic assailed our nostrils on our nature walks. Shy violets, cheeky primroses and graceful bluebells all had their place, even the wild daffodil and hyacinth could be seen and enjoyed.

The gamekeepers on the Scadbury estate reared partridge, pheasant and woodcock for shoots which were held regularly. One of our dogs was shot for straying into the woods disturbing the game. During hard winters snipe, golden plovers and lapwing took refuge in the woods and fields. The large birds which are now so common in this area, such as crow, jay and magpie, were then extremely rare whilst linnets, greenfinches, nightjars and wood-peckers were plentiful. The undulating flight of the handsome green wood-pecker was as distinctive as its laughing 'yaffle' cry. The cuckoo, which has almost disappeared from Chislehurst, was often heard heralding the spring, simultaneously calling from all points of the compass. I associate that idiotic call with the death of my father in 1923. It was during a hot spell in April with the windows flung open. The call of the cuckoo filled the house as my father lay so ill with pneumonia. They seemed to be mocking our sorrow. When someone was seriously ill it was usual practice to spread straw in the road to minimise the noise of cartwheels and to show considera-tion. Similar respect was shown when a funeral cortege passed by: local tradesmen temporarily closed their shops, blinds were drawn and the owner stood bare-headed at the door.

We heard the drumming of the lesser spotted woodpecker in the spring and saw the holes in the lawn which indicated where the green woodpecker thrust his beak for insects and grubs. If all was quiet around the Overflow or Rush Pond you could sometimes be rewarded with a blue flash as a kingfisher dived to the water or scurried for shelter. On securing a wriggling stickleback it was held by the tail and firmly thwacked against a stone to render it senseless before it was swallowed whole. As children on these school trips we usually made too much noise to see this rare and beautiful

An early bus

sight. There were no mallards on the ponds; perhaps there were too many hungry families for them to survive for any length of time.

Carts and trolleys were always great fun and your popularity was assured if you were the owner of such a vehicle. A pair of wheels could be bought for 2d from Julls, the ironmonger next door (now part of the Sydney Garage). It was my ambition to own such an article which led me into dire trouble with my parents.

One morning, when I could hear my mother's voice upstairs occupied with some household task, I looked around to see if my father was about and seeing the coast was clear crept into the kitchen. The object of this nefarious expedition was standing on the top shelf of the dresser, Uncle Sam the metal money box standing twelve inches high with traditional blue coat, top hat and stars with stripes across his waistcoat. We all fed our pennies into Uncle Sam, his appetite was insatiable. Many times I mentally rebelled at being unable to spend my hard earned pocket money but had always eventually acquiesced.

Quickly I climbed on to the table, panic beginning to rise in my breast as I worked frantically at the narrow slit with a pointed knife. With final desperation I delivered the two pennies and hastily replaced Uncle Sam in his niche.

Familiar noises from the bakehouse helped to calm my vaulting heart and before my courage failed me I ran next door and made my purchase. I had already procured a strong wooden box and straightened out some old nails. The trolley had just been completed when my mother's shadow fell across the stable door. She speedily deduced how I had come by this new possession. It was not the sharp smack around my bare knees that I feared and hardly felt, but the cold retribution of my father which would surely follow. The shame of the disclosure to my brother and sisters and the look of disappointment on my father's face caused me to shed tears of hopelessness whilst I waited in my room for my father's step on the stairs.

If there had been a snowfall tobogganing was allowed over the golf course for some, but not for we lesser mortals however. We made a spectacular run down the slope by the huge black poplar (still standing) straight on to Prickend Pond. There was no island in the centre at that time and with a good push and a lot of luck one could reach the further side in one go. Most people owned skates which were made of wood and screwed into the thick leather soles of shoes. Private enterprise boomed as unemployed men jostled for the privilege of providing a chair to lace up boots and fix skates. The ice was kept swept for a few coppers and no one was anti-social enough to throw stones or broken ice on to the surface.

As the original school of St Nicholas in 1836 was viewed as an institution 'for the education of the poor in the principles of the established church' attendance at church was therefore obligatory. Each Thursday the whole school, in an orderly crocodile, crossed to the Parish Church for a special children's service. The path, which can even now be traced across the common, was constructed for this purpose. The children from St Michael's Orphanage adjacent to the school also attended.

When my elder sister Hilda died in 1908 my younger sister and I watched the entire school set out for the church to attend her funeral, Mr and Mrs Greenfield, the headmaster and mistress, having kindly allowed Dorothy and I to stay for a few days at their house at Pendine until after the interrment. Hilda was a good scholar and had recently won a scholarship to Bromley County School which had just opened in Nightingale Lane. Despite the fact that she had been given a senior examination paper in error she did sufficiently well to win a free place.

Sometimes we would walk down to Botany Bay, the curiously named area beyond Hawkwood Lane. Tong Farm of ancient origin was originally Tong Court, now Towncourt which belongs to the manor of that name. We enjoyed the added excitement of walking over the 'three bridges' to Petts Wood, at that time all fields and woods. We were forbidden by our teachers to stand on the bridge when a steam train thundered beneath. Imagine the soot blackened imps who would have returned to school if this had been allowed. Here wild sweetpeas entwined the fence, shaded by maple and sycamore. In the distance the magnificent avenue of limes belonging to Hawkwood House was clearly visible. They are still to be seen by those who walk the three bridges to Petts Wood.

There were several places where the song of the nightingale could always be heard. The sweet melodious sound echoed across the open country from the lime avenue at Camden Place and was plainly heard when walking home

Hawkwood

from the station after the last train. The coppice at the top of Holbrook Lane was another haunt of this plain but sweet toned bird.

All these treasures were to be enjoyed on our doorstep and the children were encouraged to recognise our local flora and fauna and to be familiar with our environment.

'The Pit', as now, was the centre of our games and sports. In my school-days there was a pond situated in one corner, again probably due to the excavation of gravel. No special clothes were worn for games and liberal quantities of mud were spread over our boots and clothes in inclement weather. Cricket and football were the only games played officially, although the setting was used for many other childish games. Many of the girls could wield a useful cricket bat and were much sought after when playing in teams.

Our toys were simple and ran the same crazes that periodically overtake my modern counterparts. Peg tops, brightly painted, were wound up with string on a whip. By various techniques they were thrown spinning to the ground, rotating wildly, whilst their owners whipped and beat them in an effort to keep them spinning.

Boys ran with iron hoops driven by a hook with skids attached. Energetic use wore away the hooks which were repaired at the nearest blacksmith.

Girls had larger hoops which were propelled with sticks. Another favourite was marbles and particularly coveted were the large glass alleys. All cigarettes had cards inside the packet and collections were diligently sought after. Sets varied much in content — famous people, sportsmen, ships, butterflies, kings and queens and wild flowers to name but a few. Some were educational and formed a mini encyclopaedia when pasted into an album with flour and water paste. Any 'doubles' which could not be swapped were balanced on the side of a clenched fist and flicked with the other. Needless to say, the one whose card flew the furthest won the game. Another perennial favourite was hopscotch, the numbers and squares being scored into the earth and dust with a stick.

The big trees under which the children now play at break time were just right for 'Puss puss, do you want a drink of water', a statue type game, looking out from behind to see if you can catch someone moving. The row of white posts by Whinfield were the appropriate height for small boys and girls who leapfrogged with gusto, ripping and tearing petticoats and trousers. Five good sized screws were needed for 'Cherry oggs', another simple game. The screws were used as skittles to be bowled over by cherry stones. This game was seasonal and was played frantically as long as the cherry season lasted. Another seasonal game was conkers and a considerable amount of status could be gained if you had a durable specimen. The life of a conker could be prolonged and enhanced by slow drying in a cool oven and leaving for a week. If used too soon it was brittle and would fall easy prey to the opposition. Everyone had their own theories for hardening off conkers, soaking in vinegar and painting with paraffin were all tried experiments.

One day each summer was reserved for a trip to Hastings or Ramsgate. The latter at that time was the prime fishing port in Kent and was of considerable size and importance. Dozens of fishing boats were moored in the harbour. Provided with sandwiches and a few coppers from our mothers we set off with great expectations from Chislehurst Station. On one such occasion, playing around in the railway carriage, I dropped my money out of the open window. I was appalled and had an instant vision of myself abandoned by my classmates on a strange station platform. After a well deserved rebuke from my teacher there was a quick whip-round amongst my pals and I was solvent once again.

Sunday School was at 2 pm when we were set to learn by heart the collect for the day. At three o'clock we crossed from the school to the church where the Rector gave an address. If there was to be a Christening we were allowed to watch provided we behaved. Attending Sunday School for the first time at the age of five I was taken in the care of an older girl. I was so apprehensive I forgot to remove my cap and one of the teachers wrenched it from my head and threw it to the ground. My ensuing terror rendered me incapable to memorise even the shortest text for the Rector.

My wife's sister, Sybil, as the Good Fairy in 'Red Riding Hood'

"Red Riding Hood" at Chislehurst. 1913.

The full cast of 'Red Riding Hood' performed at the Village Hall

50

Sunday School outing to Ramsgate for the day. The line of children stretched the length of the High Street.

Sunday School was well attended and consisted of eight classes. The Misses Sophie and Agnes Tiarks, Gibson, Webb and Glassop were but a few of the stalwarts who maintained the Sunday School at a high level for many years.

Each Christmas the Sunday School arranged a visit to the Pantomime in London, usually at the Lyceum Theatre. The children from St Michael's Orphanage joined us and the choirboys were always included. After the show we were taken to Gatti's for a meal. It was all a great adventure.

We gave an annual show for our parents in the Village Hall at Christmas, putting on simple sketches and singing carols. Silent Night, In the Deep Midwinter and Once in Royal David's City echoed around the high pitched timber roof with our childish treble voices.

The Village Hall was built in 1867 in the style of a Swiss chalet, the steep roof reaching nearly to the ground and surmounted by a spirelet. Unfortunately it was burned to the ground in 1976 to be replaced by a much smaller building of wood. The old hall was a centre of social life in the village. Plays, concerts, sales of work, fairs, lectures, magic lantern shows, whist drives and meetings of all kinds drew together all strata of society. There was a sale of work in December and a small charge was made for admission to the cornucopia of goodies assembled by the local populace. Private individuals made homemade jams, jellies, curds and cakes. Laces and linens, babies, childrens and adults clothes beautifully hand worked

51

The Village Hall, where so much of our social life took place

Miss Sophie Tiarks launching the Boy Scouts punt on Prickend Pond. This attracted a great deal of interest as can be seen by the crowd of bystanders. Chislehurst Boy Scouts were one of the first groups in the country and were extremely successful.

were for sale. Embroidery and smocking were greatly favoured, as were anti-macassars and hand-worked samplers. Local traders were prevailed upon to give generously of their own particular produce — joints of meat, poultry, a brace of pheasants and a cooked ham, cartons of golden rich cream, honey from local hives, fancy bread and still more cakes. Fruit and vegetables were in abundance, potted plants and wreaths of holly, muscatels and almonds and round fat Christmas puddings jostling together in snowy cloths.

Miss Sophie Tiarks provided the money to build the Village Hall Annexe where she ran, unaided, a boys club for 25 years. She also presented a rowing boat to the Scouts and this she launched with due ceremony into Prickend Pond. It was here she could frequently be seen teaching the boys to row and manoeuvre the small craft amid much splashing and laughter.

The Cottagers Vegetable and Flower Show dates from 1841 and was held annually in the Rectory meadow, now Walnut Tree Close. A marquee housed the exhibits and a high standard of produce was reached. Many of those competing were professional gardeners from the big houses. They had every facility with heated greenhouses etc, to help them produce good quality fruit, vegetables and flowers although the humble allotment owner was a creditable competitor. The ladies displayed their artistic ability with flower arrangements and children ran races such as egg and spoon, obstacle and relay. Pageants were usually performed by the children and some historical interest, the landing of St Augustine in England bringing Christianity to these shores or the knighting of Sir Walter Raleigh by Queen Elizabeth. Bunting was hung around from tree to tree and it mattered not which nations' flags were flown as long as the Union Jack was predominant.

For ten years I was a choirboy at St Nicholas Church and was a server until I entered the Army in 1917 at the age of 19. Choirboys earned £3 per quarter and 10s extra for weddings and funerals. We attended three choir practices per week, Monday and Wednesday 6.30 pm until 7.30 pm and Friday 6.30 pm until 9.30 pm. It was a large choir by today's standards. The boys arrived at 6.30 pm to practice alone before the men who came later. Bass, tenors, altos and sopranos were trained by Mr Hodsall who was organist as well as choir master. 'Tommy' Atkins, the butcher on Royal Parade, had a fine voice. His throat was always well lubricated at the Bulls Head before he hurried, late, into the choir stalls straightening his tie and running a hand through his thick blond hair.

On special occasions Arthur Melville came from the St Paul's Cathedral choir to sing the Easter Anthem. My first solo was 'See amid the winter snow', my nervous treble rising through the evergreen decorated church. Christmas candles poured a soft illumination throughout the ancient nave, warming the rich timber screen and throwing figures into deep relief. The other server, Billy Steptoe, and myself enjoyed the seasonal processions holding the Rector's cope. Billy and I 'took the King's shilling' together at

A Pageant in the Rectory Meadow 'The Bringing of Christianity to England by Saint Augustine'. My sister and myself took part.

A view of the High Street taken from the roof of Coolings shop, 39 High Street. The Bank Holiday coconut shies are on the right.

Woolwich in 1917. He was one of the many who fell in the Great War. Sadly his brother was killed and another seriously wounded. A commemorative window to Billy was placed over the priest's door in the chancel.

At weddings the bride was met by the clergy at the west door of the church on a red carpet and under a red and white striped awning. At funerals the body was received by the Rector at the lych gate and together with the choir was escorted into church.

Prior to Christmas many of the choirboys went singing carols at some of the big houses. Well scrubbed and with hair brushed flat we presented ourselves at the front door, a rare privilege. Tradesmen always, always, used the rear entrance leaving the horse and van in the road at the end of often long drives.

Pulling off our caps we rang the bell and heard it echo through the vast hall and disappear into the depths below. The door was opened by a uniformed parlour maid in a dark dress with a white frilly apron and cap. We would explain we were choirboys from St Nicholas and would the master and mistress care to hear some carols. Usually we were ushered into the drawingroom where the family were drawn up before a roaring fire. Thick exotic carpets covered the floors and heavily fringed silk curtains draped the long windows. Gilt framed oil paintings vied for space on the panelled walls and tapestry covered the comfortable chairs. Draught created by the closing door caused the crystals to jingle in the chandeliers which hung from the heavily decorated plaster ceiling. After much throat clearing we sang the most popular of the old carols and any others which were requested. Once finished the parlour maid ushered us out taking us below stairs to the servants hall for a mug of hot orange and a mince-pie. It was not until we were well outside in the moonlight that we counted the spoils of the evening.

The tiny weatherboarded shop adjacent to the Bulls Head was run by Miss Rabbit and her niece Lucy. The shop was minute but sold all manner of goods. Seldom had we money enough for sweets but after carol singing we indulged ourselves with hot cordials or some marsh mallows. There were sherbet dabs and tiger nuts, powdery bon bons and shiny sherbet cushions in many colours.

Chislehurst was agog on Bank Holidays. At Mill Place, the Cockpit and Prickend various stalls and coconut shies were set up. There was intense competition amongst the older boys to see who could accumulate the greatest number of coconuts. Stalls sold minerals and sweets. Grey stone jars kept ginger beer and lemonade delightfully cold whilst the marble and wire tops insured the fizz kept effervescing. Toy windmills were popular with children as were gas filled balloons and toy birds flying on sticks. Many a wail was heard when an unwary child let go of the balloon string which was carried rapidly aloft. Old Mr Boswell walked his donkeys from

The Oddfellows Fete, one of many festivities held annually on the common, 1906

Long queues waiting for the bus on Whit Monday Bank Holiday

Farnborough to provide donkey rides for the children and in the evening there was dancing on the green.

These celebrations were all that remained of the old fair which was held annually on the Wednesday and Thursday of Whitsun week.

A continuous line of stalls and booths was assembled between Camden Court and the Tigers Head, whilst other exhibitions were held about the village green. Jockeys wearing racing colours took part in horse races which started half way down the broad walk leading to the Rush Pond. They skirted the common along by Heathfield, crossed the main road and up the stony path towards St Nicholas School, finishing at the gates of Camden Court (now Camden Close). Many of the old locals refer to this first part of the race course by that name. The Fair gradually deteriorated and our Bank Holiday celebrations became more modest and considerably less rowdy.

Balloons were flown regularly from the Crystal Palace. Enthusiastic balloonists were swept aloft passing overhead and often being carried for many miles on the air currents and prevailing winds. However, through lack of wind they sometimes landed prematurely. The roar of the flames producing the hot air was perfectly audible as they struggled to keep the craft airborne. Sometimes they landed with a bump giving amusement to the pursuing children. Each Thursday brought a firework display at the Palace which could be watched with appreciation from the high ground at the cricket field or from the summit of Summer Hill.

Bank Holidays were a busy time for all our family and staff. Heavy urns filled with water were lifted on to the kitchen stove to provide boiling water for the teas served in our garden. It was not unusual to cater for 200 on a Bank Holiday afternoon. For one shilling (5p) per head customers were provided with a pot of tea, rolls, butter and jam with assorted cakes. Our cooks came in early in the morning to make fresh cakes for the afternoon teas. Cold lunches were supplied, consisting of ham, hot potatoes and salad followed by apple pie and custard. This epicurean delight cost 1s 6d (7½p). Outside our front gate I assembled a makeshift counter with trestles and boards covered with a white tablecloth. Here I sold soft drinks and sweets, hoping to attract trade away from Miss Rabbit's opposite.

Sometimes customers would complain about the price and refuse to pay. I was sent off to find our village 'bobby' but the threat was usually sufficient to make them pay up. It was always possible to find our policeman as his beat and timing were as regular as clockwork. Leaving the Police Station in the High Street he walked across the common to Royal Parade and down St Paul's Cray Road to Manor Park corner, then up Manor Park Road at a leisurely pace past the Governesses Institute (a row of red brick cottages specially built to accommodate retired governesses), skirted the churchyard and on to Church Row, across the common to Kemnal Road and with a measured tread into Ashfield Lane and back to the Police Station.

A trip by my parents in a charabanc

At the time of Harvest Festival many of the gentry ordered wheatsheaves made of bread to decorate the altar. Each ear of corn was cut into shape from the soft dough with a pair of scissors. It was brushed over with hot flour water and salt solution which gave the sheaf a golden finish when baked. The culmination of hours of work was a burnished sheaf of corn to enrich the decoration of one of our local churches for the thanksgiving of harvest.

Dances were held regularly at the Village Hall which was decorated with flowers for the occasion. Evergreens and bunting were arranged by the ladies. Proceedings were all rather formal by today's standards, gentlemen wearing white gloves and asking permission for a partner to dance. Girls usually had a programme of dances and you had to get in quickly as the pretty girls were soon booked up. Waltzing was the favourite whilst much energy was expended in the more robust polka, Lancers and the gallop. American barn dances were beginning to take their place in the programme whilst Highland Reels and Sir Roger de Coverley still featured prominently. Only soft drinks and light refreshments were served. Gas lights provided the illumination for the hall and stage.

Our pleasures were simple and enjoyed within the home. Periodically my parents had a musical evening and whist drive. In an appalling voice my father would render 'Let me like a soldier fall' or 'The Lost Chord' whilst my sister played the piano accompaniment and I turned the music sheets. This was followed by 'Home Sweet Home', the 'Indian Love Lyrics' or patriotic songs which caused a moist eye or two. The lusty singing of 'Onward Christian Soldiers' stirred the zealous breast but 'Ta-ra-ra-boom-de-ay', which swept the country at that time, was considered rather risqué by my parents and was not encouraged. We all loved the current musical comedy songs, so romantic and evocative of that era. The cost of a phonograph record of Adelina Patti was one pound, a considerable sum for those days. Recitations and monologues had to be endured especially if asked to perform ourselves.

Most of my contemporaries suffered the agonies of learning to play the piano, some even enjoying the experience and becoming proficient enough to perform before visitors. Some of the men harmonised and improvised having no inhibitions as to the quality of the voice. For a special treat my father gave a showing of his magic lantern. Images were projected and illuminated on a sheet stretched across the wall bringing to life our fairy stories, animal slides and life in other countries.

These social occasions were improved by refreshments prepared by my mother, sausage rolls, filled vol-au-vents and the inevitable sardine and relish sandwiches. Tea and coffee were acceptable as was a little port or sherry. Taking the stoppers from the decanters and sniffing made me realise what evil smelling liquid adults would drink.

Charades was another favourite pastime. Shrieks of merriment rang out as we dressed up and acted out each syllable of the word. Riddles, conundrums, palindromes and puzzles all helped to keep our minds constructive and alive. The men played cribbage and vingt-et-un and many hours were spent trying to eliminate all the marbles in solitaire.

In 1917 my father ventured into politics and topped the poll at the local elections standing as an Independent. He was rash enough to vote in favour of a bus service on Sundays to run between the Bulls Head and Woolwich. The thought of public transport operating in Chislehurst on the sabbath was not popular and the following week he lost two hundred and fifty customers.

When I reached the age of twelve my parents thought deeply as to which direction my education should take. Seeing I had no particular aptitude for anything academic they thought it advisable for me to attend a different school with a wider curriculum with the hope I might show some promise in one direction or the other.

The old house at Farringtons

The cottage in Bull Lane now called Handley Green

A CONTINUATION OF CHILDHOOD
INCORPORATING PERRY STREET

When I was twelve years old I was sent to Sidcup Hall, an establishment owned by the Farnfield family. Mr Farnfield had six sons all of whom taught at the school. At one time or another they were all in the University football team for Cambridge. Later they ran their own team called the New Crusaders. They attracted some famous opposing clubs, the Corinthian Casuals, the Norsemen and the Civil Service from the Southern Amateur League. Cambridge University regularly contributed players to their team. I thrived on the sport but hated to study.

The school building is now known as Sidcup Place, which is part of the local council office for the Bexley Borough. When I attended meetings for the Food Control during the Second World War my thoughts often drifted back to my days at school, for the council chamber was our old school dining room.

I walked to and from school daily starting off down Bull Lane past Hurstmead and Handley Green. Mr Koenig lived in the latter and kept some handsome horses in the paddock. The house was then known as The Cottage and was built in 1829. It is full of character. Opposite was the Working Mens Club founded in 1867 and rebuilt in the present attractive style by the generous patronage of several wealthy gentlemen of Chislehurst. Billiards and snooker were played and a rifle range, which ran the whole length of the upper floor, provided facilities for those who wished to improve as shots. There was a well kept bowling green at the rear and a generously stocked bar.

Next to the Club were four acres of allotment gardens divided into fifty-two plots each costing 10s (50p) per annum to rent. Thankfully it is still used for this purpose. Due to the quality of the soil and the industry of the plot holders much good produce is still grown today.

Where we now see Hollybrake Close was the fine old Georgian mansion of Hollybrake. It lay well back from the road behind mature trees and a shrubbery with a well weeded gravel drive leading to the front door. It was once a farm, the deeds reaching back to the seventeenth century.
Miss Pentlow, her daughter, lived there and tended a lovely cottage garden until she died at the age of 94 in 1988.

Her father was employed as a forester for Earl Sydney who was then Lord of the Manor of Scadbury and Frognal. She tells a tale full of moral implications.

Farringtons Girls' School, May 1911. The school was being built when I passed on my way to school at Sidcup. Queen Mary opened the extension on June 30th 1925.

One hot summer day Mr Pentlow and another employee of Earl Sydney had been hard at work all morning. Walking up Perry Street an acquaintance invited them into the Sydney Arms for a beer to ease their thirst. After first refusing the invitation they were finally prevailed upon and thankfully entered the inn and ordered a pint. It slipped down their parched throats as nectar and they hastily returned to work. The next day Mr Pentlow was summoned by the Earl who accused him of drinking during his employer's time. He did not deny the charge and said by way of mitigation that it was an unusually hot day. The Earl retorted that at least he was not a liar. His friend had denied all knowledge of the incident and was summarily dismissed from his job.

The building of the five handsome houses on Shepherds Green had just begun and beyond were the Malt House Cottages surrounded by fields. The building of Farringtons School had also just started but the estate was empty and overgrown. After long years of desolation Farringtons land was sold to the Girls College Association on December 17th 1909. A school was opened there on Thursday September 21st 1911. It had been a lovely estate with rhododendrons and blue cedars and had quite a history. Unlike Scadbury there are some pictures and illustrations of this old miniature mansion in its heyday. The design was uniform and elegant, three storeys high with a deep extended cornice. Inside there were beautiful, lofty embossed ceilings and heavily carved doorcases, chimney-pieces and panelled walls, the latter of which were moved to Frognal.

Bluebells at Scadbury, opened to the public on certain occasions

A general view of Chislehurst Common

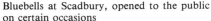

Thomas Farringdon is the first owner of whom there were records. His son fought with the Duke of Marlborough at Ramilles in 1706. The third Thomas was implicated in the disgraceful behaviour in St Nicholas Church when uproar ensued after he and Sir Edward Bettenson thought there was a Jacobite plot and tried to prevent the collection being taken to the altar. Edward himself was a heavy gambler and had to sell oak trees from Scadbury to pay his debts.

Eventually Charles and Mary Townshend, brother and sister, inherited Farringtons and lived there, much loved by the locals, until their deaths in 1799 and 1821 respectively. It was from that time the estate fell into disrepair and was left empty and unused until it was demolished. Before the advent of the school the estate formed the entrance to Scadbury from the south. Tickets were issued by Mr Townshend to the favoured and respectable to walk through his estate to see the bluebells in the spring.

Opposite Farringtons on the left of Perry Street was the mansion of Homewood with a lodge facing the road. The house was pulled down in the twenties and the ground incorporated into the Foxbury estate.

Perry Street is one of the oldest mentioned in Chislehurst's history. It probably derived its name from the close proximity of many pear orchards

Homewood Estate, Perry Street, later incorporated into Foxbury Estate

Homewood, Perry Street

in that area. Beyond Bettrington was the conglomeration of cottages and houses which constituted the hamlet. A corrugated iron church, known rather irreverently as the 'tin tabernacle' fulfilled the spiritual needs of the inhabitants. A curate from St Nicholas Parish Church took services there regularly. The chapel and two tiny cottages stood where we now have Wykham Court. The cottage rent was 2s 6d (12½p) per week. Just this side of the Sydney Arms was Cleverley's cottage and opposite was an ancient timber-framed house with a deep pitched roof. Backed by the dark dense woods of Scadbury it reminded me of the witch's house in Hansel and Gretel.

An advertisement from Kelly's Directory for the Sydney Arms is of some interest:

SYDNEY ARMS HOTEL
11 Miles from London Bridge
GROUNDS — GARDEN — ROSARY

Constitutes one of the prettiest spots in the prettiest county of England — one mile from the railway station. Visitors will find every amusement both indoors and out. Croquet — cricket — bowls — skittles — bagatelle — quoits — swings etc. The cuisine under management of a professed cook will be found perfect in every essential. The wines and spirits are very superior quality carefully selected such as to meet approbation.

Tariff post free on application.

Opposite Ringer's cottage there was a rear lodge to Homewood where the traders came and went. Charlie Ringer owned and ran a laundry and lines of drying clothes flapped in the fresh breeze beside the house. Behind were sheds where women washed and ironed amid the steam and smell of Sunlight soap. They wrestled with cumbersome mangles and heavy loads of washing, pegged out wet clothes and damped down the dry. They boiled sheets and starched collars, put irons on to heat and spat on them to see if they were hot. A bull terrier was tied up outside watching with sly pink eyes and waiting for an opportunity to attack. He had a mighty long chain and it was well to cover your rear when approaching the house. The women sang, chatted and argued as they worked and Charlie's cows chewed the cud in an adjoining meadow waiting to be milked. Chickens and bantams foraged noisily amongst the hollyhocks and golden rod in the garden. In the yard stood two aged carts which were used for the collection and delivery of linen.

The old school house was built by Lady Sydney as a dame's school for the nearby children. It was not in use for that purpose when I travelled Perry Street to school. Opposite was a long brick wall of considerable height which enclosed the kitchen garden of Homewood. There were a few more

Baxter's Forge in Perry Street, now a petrol station

cottages and houses on either side of the road and then there was Beaver-wood Farm (now Hoblands Close). It was mainly a dairy farm and the bull could frequently be heard bellowing from his stall. A massive boar sired endless litters of squealing pink piglets and a self-opinionated cockerel crowed from the summit of a gargantuan dung heap.

The Western Motor Works were under construction. They bear an interesting history which warrants further comment.

At the turn of the century drivers could be prosecuted for driving at eight miles per hour without a man walking twenty yards ahead with a red flag. Cars were not welcomed by all and manufacturers had many problems overcoming prejudice in trying to establish the industry. Roads were poor, there was the speed limit, toll roads and bridges. The complex construction of a successful motor car with all the problems was an immense undertaking. It was a start when in 1905 Parliament repealed the Red Flag Act of 1865.

In 1904 Hugh Marsham Townshend was given a 15 hp Panard by his father as a wedding present. It was supplied by C.S. Rolls of Rolls Royce fame who, incidentally, was a cousin of Mr Hugh. His younger brother, Ferdinand, became particularly enthusiastic over the Panard and in the motor car generally. He started a works of his own in the stables of Frognal House. Two Rolls trained men joined the staff, Mr Arthur Priest and

Mr H.C. Bennett, and the business prospered. There was little passing trade, mechanics being sent to the car owner's house if the car could not be fetched to the works. Spares were carried in the car and blacksmiths, cycle shops and oil shops sold cans of petrol.

Mr C.R. Hodsdon, who began his apprenticeship in 1907, remembered the small granary in the stable yard in Frognal which served as an office. The pride of the establishment was the machine workshop which enabled everything necessary to be produced short of casting a cylinder block. The gleaming coachwork, burnished brass and studded leather were a joy to behold in the Napiers, Daimlers, Rovers, Durracqs, Fiats, Stars, Austins and later Vauxhalls.

It was not long before it became apparent the present premises were not large enough to cope with the volume of work and in 1909 the first purpose built Motor Car Service Station in the country was built in Perry Street. The construction was robust. This was particularly necessary in the roof timbers for the removal of car bodies which was the easiest method of reaching the engine etc. The workshop was illuminated by five Blanchard paraffin incandescent lamps and the works were centrally heated.

The number of motor vehicles nationally increased from 17,860 in 1904 to over 100,000 in 1909. During the Great War the equipment at the Western Motor Works was found to be ideal for the production of shell caps and many hundreds of thousands were manufactured.

In due course cars were converted from petrol to coal gas and to cope with the increased demand a special gas main was installed. Every time these containers were filled the gas pressure dropped and Charlie Ringer's gas operated laundry plant broke down.

Unhappily Mr Ferdinand was killed in the war and the Western Motor Works passed to Mr Hugh who in 1920 handed over to H.C. Bennett. The old Panard was given to Mr Bennett in 1954 and competes annually in the London to Brighton run. She can be seen with her Veteran Car Club inscription proudly displayed amongst her modern less thoroughbred counterparts in the Perry Street Showrooms.

Beyond the garage was Baxter's Forge, one of the many in use in Chislehurst. In the days when 95 per cent of the population travelled by horse-drawn vehicles there was plenty of work shoeing horses and repairing equipment. I can well recall the acrid smell of singeing horse hoof and remember with pleasure watching the blacksmith at work. Evocative sounds, the clanging hammer on anvil, the rush of air from the bellows resurrecting the charcoal embers into a roaring inferno. No child could resist the sizzle of a red hot horseshoe when plunged into water and the ensuing wreaths of steam which encircled the dark interior of the forge. After school a group of children could be seen hanging around the stable door enjoying the eternal scene. I regularly rode our horse barebacked to this forge to have him shod. Opposite was a glass covered workshop where

Frogpool Farm, Perry Street

The thatched cottages in Perry Street, 1905

repairs were carried out on coaches and carriages. Badges and coats of arms were expertly applied by hand to the equipage.

Cadlands is an old house on the opposite side of the road which takes its name from the ancient field on which it was built. It was the last house on the right hand side of the road before Frognal House. Frogpool Farm, originally a seventeenth century farmhouse, stands on the edge of the Chislehurst parish boundary and is in good shape today.

Lastly there were the two thatched cottages over which recently there has been much discussion due to the encroachment of land development and road widening. Watercress was gathered in the nearby stream and sold in the village.

There was no A20, in fact no road at all, only the lane which led to Sidcup. My route was through the 'kissing gate' and across the fields to Sidcup Hall. As I was some distance from home I stayed for school dinners. It was an abomination to me as I disliked the meals provided. To ensure I cleared my plate I was made to sit at the Headmaster's table. I alternated between fear of disapproval if I did not do as I was told or the inevitable heaving of the stomach if I did. As my parents were paying school fees for my attendance it added to my sense of guilt.

An estimate written by my father to the headmaster, S. Farnfield Esquire is as follows:

Royal Parade
Chislehurst
17.1.12

Dear Sir,

Many thanks for your kind offer of today and it affords me great pleasure to give you the following quotations:

White or Brown Bread @ 6d per 4 lb

Flour, Best White @ 36/6 per 280 lb

Slab Cake from 6d per lb

Various buns and scones 28 for 1/- (5p)

All goods to be weighed in at the time of delivery and any short weight to be made up each month.

I am, Sir,
Yours faithfully,
J.A. BATTLE

The fees would have been deducted from the bill as this was usual practice.

The Farnfield family eventually moved from Sidcup Hall to Bickley Hall, a large house and grounds suitable for a school at the top of Chislehurst Road, Bickley. A modern housing estate now occupies the site.

Prickend Bonfire, November 11th 1921

The Bonfire at the Cockpit 1908. This photo includes my sister, Rosie Atkins and myself. The guy is Mrs Pankhurst, the suffragette. Note the Telegraph Boy with his bicycle on the extreme right of the picture.

THE BONFIRE

We had three permanent common keepers who maintained order on the commons in every way. They patrolled the area continuously, particularly at weekends. As now, they were employed by the Chislehurst Commons Conservators. Smartly turned out in brown corduroy breeches and jackets they carried a stick which could be deftly wielded if you misbehaved. Their hats were small brimmed and jaunty and there was a brass CCC badge fixed to the lapel of their coats.

The common was far less wooded than at present and much was covered with gorse, or furze as we called it. Visitors walked in the woods and picnicked on the grass. Riders frequented the paths and local children climbed trees, fished for tadpoles and dammed up streams. In the interests of good husbandry dead wood was cut away and gorse pruned back to promote new growth. Trees had the space to develop and mature in their full glory, majestic in size and strength. After the autumn pruning waste growth would lie about waiting for the children to 'drag' for their local bonfire. Enormous rivalry existed between the inhabitants of Mill Place, Royal Parade and Prickend for the biggest and grandest bonfire. This activity served a dual purpose in clearing the commons of dead growth and creating focal points of social activity on November 5th. The sites used were on the high ground above the Ramblers' Rest, adjacent to the Cockpit and above the pond at Prickend.

This was one evening of the year in which the children were intensely involved. The bonfire towered above them turning them into Lilliputians. Warmly cocooned in woolly hats and scarves, with chilly hands thrust firmly into their pockets, they waited in silent anticipation for the magic moment. For them the bonfire had a special significance. Many long hours of back breaking labour had gone into making theirs the largest and most magnificent in the area. With hoary breath bursting from straining lungs they heaved and pushed the withered branches, shouting encouragement to each other in the cold, crisp winter air. Due to the unpopularity of the Kaiser he was often chosen as the guy and to hold the high position of ridicule. He sat with stiff immobility surmounted with a spiked Prussian helmet.

Moses Lines gave a hock of bacon to the wife of one man represented as a guy to compensate for her embarrassment and discomfiture. Another year it would be Mrs Pankhurst, the suffragette, and sometimes it was the turn of an unpopular 'bobby'.

November 5th 1909. Perhaps this effigy was the one which prompted Mr Lines to give the victim's wife a hock of bacon as a consolation for the indignity of being burnt as a guy.

Within the circle of spectators there was a sudden contraction as the head commons keeper bent to ignite the oil soaked rags at the base of the bonfire. Quickly the lower branches were engulfed by the eager flames. With terrifying rapidity the whole edifice was ablaze making the surrounding area appear black. An observer viewing from a distance could imagine a tableau before him floating in space with minute figures gyrating at the base.

The crowd became hushed at the uncontrollable power unleashed before them and stood back in awe as Kaiser Bill was consumed with hideous grimaces and contortions. Black buttoned boots drummed faster with exhilaration as their owners were stimulated by the sharp staccato cracks of the tinder yielding to the fire. Rockets soared upwards with a whoosh, bursting with exuberance in the inky sky. Catherine wheels turned in fiery revolution sending out showers of sparks raining to the ground. Squibs sent children screaming as they tried to anticipate the direction of their next jumps. Even the most timid child held a sparkler in one hand whilst trying to cover both ears at once with the other hand.

With a roar the centre of the conflagration collapsed, sending myriads of sparks skywards as inverted golden rain.

Suddenly the mood changed from one of expectation to mild disillusion. It had gone and with it the comradeship of those who had built and shared it. All that remained the following morning were some twisted timbers and a pile of smouldering grey ash blowing in the wind.

ROYAL PARADE

Although much of Royal Parade was built in the 1860s it takes its name from the Imperial family of France who lived at Camden Place in the 1870s.

The Bull Inn is marked on the oldest maps of Chislehurst and was at one time connected with Warwick the Kingmaker. It probably derived its sign from the badge of the Nevill family during the Wars of the Roses who were at that time Lord of the Manor in Chislehurst. Always a comfortable inn it comprised letting rooms, a dining room, billiard room, a saloon and public bar. It was then a free house under management. The Adam Room is the oldest part of the present building.

Stabling at the side and rear of the inn was let to Fields who ran an extensive coach hire business and livery stables. My father often hired an extra horse from them if we were particularly busy. Fields were granted leases at all the other public houses including the White Horse, the Queen and Tiger's Head, the Gordon and Sydney Arms, The Crown and, of course, the station. There the cabbies had a wooden cabin where they drank tea, cooked food and waited for the 'phone to ring for hire. Each place had its own fly-master who saw the horses were well groomed and the tack cleaned and maintained.

The musical comedy was at the height of popularity at this time. The Maid of the Mountains, The Merry Widow, The White Horse Inn, The Gipsy Princess, The Chocolate Soldier, Floradora & Our Miss Gibbs were performed at the Gaiety, Adelphi and Dalys Theatres. Music Halls were filled to capacity, the robust humour popular with the masses. The low cost of train fares, 2s 6d (12½p) return to Charing Cross, enabled us to enjoy many of these shows and on returning to Chislehurst late at night a pony and trap of Fields could be relied upon to convey us home in comfort, whatever the weather.

In London the minimum fare for a hansom was a shilling (5p). This took you anywhere up to two miles after which you paid more. Motor cabs minimum fares were 8d, but for longer distances they were more expensive than the hansoms. There was always the brightly coloured omnibuses or the 2d Tube. We always consider London these days to be packed with traffic and endless traffic jams. It was much the same early this century, the mixture of motor and horse drawn vehicles causing chaos.

Chislehurst Station approach was crowded with assorted equipages, broughams, landaus, gigs, flies, victorias or coaches for four persons. Most had liveried coach and footmen waiting for their masters' return from the City or their mistresses' from the West End stores and matinees.

Heavy horses pulling timber outside the Bull Hotel

ESTABLISHED 1864.

GEORGE FIELD,

Job Master and Fly Proprietor,

THE BICKLEY HOTEL,
CROWN HOTEL, FOX & HOUNDS, TIGER'S HEAD,
AND BULL HOTEL, CHISLEHURST.

LANDAUS, VICTORIAS & BROUGHAMS. OPEN AND CLOSE CARRIAGES ON HIRE.
Ralli Carts. Saddle Horses. Polo Ponies and Hunters.
ORDERS PROMPTLY ATTENDED TO. CHARGES MODERATE.

Business card for George Field, Job Master and Fly Proprietor

The Water Tower. Martin's Bank is on the right hand side of the picture, the Golden Grasshopper being prominently displayed.

There was usually great competition amongst the experienced coachmen to race each other up Summer Hill, spurring on their snorting, sweating charges to be first through the Water Arch which spanned the road at the summit. Only one vehicle at a time could proceed through and common courtesy was often stretched to the limit if someone was coming in the opposite direction who was in a hurry to catch a train. Colourful language would fly from one to another, forcing a passage through the restricted entrance. When there was heavy frost or ice on the hills horses were shod with special square headed nails driven into their shoes. This enabled the horse to obtain a better grip on the slippery surface. Their heaving lungs emitted streams of steaming breath through flaring nostrils like angry dragons eager for a kill. Coal carts climbed up the hill after loading at the station yard, traversing from one side to the other to minimise the gradient and to ease the load. Sometimes the horses were chained together for added strength.

Fields also let out a horse and groom under contract for doctors, London trips or for holidays. A two-horse brake was run from the station to Bromley each Thursday, Market Day, at the cost of 6d return per person.

The roads were not made up and were of earth covered in tar with gravel chippings or sand well pounded down by a heavy steamroller. A barrel shaped contraption which contained the tar was heated from a fire underneath, the excess moisture escaping through a chimney on top. The tar was drawn off by the bucket and thrown on to the road and covered with sand.

Walter Atkins (Tommy) outside his shop at 17 Royal Parade. Note the fine Minton tiles which were in colour.

Walter Atkins' shop with his son Bernard at the door

This was always done in warm weather to keep the tar moveable and to prevent it thickening. The roads were in this state until macadam was invented and generally introduced for road surfaces after the Great War.

Royal Parade was swept daily by the local council and the sweepings tipped into the gutter for the chickens to peck over.

Outside the Bull's Head Fields horses stood patiently, nibbling in their nose bags and waiting for hire. Occasionally they stamped their hooves and shifted their weight, snorting and blowing out chaff and oats.

Our chickens frequently crossed the road and standing under these docile creatures waited for an additional supplement to their diet, fighting noisily over every grain dropped. Many a plump Buff Orpington graced our dinner table, grown fat on the unconscious generosity of the horses. White and Black Leghorns and Plymouth Rocks were some of the more popular breeds, as were the strutting Faverells showing off fine, fluffy feathered legs to the famous Wyandots. Many people kept chickens and were not a bit squeamish about rearing them for food. Sometimes ducks, which were kept in the garden, were added to the livestock. There were the popular White Aylesburys, Khaki Campbells and the Indian Runners, easily recognisable by a distinctive upright waddle.

But I digress and must return to Royal Parade. Beyond the stables was Miss Rabbit's shop which I have already mentioned. Alongside the shop was an alley known locally as Rabbit's Alley but officially, I believe, named Parade Cottages. These were four in number and inhabited by old Mrs Rayment, Mr and Mrs Booker and the Warren and Kentall families. An intriguing notice bearing the words 'Ancient Lights' was nailed to the wall. This prevented any encroachment of their light.

Next door was Atkins, the butcher. Only a small place but well set up and known a little ostentatiously as Aberdeen House, Scotch beef being a speciality. Beneath the shop window were scenes of the Scottish Highlands depicting Highland cattle in their natural environment. The colours of these Minton tiles were particularly fine and survived until recently. Heavy round moonlike gas lamps hung above illuminating the name ATKINS in bold gold letters. The floor was wooden, as were the thick blocks of hornbeam used for cutting and serving meat. As was customary, the floor was covered in sawdust to soak up any excess grease and blood that dripped from the huge hind and fore quarters suspended on murderous meat hooks. Joints of meat were arranged in the window which was pushed open to show legs and shoulders of lamb and pork, sweetbreads, pigs heads, loins and necks, kidneys in snowy suet, soft white tripe, striped oxtails and neatly trimmed cutlets.

Walter Atkins, who was later to become my father-in-law, was a character. He hailed from Norfolk of farming stock. He was one of a large family so he came to London to seek his fortune. He settled in Sydenham and became a journeyman butcher. Here he met and married Anne Newman

The Old Hill showing the Imperial Arms and the Organ Works (centre left). The entrance to Kangaroo Walk is seen on the right, 1911.

The brake which ran to Bromley on Thursdays (Market Day). The fare 6d return.

from St Leonards-on-Sea who was in service in Sydenham as a cook. In answer to an advertisement for a job in Chislehurst he took up a position with Mr Foat who owned a butcher's shop at the top of Old Hill. Behind was a slaughter house where they killed and hung the meat. Sheep, pigs and bullocks could frequently be seen driven into the shed at the rear where the unsuspecting creatures met their end. The house is now a private residence but the protruding shop window is clearly discernible. Walter took a cottage in Mill Place and added to his growing family.

By chance, Sir William Willett loaned him sufficient money to set up his butchery business on Royal Parade. This was by no means an unusual practice as many local tradesmen were originally backed financially by the local gentry. It was not as philanthropic as it may at first appear as current rates of interest were charged on individual loans. Nevertheless, sufficient faith was placed in the trader, who very often had little collateral, and it was a method by which industrious people could become shopkeepers and property owners.

Walter worked hard and played hard and was especially fond of whisky. The close proximity of the Bull and the liberal opening hours at Smithfield did nothing to cool his hot temper. He left for Smithfield at four o'clock in the morning with a two horse van three times a week. He selected, paid cash for, and brought back his own chosen carcasses. During the Great War, Rosie, his third daughter who became my wife, drove him to Grove Park station to pick up the 4 am train for London.

He was always smartly dressed, wearing a white coat, oversleeves and spotless apron. In winter the white coat was changed to a warmer one of dark grey. The long oversleeves protected the coat sleeves from soiling and could be changed frequently. Laundry was collected in baskets and delivered weekly by Podgers Laundry of Homesdale Road, Bromley.

Walter, inevitably known locally as Tommy, had three floats with fast horses which were sent out and around to collect orders for lunch. At 10.30 am they were back at the shop as orders were executed and delivered to enable the cook to prepare the midday meal. Orders for dinner were gathered and delivered later. Often Walter had a genial lunch hour at the Bull and returned to work roaring but always capable of doing his job and turning on his undoubted charm to the ladies. If an unfortunate dog chose to lift his leg near the shop door a knife came hurtling after the offender. The dog slunk away looking around resentfully only to be lured back by the irresistible aroma of raw meat. On one memorable occasion a cash register came forcefully through the plate glass door. This quietened everyone down for the remainder of the day.

From time to time he inflicted horrendous cuts on his hands, once decapitating a finger. Making no fuss he poured neat iodine over the troublesome member, wrapped it in a towel and trotted down to Dr Tallent at Walton Lodge for a stitch or two. Rosie sat in the desk and kept the books and took

Walter Atkins with first commercial vehicle in Chislehurst. Bernard, his eldest son, was killed during the First World War.

Ivan with our primrose and green van

the cash. Almost everything was sold on credit and weekly or monthly books were kept. She was very quick with figures and could simultaneously tot up £ s d on a till roll, and added an extra 6d per pound to the bill of any customer who made the mistake of saying the previous weekend's joint was delicious.

New Zealand lamb and mutton were approximately 4d a pound cheaper than English at 9½d per lb. Sheep between four and five years old were best for mutton and wether mutton was preferred to that of ewe. Three-and-a-half to four-and-a-half months was the age to slaughter calves and it was common practice to bleed them before killing. Veal fillet was around 10d per lb and legs of pork 9d per lb. Sucking pigs were at their best about five weeks old and were cooked at once rather than hanging as was usual. Flesh of beef should be well marbled with fat, red in colour with creamy white fat. Ribs of beef were 8½d and rump steak 1s per lb. A whole ox tongue was a great luxury at 3s 6s (18p). Saddles and racks of lamb, barons of beef and grass lamb were eaten from Easter to Michaelmas. Venison was dusted with ginger and pepper to keep away flies whilst hanging. The condition of the flesh was determined by plunging a knife into the haunch and having a good sniff.

The shop was scrubbed out daily, as were the floats and baskets. This was just as well as the meat, once prepared for delivery, was weighed, priced, ticketed with a small metal skewer and put into the basket with no wrapping.

Three times a week Carlo Gatti delivered eight to ten huge blocks of ice covered with sacking. It was heaved through the shop and lowered into a square sunken ice box in the passage between the shop and the parlour. Walter was very proud of his mini fridge and kept as much meat as possible under these conditions. It was especially useful when the new chilled meat was imported from the Argentine. Chilled could always be passed off as fresh meat and a correspondingly high price charged. He was ever alive to the possibility of making extra money; if the customer was satisfied so was his conscience.

One warm afternoon the piano teacher, Mr Grey, arrived to give the girls a music lesson. He passed through the shop for this express purpose. Carlo Gatti was delivering at the same time and this proved to be unfortunate. The trap door had been left open and Mr Grey's rapid descent was seen by the deliveryman who was appalled at the noise and language which issued from the depths. Leaving him to flounder amongst the ice blocks and chops he rushed into the shop exclaiming in a charming mixture of Italian and English, 'De leader ob de band, he fallen down de 'ole!'

The excavation was insulated and fitted with a drain or soak-away to cope with the slowly melting ice. As in the ice houses of some of the big houses, the ice melted very slowly and kept the ice house chilled for months.

Ice was also delivered to the shop next door, which was a fishmonger.

A display given by Chislehurst Fire Brigade, 1912

There was another fish shop and poulterer further down Royal Parade where we now have Petite Fleur Restaurant. The ice slabs were placed on the open marble slab where fish were artistically arranged and decorated with parsley.

Trout was not sold after September 7th but mullet, tench, carp, bass, barbel, mussels, sprats, thornback and sturgeon were widely bought, as well as the more common haddock, cod, herring and soles, etc. August 4th was the earliest date for the sale of oysters. The small shelled variety, Byfleet, Colchester and Milfords were the finest in flavour. The larger Torbay oysters were considered only suitable for soups, sauces and adding to beef-steak puddings.

Mr Burton, the builder, lived over the shop where Jimmy Payne had a repair garage. He was Chief of the Fire Brigade and was frequently seen leaving home in a hurry in answer to the alerting maroons which thundered out from the Police Station. The turncock and police were notified immediately in the event of a fire. The brigade was manned by a volunteer force, gardeners, carpenters, bricklayers, shopkeepers, all of whom left their jobs on a variety of transport to man the fire engine which was housed near the Tiger's Head. Horses were brought from the stables at the pub by eager volunteers clad in their metal helmets and clutching an axe or shovel. There was another appliance at the rear of the Police Station in the High Street.

Whur, the family tailor, lived in the house which is now an exclusive dress shop. Behind the house were workrooms where the tailors sat traditionally cross-legged as they worked, hand stitching the garments. Mr Whur had a thriving trade for servants' liveries finished off with velvet, gold braid and with hand worked buttonholes. Pressing played an important part in the excellence of the finished article. Gas jets were continually heating the flat irons which were spat on, the sizzling test for heat, and were used in constant rotation. I can still recall the smell of stale tobacco smoke trapped in the busy workrooms, the blue haze lingering over the head of the treddle machinist.

The steep roof and dominant chimneys of the lovely Queen Anne house was the residence of Doctor Tallent, a much loved and respected member of the community. The green Brazilian parrot which hung by the door to the surgery screeched instructions to all who called, imitating the doctor and confusing the servants. The doctor was a distinguished looking man with a smooth dome of a head and a refined air. His wife was a handsome lady some years younger than he, dressed stylishly in picture hats and lovely colours. She was interested in amateur theatricals which were regularly produced at the village hall. There were comedies, straight plays and musical comedies which were produced with a high degree of profession-alism and dash. Walton Lodge had an attractive walled garden and a staff which kept the establishment in pristine condition. The cellar of the house is said to have contained a spring, the water level of which fluctuated when the hydraulic organ was started up in the church. The organ also affected the pressure of water in the stream which runs across the common to the Rush Pond. This was a regular signal that the sermon was over and the last hymn had begun.

In common with most of the big houses, Tallents employed morning girls and boys. They cleaned shoes and steps, laid fires, fetched in coal, carried hot water and emptied wash basins before they went to school. All this for 2s 6d (12½p) per week and, in some fortunate cases, a bite of breakfast.

Dr Tallent drove a tall dog cart on his rounds with a groom to hold an umbrella over him on wet days. When snow lay thickly on the roads a sleigh was hitched to his horse which cantered easily over the soft surface drawing the doctor behind with effortless grace and a pleasant jingle. It was he who possessed one of the early motor cars, purchased for him by grateful patients. Dr Lawson, who lived on the Old Hill, was a different kettle of fish. He drove a spirited strawberry roan belonging to Sir Patteson Nicholls of Fallowfield. Sir Patteson's polo playing sons could not hold it in so it was presented to the doctor to curb its exuberance with the regular exercise. It was many years before Dr Lawson finally succumbed to motorised transport. Sir Patteson Nicholls exercised his ponies daily on the 'race course', the old name for the wide path which runs from the Rush Pond to Bromley Lane.

Cooling, Fishmonger and Poulterer, 1872, later Bastables. George Cooling standing in front of the shop owned by his brother. It was managed by him before moving to the High Street. Note the delivery carts.

General view of Royal Parade looking north. The road surface was unmade. Waters Printing Works is advertised. The Methodist Church is visible in the distance.

A representative doctor's account is reproduced as follows:

Chislehurst
(and St Mary Cray)
24th October 1894

Mr Aplin,
    To Wade, Battiscombe & Lawson
1894

For Professional Attendance	£	s	d
January Mrs.	2	3	9
February "	3	1	3
April "		10	6
" Infant		3	6
May "		18	6
June "	3	6	6
May & June, Servants		7	6
	10	11	6

1894

Maid, Rose Clarke, May		5	0
Maid June		2	6
		7	6

The cottages adjoining Walton Lodge had been at some time a post office, butcher's shop and a slaughter house. During the middle 1800s the ground beyond the cottages towards the present War Memorial was let on a builder's lease and shops were constructed as far as the present antique shop at the end of Royal Parade. Lidstone, another butcher, was built with a slaughter house behind. The site is now occupied by Dragonara, the establishment which houses fine Chinese furniture and porcelain. Livestock for slaughter were hand driven along the Parade and from time to time broke free, scattering over the village pound opposite. Sometimes they proved difficult to round up, children and dogs adding to the chaos in their efforts to help.

Bastables, the fishmonger and poulterer already mentioned, was the next shop in line and they had another shop in West Chislehurst. Their service included full daily delivery, often travelling as far as High Elms, at Downe, the home of Lord Avebury, and Brunner Mond's residence at Coombe Park, Sundridge. Poultry and game hung on a high rail outside the shop and was often left out all night which speaks volumes for the honesty of the local populace. Geese were more commonly eaten than now and any bird over twelve months old was not considered suitable for the table. Ducks were 2s 6d each, chickens 3s. Pigeons shot on the local estates only fetched 9d but turkeys were approximately 10s. Gamekeepers kept the shop supplied with rabbits which could be bought as cheaply at 6d. Our mothers knew how to discriminate between young and old game, the spurs on the old birds being long and pointed and those of the young rounded and short. Tame ducks had yellow feet but wild ones were red. Pheasants were plentiful in the area but were not available until October 1st and grouse not before the 18th. Woodcock until fairly recently could be found in the Scadbury estate and even the legendary capercaillie were obtainable until December 20th, although not indigenous to the area.

A cabinet maker and upholsterer, Mr Martin, had the shop which is now Wrought Iron House. He was soon followed by Mr and Mrs Humberstone who carried on the business and lived above. A saddlers was next in the row, owned by Mr Sibley. This shop was a constant delight to me, smelling comfortably of new leather impregnated with saddle soap. Reins, harnesses and glistening horse brasses hung on the walls and new saddles of every size and description were offered for sale. Everything was there for the well turned out horse — riding and driving whips, brushes and horse clothing, chamois leathers and thick wool knee rugs. No commission was too insignificant for Mr Sibley to undertake, restoring and repairing anything within his trade. Many times he rebound the handle on my cricket bat whilst I waited, or stitched up a broken handle on a leather suitcase or Gladstone bag.

The Waters family, until comparatively recently, owned the book shop for three generations. They printed on the premises, including wedding and funeral cards, a speciality when they were in vogue. Papers were delivered daily and at Christmas time, in addition to books, there were toys for sale. The now Chislehurst Antiques was a boot and shoe shop owned by Mr Wise. He also had another shop in Chislehurst West, next to the Queen's Head, where he sold a cheaper range of shoes. He lived with his wife and daughter above the shop. Unfortunately he suffered with some peculiarity of the voice which resounded as a bark from the roof of his mouth. In addition he was rather deaf so a visit to Mr Wise called for a great deal of self control on the part of giggle prone children. No one was allowed to leave his shop in a pair of ill-fitting shoes. It was his pride to be familiar with the last of each of his customers and he kept shoes in stock for any particular fitting needed. On request a boy on a bicycle brought a basket full of shoes on approval which were collected a few days later when your choice had been made. Leisurely shopping indeed.

Next door was Wells and Lea, drapers and haberdashers, where everything was sold from pins to blankets, shirts to feathers. The business was originally situated on Church Row but moved to the main parade of shops which had more potential. An advertisement of theirs in Kelly's Directory is of relevant interest.

WELLS AND LEA
ROYAL PARADE

SILK MERCERS — DRAPERS
FAMILY LINEN WAREHOUSE
ENGLISH AND FOREIGN DRESS GOODS — SILKS —
   VELVETS and VELVETEENS
MILLINERY — FUR & BEAVER HATS — CHIP STRAWS —
SHAPES and all newest novelties — LACE — FLOWERS —
FEATHERS — HOSIERY — UMBRELLAS — GLOVES —
TRIMMINGS & HABERDASHERY — LADIES
UNDERCLOTHING — CALICOES & HOUSEHOLD LINEN
— FLANNELS — BLANKETS — HORROCKS LONG
CLOTHS — CREWDSONS CALICOES.
GENTLEMEN'S SHIRTS — TIES — PANTS — GLOVES etc.
AGENT FOR PHOENIX FIRE INSURANCE.

The large double fronted shop was Coffin's, a high class grocers with a drive in (now Donna Alexandra Mews) for vehicles and horses loading and delivering.

The small side shop, until recently occupied by the National Trust, was part of the same premises and sold crockery and china. Mr Coffin had stabling for six horses and delivery carts at the rear. The forecourt, which now provides car parking space, was once bustling with activity as drivers took out their fast carts to collect orders before 12 o'clock to be delivered after lunch. The trees growing along the frontage were enclosed by iron railings, a necessary precaution with so many horses with a fancy for fresh green leaves.

Most grocery items were bought in bulk — butter, sugar, lard, rice, barley, dried fruit and tea etc — and were weighed off and packaged. I derived much pleasure from the dexterity of the assistant on the provision counter. Several varieties of butter were available, again in 56 lb blocks. It was cut, moulded and patted into shape in no time. Scottish butter was pressed into a heavy wooden mould imprinting a thistle on the glowing surface. Perhaps a customer had a taste for extra salt, in which case the butter was flattened, sprinkled with salt, rolled and turned like puff pastry until the salt was evenly distributed. Ham was home cooked and cut on the bone, the type being identified by the shape, a York ham being flatter than a Westmorland or Hampshire and all subtly varying in flavour. Other gammons and sides of bacon hung on hooks suspended from a brass rail which ran around the shop. Hard fat cheeses sat smiling on the marble slab, unaware of imminent decapitation with a deftly handled cheese wire. It required skill to cut up a large cheese to accurate weight without wastage. Home cooked brawn and pressed ox tongue were also prepared on the premises. On reflection it was incredible how all these foods were kept without refrigeration. Strict rotation and management of fresh foods were necessary if extensive wastage was to be avoided.

Mr Prebble standing on the step of his Pharmacy with his partner Mr Allan Bone

Algy, who was the provision assistant, turned the handle of the mighty bacon slicer, back and streaky rashers rippling from the relentless blade to be carefully wrapped in greaseproof and again in white paper and tied neatly with string. All this whilst he quietly enquired of the family, the weather and the runner bean crop. His hair was thinning and his droopy moustache showed the yellow singe marks of an habitual smoker. Mostly he was kind and even tempered but he could give way to an occasional lapse of the tongue if the weather was damp and his bunions played up.

Huge gold and black containers were filled with tea, varieties from the Orient, Assam, Pekoe, Darjeeling and China. Many people had a mixture of tea thus effecting their own particular brand. Everything was weighed on hand scales and amounts per pound reckoned up by the assistant. He was smartly dressed in a dark overall covered by a freshly laundered starched apron and elasticated sleeve covers.

Most customers ran credit and book-keeping was a time consuming task. Each client had their own book with items entered daily or weekly. It was common for many of the big houses to run credit for twelve months and if the annual payment day was missed another twelve months could elapse before recompense was received. In these days of cash and carry where the customer does most of the work it seems inconceivable that businesses then could be profitable with so many unnecessary outgoings.

Every imaginable dried fruit was available at Coffin's. Apricots, peaches, sultanas, raisins, candied peel, cherries, the aroma blending with that of freshly ground coffee beans all combined to create the unmistakable sweet savour of an old grocers shop. Again the floor was of untreated white wood which was cleaned to perfection daily. Service and quality were the bywords of the small shopkeepers and it was not unusual to see delivery carts going about their business at 9 o'clock on a Saturday evening.

Mr and Mrs Coffin were a grand old couple and lived above the shop. The front door was situated to the side of the shop and opened into a dark, cavernous hall with stairs winding upwards to the rear. In the centre, against the wall, was a heavy mahogany sideboard with a mirror above which reflected my terrified face, for over was a set of horns protruding from the wall. To my limited comprehension they must surely have belonged to the Minataur but I realised my mistake as I grew older and the horns grew smaller.

Every morning after breakfast my father and Mr Coffin took their terriers for a run on the common. In the evening this was repeated with Mr and Mrs Coffin taking the air. He invariably walked several paces ahead of her and never slowed to allow her to catch up. She never endeavoured to bridge the gap so the walk was concluded in amiable silence.

Mr Burton, the builder, had a second shop where Mr Easden's shop is now situated. To the right was a drive-in entrance for the collection of sand, cement, gravel and bricks, all the materials needed by builders.

The Francis family lived over the tobacconist shop and had a barbers at the rear. There was usually a queue on Saturday mornings for this service and the boys had to wait. It was all very basic; a quick trim all round, clippers up the back and sides, a deft brush off the shoulders and 2d in the till. Snuff was widely taken by the customers, eagerly exchanging local chit-chat and gossip whilst they waited their turn. There was a good range of scented and medicated snuffs from which to choose and Woodbines were purchased at 2d for ten.

Where we now have a delicatessen there was Welfords Dairy. The main depot was in the High Street (next to the Fox and Hounds). The raw milk had poor keeping quality although the flavour was rich and the cream content high. This necessitated two milk deliveries a day. The lack of pasteurization caused milk to 'turn' in hours, particularly during hot or thundery weather. The milkman wore a capacious blue and white striped apron and usually a straw boater. He pushed a heavy brass churn along on two wheels and dispensed milk into your own container in any quantity required. Jugs and basins, covered in muslin weighted down with coloured beads, were left on the doorstep to await the arrival of the milkman. He knocked at each door calling out his arrival and passed the time of day with

Royal Parade from the Village Pound. Prebble, Chemist, Welfords Dairy, Francis Barbers are the first three shops illustrated.

his customers. Personal contact was important. The milk was local, much of it coming from a farm in Hawthorn Road, Bickley, which boasted a fine Jersey herd. Cream came from Surrey Dairies in gills and was always double cream. Single cream was not produced. Skimmed milk could be purchased cheaply and buttermilk was often bought as a hopeful cure for freckles.

The last shop on Royal Parade was Wing, Aplin & Co, the chemist, later Prebble and Bone. The symbolical glass jars of coloured liquid stood on each side of the shop windows. They had a branch shop in the High Street and another at Lower Camden. Here again were many evocative smells and scents recalling many tumbles, scratches and burns which were treated with iodine, disinfectant and witch-hazel. There was camphorated oil for easing tight chests, lemon and glycerine for smarting throats. Grey stone hot water bottles, steam kettles for croup, discreetly hidden bed pans and paraphernalia for enemas. Eye baths, suffocating rolls of cotton wool, Parrishes chemical food (a popular tonic for children), cod liver oil and malt clogging the teeth and tongue and slipping deliciously down the throat. Senna pods, syrup of figs and Epsom Salts to cope with that generation's preoccupation with the 'compulsory' daily action of the bowels. An infinite variety of cough cures which defied you to cough, twists of barley sugar and arrowroot to settle the stomach. Prescriptions were dispensed into glass bottles marked out for dosage and sealed with a cork. Empty bottles were carefully collected as money was refunded on all bottles returned in good condition. Above all, the chemist dressed cuts and bruises, strapped up sprains, took foreign bodies from watering eyes and made up soothing potions for fractious children. His confidence and reassurance was a great comfort and support to all who sought his assistance.

Prescriptions were recorded in full by the chemist as written out by the doctor. Some make interesting reading. One for Master S. Chubb consisted of a mixture containing potassium iodide and syrup aurant with the instructions that two teaspoonfuls were to be taken with a teaspoon of lemon juice and a dessertspoonful of cod liver oil daily at 10 am. Nowadays vitamins would be prescribed. Often pills were directed to be silvered at the cost of one and fourpence per dozen. A bottle of mixture for whooping cough could be bought for 2s 6d and a lotion for ringworm at 1s 6d. Furniture polish was made up consisting of spirits of wine, salts, lavender and turpentine, white resin, linseed oil and distilled vinegar. They also had an effective recipe for removing the stains from marble for the price of 1s. The instructions read, 'Wet the spots with the mixture and in a few minutes rub with a soft linen cloth till they disappear'. Sometimes the directions on the medicine bottles were most particular. 'To be applied to arms and hands on soft linen rag cut into strips after scales have been removed by anointing with olive oil and bathing with thin gruel.' Other requests included a concoction to destroy flies, solutions for bugs, pills for puppies, tartar emetics and horse balls to cure equine ailments. Many had cautionary labels warning of poisons and there were different coloured bottles for prescriptions for external use.

Dr Scott's pills were prominently advertised as an 'Effective General Family Medicine without Mercury. Being as mild and tonic in their action as they are certain in their curative effects of the following ailments in both sexes or children — Bilious and Liver Complaints, Indigestion, Wind, Spasms, Foul Breath, Nervous Depression, Irritability, Lassitude, Loss of Appetite, Dyspepsia, Heartburn, Sour Eructations, Lowness of Spirits with Sensation of Fullness at the Pit of the Stomach, Giddiness, Dizziness of the Eyes, Habitual Costiveness, Piles and all other symptoms which none but the Sufferer can describe. In boxes 1/1½ and three times the quantity in one 2/9. Do not be persuaded by anyone to buy any other Medicine instead but insist on having the right thing which is wrapped in a square green package.' It appears inconceivable that anyone could possibly suffer illness with such a miraculous remedy at hand.

The indenture of an apprentice for training in Pharmacy was for four years, a premium of £65 being paid. It was a binding legal document signed and sealed by the interested parties and witnesses. The apprentice swore to serve his master faithfully, keep his secrets, obey his commands, do no damage to his property or interests, waste not his goods, shall not play at the dice tables or cards, haunt taverns nor playhouses, he shall not buy or sell or absent himself day or night unlawfully. Infringement of any of these conditions and he could be instantly dismissed.

Wing, Aplin & Co agreed to teach the apprentice the art, trade and business of Chemist and Druggist and give him every opportunity for advancement and study. They were also responsible for finding sufficient meat, drink and lodging during the four year period. In consideration of good faith and conduct they agreed to pay the said apprentice 1s per week. This could be withdrawn at any time for misconduct or damage to the firm's utensils, any cost being defrayed from the 1s allowance.

The apprentice's father undertook to provide necessary clothing, medicine and medical attendance, together with the premium. Such was the method by which young persons acquired a professional training.

Opposite the chemist's shop, as now, was the Village Pound, originally intended to enclose and confine stray cattle. It contained several commemorative trees and was surrounded by iron chains. Verging the side road by the Shaws was Burlington, the home of Mr Nettleton Balme, one of our local worthies to whom we are eternally grateful for acquiring the commons for us to enjoy in perpetuity. The Gulf Garage was originally two separate shops comprising Sydney Place. The one adjacent to my own home was Julls, ironmongers and blacksmith. They sold anything and everything and often organised raffles gainfully to dispose of any unusual item. My mother won a beautiful German clock for the price of a 6d ticket. It stood over two feet tall in a heavily carved wooden case. At each half hour doors flew open and a pair of trumpeters in scarlet and gold blew a tune.

I frequently woke early in the morning to the clanging of the hammer striking the anvil and the clopping of horses hooves as they arrived to be shod. For 3d I bought a superb golf club unknown to my mother. It was the pride of my life for a few days until she saw me taking an imaginary swing with it. I shed a few salty tears of resentment when she snapped it in two across her knee. Her respect for the Victorian virtue of thrift did not allow for indulgence in such things. To a child the shop was full of potential treasures. Lift an old brass fender and underneath find a solitaire set of fine glass alleys. There were all sizes of wheels, ropes, ball bearings, screws and nails, turpentine, paraffin lamps, picture frames and gas mantles all jostling together in wondrous disarray. Mr Jull could produce anything, it seemed, even to bookie services when necessary. Although highly illegal it was common knowledge that here a few bob could be won or lost.

Kings Dairy was next door to Julls but was soon taken over by Perkins, a greengrocer and fruiterer. Mr Perkins worked the kitchen garden at Coopers and sold the produce fresh in his shop. Potatoes were 5s per bushel and marrows 1s per dozen. In those days all food was eaten in season and in consequence after frost in early winter crisp white celery was delicious. Parsnips also thrived on a cold snap, becoming firmer and fuller flavoured. Hothouse grapes were in the shops by February. Many of the large gardens were blessed with walnut trees which often grew to an immense size. Pickling was done in August whilst the nuts were still young and tender.

HOLBROOK HOUSE

Holbrook House, St Paul's Cray Road

Glebe Cottage stood, as now, on the corner of Church Lane and St Paul's Cray Road. Originally known as the Old Rectory, it probably fulfilled this function for many years before the Georgian Rectory was built in Manor Park Road. The present cottage was put up in the 1870s at a similar time as the building of the Clergy House next door. Glebe Cottage had a substantial garden at the rear, extending as far as the Village Hall annexe which was built by Miss Sophie Tiarks for a boys' club. The garden was worked for profit and produced an abundance of soft fruit. My mother had jam and bottling sessions during the soft fruit season and later was the time to salt down runner beans in stone jars. Juicy apples and pears came next in season, one apple being called the Bascombe Mystery. The tale is told of young George Henry Bascombe who, when caught eating the forbidden fruit in his grandfather's garden, dropped the apple behind him and ground it in the earth with his heel to hide the evidence. The tree resulting from this incident survived until recently and now an offspring carries on the tradition.

The Clergy House was the home of the three curates and organist from St Nicholas Church. A husband and wife looked after the house, cooked the meals and tended the garden. The Parish Church provided clergy for St John's Church at Mill Place and the Chapel at Ease in Perry Street. Christ Church had a parish created from that of St Nicholas and part of St George's at Bickley.

Sir Alfred Bowers lived at The Grange, now called Chesil House, as I have already mentioned. Beyond, looking down St Paul's Cray Road, were several red brick houses built on to the boundary wall. These were and still are very pleasing in appearance and had good gardens backing on to the property in Manor Park Road.

Holbrook House, now elegant flats in Regency style, was on the opposite side of the road behind a strip of St Paul's Cray Common. Undoubtedly when the old road ran through the common to St Mary Cray the mansion was much nearer the road. It was built in the early seventeenth century and has been owned at some time in its history by the Poyntell, Stainmore and Barnard families. Hence the name of the roads off Holbrook Lane. It was commandeered by the military in the last war and suffered considerable damage, being pulled down a few years later. Now we are more aware of conservation of our old houses no doubt it would have been preserved.

On the other side of the road was Saxbys, which thankfully is in good repair. Dating from 1685 it has in turn been an orphanage and a dairy farm, as well as being a private residence. At one time Prince Eddy and Prince Albert, the future Edward VIII and George VI, could be seen playing in the garden. Their tutor was a friend of Mr Herbert Murton then in possession. Three large Victorian houses filled the space between Saxbys and Manor Park Road. Two are there now, St Nicholas Lodge and Wayside. Fair Oaks at the corner was demolished to make way for a modern home.

Manor Park was another road of quality houses. Both Pelham and The Gorse were requisitioned as hospitals for Belgian soldiers during the First World War. On one side of the road were Lepel, Walpole, Hartley, Pelham, Manor Place and Walsingham, and on the other Brakenside, The Gorse, Cookham Dene and numerous lodges. Most of these places have retained their original names. Each year the gardener at Cookham Dene produced a magnificent display of polyanthus which thickly lined the drive and approach to the house with their cheerful brilliance.

I pass on to St Nicholas Church which I think merits a chapter to itself.

THE PARISH CHURCH OF ST NICHOLAS

Much of the history of Chislehurst can be traced by a visit to our lovely parish church of St Nicholas. Here enshrined in timeless serenity lie the famous and not so famous of our past and our spiritual heritage.

The structure is typical of Kent with rough hewn flint walls and a broach-spire. This building, however, is not the first to stand on this site as a Saxon window was uncovered in 1957 revealing the presence of an earlier building.

The land was part of the Crown possessions and was granted to St Andrew's Priory by King Edgar the Magnificent, referring to Cyselhurst as the land boundary A.D.958 – 975. In 1089 Gundulph, Bishop of Rochester, in gifts to St Andrew's granted the monks churches in which Chislehurst was mentioned. The church was probably built between 1070 and 1089 and of this building there is no trace but the Norman font and a bracket in the Scadbury Chapel dating from 1180.

When Thomas Walsingham and his son arrived at Scadbury they soon made their presence felt and under the Rector, Alan Porter, practically rebuilt the church some time in the middle of the fifteenth century. About this time the churchyard was enclosed.

The church suffered in common with others at the hands of the Puritans at the time of the Civil War. Brasses were torn from their places, decorations erased and stained glass windows smashed. The period of the Restoration in 1660 was marked by a tablet placed on the chancel screen. One side bore the arms of Wales and the other the Kings with France and England quartered. The arms of Charles II and his wife Catherine of Braganza were portrayed by a shield bearing the arms of Great Britain impaling those of Portugal. Underneath was a harp and thistle, each crowned. These, together with galleries, high pews, lion and unicorn and other Stuart and Georgian relics, were removed during the rebuilding in the middle of the nineteenth century by Rev. Canon Murray.

St Nicholas had some notable rectors. Alan Porter's demi-brass was on the north side of the sanctuary. He was rector from 1446-1482 and was responsible for the church rebuilding at that time.

Another rector, John Welbone, in 1534 was chaplain to Henry VIII, putting his signature to the declaration renouncing the authority of the Pope. The Reformation brought about many changes, services being conducted in English in place of Latin. Many of the altar ornaments were removed but the screen across the nave and around the Scadbury Chapel was allowed to remain.

Although this photograph was taken after the Great War it does record many features which are mentioned in my story. The Rectory Meadow is the open space in the lower part of the picture.

During his years as rector from 1586 – 1630, Richard Harvey transcribed the parish records. The originals are still in existence in the county archives at Maidstone. He would not accept the adoption of the new Gregorian Calendar and continued to date according to the Julian. Christopher Marlowe was his contemporary at Cambridge and complained of the length of Harvey's sermons when he was staying with the Walsinghams at Scadbury. Marlowe was the son of poor parents but his brilliant mind won him a scholarship at King's School, Canterbury, and another to Cambridge. Even before he left the university he was acclaimed as a remarkable poet and playwright.

Often employed on secret missions abroad by Sir Francis Walsingham, his many absences caused doubts in the minds of the university authorities. Unfortunately Marlowe could not dispel these fears as he was sworn to secrecy. When he was due to receive his M.A. the university were going to pass him by until the Privy Council reminded them of the great services he had rendered to Queen Elizabeth, unknown to them. The degree was granted at once. Walsingham's nephew was also employed on secret overseas missions. Perhaps they hatched their many plans together at Scadbury.

This was probably how Thomas Walsingham became his patron. Marlowe died at the age of 29 in an inn at Deptford after a brawl, thus cutting short a promising career.

Records show the plague present in Chislehurst in 1606. Fifty-six people died in two weeks, quite a considerable number in such a small village.

It was thought George Wilson, rector from 1683-1719, was a Jacobite supporting the Stuart cause. He allowed a charity sermon to be preached to raise alms for the poor children of St Ann's, Aldersgate. A party of ragged children marching through the village alarmed the justices. Sir Thomas Farrington fought the church wardens in an attempt to stop the presentation of the alms, believing them to be used for the Jacobites. Although this unruly uproar in the church did not succeed, the preacher and guardians of the children were fined for extortion, conspiracy, fraud and sedition.

Thomas More rebuilt the Rectory and a stone to this effect is inscribed in the south wall of the chancel. A stone with T.1735.M could be seen under the canopy of the garden door of the old rectory until it was demolished in 1961. In commemoration these initials are recorded in a stone by the door of the present Rectory.

Rector for 47 years 1769-1815, Francis Woolaston was an ardent student of theology and astronomy, writing books on these subjects. Rejoicing in the signing of the Treaty of Paris in 1814 it was he who entertained between 1,300 and 2,000 people on the village green with the assistance of the landlord of the Tigers Head. He had seventeen children, one of his daughters providing us with some contemporary pictures of the old church showing box pews and two galleries against the west wall. One was for tenants and the other, just beneath the roof, for singers and musicians. One can imagine the jolly celebrations which took place. A clock which was installed in 1786 was given by Richard Barwell, the owner of Homewood in Perry Street, on condition he could divert a footpath within his grounds leading to Perry Street. The path henceforth was known as Clock Alley. The present clock was presented by Dent & Stons Ltd of London in 1857 and was used as a prototype for Big Ben. In the time of Francis Woolaston the high box pews housed families who provided their own chairs and cushions and sometimes fires with chimneys through the roof. It was not unknown for dogs to accompany the families to church, barking and growling or curling up asleep on a cushion.

Francis Dawson, 1815 – 1840, who succeeded Francis Woolaston, allowed his curate to live at the Rectory and let out the garden as a potato field. He enjoyed several 'livings' and was seldom seen in the parish. Services were only held on Sundays and Holy Communion was celebrated but six times a year.

Undoubtedly the most well known and well loved incumbent was Francis Murray, rector for 56 years. The son and grandson of a bishop, his father was Lord George Murray, brother of John, Fourth Duke of Athole. It was

The Rectory in Manor Park Road

this worthy gentleman who invented the shutter telegraph. At one time his father was Bishop of Rochester and resided for a while at the Bishop's Palace in Bromley. Later he was appointed in charge of Herts and Essex when they were separated from the London See in 1845. Bromley Palace and the land attached were then sold.

Francis Murray tells of the primitive communications of those days. He and his brother were in a coach with their father in the Old Kent Road when they came to a place where the new Greenwich railway was being constructed in 1836. Curious to see exactly what a railway looked like they climbed a ladder and had a look. The following year he made a journey from Whitstable to Canterbury, the train being drawn partly by rope and partly by locomotive.

When he first arrived in Chislehurst in 1846 the only method of transport to London was a poor coach and a pair of horses driven by 'Old Gates' from Orpington. It went through St Mary Cray to Chislehurst and on to the railway at Greenwich returning the same evening. 'Old Gates' was the slowest of the slow only once showing any urgency when his horse took fright and ran off causing an upset. Gates sustained a broken leg and the provisions for a ball supper that he had on board were scattered all over the road. There was also a four-horse coach in the Footscray Road which ran from Maidstone to Greenwich each day. Frequently my sister and I walked down Kemnal Road and across the fields to meet my brother coming down from London for Sunday lunch. From 1852 – 1860 two omnibuses ran daily from Chislehurst to Greenwich.

In 1857 the railway was built as far as Beckenham by the London Chatham and Dover Railway, and by the following year it was carried as far as Bickley. The first railway for Chislehurst was in 1865, the South Eastern Railway opening the station at the foot of the Old Hill. It was at this time that a determined effort was made to provide good sites for homes for the gentry and Lubbock Road was developed.

Canon Murray restored the church to its present appearance adding the south aisle. He extended the chancel and added the chancel arch and a vestry. The two galleries formerly housing the tenants, singers and instrumentalists were removed, the roof timbers were exposed and new pews installed. The first organ was in place in 1856 which did yeoman service until the next one was donated in 1900. The church was reconsecrated in 1849 but was severely damaged by fire in 1857. A workman who had climbed into the tower to look for his friend coming from Prickend must have dropped a match amongst some sacking where it smouldered all night. The resulting fire was not discovered until 5.30 am. A man walking to work through the churchyard saw the smoke and ran to the Rectory and aroused the Rector with cries of 'Fire, fire!' A chimneysweep about his work in the early hours had seen nothing amiss and a lady, unable to sleep, looked out of her window to the church and thought she saw a light but assumed it to be a reflection from the early morning sun.

Canon Murray rushed to the scene and directed the fire-fighting operations. The wooden shingles of the spire roared and crackled with the heat and were soon burned away revealing the bare ribs of the spire. The six bells followed the destruction by crashing to the ground. The oldest of the bells bore an inscription of 1607 and one could visualise the history of which it could tell.

A long line of parishioners soon appeared and moved 2,000 buckets of water in a continuous chain from the numerous home wells in Church Row. It was this mammoth effort, together with a lucky change of wind, which saved the remainder of the church. By twelve o'clock the Rector was able to offer a Te Deum in thanksgiving for the preservation of the building. Within a year all had been restored, the tower and spire having been raised about five feet to improve the appearance. The lych gate was built in 1866, the Village Hall in 1867 and the Clergy House for the curates was acquired in 1877.

Some old cottages were removed from the south east side of the churchyard, the site being absorbed into the church land. The lych gate was moved to its present position in the same year. It was to celebrate Queen Victoria's Jubilee that the chancel was lengthened and the lovely east window inserted and a new alabaster reredos placed in position to replace the old.

St Nicholas Church

In August 1899 nearly 800 people paid for admission into the Rectory field to see Mr Cyril Shadbolt, the Rector and a representative from the Kentish Times take off in a balloon. The £18 raised was donated to Cray Valley Hospital. Parishioners were horrified to see their elderly Rector step into the balloon car showing his determination to take part in the flight. Because of the difficulty in filling the balloon with sufficient gas the passengers were asked to alight and many entreaties were made to persuade the Rector to change his mind. However, the balloon slowly filled and the Rector donned a thick woolly cardigan and disengaged his coat tails from which his anxious parishioners persistently clung. Mr Shadbolt gave the order to release the restraining ropes and although still short of gas the balloon rose rapidly to 1,000 feet and disappeared into the clouds. The crowd dispersed to the Village Hall to listen to a recitation by a Mr Brandon to complete the afternoon's entertainment.

The intrepid aviators eventually came to rest on a patch of grass next to a coal yard in Becton on the Isle of Dogs. The Rector's clerical hat was squashed flat by the exuberant East End crowd which mobbed them for souvenirs as they landed. It was with some difficulty that the occupants extracted themselves and deflated the balloon. With great relief the parishioners found the Rector present as usual in church the following day.

The Rector outlived Queen Victoria by one year having lived, like her, through the Imperial years of Britain.

Canon Dawson took the old Rector's place in 1902 and was Rector when I was in the choir at St Nicholas. The Lady Chapel was commemorated as a War Memorial Chapel after the Great War, recording the names of fifty-one of those who died in the service of their country.

At the eastern end of the North Aisle is the Scadbury Chapel which reflects much of the history of the occupants of the Manor.

One tablet on the Walsingham tomb commemorates Sir Edmund Walsingham, Lord Lieutenant of the Tower of London for twenty-two years. He witnessed the executions of two Queens, Anne Boleyn and Katherine Howard, the ill-fated wives of Henry VIII, and many others who perished during that bloody era. His sword and tiger crested helm were displayed on a bracket above the tomb. Painted on the walls are the badges of Henry VI and Edward IV, two rivals in the Wars of the Roses. It is supposed they were placed there on the orders of the second Thomas Walsingham when he enlarged the church. As both kings ruled twice one supposes he was covering both options hoping not to cause offence to either side. Some say they were put there by William Camden, the antiquary, and others contend both symbols were shown as the manor of Chislehurst was held successively by a Lancastrian and a Yorkist.

The sculptor engaged on the effigy of Earl Sydney died before it was finished but the work was completed by his pupil who later became an R.A. In 1956 an American, Mr Calvin Hoffman, gained permission for the Walsingham tomb to be opened in the expectation of finding the manuscripts of Christopher Marlowe. Mr Hoffman maintained that Marlowe was the true author of Shakespeare's works, but nothing was found to support the theory. Alas, Chislehurst is not likely to become another Stratford-upon-Avon. A further excavation was carried out more recently, again revealing nothing more instructive to this point.

St Nicholas Church has stood on its lovely site overlooking the village green for 1,000 years, administering the sacraments, comforting the needy, witnessing wars, commemorations and celebrations and guiding the daily round of the parishioners. It has faithfully served our spiritual needs and provided the village with a basic continuity in which our faith in the future is constantly renewed.

The High Street in 1920

Chislehurst Village, 1907

THE HIGH STREET

The High Street has not altered greatly in appearance during my life time. Almost all the transport was horse drawn. The forecourts, now crowded with parked cars, provided space for the occasional pony and trap, a delivery van or a customer's carriage. Horse chestnut trees were then, as now, a popular tree with which to grace the High Street. The mass of white or pink chandeliers opening out from bursting buds into a glorious show of bloom in the spring, shedding rich brown 'conkers' in the autumn. Fresh trees were planted and protected from hungry horses by iron railings as the old ones became diseased and unsafe. The magnificent plane tree in front of the Police Station was but a sapling early this century. A comprehensive range of shops provided the village with almost all its needs without the necessity of travelling to Bromley, as later became the usual habit.

Every type of food shop catered for the public needs: dairies, butchers, bakers, fishmongers, grocers, greengrocers and fruiterers. The latter advertised locally grown hothouse grapes, preserved bottled fruit, fresh vegetables daily, bouquets, coal and coke.

Individual grocers became known for a particular variety of produce, hence Aylesbury, Devon and Dorset butters delivered twice weekly and siftings of finest tea at 1s 4d and 1s 8d per lb. Some were agents for J. Schweppes and Co. or specialised in varieties of bacon and hams. Huntley & Palmers delivered cakes and biscuits weekly. A cheesemonger was agent for Wills of Bristol selling Three Castles tobacco. Nearly all grocers sold china and earthenware. Large crocks for storing bread and flour were also used for wine making. Many unlikely shopkeepers were agents for insurance companies.

Butchers advertised fresh sausages daily and bakers Vienna and granulated bread, fancy biscuits and wedding cakes. Family millers and corn chandlers catered for the needs of the horse whilst saddlers and harness makers maintained the tack. Coach builders and wheelwrights coped with the equipage and forges with shoeing and repairs to vans etc.

Drapers and mercers stocked all manner of linen and materials of all kinds, both British and foreign. Gentlemen's outfitters provided shirts, ties, pants, Dents gloves etc. Trousers were made to measure for 12s 6d (63p) and suits for two guineas (£2.10). Tailors made up liveries, ladies jackets and riding jackets. Suits and coats were turned, the garment being unpicked, cleaned, pressed and made up again reversing the material. Cleaning and repairs were also undertaken.

Hollington and Hornbrook House. The latter was a V.A.D. hospital during the First World War. Formerly it was a private school for boys.

Brigdens, Corn Merchants, and Lash's Forge in the High Street

Feet were particularly well looked after with good stocks of boots and shoes either ready made or made to measure. The bootmaker soon knew the last required and henceforth would only supply the correct fitting. Top boots were sold for liveries and cork soled boots for winter wear, dress and evening shoes for special occasions. Boots called 'straights' were designed to be worn on either foot. Slippers were hand worked and carefully mounted and repairs of all kinds were executed promptly and efficiently.

There were numerous builders and decorators offering a comprehensive service which would be envied today. Work was undertaken by skilled craftsmen who had served apprenticeships. These entailed long years of training under a skilled man with pitifully low wages. The employer virtually owned the lad until he worked out his time of full qualification. Quoting from an advertisement of the time —

PLUMBING — FITTING OPEN & CLOSED RANGES — GAS & HOT WATER FITTED — WATER CLOSETS FITTED & REPAIRED — WRITERS — GRAINERS — GILDERS — FRENCH & ENGLISH PAPER HUNG — AGENTS FOR FURNITURE MAKERS — CARVED WOOD MANTEL-PIECES — SPECIALISTS IN PARQUET FLOORS — BORDERS & DADOS — PROVIDE MINTON TILES — MOSAIC PAVEMENTS — STAINED GLASS & LEADED LIGHTS — LIMOGES & DOULTON WARE — SPRING ROLLER & VENETIAN BLINDS — GREENHOUSES CONSTRUCTED.

They were frequently agents for coal and coke, selling it by eight ton truckloads.

Ironmongery covered a vast range of goods and services. They were also locksmiths, bell hangers, gas fitters, sold or hired baths, delivered oil and benzoline, ground mowers and repaired all manner of iron ware, usually having a smithy at the rear.

Upholsterers re-covered chairs stuffing them with horsehair and seats were recaned. Carpets were collected for cleaning and returned and umbrellas steamed, repaired or re-covered. Hairdressers, apart from barbers, made up customers own hair and created ornamental hair pieces. Long hair was regularly singed to prevent the ends from splitting. Schools and families were waited upon in their own establishments if necessary. Cut throat razors were ground and set.

Stationers reckoned to compete with London with prices for paper items as well as bibles, prayer books, church service and hymn books.

Local craftsmen included stone masons, chair and ladder makers, manufacturers of bricks and tiles, whilst nurserymen, fruit growers, carriers, photographers and chimney sweeps were all part of the High Street scene. All these crafts and trades provided a service to the local populace and

General view of the High Street, 1907

Local postmen at the General Post Office

employment for all. Such a comprehensive variety of services available illustrate the self sufficiency of Chislehurst, as were many villages at that time.

At the junction with the main road and Prince Imperial Road was Hollington, a mansion overlooking the golf course at the rear. It was owned by Mr Tiechman, the son of Mr Tiechman of Sitka. The Midland Bank is situated on what was the kitchen garden. Later Mr Arthur Cooling leased the land as part of his nursery.

Hornbrook House next door was another house used as a hospital during the Great War and was subsequently taken over by the Red Cross Society. The house was let for weddings and other functions having a spacious garden at the back (now a public car park). In 1883 it was a school for young gentlemen who were well grounded in the classics and mathematics and were prepared for public schools. Boarders were taken up to the age of fifteen years and were charged fifty to eighty guineas per year.

Brigden was a corn chandler with the first shop at the top of the village. Behind the high wooden gates there were stables and three well turned out vans which delivered fodder, trusses of hay and straw, flour and corn. Each Sunday morning beer was dispensed liberally to gardeners, coachmen and grooms in the hope of gaining new customers and ensuring against losing the old ones.

Lash's ancient forge was next door where coaches were built, repaired and painted, umpteen coats of paint being applied by hand to give the vehicle a surface like glass, hard and glossy. Coats of arms and other decorations were professionally added to grace the coach. What a joy to watch a wheelwright construct a wheel of wood and band it with iron. The forge stood 'under the spreading chestnut tree' as in the famous poem, several of the family working together for three generations until 1960. The stable doors were always flung open to the elements and the ringing of hammer on anvil could be heard far off. Bellows coaxed the dying embers into a roaring inferno, sighing and moaning as the shoe became red hot. Great tongs held it on the anvil as the sweating smith battered it into shape. Hitching up his soiled leather apron and wiping the sweat from his brow the smith fitted the shoe, sizzling and scorching, to the pithy part of the hoof. Thick smoke arose obscuring the view of the smith striking home the nails in the shoe. Horses, from thoroughbreds to cart horses, stamped their hooves with boredom or impatience whilst awaiting the time of the blacksmith.

Built at the turn of the century the Post Office replaced some old but attractive cottages with small front gardens. Prior to this the sub office was on the corner of Camden Grove opposite the Fox and Hounds. Riders, the builders, had an office in this part of the High Street and there was a draper and a tailor. Camden Grove was an unmade road and was eventually surfaced for £200. The present pet shop was a toy emporium and was also a sub

Old Cherry Tree Tea Rooms, now ladies and gents hairdressing

High Street, showing the Coffee Tavern and Coolings

First bus for Chislehurst

post office before the main office was opened. The Fox and Hounds was a very old hostelry on the corner of Camden Grove. It was destroyed during the Battle of Britain but there was business as usual for the duration of the war in the stables behind. In due course it was rebuilt in the present style but lost much of the original atmosphere as a 'local'. At the same time another bomb finished off Dean's, the high class family grocer (now the Victoria Wine Co.). Another caused a large crater in the main road outside St Mary Hall and yet another damaged the Annunciation church porch.

Welfords main dairy was at 23 High Street behind which was extensive stabling for horses and covering for carts. The houses of Stockmans Row are probably the oldest buildings in the High Street apart from the Queens Head. They were originally a row of eighteenth century cottages but over the years shops have been added which has spoilt the original appearance. Frontal shop development occurred throughout the High Street on the western side.

Mr Pepper was the owner of the first of the shops in Stockmans Row. He sold sweets in the front and had a barber's shop behind. He was a credit to his profession being of immaculate appearance with a carefully waxed moustache. This was fashionable at the time and many men drank from special moustache cups to ensure the moustache was not soiled by drink or drooped by heat. A draper, Murrels, then Keith's, a family butcher. Dean's, as previously mentioned, was a grocers run by two brothers, one

George Cooling (Grandfather Cooling) outside his shop in the High Street with his newspaper boys and the wholesale delivery van, 1910

George Cooling with his family at the rear of the High Street on land which is now part of the Garden Centre. The wooden cottages on the right have since been demolished.

One of the early buses for Chislehurst

slim and quiet, the other rotund and jolly. The present dress shop was an attractive detached house covered in ivy with starched lace curtains at the windows and neat white railings enclosing the front garden. The Cherry Tree tea rooms provided refreshments for travellers and coachmen, catering at the weekends for cycling parties.

Opposite the Queens Head was Marsh, the bakers. Bread was baked in an old side flue oven in a bakery to the rear of the shop. Wedding cakes were made to order and mould sponges and luncheon cakes were a speciality. Behind was Danzig Place comprising some ancient wooden cottages.

Sadly we have recently seen the disappearance of the Cooling family who, as newsagents and stationers, were in business in the High Street for three generations. Great grandfather Cooling hailed originally from Lincolnshire of farming stock. It was one of his sons who opened the poulterers shop on Royal Parade and displayed such a wonderful array of poultry and game outside the shop. As with most meat and fish shops, goods were hung up in the open or presented on marble slabs packed with ice.

Grandfather Cooling, then a young man, was employed as a valet at Ripon in Yorkshire. He came south to help his brother on Royal Parade. Seeing a fish shop for sale in the High Street he started in business on his own account. He transferred to the newsagents and stationers premises at the turn of the century. Grandfather Cooling always wore a silk cravat with a diamond pin and lived with Mrs Cooling and their ten children above the shop. The eldest son took up photography commercially as an addition to

The Cooling family assisting Arthur Cooling on his smallholding in Belmont Lane

Mr Arthur Cooling and Mr Boyce outside St Mary Hall

Another Coronation picture in the High Street

the existing business but unhappily he was killed in the Great War and that part of the business lapsed.

Miss Cooling, the eldest child, was until recently still with us, dying at the ripe old age of 93. She would tell of the quietness of the High Street and the lack of traffic. It was quite safe to mark out for hopscotch in the middle of the road after 6 pm as no wheeled traffic passed through the village after that hour.

Another son, Arthur, ploughed up the land at Belmont Lane to raise potatoes during the food shortages in 1914 to 1918. These humble beginnings were the origin of the thriving nursery we know in Willow Grove owned by his son Michael. Although a full-time postman Arthur found the time and energy gradually to develop the site at Willow Grove and promote the business. He was also responsible for the formation of the Poultry Society, the largest club in Chislehurst at the time. Two shows were held annually in St Mary Hall. He prided himself on his ability to dispatch a chicken efficiently and humanely in double quick time. His services were much in demand.

Next to Coolings newsagents was Bastable, another wet fish shop with marble slabs, shuttered windows and a row of gas lights under the front porch. Fresh fish was delivered each day from Billingsgate to the orders of Mr Bastable who visited the market daily at the crack of dawn.

Beyond was Fleggs, saddler, harness maker and shoe repairer. Anything was repaired if it was humanly possible. Leather cases, portmanteaux and

Wilson, Corn Merchant, at the corner of Willow Grove

Wilson, Corn Merchants, on the corner of Willow Grove. The site is now occupied by the Abbey National Building Society.

Gladstone bags were restitched and patched. Saddles were renewed with fresh leather and saddle soap was liberally applied. Footballs were mended and fat round studs driven into the footballers' boots. Rows of neatly repaired boots and shoes awaited collection or delivery. Top boots for liveries, riding boots, dress and evening shoes all awaited the attention of Mr Flegg.

The premises adjoining the Police Station were at one time a temperance hotel and the basement was utilised for people to take baths for a few pence. No doubt this facility was extremely useful as most working class homes had no bathrooms, let alone a bath, and many people had manual jobs.

Basements and cellars housed the coke and coal supply for the house, coal being the main source of energy. Access was gained by a heavy metal lid in the pavement opening up to a cavernous place beneath. The coalman shouldered a hundredweight bag and aimed with deadly accuracy over his shoulder through the narrow hole to the cellar below. A quick sweep around and the load was safely delivered.

The new Police Station was opened in 1893 replacing the old police house at the top of the Old Hill adjacent to the Imperial Arms. It is easily recognised by the double door which at one time opened into the court house. The new station was much more spacious and housed the Inspector's family. The complement of police for Chislehurst early in this century was forty-nine. In the advent of a reported fire several maroons were let off with tremendous report alerting all the volunteers to report for duty.

Next door was Shears the butcher. On the forecourt in front of the shop livestock was kept in pens awaiting slaughter. One way of keeping meat fresh as it was not killed until needed! There was a gentlemen's outfitter then Rouch the draper. At the end of that block was another branch of Wing, Aplin & Co, the chemist.

On the corner of Willow Grove was a little old shop set well back from the road with a barn and hayloft to the rear. This belonged to Mr Wilson, corn chandler, a genial old man with whiskers and a tiny wife with a nipped in waist. An interesting advertisement appeared in Kelly's Directory indicating the humility shown by traders to gentry in years gone by.

WILLIAM WILSON
FAMILY MILLER, CORNCHANDLER etc DESIRES GRATE-
FULLY TO ACKNOWLEDGE THE LONG ACQUAINTANCE
OF PATRONAGE WITH WHICH HE HAD BEEN
FAVOURED AND WHILST RESPECTFULLY SOLICITING
THE RENEWAL OF SAME ASSURES HIS PATRONS THAT
THEIR COMMANDS WILL ALWAYS RECEIVE HIS
CAREFUL AND CONSTANT ATTENTION.
GENUINE COUNTRY HOUSEHOLD FLOUR
HAY, STRAW, CLOVER etc.

Another grocer was situated on the opposite corner of Willow Grove and then was Miss Stringer's school for young ladies.

Burlington Lodge, High Street, with the intrepid Mr Pierce (Postman, retired) standing by his front gate

Burlington Lodge is the centre building in this row of Victorian houses. Sainsburys now occupy this site.

Empire Day at the Annunciation School. The roof of the mineral waters building in Park Road can be seen above the trees. Two of the cottages in the foreground were destroyed by enemy action during the last war.

St Mary Hall was built in 1877 and housed many local functions and exhibitions. The school was to the rear. A welcome drink of cool, clear water could be obtained from an ornate drinking fountain which had an ancient iron cup on a chain. There was a similar fountain on the edge of the churchyard of St Nicholas. Opposite the Annunciation Church was a row of varied Victorian villas, one of which was Tile House, an orphanage for the Waifs and Strays. Burlington Lodge was built by Mr Pierce, a postman who earned 10s per week. It was a sizeable house with a front and back staircase with the best rooms in the front. These were let to paying guests which enabled him to pay his mortgage. I cannot but admire his nerve and business acumen.

Proceeding towards Red Hill Whitelegg's nursery spread over the open ground now occupied by Empress Drive and verging on the main road as far as the present library. A riot of colour and perfume permeated the summer air competing with a nearby piggery. Another small pond was at the foot of Red Hill and an old cottage halfway up where the Browning family lived. It was reputed that they paid their rent in the form of two chickens per annum to the Lord of the Manor. Kennard and Trill had a coal yard part way up the hill and lived in a cottage adjoining.

Across the road was Burlington Parade which contained a variety of shops. This row was built by a Mr Squires who had invested money in the gold fields of South Africa. The company had a gold strike and the shares boomed. The town near where this gamble paid off was called Burlington

117

Brownings Ivy Cottage on Red Hill. Mr C. Browning with Reg and Win, 1907.

Mrs Trill in front of Friendly Cottage, Kennard & Trill, Coal Merchant, 1907

Red Hill tooking towards the High Street

and to put a seal to his good luck he built Burlington Parade as an investment. One of the early Co-operative stores was here — the larger more modern version was built in the thirties on land which was once the nursery.

There was a bakers with a primitive bakehouse. I well remember the oven being lit with a smouldering rag in a tin of oil. The stables were to the rear where stood an ancient nag and pony cart for deliveries. Next door was a butcher who kept a handsome parrot in his shop. It was here where Mr Rex Pierce tells how as a small boy he and his friends would blow up a pig's bladder like a balloon.

There was another draper, shoe shop, newsagent and grocer. This block and the nearby houses were built on land previously occupied by Red Hill farm. Part of the orchard was still in being when it was all bulldozed to the ground to make way for a car park. A tributary of the Ravensbourne ran alongside the vicarage fence and out to Belmont Lane.

Behind the newsagent was another forge where Mr Robert Head's father was blacksmith. I find the following wording of the boy's indenture an interesting document:

This Indenture made the *eight* day of *July*

one thousand eight hundred and ninety *two*
Witnesseth That *William Arthur Leonard Head*
of *Bromley*
in the County of *Kent*
Son of *John Head Butcher*

by and with the consent and approbation of his *Father John Head* testified
by *his* executing these Presents, doth put himself Apprentice to
Horton Brooks and Son
of *Crayford*
in the *County* of *Kent*
to learn the Art, Trade or Business of *Blacksmiths*

and with him after the manner of an Apprentice to serve from the *Twenty Six* day of *November One thousand eight hundred* until the full end and term of *five* years from thence next following, fully to be complete and ended. During which term the said Apprentice his Master faithfully shall serve, his secrets keep, and his lawful commands obey;—he shall do no damage to his said Master or his Goods, nor suffer it to be done by others, but shall forthwith give notice to his said Master of the same, when necessary;—he shall not waste the Goods of his said Master, nor lend them unlawfully to any; nor shall he do any act whereby his said Master may sustain any loss, with his own Goods or others' during the said term;—without Licence of his said Master, he shall neither buy nor sell during his Apprenticeship; nor shall he absent himself from his said Master's service day or night unlawfully; but in all things as a faithful Apprentice shall behave himself towards his said Master and others, during the said term. And the said

his said Apprentice in the Art, Trade, or
Business of *Blacksmiths*
which he useth by the best means in his power shall teach and instruct or cause to be taught and instructed;—the said *and finding the said apprentice sufficient meat drink and* will pay the said Apprentice the Wages following—that is to say *& so itgoing two shillings per week during the first year, two shillings per week during the second year, three shillings per week during the third year, four shillings per week during the fourth year and five shillings per week during the fifth year and the said John Head agrees to find and provide the said apprentice with proper and sufficient clothes, washing, mending, medicine, medical attendance and all other necessaries except board and lodging during the said term*
These presents shall be handed over to the said *William Arthur Leonard Head*
on the completion of the said term, with a Certificate of such service endorsed thereon.
AND for the true performance of all and every of the said Covenants and Agreements the said Parties bind themselves by these Presents. IN WITNESS whereof the said parties have hereunto set their Hands and Seals the day and year first above written.

Signed, Sealed and Delivered in the presence of

William Arthur Leonard Head
John Head
Horton Brooks & Son
Signed *Charles Webb*

William Arthur Leonard Head

John Head

Horton Brooks & Son

BOYS APPRENTICESHIP
INDENTURE

THIS INDENTURE made the eighth day of July one thousand eight hundred and ninety six
WITNESSETH that William Arthur Leonard Head of BROMLEY
in the County of Kent
Son of John Head Butcher
by and with the consent and approbation of his Father John Head testified by his executing these Presents doth put himself Apprentice to

Horton Brooks & Son
of Crayford in the County of Kent

to learn the Art Trade or Business of BLACKSMITH and with him after the manner of an Apprentice to serve from the Twenty Six day of November one thousand eight hundred and ninety five the full term of five years from thence next following fully to be complete and ended. During which term the said Apprentice his Master faithfully shall serve, his secrets kept and his lawful commands obey:— he shall not waste the goods of his said master, nor lend them unlawfully to any, nor shall he do any act whereby his said Master may sustain any loss with his own goods or other's during the said term; without Licence of his said Master he shall neither buy or sell during his Apprenticeship, nor shall he absent himself from his said Master's service day or night unlawfully but in all things as a faithful Apprentice shall behave himself towards his said Master and others during the said terms. And the said Horton Brooks and son and his said Apprentice in the Art Trade or business of BLACKSMITH which he useth by the best means in his power shall teach and instruct or cause to be taught and instructed and finding the said Apprentice sufficient meat drink and lodging and will pay the said Apprentice the Wages following that is to say:—

One shilling per week during the first year
Two shillings per week during the second year
Three shillings per week during the third year
Four shillings per week during the fourth year
Five shillings per week during the fifth year
and the said John Head agrees to find and provide the said Apprentice with proper and sufficient clothes, washing, mending, medicines, medical attendance and all other necessaries except board and lodging during the said term. The presents shall be handed over to the said William Arthur Leonard Head on the completion of the said term with a Certificate of such service endorsed thereon AND for the true performance of all and every of the said Covenants and Agreements the said Parties bind themelves by these Presents
IN WITNESS whereof the said parties have hereunto set their Hands and Seals the day and year first above written.
Signed and sealed in the presence of

William Arthur Leonard Head	William Arthur Leonard Head
John Head	John Head
Horton Brooks & Son	Horton Brooks & Son
Signed Charles Webster	

To cater for the spiritual needs of the people of Prickend in the middle of the nineteenth century a curate from St Nicholas conducted services in one of the cottages in Chapel or Cross Lane (Park Road). In time a mission chapel was built which sufficed for another ten years, but the increasing

The Annunciation Church and the pond at the foot of Red Hill

Burlington Terrace and Parade

My first commercial vehicle somewhat later, 1925

population made it necessary to build a more permanent place of worship. The foundation stone of the Annunciation Church was laid in 1868 and it was completed and consecrated in 1870. Much of the funds to meet the building costs were provided by the Rector, Canon Murray, from the proceeds of compiling the hymns Ancient and Modern. The foundations of the tower were laid but it was not completed until the early 1930s. It was originally intended to have a spire. The Annunciation Church was the first to bear that name since the Reformation. A short distance behind are the almshouses which are half timbered and quite picturesque. They were founded in 1881 by the Misses Anderdon, the sisters-in-law of the Rector, the Reverend Murray.

Some of the old cottages beyond the church towards Park Road were wrecked during the blitz in 1940. A few are still in evidence and are known as Wellfield Place.

White & Bushell, ironmongers, was situated on the corner of Park Road and the High Street and occupied a large site. They were a very old established business. Their advertisement in Kelly's Directory reads as follows:

WHITE AND BUSHELL
Shoeing and Jobbing Smiths
Locksmiths, Bell Hangars and Gas Fitters
Horses shod with care and attention
All kinds of Lawn mowers ground and repaired.

George Streatfield, General Carrier, Queens Road

George Streatfield, General Carriers, Queens Road

View of High Street showing the large tree on the forecourt of the Queens Head

Almost anything could be found here, eventually! Huge balls of rope or twine, chains, buckets, baths, brushes, mops, tools of all kinds, scissors, shears, lawn mowers and dustbins, penknives, gas mantles, aladdin lamps and hearthstone could be seen, filling every space, shelf or box, even hanging from the ceiling. Rows and rows of wooden drawers contained nuts, bolts, screws and tacks, which were sold by the pound. The indefinable conglomerate of tarred rope, paint, paraffin, turpentine and a hundred and one other items resulted in a most satisfying ironmonger's aroma. Stock was piled high in chaotic disarray but the family who served in the shop knew where to find everything and time was of no importance. They decorated and plumbed, were grainers and gilders, hung paper and fitted ranges. Their versatility was endless. The smithy at the rear could execute any repairs which were both collected and delivered.

Next door was the International Stores, one of the first chain stores. Later, Fishers had a dairy on that site selling and delivering milk from their own cows which browsed the fields which surrounded Chislehurst. One such place was Beaverwood Farm, where Hoblands End is now situated. The cows meandered carelessly across Perry Street with the dog barking frantically at their heels, edging them slowly into the farmyard and ultimately into their stalls for milking.

Continuing up the High Street we came to Bulley's, builder and undertaker, with painters and decorators doubling up as pall bearers. Mr Rice

Tree blown down in gale, September 30th 1911

The Chislehurst Band in front of the Queens Head. Frequently referred to by the locals as the 'Thirsty Dozen' since they spent as much time inside the Queens Head as out, 1909.

had a cycle shop and garage next door to Judd's Emporium which advertised millinery and costumes from the windows above. They had a small departmental store beneath. There was yet another grocer and then there was Queens Passage which housed another tin tabernacle and led to the cottages of Queens Road. On the other side of the passage was Hilda Daw's sweet shop where she dispensed goodies into conical shaped paper bags. Further along was Mr Mann, the jeweller, watchmaker and repairer. The chiming of numerous clocks varying in tone and volume greeted you if you entered the shop upon the hour. Mr Wise's other shoe shop was next door to the Queen's Head.

The Queen's Head is the oldest building in the village. The central part is Georgian but the northern end is much older and until recent years contained two inches thick oaken vats which dated from Stuart times. They advertised as follows:

QUEENS HEAD HOTEL
CHISLEHURST WEST
J. C. RAINE, PROPRIETOR
WINE VAULTS — SPIRIT STORES
BASS'S ALE IN BOTTLES
GUINNESS'S STOUT
COMFORTABLE APARTMENTS OVERLOOKING TASTEFUL
GARDENS and RURAL SCENERY
GOOD STABLING

Each Saturday the Chislehurst Band played on the forecourt of the Queen's Head retiring to the pub to renew their energies and lubricate their throats. They became known as the 'Thirsty Dozen'.

On Saturday nights it was a common sight to see enraged wives waiting outside the pub for their errant husbands to emerge. Some were belaboured with sticks accompanied with colourful language. Others incapable of walking were wheeled to the Police Station cells on a bier to sleep it off overnight. Sometimes the police wheeled their unconscious load from the Bull or Tigers Head or picked them up senseless by the roadside.

Buses terminated at the Queen's Head. A white steam bus plied between Lewisham and Sidcup in 1908. The first weekday service began in 1916 to take war workers to the Woolwich Arsenal and operated between Forest Hill and Woolwich.

Prickend Pond and the other ponds in the area were created by the excavation of gravel. It must be well supplied with several springs as it never dried out completely even in drought conditions. On the southern slope stood a massive black poplar which shed a blizzard of windborne seeds as ephemeral threads to settle in snowdrifts by the roadside. Many of these embryo saplings wafted hither and thither in the thermal currents eventually to root in some hospitable soil. The retaining wall was built along the

Prickend Pond and part of the High Street

northern edge of the pond in 1900 because complaints were made that the pond was insanitary and in the following year posts and bars were placed along the eastern side to prevent vehicles going off the road. Sometimes cows cooled their heels in the refreshing water before being driven in for milking. And so on to the common again.

STREET TRADERS,
PERFORMERS AND ENTERTAINERS

Street traders and performers added greatly to the colour and general fun of parochial village life and, as a child, I looked forward to their arrival each week.

Every Tuesday morning an old man, or he seemed old to me, arrived with a hurdy-gurdy on his back. He was of small stature with a beard and was none too clean, but the sound produced from that instrument was music to my ears. A 'man of the road' had glamour for any youngster, seeing only the fun and none of the squalor of his existence. The afternoon peace was disturbed by the arrival of an Italian gentleman and his wife. He pushed a magnificent, highly decorated barrel-organ and she collected the pennies in her tambourine. She was dressed loudly in bright colours, a shawl with a deep fringe around her bare shoulders and fancy combs in her dark hair. Black eyes flashed boldly and golden earrings tinkled as she danced before the men, daring them to throw her money as her husband turned the handle to churn out the melody. The sound of a barrel-organ creates the most evocative of memories and one cannot hear the music without recalling the long lost days.

With a horse drawn barrel-organ came a man who had lost an arm and leg in the construction of the second tunnel at Elmstead Woods. He lay on the low cart and turned the handle in an exhausted fashion. His must have been a meagre living and a miserable existence.

Thursday was the day the tin whistler called. He could play anything on his primitive tin whistle and could coax forth both popular and classical music. For a few extra coppers he would render Mendelssohn's Moonlight Sonata or some part of Mozart or Beethoven and Tommy Atkins could be heard harmonising his tenor voice with the magical whistle.

Less frequently we were visited by a team who performed with the diabolo, a game with a double cone spun in the air by a cord on two handles, an adaptation of the old game of the devil on two sticks. This produced a craze for the ownership of one of these toys and many youngsters became most proficient.

The summer months brought the Hokey Pokey Man and he was most welcome. The horse and cart stopped on our forecourt and the Italian producer of this water ice dispensed liberal quantities of this coloured, dubious concoction to all who gathered around with their money. Produced under questionable conditions my mother forbade us to eat it and looked disapprovingly as Tommy Atkins appeared with a huge bowlful for his family. We made icecream in our bakery and it was delicious. It was produced by blending pure egg custard with fresh double cream which was then hand churned until it thickened. Ice was obtained from the fish shop, split with an ice pick and packed in the container together with freezing salt. In this way it was sent out for parties and dances.

On winter Sundays a man arrived with a large tray of crumpets and muffins covered with a green baize cloth, ringing a bell to attract attention. Once again we were not allowed any of these as he was in direct competition to my father. Such defection would be considered the height of disloyalty. Crumpet making was a simple process. Thin white batter was poured into rings placed on the hot plate. When the bubbles appeared they were cooked, removed and put on racks to cool.

Sunday also brought the man who sold shrimps, prawns, winkles, cockles and whelks. He carried them in a basket over his arm and measured them out in half and one pint quantities directly into your dish. He had no expensive wrapping costs.

Kate sat by Coffin's side door with her flowers ranged about her, in bundles tied with bass. Above her head the swallows wheeled and turned alighting nimbly into the compact mud nests which ranged along the wall beneath the eaves. Kate was a flower seller par excellence arriving on a Thursday complete with stock and a clean check apron. Gentlemen bought bunches of irises and tulips for their wives, and young lads a single rose for their sweethearts. She made up special posies for children to give their mothers on Mothering Sunday or other special occasions.

Once a week Mr Dotter drove his pony and trap from Bromley to wind the clocks in the big houses. He was as regular as his timepieces, arriving at precisely the same time each Monday morning.

The knife grinder sat on the seat of his trolley and pedalled to drive the sandstone wheel which sharpened scissors and knives amid a shower of sparks. Sometimes he sat cross-legged at the kerbside, mending mats, recaning chairs and making general furniture repairs. He was a bachelor and lived in a lodging house in St Mary Cray.

There was an aura of magic about the lamplighter. At dusk and dawn he moved from lamp to lamp turning the gas taps on and off. Opening the side window of the lamp he pulled a chain with a hook at the end of a long pole, thus releasing the gas and causing the lamp to burst into light. If requested he would give you a call in the mornings to make sure you did not 'lie in' when you were meant to be up and about.

There was no street lighting in Chislehurst until 1885, when a meeting was held to discuss the matter. The ratepayers were against gas lighting, chargeable on the rates, so it was decided to use oil lamps fixed to householders property who had frontages on the public roads, the expenses being defrayed by them on a voluntary basis.

Later the only street lights in Chislehurst were from Manor Park corner to the end of Royal Parade, with some more along the High Street, as most traders provided lamps over their own shops.

I can vividly remember my parents rousing from bed my sister and myself to witness the phenomenon of Halley's Comet in 1910. An orange, fiery ball trailing a long tail as a fox's brush, soared across the inky blackness of the night sky.

Rag and bone men called frequently, collecting old rags, bones and metal of all kinds. Usually they came from Deptford, often walking the distance pushing a hand barrow. The more affluent coaxed a weary horse with a loaded cart back and forth, the streets echoing with their cry.

Sometimes, when times were hard, groups of unemployed men ranged the streets, singing of their plight. Some charitable folk gave them money to help alleviate their immediate need and that of their families.

The Brett Smith family were noted for ringing hand bells. At Christmas they performed in people's homes, ringing in the festive season with the joyous sound of tinkling bells and greeting the New Year with rejoicing and optimism.

Gypsies were frequent visitors to Chislehurst and had permanent encampments in Crofton Lane and Corks Meadow, St Mary Cray. These sites were littered with painted caravans, lean-to tents and makeshift sheds. There were plenty of smoke blackened children everywhere. The women canvassed the village with paper flowers and clothes pegs, their voluminous skirts swirling the dust. Combs confined their braided hair and shawls were wrapped around their shoulders. Always ready to tell your fortune they would round on you or lay a curse on you if their palms were not crossed with silver. We were always more wary of the men as nothing was considered safe whilst they were about. Piebald horses were tethered near the caravans and hungry looking lurchers wandered amid the rubbish. When the head of the family died the caravan was burned according to custom.

Sometimes the gypsies would depart suddenly, trailing along with buckets swinging from the carts and caravans and drays piled high with scrap. The lean dogs followed and the grubby, noisy children ran alongside.

These comings and goings brought colour and variety to our simple lives, each visitor bringing a breath of another world into our village and a touch of glamour to our lives.

The drive leading to Scadbury. The Lodge, the home of Mr and Mrs Thornbury, 1906.

Dabners Cottage and bakery on St Paul's Cray Common

THE DAILY ROUND

After an early morning start in the bakery, by 7 am I was delivering fresh bread to Scadbury and the surrounding cottages. Winter and summer, wet or fine, and loaded with baskets across my back and on each arm, I pedalled through the deserted woods before the dew was off the grass. Opening the gates I passed the old thatched lodge with lancet windows where lived Mr Thornbury, the gamekeeper. The lodge was immaculate as was the vegetable garden on the opposite side of the drive. Here also were the chickens and outhouses which contained Mrs Thornbury's home made wine. In May the woods of the estate were gracefully carpeted with blue-bells, a wonderful sight beneath the fresh canopy of beeches and oaks. On certain days invitations were issued for visitors to come and share in the beauty of the unspoiled woods, and countless carriages and traps could be seen moving along the long drive to the house. Autumn was the season for organised shooting parties with local lads employed as beaters. Pheasants, partridge and woodcock were reared in the woods for such an occasion. The still autumn air was disturbed by excited dogs wheeling around their masters, sniffing the air and waiting for the command to 'fetch'.

On leaving the Scadbury estate I passed along the wide path in St Paul's Cray Common which was originally the main road from Chislehurst to St Mary Cray. Each side was bordered with fine old oak trees resembling the pillars of a lofty cathedral. The analogy was further extended when shafts of sunlight penetrated the branches throwing rays of light to the moss covered nave below as if from a clerestory above. On my right was Dabner's Cottage, smoke curling lazily from the chimney. Before the present road was cut from Chislehurst to Orpington Dabner's Cottage faced the main road which went to St Mary Cray. The new road passed behind the cottage which was then back to front. Originally built as a smithy in 1790, this typical old weather-boarded house was also a bakery. There was a primitive oven fired with faggots collected on the common, the bread being baked on the dying embers. When Dabners closed down my father bought the business for £70 which included all the customers as well as the tins and trays.

Beyond were three cottages, part of which was once the Robin Hood Inn, near Hoblingwell Wood. This name is Anglo-Saxon and means the wood round the well of the hob-goblins. Hob or Rob was the pagan god of nature, the name gradually evolving into Robin Goodfellow whose name was associated with the outlaw of Sherwood Forest. These links with pre-Christian times leave a tangible aura in these magic places of the past. It is

The Manor House, Manor Park Road

not too fanciful to imagine generations of simple folk partaking of simple ale at the Robin Hood Inn after dressing the well.

Beyond lay Bridger's farm which supplied much of our milk in Chislehurst. The apex of the hill, now St Paul's Wood Hill, opened on to a panoramic view of strawberry fields, orchards and, in the distance, hop fields. Poor folk from far and wide came to earn money picking fruit in season. They were allowed to take home whatever fruit they could carry. Shoes, caps and handkerchiefs were used to convey home the 'perks' of the job. Once the fields were officially picked the locals could move in and clear any fruit which was left free of charge. A fruit picker's wage was between 10s and 15s per week.

The mansion of Marlings was owned by the Berens family, hence the modern names of Berens Way and Kevington Drive, Kevington being the family seat in St Mary Cray. The house of Marlings stood back from the main road just past Leesons Corner on the left hand side of the road in the direction of Orpington.

The cottage in the woods, now the property of the National Trust, once witnessed the brutal murder of a husband and wife who were employees of the Berens family.

Returning across the common I came to Manor Park, a fine road of Victorian houses with well maintained gardens and well run homes. The Manor House in Manor Park Road is a misnomer as Chislehurst has never had a manor house in its history. Mr G.H. Bascomb acquired the property in 1849, made many modern additions and gave it the status of a Manor House. The one time owner, Mr Perdicarris, was taken prisoner by brigands when on business abroad and was held to ransom for some considerable time.

My daily deliveries around the area enabled me to observe in some detail the local houses and the daily lives of the people involved. Although I did not call at each house an extensive area was covered each day and an even greater area was encompassed when Petts Wood was developed in the nineteen twenties and thirties.

Each morning Sir William Willett was out riding the common on a handsome horse. He always shouted 'Good morning, young Battle, all these lovely hours of sunshine wasted with folk still in bed'.

Early one winter morning I was out delivering on foot with our pet terrier, Punch. He barked at the galloping horse of Sir Leonard Powell from Heatherbank causing it to rear violently almost unseating the rider. Sir Leonard chased me on horseback brandishing his whip and shouting abuse. I turned on my heels and ran, only reaching the sanctuary of the churchyard in the nick of time.

After saddling our horse, Ivan, and putting him between the shafts I loaded the van with white and brown bread, milk and currant loaves and flour. This was sold by the peck and half quartern (14 lb or 3½ lb). My first customers were along Royal Parade which I have already described. Swinging right into Bromley Lane I called on the old homes facing the common. Miss Barnes at Rose Lawn ran a training school for domestic servants and was an agency for the employment of the young trainees. There was also an orphanage for the Waifs and Strays. After the last house, Woodbury owned by Dr Brennen MD, was Brettenby which is now the Duke of Kent Court, the Masonic home for the elderly. The Robinsons, who were in residence then, lost twin boys, drowned whilst on holiday in Cornwall. It was a great local tragedy.

Across the road was Sunnymead, a fine example of mid to late Victorian architecture. During the First World War Lady Wadia would entertain the officers and men of the Royal Artillery when they towed their guns from Woolwich to Chislehurst common for practice. She sent her staff to our shop to buy up all the cakes and buns to feed the hungry soldiers.

Fairlight, another Victorian gem, lay behind Sunnymead. A fierce Pomeranian dog roamed the garden which snapped persistently at my heels as I walked down the long gravel drive. Frequently a baker's basket was the only protection from over-zealous house dogs. Outside three mature monkey puzzle trees provided an ideal challenge for agile children to climb.

It was Sir Patteson Nickalls who resided at Fallowfield in Ashfield Lane. He was renowned for his polo ponies which grazed in the paddock next to Miss Pentlow's cottage in Bull Lane. Mr Meers lived in Shepherds Green,

Church Row showing from left Council Offices, Telegraph Office, Post Office, Wells & Lea before they moved to Royal Parade

the fourth house on that particular triangle of land. Until recently it was Farringtons Junior School. He was passionately fond of church music and had a magnificent organ installed in the house. This wonderful instrument was built at the Organ Works next to the Imperial Arms on the Old Hill and was taken to Sydney, Australia, for their cathedral. The organ builder, Mr Whitely, travelled to Sydney himself personally to oversee the installation. Imagine the consternation of everyone when the completed organ barely produced a squeak. After much deliberation it was discovered that the extreme change in climatic conditions was responsible for the trouble. After adjustments and a period of acclimatisation the organ was finally coaxed into its full tone and volume. To the best of my knowledge it is still doing the same today.

On Mr Meers' death Miss Meers moved to Achlian, a genuine Georgian house on Church Row. She was a generous benefactor to Chislehurst, especially to the church of St Nicholas, and was an authority on local history. She could entertain one and all with many tales and anecdotes.

These four houses were classics of their type. Light and spacious with colourful mosaic tiled floors, lofty ornate plaster ceilings and richly coloured leaded lights.

Returning to the Village Pound I took the horse and van along Church Row. The first shop was run by the Misses Taylor. It was a high quality confectionery business and when finances permitted I could purchase eight marshmallows for 1d. Next door was Andrews, the greengrocer, now the Sub Post Office.

The first house on Church Row was the Council Offices, presided over by Mr Knight, Clerk of the Council. He employed a husband and wife, Mr and Mrs Capon, as foreman of works and housekeeper respectively. The council yard was on the common near the Rush Pond, opposite Oak Cottage. Woods of Crockenhill were the contractors often used and it was here they left the steam roller, granite chippings, barrels of tar and any other equipment needed for the job. The workmen lived in a wooden caravan on the common until the contract was completed.

The next house was the Telegraph Office where the Telegraph Boys in navy blue uniforms and pill box hats stood at the ready with bicycles to deliver the messages. I remember being sent there as a child by one of our pastry cooks to watch for the telegrams to come along the wires. In my innocence I visualised little envelopes containing the messages travelling along from one telegraph pole to the next. I spent many hours patiently waiting until I was enlightened by a puzzled passer-by seeing my upward unwavering gaze. The next cottage housed the General Post Office and was the main office for Chislehurst before the building of the present one in the High Street in 1908. We had four posts a day — 7.30 am, 10 am, 2.30 pm and 7 pm, and four collections, the last one being at 9.30 pm, Sundays 6.20 pm. Telegrams could be sent from 8 am to 8 pm and on Sundays from 8 am until 10 am. It cost 1d to send a letter weighing 1 oz and rose ½d for every subsequent 2 oz.

A draper's came between the Post Office and Mr Edey, the dentist at Jasmine Cottage. Such a pretty house for such a dolourous visit. It was taken for granted one had to endure pain and discomfort if teeth were to be put in order. Continuing up Church Row there was a group of small cottages housing Parrats, corn and coal merchants, the carrier who delivered parcels from the station, and Mr Lambourne who was coachman for Sir Travers Hawes at Nizels in Kemnal Road. The stabling for the horses was also here so they could be tended if sick or needy by the resident coachman who lived above. In some of the places further along the road rooms were let to gentlemen or paying guests were taken in. At one time one house was used as a preparatory school for Coed-bel Girls' School in Lubbock Road. Mr Pattison, who lived at Pirbright, had some appointment in the Royal Household. Most of the Georgian buildings were built of Chislehurst bricks from Pascals brickyard on White Horse Hill and nearly all of them had deep wells in the garden. It was these home wells which provided sufficient water to douse the blaze which severely damaged St Nicholas Church in 1857.

There has been an inn on the island of land now occupied by the Tiger's Head since the fifteenth century. The sign probably derived from the coat of arms of the Walsingham family. In the early 1900s it was a comfortable hostelry, popular with cyclists who came into the country for the day. It was

Rectory Cottages

Coopers in Hawkwood Lane

the landlord of the Tiger's Head who provided the feast for 1,000 parishioners on the village green to celebrate the Treaty of Paris in 1814. Virtually the whole village was entertained with the hope that Napoleon had at last been defeated. The grubbing, burning, levelling and sowing of the eight acres to form the cricket ground incurred a debt of £191 in 1822. A dinner was held at the Tiger's Head to consider ways of recovering the money. It was ordered for 6 pm on Saturday April 22nd at the cost of 4s per head. It was decided the annual subscription for the Cricket Club would be £2. The landlord, himself being a useful cricketer, kept the Club's wine in safe keeping, allowing a pint for each player, man or boy. One cannot but speculate as to the condition of the players when they returned to play after an early lunch with such a liberal quantity of liquid refreshment. Successive landlords maintained the tradition.

Continuing behind the Tiger's Head and before reaching the five Rectory Cottages was the Fire Station. The fire brigade was established in 1868 but did not have its first call for active service until ten years later. When maroons alerted the neighbourhood of a fire horses were taken from the stables at the Tiger's Head and harnessed to the nearby fire appliance, to be up and away with bells ringing and helmets sparkling. One of the Rectory cottages was formerly a school and later became the first station of the new police. Unfortunately No.1 was destroyed by a bomb during the Second World War. The owner was taking a bath at the time and was hurled into the garden as naked as he was born, none the worse for his experience.

Further along Hawkwood Lane was Coopers, another fine Georgian mansion. Within the estate were some magnificent cedar trees, most of which survive today. Coopers was one of the houses in the area which had an ice house, maintaining cold storage conditions throughout the summer months.

One of the owners, Captain Henry Bowden of the Scots Fusilier Guards, was a convert to the Roman Catholic faith. He took part in the Battle of Waterloo and later, this time allied to the French in the Crimean War. Bowden was married twice. His first wife, Emma, was the daughter of George Norman, a well known personage of Bromley Common. His second wife, Marianne Catherine, daughter of Major Sir Montague Burgoyne, was of direct descent from Edward III. It was Henry Bowden who was responsible for bringing back to Chislehurst the public celebration of the mass after three hundred years. He donated the land and endowed the work for the building of the little church of St Mary. It took but nine months to complete and was consecrated on August 8th 1854. The early congregations consisted of the Bowden family, Irish quarrymen engaged in building the Elmstead Woods tunnel, workers from the paper mills in the Crays and farm labourers.

The arrival of the French exiles in 1871 with their attendant court greatly enriched the finances of the church and beautified the interior. The parish

ST MARVE (RC) CHURCH

St Mary's Church, Crown Lane

priest, sitting astride his horse and wearing a tall hat and tails, would meet the Empress at the church gate. On one occasion, bending low over her proffered hand, he lost his balance and slid to the ground thoroughly losing his composure.

Lord Robert Cavendish was at one time resident at Coopers and it was at this time that Mr Gladstone was a frequent visitor. Morley was the next owner, responsible for the building of Morley Cottages opposite. It is indeed fortunate the name of Coopers is perpetuated in the name of the school now installed, together with the Marjorie McClure School for handicapped children. As already mentioned the productive kitchen garden was worked by Mr Perkins, a greengrocer on Royal Parade. It yielded first class produce, being well tended and protected by a mellow brick wall. Sometimes luscious fruit hung over the wall from a gargantuan fig tree, tempting enough to be lifted from the tree and taken home. The asparagus beds were particularly fine, producing a profitable crop in June.

The present Bansome Wood Stables take their name from an ancient field title. Other lovely sounding names crop up such as Cadlands, Peasons Plain, Hoblingwell Woods, Cooks Parlour, Druggers Land, Wilkettle and Winters Hole to name but a few. Little and Great Thrift in Petts Wood and Thornet Wood Road are clearly named after the ancient woods of that name.

At the end of Hawkwood Lane was a conglomeration of Georgian and earlier buildings which formed Hawkwood House. Originally a small farm it was gradually enlarged over the centuries to become a very large house with beautiful gardens and a magnificent avenue of lime trees. These limes can still be seen, the rooks cawing noisily from the rookery above.

The bread for the house was kept in a huge wooden box in the cellar. Before ordering each day the cook, a short stout fussy woman, stood with arms akimbo at the top of the steps demanding to know how much bread was left from the previous day's delivery before ordering a further eight or ten loaves. For a household of hungry servants bread provided the basis for their meals. Cooking for large families and staff the huge joints of meat produced quantities of delicious dripping. The cooks parcelled it up in 2d packets and gave it to the tradesmen to sell whilst on their daily rounds. Many of the poorer people in Mill Place, Park Road and the farm cottages were eager to buy the tasty and inexpensive spread. This was considered the cook's 'perks', as it was for the bakers who cooked joints for customers. The train which left Chislehurst Station at 2.30 pm on Sundays carrying the cooks with their profits to London was known locally as 'the dripping train'.

Hawkwood Lane led into Botany Bay. Here were Hawkwood Farm and the ancient Tongs Farm, together with several small cottages for the farm workers. They were homely but primitive, water being obtained from an outside pump. The right of way eventually led to Towncourt, now a developed area of Petts Wood, via the three railway bridges. In autumn golden corn waved in the gentle breeze where it was harvested and stacked in ricks awaiting the arrival of the threshing machine which came from contractors in Crockenhill. Across the fields was an uninterrupted landscape of woods and pastures in the direction of Orpington and Bickley.

Each year the steam thresher arrived with a team of men who travelled the county contracting for the hire of the machine. The men, many of them ex-soldiers from the Boer War, lived rough, sometimes in lofts and barns or using a caravan which they brought with them. Food was basic. Very basic! I have seen men fry eggs on their shovels and bake swedes in the hot coals of the threshing machine. Earth was rubbed from the swede, the top removed and it was put to cook for the morning in the coals of the steam engine. At midday it was taken out, the soot rubbed off, split open and with the addition of a little margarine or butter made a gourmet's delight. Bully beef was a favourite with the ex-soldiers who turned it into a stew by adding water and vegetables. Beer could be bought for 2d per pint and tobacco for their pipes at 3½d per ½oz. The brew-up was cheap as tea was 4d per quarter pound and sugar 2d per lb.

I have never seen so many rats and mice which appeared when the thatch was taken off the rick. An army of rodents spilled to the ground scattering to all points of the compass. Pandemonium ensued as workers, children,

Rosemary and Jessamine Cottages in Morley Road

dogs and cats descended for the kill. It was not considered unsuitable for children to join in this gory pastime and farmers gave rewards for the greatest number killed.

Straw from the bearded wheat was used in the manufacture of women's straw hats and had to be collected and bundled separately. Other straw was finely chopped up and used for filling palliasses. The men who worked the threshing machines made their shaving brushes from the self binder string from a sheaf and never suffered from skin complaints which were sometimes contracted by those who used an ordinary lather brush. With the advent of the modern combine harvester the old thresher and its large troupe of followers disappeared.

The public footpath leading to Goshill Road was contained by a close metal fence of vertical slats which gave rise to the name of Birdcage Walk. This footpath is open to the public and is administered by the National Trust.

Along Morley Road I called at Norman Cottage, a truly delightful house built towards the end of the eighteenth century. One of the earlier owners was a carpenter and retailer of beer and it is thought at one time to have been an ale house named the 'Union Jack'. Later it became an orphanage for small boys. The interior contained some good panelling and at the time I am recording was the home of Mr Tod, a stockbroker. He had previously lived at Rose Cottage, an attractive Regency house near the west side of the

Tiger's Head. An earlier owner of Norman Cottage built two weather-boarded houses adjoining named Rosemary and Jessamine Cottages. In the spring the Mitchum family erected a small marquee in the front garden where they served afternoon teas and light refreshments. A flying bomb put an end to both and severely damaged The Ivy House next door. This square classically Georgian house was of three storeys surrounded by a yew hedge with a massive yew archway over the gate. This was the home of the Nussey family. Old Mr Nussey was Apothecary and Physician in Ordinary to three successive monarchs, George IV, William IV and Queen Victoria. When the war damage was repaired Ivy House was reduced to two storeys and had lost the famous yew arch. Crown Lane lay behind, mostly workmen's cottages and homes of gardeners, coachmen and grooms.

Old Crown Cottage was an ancient timbered property. As the Crown Inn in the Middle Ages it was the last hostelry for pilgrims en route for Canterbury before they plunged into the wilds of Kent and ran the gauntlet of robbers and highwaymen. For many years it was used as a halfway house for smugglers. In consequence Miss Martin, the daughter of the banker at Camden Court, had the cellars bricked up to rid the house of the smell of spirits when she came into ownership. The ceilings were low, the beams heavy and black with age and the floor level was two feet below ground level. The whole place was permeated with an air of antiquity and history. Here again the same V1 destroyed the house completely, also Well Cottage alongside. It was rebuilt using much of the old timbers and materials. The present Crown Hotel was built in 1874 moving there from the previous position in Crown Lane.

The mellow Georgian house of Bishops Well stood at the corner of Crown and Watts Lanes. It had a classical pillared porch and a door in keeping with the design of that period. The bricked-in windows on Watts Lane side bore witness to the crippling window tax of the past and several leafy elms shaded the front aspect. Fixed to one of these was a lantern lit each night by the owners to give a welcoming glow to travellers on dark winter evenings. The inevitable iron railings secured the front boundary. Bishops Well took its name from the ancient well enclosed in the garden of old Crown Cottage, the public having right of access. This was one of many springs which were consecrated by former Bishops of Rochester when in residence at Bromley Place. One owner, a Mr Woolaston, grandson of Rector Woolaston, was a foremost authority on ferns, creating a beautiful botanical garden at Bishops Well.

Camden Court, formerly known as Cannister House, was not a particularly attractive building although it was large and included stables, a coach house, greenhouses and all the trappings of a gentleman's residence. At one time a previous owner tried to enclose a line of limes which still border the western side of the estate. This was frustrated by a meeting of the vestry which controlled local affairs. Even in those far-off times democracy was seen to be working.

Camden Court, now replaced by Camden Close

A similar example is illustrated in a story told of a naval lieutenant who, not wishing to lose a treasured servant to a sailor by whom she was loved, arranged for the Press Gang to arrive and seize the young man. Villagers heard of the plot and fought a battle with the gang who fled the field defeated.

When I called at Camden Court it was Bishop Bilborough who was in residence, faithfully served by his cheerful Scots housekeeper Jeannie. I can still recall her shrill call and see her shining rosy face devoid of any make-up. Her unruly hair was skewered with countless pins which were in perpetual danger of falling out. Now of course there are many houses in Camden Close, attractive and varied being built mostly of old materials and of period design.

The two houses facing south, Seafield and Athelney, have deep gables in the French style built for exiles of the French court and a reminder to us of their brief stay in Chislehurst.

The White House has little of the original seventeenth century building left apart from the hall, the room above and the cellar beneath. It has been greatly added to over the years resulting in a very interesting house of charm and character which has witnessed much of Chislehurst's history due to its proximity to the village green. The field behind the White House on which the Crown Hotel now stands provided grazing for donkeys. The owner was greatly in demand to carry passengers' luggage to Bickley Station before the station at Chislehurst was opened.

I then arrived at St Nicholas School which warrants special mention.

ST NICHOLAS SCHOOL

St Nicholas School was where I spent my first school years, as so many local children have before and after me. It might be of interest to delve a little deeper into the school's origins in view of the number of people who have personal connections with the school, past and present.

By the early nineteenth century it appears that two schools were established, the boys at Prickend and the girls in the workhouse near the present school. In 1835 Viscount Sydney, Lord of the Manor, leased a site for the sum of 1s per annum for the building of a National School for the education of the poor in the principles of the established church. By 1836 a schoolroom and master's house were built on the present site of the school and opened for both girls and boys. The boys' education was limited to reading, writing and arithmetic while book learning took second place to plain needlework for the girls.

After complaints by Her Majesty's Inspectors a new school building was contemplated. The committee which ran the school was responsible for the building, appointing staff, supplying books, furniture, light and heat. Finances came from three main sources; subscriptions from local residents, grants administered by the Education Department and 'pence' from the children's parents, 3d being the average cost but it proved to be too much for the large families whose fathers probably earned no more than 10s to 15s per week. Eight years after the Inspectors' complaints the new wing was opened on April 20th 1874. In September of that year gas was laid on thus 'affording every convenience'.

A school was opened at the rear of St Mary Hall in the High Street for the children of West Chislehurst in 1887 at the cost of £1,100 and two teachers were appointed. There was also a Dame's school in Perry Street, but it was very small and the children were eventually admitted to St Nicholas. An interesting comment in the school log of 1864 states 'Perry Street children are always more troublesome as a rule than others'. Another entry this time referring to a seven year old, 'Don't think she will do for this school, new to the village'.

In 1877 Mill Place School opened to accommodate the rapid increase of children into the area, probably due to the arrival of Louis Napoleon and his entourage at Camden Place. Christ Church School closed in 1907 necessitating a further extension of St Nicholas' classrooms.

The headmistress of St Nicholas School wrote in the log book, 'Chislehurst children are certainly the dullest children I have heard, not for the want of proper instruction but dull, sluggish understanding, beware!' 'A penny taken off the table, searched every pocket. Found by Emily Mills in the pencil box in the cupboard. Who put it there?'

By the end of the nineteenth century over 200 children attended St Nicholas School, the population of Chislehurst having grown from 1,217 in 1801 to 5,069 in 1891.

The original school was built in 1836, a new wing in 1874 and the final enlargement by 1907 joined the two wings. By this time the Sydney plot had been completely covered and to this day the only hope for extension is upward.

The sexes were segregated in school and during recreation. Coal stoves were the sole form of heating, lit in October and ceasing at the beginning of April, regardless of the temperature. '21.1.1907 Flues blocked by soot. Thermometer stood at 32 degrees at 9.30 am and all day. Children remained in school, permitted to wear hats and coats.'

Throughout the period the school was used for Urban and General Elections as a polling station. It also housed an annual Chislehurst Industrial Exhibition. The title appears to be confusing as it showed local arts and crafts as well as needlework from the girls and woodwork from the boys. The whole quadrangle was roofed in which made an admirable picture gallery, the pictures being lent by some well known artists. The boys' classroom exhibited porcelain, silver work, bronzes and oriental lacquers. There was a Natural History Room showing collections of insects and fossils, minerals and precious stones. The girls exhibited water colours and wood carvings.

The committee governing the school was dissolved in 1904 when the school came under the control of the Kent Education Committee. '3.7.1903. Holiday to allow inventory of school effects being taken for the K.E.C.'

Eighteen seventy-six saw the school boards invested with the authority to enforce attendance with the acceptance of a government grant in 1891. There was no excuse such as want of money to stand in the way of the solemn duty of parents to have their children well educated. The school income was increased by £200 per annum in 1899 in respect of the inflow of children from St Michael's Orphanage nearby.

Early education was ruled by the acceptance of two assumptions. There was general agreement with the notion of original sin and children were thought to be essentially biased towards evil. Education, therefore, was believed to be a process of redemption. Along with this belief was the philosophy believing that at birth the mind of a child was a blank sheet. Education was thought to have the unique opportunity to produce any kind of adult one wished. No wonder days at St Nicholas School were spent learning and reciting the catechism and passages from the Bible with visits from the Rector and to the church at least once a week.

To qualify for examinations children had to attend 250 days in the year. Unfortunately children were often taken away from school to help at home, in the fields or to do seasonal work. '17.9.96. Several children left school today to go hopping.'

Attendances were always markedly lower after holidays due to the fact children were fruit picking and would return when it was completed.

By the end of the century there was an extension in the number of subjects taught. Girls were instructed in Domestic Economy, rules of health, poetry, history, geography, elementary science and botany in addition to the three 'Rs'. In 1906 children's essays were submitted in the RSPCA competition, the practice continuing for several years. My sister Hilda submitted an entry in 1907 and I have the original copy. Art and P.T. were additions to the syllabus which soon followed.

In 1907 provisions were made for the pupils to gain scholarships in secondary schools but St Nicholas School was slow to take advantage of this arrangement. The first success was in 1914 when a boy won his way to Bromley County School.

November 1896 saw the school closed for an indefinite period because of a measles epidemic. Scarlet Fever caused another closure for three weeks in 1904 but due to the fact some children returned before fully recovered it was closed down again from November 11th until December 12th. In 1907 a private member's bill made provision for medical examinations. This revealed ringworm in 40 per cent of the children and a child with bruising on the face was referred to the NSPCC.

Miss Taylor, headmistress until 1864, probably received an annual income between £40 and £50. Mr Eggleston and his wife, who were in residence for thirty-eight years, earned £100 and £60 respectively. In 1897 the newly appointed Greenfields received £180 in total.

Discipline was strictly enforced and corporal punishment was in the form of six strokes of the cane given for thieving in local shops, four strokes administered for bullying, all being entered in the log book. One wonders the precise situation which prompted this entry: 'Emily Holland set fire to herself in the dinner hour. Told never to have dinner at school again.'

By 1923 the girls attendance numbers had fallen and in consequence they were sent to the Annunciation School. Boys stayed on at St Nicholas. The authorities did not return to the coeducational system until 1951.

ST MICHAEL'S ORPHANAGE

St Michael's Orphanage began as the local workhouse where spinning was the principle industry. Sail and rope making and other hempen articles were made to order, the Master of the Workhouse receiving ten per cent of the return for the business done. During the Napoleonic wars, when food was scarce and expensive, the inmates of the workhouse were put to work clearing gorse and scrub from the common for the purpose of growing potatoes. The wide path on the western side of the common, which is still in existence, is the remaining evidence of this experiment.

When the Bromley Workhouse was built (now part of Farnborough Hospital) the building at Chislehurst was no longer needed and it was let, until purchased for an orphanage in 1861. It housed 50 children from various classes of society but mostly from trade and service. They all attended the National School with the other children.

The orphanage was first opened in one of a pair of cottages (now Saxbys) on St Paul's Cray Common, being run by two worthy ladies, sisters-in-law of Canon Murray. This institution was the first of its kind to have close connections with the Church of England and many local ladies have worked hard over the years to raise money for the funds of St Michael's Orphanage. The two Miss Anderdons managed the establishment for forty years and in 1897 the surviving sister handed it over to the Church of England Waifs and Strays Society. These two worthy ladies were also responsible for the founding of the Annunciation Almshouses in 1881, a picturesque row of half timbered cottages situated on the fringe of the churchyard.

DAILY ROUND CONTINUED

I cannot leave the village green without reference to the cockpit on the open ground to the west of St Nicholas Church. It is considered one of the finest examples of its kind in the country, being 120 feet in diameter and 4½ feet deep with gently sloping sides. The inner circle is 95 feet in diameter surrounded by a raised path 12 feet wide. Thankfully cock fighting was abolished in 1834 and after it was used for bull and badger baiting it witnessed the less cruel sports of cudgelling and single stick bouts at the annual fair. Patches of purple and blue indicated rose bay willow herbs and delicate harebells. In summer the lark's throbbing throat proclaimed its joy higher and higher in the summer sky until it was but a distant speck. The cockpit and surrounding village green were a focal point where villagers were drawn in times of stress, thanksgiving or celebration.

Urging the horse into a quick trot I left School Road and joined Bromley Road near the Overflow. This lane has since been filled and become part of the common, as several others have done.

There were only six houses at the top end of Camden Park Road facing the golf course all of which were built by William Willett. At the time of building each house had to sell for £1,500 or over, a considerable sum in those early days. The initial letter of each house in turn spelt Camden, thus Camden Holt, Avonhurst, Mountfield, Derwent House, Elmbank, but the last name escapes me. Perhaps a reader with a long memory can provide the answer? This nameless last house eventually became Bonchester and was the home of Sir Malcolm Campbell's parents. As a pilot in the First World War he landed his plane on Chislehurst cricket ground and people flocked to see this unusual sight. A ring of small boys, hands in pockets, stood around in awe of this glamorous figure who climbed from the cockpit in leather jacket and goggles.

On November 5th some of the local children were invited to join in the private firework display which was given annually at Avonhurst. Derwent House was the venue for the children's Sunday School Party. Here we were entertained to a sumptuous tea and all participated in games and races.

Again, there were only six houses with extensive grounds sited around the Cricket Ground; Rosemount, Chipstead, Leweston, Hawthorn, Mayfield and Millfield, the last being the site of the old windmill. Strategically placed on the hill summit, the mill had been built in 1796 by the Rector, Lord Sydney and other local gentlemen who took shares in the undertaking. It was meant primarily for the convenience of the parishioners and the poor had the privilege of having their corn ground at 1d per bushel on Mondays

The old mill at the summit of Summer Hill

Mill Place, showing an enclosure for animals

and Tuesdays. Two stones were reserved for this specific purpose. The Rector eventually transferred his shares to the parish which formed the basis of an endowment for the school.

The mill came into the possession of Mr Bascombe in 1868 and as it was in a poor state of repair he announced he was going to pull it down. He erected a fence around the mill and an indignant crowd of villagers promptly removed it as they had recently been granted the land for common and public use. By compromise Henry George Bascombe gave back part of the land but had the old mill razed to the ground in one piece. The mill was said to have been visible from Lewisham, a lovely sight on the high ground with the sails turning in the wind. From the top of the hill there was an uninterrupted view across London via Crystal Palace and Dulwich. Although the mill was destroyed in 1868 the area of small cottages originally housing railway and mill workers is still known as Mill Place. It was a complete community and retains that quality which must be delightful for those who live in those steeply terraced homes. A general shop served the needs of the cottagers and a covered well to the south of the Ramblers Rest was an ideal place for the women to chat and gossip. St John's Church was built as a chapel at ease to St Nicholas and services were held regularly on Sundays and a sermon preached.

Close by was the Ramblers Rest, one of the most popular pubs in the county. It was somewhat smaller than it is today but of the same weatherboarded appearance. I believe then it was only a beer house. Above on the higher ground, where many today sit and enjoy their drinks on a warm day, were rows of washing lines. What an ideal place for the Monday wash to stress and strain against the brisk winds sending the split pegs flying. It was the gypsies who sold such items, calling from door to door with hand whittled pegs.

We are more than fortunate in having such a beautiful cricket ground. The West Kent Cricket Club was formed in 1822 and played at Princes Plain on Bromley Common. This was lost by enclosure but by the good offices of some influential members they acquired the use of the present one at Chislehurst, under certain safeguards, for public use.

West Kent Cricket Week was an event to be anticipated with pleasure. Very much a victim of the weather it could be a delight or a wash-out. Marquees were erected on the cricket ground where members, players and guests were lavishly entertained. A certain aroma trapped within the confines of a marquee is synonymous with pleasurable outside activities. Matting on the grass kept dry and warm the well shod feet of the ladies. Elegant fashions were displayed by the ladies anxious to show off their finery, including wide straw hats piled high with flowers and birds and frivolous, frilly parasols twirling gaily in the sunshine. Quantities of strawberries and cream and iced coffee were demolished by the spectators as they debated the relative merits of one or other of the players. The laden tables

The famous gates of Camden Place and the avenue of lime trees

festooned with greenery were soon emptied whilst the steaming urns
whistled away to provide hot water for the tea. Some of the local children,
hoping to see the sights within, were hustled away by the champagne serving
waiters. Outside in the sunshine the villagers thronged the perimeter
bringing their own ginger pop and cakes. Visitors flocked in from miles
around when West Kent played their matches against the MCC, the Royal
Artillery and the Royal Military Academy from Woolwich. W.G. Grace
lived in Mottingham and was a frequent visiting player. Gentry arrived in
carriages, the country folk in decorated wagons or on foot.

A grand ball was held in the evening of the last night of Cricket Week at
Camden Place. Successive carriages crunched up the gravel drive through
the famous gates which dated from the Paris Exposition of 1867. Grandly
wrought in iron the lamps illuminated the gold crowns above. They were
taken with all the other wrought iron and cast iron railings for the war
effort in 1940. Towards the house was the noted avenue of sweetly scented
limes, past which the carriages glided carrying ladies in their finest gowns
and men in white tie and tails. Many a man sported a boiled shirt that night
and wore immaculate white gloves for dancing. It was well into the early
hours of the morning when the revellers were collected by patient coachmen
ready to drive them home, lamps flickering and glowing in the warm
summer night. They did not spare a thought for the unhappy victims as they
passed the site of the old gibbet at the junction of Bromley Road and Watts

Lane. Ghosts of tortured souls haunt that corner; no wonder the commemorative pink horse chestnut tree which marks the spot refuses to thrive.

Spanning the Bromley Road was the water arch already mentioned, built as a water tower and toll gate. It was never used for either purpose. Not a building of particular architectural merit although it was typically Victorian gothic with red brick turrets at each end. Two families were domiciled within, their homes comprising several floors. Traffic could pass through singly and there was a separate arch for pedestrians. We, the public, unfortunately were too slow to react to the news of its impending demolition and opposition came too late. It was pulled down in 1962 and is remembered by a plaque at the top of the hill.

It was at the apex of the Old Hill and Bromley Road where I eased old Ivan to the water trough to slake his thirst. With the demise of horse drawn vehicles the trough is now filled with flowers.

On the left beyond the Water Arch was Ravenshill, a house set in spacious grounds with a lovely garden and heated greenhouses. Once inside the gate any one of three dogs came to the attack which called for some dextrous work with the bread basket for defence purposes. Cromlix was the next house and further down the hill was Heatherbank, set well back from the road. This was the stately establishment of Sir Leonard Powell which was reached by a curved uphill drive. In spring the grassy slopes were carpeted with daffodils and narcissi. Down the drive at full speed galloped his coach and four, a liveried coachman in front and another behind blowing a horn. They flew through the Water Arch at a spanking pace, everything and everyone moving aside to let this magnificence go by. Spirited Dalmatian dogs were frequently seen running alongside the coaches and carriages. Black and white and liver and white these sporting dogs were originally bred to protect the travellers from the dangers of the road.

Set well back from the road, behind rhododendrons and laurels, was Avalon, now owned by the Salvation Army but then a private house of unusual style. There were only two cottages to be served in Gosshill Road then a fast trot up Bickley hill, past the station-master's house and Merevale on the right. My goal was East Hill, a mansion at the summit of the hill, now an estate of houses. It belonged to Joynsons, the paper mill owners from St Mary Cray.

Back to the station and along to Lower Camden where lived a community of Germans who were badly treated by some local residents during the Great War. Several of the families with German names had them changed by deed poll, resulting sometimes with a brother having one name and a sister another. The German bakery produced a variety of bread and pastries typical of their homeland. The bakehouse was underground and it was possible to see the men at work through a grill in the pavement at the front of the shop. Wonderful aromas of freshly baked bread and cakes wafted upwards to my appreciative nose.

Lower Camden in 1906

Coed-Bel, Lubbock Road, a private school for young ladies, 1905

Lubbock Road was named after Sir John Lubbock who lived at Lamas and was the founder of Bank Holidays. He became the first Lord Avebury. Worsketts, of the London glove company, were in residence in my time. St Hugh's Prep School originated at Lamas. To reach the house of Camden Hill, now Great Ash, I left the horse and van at the end of a long, long, steep drive and climbed the hill carrying my basket. If my basket did not contain the exact requirements of the cook it was a long trudge back to the van and an even more onerous climb back again. It was no wonder I needed my shoes repaired every two weeks. Pieces of thick leather were nailed over the worn parts of the sole to save the expense of a complete resole. This primitive method of repair was aptly called 'clumping'.

Mr and Mrs Fehr lived at Hatton House, now the site of numerous flats. Long after the car had become every man's method of transport Mr and Mrs Fehr still went abroad in a victoria. Mr Clifford Platt of Leesons tells of the occasion on walking home from the station during the Second World War he saw Mr Fehr's victoria drawn up outside the house of his masseuse, Miss Marjorie Astell. On the box sat his coachman, old Egglesfield, his top hat on the seat beside him, a tin hat on his head with a flying bomb roaring across the sky.

Abbeyfield was a Red Cross Hospital between 1914 and 1918, as was the church hall at Christ Church. It was the generosity of residents in Chislehurst and Bickley which enabled Christ Church to be built, taking in part of the parish of St Nicholas, Chislehurst and part of St George's, Bickley. It provided a 'lower church' service than St Nicholas or the Annunciation Church and helped to provide for the spiritual needs of a fast rising population in that area. Lord Sydney laid the foundation stone in 1871 and it was consecrated the following year by the Archbishop of Canterbury. It is a commodious and spacious church providing seating for seven hundred parishioners.

Camden House and the Imperial interlude which put Chislehurst in the limelight with visiting royalty and dignitaries is dealt with in the appendix. It was a Mr Weston who rebuilt the house in the eighteenth century, adding acreage to his estate towards Red Hill. He planted the fine avenue of limes. The house in time came into the possession of Charles Pratt, afterwards Lord Camden. He eventually became Lord Chief Justice and a peer of the realm but was not above acquiring more adjoining land by one way or another, including the common land. There was much strong feeling expressed amongst the villagers about these enclosures and the vestry agreed no further land was to be granted to Lord Camden.

A merchant by the name of Bonar purchased the building in 1805, he and his wife being cruelly murdered by their manservant who was publicly hanged at Penenden Heath in May 1813. The tomb in the churchyard of St Nicholas bears a strange inscription insisting that their sudden death

Camden House, the former home of the Imperial Royal Family

The entrance to Whites Oakwood, Willow Grove, 1908

together was really a mercy in delivering them from the slow pains of a more natural dissolution! This was quoted by Gladstone in one of his parliamentary battles with Disraeli. Gladstone must have seen the inscription on one of his visits to Coopers. It was the Bonar's grandson who sold the mansion to Mr Strode, the gentleman who offered the residence to Napoleon III.

Crossing Yester Road I proceeded up Southill Road passing Glen Druid on the left. There were four or maybe five houses in the road. Taking a turning to the right up a stony road was Wild Croft, the residence of the Sankey family (builders merchants). Higher up was Sitka, now SIRA, Scientific Instruments Research Association. The owner, Dr Oska Teichman, tells of his father, a well known figure in the neighbourhood. He was a fur merchant by trade when Alaska was bought from the Russians in 1867 by the USA and all trading agreements lapsed. Mr Teichman, at the request of the London Fur Traders, made a dangerous journey by ship to the capital city, Sitka. He concluded new successful arrangements and the fur trade remained with this country. At the foot of Sitka drive I put a nosebag on the horse and ate my lunch, a quarter of fresh cooked ham from Deans in the village, some new bread and perhaps a couple of slices of cold plum pudding from my mother's larder. Libberters, a farm at the junction to Walden Road and Willow Grove, sold soft drinks and other refreshments. Here I purchased a bottle of Chislehurst Mineral Waters, lemonade or ginger beer which completed the feast. Chickens scratched about the yard and behind were apple and pear orchards which made a colourful show of blossom in the spring.

Mr Teichman's neighbouring house was Walden which has since become the site of Yester Park. This estate in turn joined Oakwood, the home of the De Quinceys, a proud Victorian mansion with a lake and boathouse. This family were connected with the successful breeding and showing of Sealyham Terriers. Whites, whose house was also called Oakwood, was next door. Their estate included the wood by the recreation ground near Red Hill which is still known as White's Wood. There were many other mansions in this area, amongst them Waratah, Elmstead Grange, Elmstead Knoll, Walden Manor, Elmstead Glade, Storth Oaks and Cranmore Place. Mr Solway, the gardener at Cranmore Place, produced a glorious show of roses each summer. 'Never prune before the end of March' was his advice and I have always acted upon it with benefit. He also recommended bedding out plants in the first week of June to avoid late frosts. The garden was a blaze of colour when the Primrose League Garden Party was held there each year. Beyond lay miles of open farming land and verdant woods.

Beechcroft, with its lovely views across the golf course, was owned by the Williamson family. They employed George Watto, David Livingstone's faithful negro servant who travelled from his native Africa to bring home his master's body for burial. He had been saved by Livingstone from slave traders and was in consequence devoted to his benefactor. He was a short

Wesleyan Chapel

Wesleyan Chapel, Chislehurst.

Wesleyan Chapel

The Wesleyan School, Willow Grove

man, exceedingly black, and wore a long overcoat which reached almost to the ground. Balanced precariously on a wheelbarrow he had a disconcerting habit of popping his curly black head over the fence just as you were passing. He was employed as a jobbing gardener, married a local girl and had two sons. The origin of his name appears to stem from the greeting of folk when they saw him, 'What ho my fine fellow?' He worked the pump for the organ at St Nicholas Church and Mrs Watto took in washing, delivering it on a trolley.

Pinewood, now a block of flats, and Luson House, now Foxhome Close, were also on the right approaching the village, with lovely views across the golf course. Luson House was destroyed by a flying bomb in 1944 with a tragic loss of life. Golf View was the last house on that side of the road until the semi-detached villas near the High Street.

Opposite was the Wesleyan School, originally built as a Sunday School in 1875. It was enlarged twice to make it suitable as a day school. The schoolmaster's house was built alongside for £600. The school building was typical of that period, constructed sturdily of red brick with high narrow lancet windows. Alas all was swept away to make room for Furzefield Close. Nearer to the now Sainsburys car park entrance was a small row of villas which were also demolished by a flying bomb in 1944. The Annunciation School was wrecked and St Mary Hall badly damaged.

A Bazaar at the Wesleyan Church Hall. The prices for supper were 1s roast beef or ham and 1s 6d chicken or tongue. 6d bread and butter with tea, 9d with jam and cake. Note the beautiful lace edged tablecloths.

Peace Celebrations, 1919. Miss Ethel Pierce on the extreme right.

Annual Sports held on Red Hill to the rear of where the Library now stands, 1914

There was but a handful of attractive houses in Wilderness Road, Frank Tiarks at one time lived in Roycroft. Other houses still bearing their original names were Morlands, Copley Dene and Selwyn Lodge, all built by Sir William Willett.

The executors of Mr Strode of Camden Place gave the ground for the erection of the Wesleyan Chapel, as was done for Christ Church. The Chapel was built in 1868 for the modest price of £5,800 and opened for worship the following year.

Miss Ethel Pierce of Burlington Lodge in the High Street devoted sixty years to teaching in the Sunday School and eighty years in worship. She tells of eight or more classes meeting several times on a Sunday. Bible classes for boys and girls were on Saturday mornings. If children were naughty they were relegated to the awkward squad. Once a week a special service was held on the common by the pond. The congregation were always formally dressed and gloves were a 'must', even if they were only cotton and well darned.

Early in the life of Wesleyans in Chislehurst meetings were held in the kitchens of private homes. There were house groups, Lady Chubb, later Lady Haytor, being one who provided a room for such meetings. The congregation were keen on supporting foreign missions and letters sent home from missionaries in China, India and Africa were read at classes as an example to others. A tea was given annually at Beechcroft, the event being finished off with prayers in the lovely music room.

The old White Horse before rebuilding at the end of the last century

The old White Horse Inn with the massive elm

Win Browning standing in the middle of Victoria Road, 1907

The church was very alive in those days and had devotional, social and guild sections which claimed crowded gatherings and meetings. Gradually youth clubs began to take away the young people and the character of the classes altered and decreased.

Halfway up Red Hill was a cottage and coal yard near where we now have the library. At the summit was the White Horse Inn, recently rebuilt and modernised as a typical late Victorian pub. The former structure was of early Georgian origin, a quaint and picturesque old inn of Kentish design with weatherboarding and dormer windows. Outside stood a huge pollarded elm of immense girth on which was hung the sign of the White Horse. It creaked and groaned on winter nights when the south west gales hurled themselves against the top of the hill. Here also was another horse drinking trough of granite, a relic of days gone by when all our transport was on four legs.

Behind lay the brickfield which was of some antiquity. There are documents of accounts for tiles supplied for the building of Hampton Court Palace in 1532 at the price of 25s 8d per thousand. The brickfields were closed in the 1890s due to the death of the owner after a continuity of over three hundred and fifty years. Brickfield cottages originally housed the workers who earned their living in the brickfields and others who worked in the surrounding area. It was common knowledge that police patrolled in pairs over White Horse Hill, then called Telegraph Hill, as it was known to be too risky for an unarmed officer to venture alone.

White Horse Hill (Telegraph Hill) with shop and cottages. There was open farmland on the opposite side of the road, 1910.

Green Lane decorated for the Coronation, 1911

Across the road from the White Horse Hotel was a path leading to Old Telegraph Field. Before the days of electricity Canon Murray's grandfather, Lord George Murray, Bishop of St Davids, invented a shutter telegraph. It was extensively used during the Napoleonic wars from 1796 until it was superseded by semaphore in 1822. These telegraph stations were strategically placed between the Admiralty in London and Dover and by a line of stations messages could be sent in seven minutes over that distance. Chislehurst was situated between Forest Hill and the Birchwood station. It is not too fanciful to imagine that the news of Trafalgar and Waterloo reached London by this means.

The footpath eventually led to Green Lane which was a narrow muddy track surrounded by farming land. It was free of houses apart from one or two widely separated cottages. At the foot of the hill returning towards Chislehurst was Kemnal Lane (Belmont Lane) which was then a private road leading to Foxbury. Belmont, halfway down the lane on the left, was built early in the nineteenth century. It was a small country house standing in spacious grounds surrounded by a high yew hedge. Back in Green Lane allotment gardens gave way to Victorian terraced houses on either side of the road. Each terrace was known by a different name such as Frognal Villas, Carlisle, Bickley and Marland Terrace instead of a number in Green Lane.

In one of these lived Mr Ledner, a well known painter and decorator in the area. He resided at No.1 Marland Terrace. Highly respected for his work he did much for the Tiarks family at Foxbury and the De Quinceys at Oakwood. An accomplished artist he painted many pictures, including the four seasons on the panels of a door in one of the Chislehurst houses. Perhaps someone can throw some light on the subject and recall where this was executed. The owner of Bickley Hall presented him with a porcelain faced German landing clock in token of his appreciation of Mr Ledner's worth. It is reputed to be 150 years old and still owned by the family.

At the end of the week when his workmen were paid their wages, one of Mr Ledner's daughters served each with a tankard of beer drawn from a wooden barrel. It was customary at the time for decorators to finish the final coat of plaster with milk to give a smooth and glossy surface. Due to the fact the temptation to drink the milk was irresistible, Mr Ledner mixed it with disinfectant to discourage the habit.

Two of his daughters were members of a set of lancers and all of them, eight in number with their escorts would ride to local dances in a carriage. On returning, if the gradient of the hill was too steep, the men alighted and pushed to aid the struggling horse to gain the summit.

Mr Ledner owned a somewhat macabre relic in the form of a piece of wood reputed to be part of the coffin in which the Prince Imperial was returned to England in 1879 after his tragic death in Africa. Mr Ledner, a

Mr Ledner with his staff at the rear of his home in Green Lane

The Rush Pond. On the left behind the trees was the meadow where Mrs Bowen's Jersey herd browsed.

Prickend Pond and Heathly House

grand old man, eventually moved to Brighton in 1917 where he lived and painted pictures until he was 97.

So to Mead Road, a pleasant road with some very attractive houses, Golden Mead and Sweet Meadows, names reflecting the rural ambience of the locality. Penthorpe was a private school which has maintained its scholastic connections to this day. Proceeding up the narrow lane and opposite Prickend Pond was Mead House, occupied for several generations by the Shackleton family. Sir Ernest Shackleton, the eminent Arctic explorer, died on an expedition in 1922.

Blanchard House, now rebuilt as flats for the elderly, was formerly known as Furzefield and was the home of Spinks the West End jeweller.

My next call was at a low stuccoed house, Heathly, built about 1760, just before the crossroads of Heathfield and Ashfield Lanes. The owner, Mr Bowen, was a local solicitor. His wife had acquired the adjoining meadow opposite the Rush Pond where a herd of fine Jersey cows browsed amongst the buttercups. It was a picturebook meadow surrounded by graceful elms and sturdy oaks. These provided shade for the animals who swished their tails, chewed the cud and gazed with mild curiosity at the occasional passerby. Even when the weather was wet the rising mist, diamond studded webs and dripping trees had a magic quality. The peace was disturbed from time to time by the resonant roar of the Jersey bull which caused much annoyance to the neighbours. The arrival of summer

Foxbury, Kemnal Road, the home of the Tiarks family

Dining Room

Lounge

Swimming Pool

was heralded here by the cascading song of the willow warbler and the sweet aroma of may blossom hung heavily on the still air on warm evenings. Occasionally someone would call at the back door of the house carrying an enamel can for milk and a few new laid eggs.

It was outside Heathly one day that I pulled up the horse as the bridle had worked loose. As I tried to adjust it the horse reared its head, slipping off the bridle. The horse bolted down Green Lane, the van lurching crazily from side to side with me in hot pursuit. Swerving at the last moment into Mead Road the van overturned spilling out loaves and showering flour all over the road. Tommy Atkins, the butcher, lent me his new motor van to complete the day's delivery.

Many years ago a carpenter named Ringer lived in one of Webster's old cottages. This was the heyday of smuggling and many took the chance to cheat the revenue men for the sake of a handsome profit. Ringer was renowned for his fine celery beds which were adjacent to the timber yard and in which he was reputed to store the illicit liquor. I have already mentioned Woodlands where the Webster family once lived and whose name is remembered in much of that area of Chislehurst.

On the opposite side of the road on the fringes of the common were some very fine horse chestnut trees. One of them was struck by lightning during a particularly severe storm killing a nursemaid and a child from Cookham Dene whilst they were sheltering beneath.

Turning left into Kemnal Road I came to Meadowcroft which is now Marlowe Close. What a wonderful greenhouse full of semi-tropical fruit presented itself to me on my way to the back door. Lush black grapes hung in heavy clusters and were covered in a delicate velvet bloom. Nectarines and peaches gave off a wonderful aroma and melons, round and heavy, were supported with frames and nets.

Woodheath which was next, now named Hoblands, was burned to the ground and rebuilt in its present classic style by Frank Tiarks. He owned the first swimming pool in Chislehurst. His gamekeeper lived in a nearby cottage and was responsible for the shoots and maintaining the supply of birds for this purpose. Westerland was then known as South Laund and Nizels was the home of Sir Travers Hawes who was chairman of the Chislehurst Commons Conservators for many years. A professor of theology, Dr White, lived at South Home. The two adjoining cottages housed the coachman and gardener. Lords owned Inglewood and the Payne family were at Selwood. Mr Rowan lived in the lodge and was gardener for Nelsons at South Home. Kemnal Wood and Holly Bowers are now covered with estates of houses and many flats. Pecketts, the well known authority on stamps, lived at Mulbarton Court, then known as Wivelsfield.

Foxbury I have already mentioned as the home of the Tiarks family. It was the only house on which I called which boasted of a housekeeper. Each week I collected the account in her private sitting room. A box containing the bread was large enough to accommodate twenty to thirty loaves as there

Haymaking at Foxbury, 1908. Mr Frank Tiarks in white suit. Mr Browning and Mr C. Ince on the hay wagon.

A prize bull, 'Webbington Freemason', bred at Foxbury

A later aerial photograph of Foxbury

were many servants to be fed. The head butler was chief of staff equally with the housekeeper. Footmen opened doors, helped visitors to and from their carriages and waited at table. Cook was commander in chief in the kitchen, having kitchen and scullery maids to help her. There was a lady's maid for Mrs Tiarks' personal attention and chamber, parlour and house-maids completed the indoor staff. Away from the house over the stables was the bothy which accommodated the male staff of the estate and where they fended for themselves, cooking their own meals and generally leading a bachelor existence. The 'phone connecting the bothy to the house was one of the first to be installed in the area. There was always some ribbing and ribaldry when I arrived, a close cameraderie developing amongst men living and working together.

Outside was a graveyard for the family pets. Inscribed stones were kept scrubbed clean and the grass well clipped.

Although the origins of Kemnal Manor go back to 1250, it has had an uneventful history. For centuries it belonged to New College, Oxford, and

View of Foxbury from the lakes, 1905

Websters Pond at the junction of Ashfield Lane and Kemnal Road. Fallowfield, the home of Sir Patteson Nicholls, seen between the trees.

the surrounding woods were used for charcoal burning until 1794. The house in my time had no particular claim to antiquity but it occupied one of the most ancient sites of the parish. Kemnal Road was heavily wooded and formed a right of way to Sidcup Road where the bus for London could be boarded. Beneath the massive oaks, beeches, limes and cedars rhododendrons and azaleas blazed in colour during the early summer.

The horse knew when I approached the end of the round and became skittish and eager to be off and home to his stable. A quick drive through Websters pond cleaned the dust and mud from the wheels and cooled the hooves whilst he drank his fill. With a flourish he was off at high speed, the iron bound wheels rattling and bouncing over the uneven surface of the road. Another day's work done.

Rosie Atkins, who became Mrs Battle.

CONCLUSION

In trying to collect together all these loose ends of history and memory I have attempted to paint a picture of a Kentish village, our village, during the Edwardian period.

The population at this time was around eight thousand which was small enough for most people to know many of their neighbours. Their triumphs and tragedies were known and shared by all, as were petty feuds and jealousies. There was a feeling of continuity, for ordinary people could not afford to travel far afield and children usually followed in the footsteps of their parents. A large percentage of the population worked on the land with tied cottages and this by definition produced a feeling of permanence as well as discipline dictated by the seasons.

Gentry involved themselves in local affairs and in the main were fair and charitable. They would always inquire of the family remembering names and illnesses, show an interest in the progress of one or another, give advice and perhaps loan money. A labourer, domestic, tradesman, craftsman, policeman, doctor or solicitor all fitted into a slot in the strata of society, most people accepting its inevitability, but you never forgot 'your place'. Nothing had occurred to upset the old order. The First World War had not yet erupted upon us upsetting our values and causing us to question the old ways.

Education was opening up, a few scholarships and grants were being offered. A wider range of subjects was included in a school syllabus and girls were no longer only instructed in the womanly crafts. Transport was advancing. Already cheap rail fares allowed day trips to the coast and easy access to London. A week could be spent in one of the Kent coastal towns with change from £5. Holidays for all had arrived. Cars were beginning to reach our roads in increasing numbers and forms of mechanisation to our farms. Flight was contemplated as a real possibility instead of the pipe-dream of centuries. Medical care was improving rapidly due to a wider use of anaesthetics, understanding of antiseptics and various early forms of immunisation and vaccination.

Everyone was encouraged to 'get on' or 'make good' and with a little money, a lot of hard work and a bit of luck it was possible to do so. Life was concerned with basics, having a roof over your head and enough to feed the family. Any free time or money was a bonus which was not expected but enjoyed to the full if offered. Lack of communication made us parochial and self absorbed in our own little sphere. Newspapers were our only contact with the outside world. People were nearer to nature, knowing the natural world and compromising with its foibles.

Alas we have now grown further apart. The motor car and supermarket are less sociable than a walk to the village and a chat over the grocer's counter. We have lost our innocence and have become more sophisticated, too sophisticated to enjoy the pageants in the Rectory meadow or the fun of the Bank Holiday Fair, even if present day hooliganism allowed it. The First World War began a change in attitudes and values and stimulated faster development of invention and innovation. The population doubled and trebled at an alarming rate and the property developers raced to provide the accommodation needed. Twenty-one years later the Second World War again accelerated change, altering time honoured values and traditions and gradually Chislehurst evolved from a village into a pleasant suburb. We had lost our self sufficiency.

There have always been those who have served the community in whatever capacity, who have left an indelible stamp on our village life. Little specks of Chislehurst are planted securely all round the world by the adventurous or famous. It is due to the farsightedness of our forefathers that we now enjoy the commons and our lovely cricket ground in perpetuity. They planted cedars and avenues of trees, built fine houses, beautified our churches, created our memorials and chronicled our history. Each era mirrors its successes and failures in town and village. We can look to our own and possibly come to different conclusions. Those of us who still remember, do remember the forgotten years, the happy years, the years of achievement and the years of failure. This then is the eternal saga of ever changing village life and the later development of Chislehurst is another story.

Royal Parade
Chislehurst
Nov 21. 1918

Dear Arthur.

Now that the excitement of the glorious news has subsided,
I expect you boys are getting anxious to get back to civil
life again. One problem solved, another to be solved.
"What do you think of doing". You have got to make
up your mind seriously what you want to do, and
stick to your job, and see it through.

I must get out of the bakehouse at once, as Dr. Tallent is
of the opinion, that I shall be no better unless I get out.
Are you in the mind to come back and take my place
there to help O'Brien, and do the round.

If so, I am quite willing to give you an opportunity of
doing your level best to help me in the business and
by so doing, help yourself to a position for your future.
But it means a few years of hard work and great
perseverance to put things right again.

I do not wish to influence you at all in the matter,
you must choose yourself, as you are old enough now to
know that the work of reconstructing a business, requires
grit, and strength of character, if it is to be a success.
There is a good business always to be done here, and
I should like to see it grow, and improve, as I feel
sure it would, if I had the necessary help.

I want you to seriously consider the matter as I must
get help as soon as possible, and let me know.
What you propose to do.
I do not think there would be much difficulty in
procuring your discharge if I applied for you,
but you must just make your own choice.
Mother is sending on a few things today which I dare say
will meet with your approval.
Pleased to say all are well and send their fondest love
to laddie, and the same

From your affectionate father
J A Battle

POSTSCRIPT

After the Great War my father asked me if I would like to join him in building the business. The area was developing fast and it was time for expansion.
We bought a Ford van and I canvassed the customers as they moved in,
particularly in Petts Wood. Outside catering was developed and delivery
expanded to cover a large area.

Unfortunately my father developed viral pneumonia and died early in
1923. Family affairs changed. I married and started a bakery business at
Burlington Parade in 1925. The old bakery on Royal Parade continued to
produce confectionery for the Royal Parade, Lower Camden and Orpington shops as well as the new one at Burlington. Bread was baked at the
Lower Camden and Burlington bakeries. Events continued in this way
through the Second World War years. Production was maintained throughout air raids and flying glass, shortages and synthetics. In 1945 we closed
the old bakery on Royal Parade, it no longer being financially viable.

It remained closed through the years, collecting dust and cobwebs. The
iron doors of the great oven rusted away and the ancient whitewashed walls
peeled and crumbled. At last in 1985 it suffered a metamorphosis. The
premises were sold to a firm of accountants. The oven was dismantled
revealing its massive structure and eighteenth century clay pipes amongst
the broken masonry. The floor was relaid and carpeted, the walls plastered

and hung with pictures. It had become an elegant boardroom. The old beamed kitchen, sitting-room and bedrooms became offices complete with word processors and computers. The ancient cottage is awaiting a similar awakening, to be restored to its former glory, when hollyhocks peeped over the fence and primroses clustered around the rock garden. It would be sad to see so many past years disappear without trace.

Royal Parade has changed fundamentally since those far off times. There were then two butchers, a baker, two fishmongers, a grocer, two green-grocers, a dairy, a chemist, a saddlers, upholsterers, builders, a haberdasher, ironmonger and forge, bookseller, draper, tailor, a doctor, a vet and a pub. Only the latter has stood the test of time. These days Royal Parade offers a specialist selection of shops — antiques, gift shops, baby clothes, interior decorating, up market clothes, jewellers, hairdressers and restaurants.

The fresh fish shops have gone from the High Street, so have the green-grocers and sweet shops. There is only Sainsbury's to supply our groceries. We have building societies and estate agents in profusion and a fair sprinkling of dress shops and restaurants. Traffic lights and numerous pedestrian signals regulate the teeming traffic which litters the High Street and cars fill every available space both legally and illegally.

Thanks to the continuing existence of the commons we have managed to retain some degree of individuality and have not become a 'run of the mill' suburb. Perhaps because our village has a legacy of history with roots deeply implanted in the past we can today reach out and touch the magic of a bygone age.

Appendix

GENERAL INFORMATION AND PAST HISTORY

Chislehurst in the late nineteenth century was described as 'situated in the Hundred of Rokeslie, in the Lathe of Sutton at Hone, in the County of Kent'. Distant eleven miles from London. For civil purposes Chislehurst formed one of the group of fifteen parishes which constituted the Rural District of Bromley, its local affairs being administered by a parish council. It formed part of the Parliamentary Division of Sevenoaks and in conjunction with the Crays and Orpington elected a member to the Kent County Council. For ecclesiastical purposes it was then a part of the Rural Deanery of Dartford, the much loved Reverend F.H. Murray being Rector for approximately the latter half of the nineteenth century.

Until the creation of the Greater London Boroughs in 1963 Chislehurst covered about six square miles, bounded on the west by Bromley, north by Eltham, on the east by the Crays and by Orpington in the south. This rural parish was divided into two parts by the common. The north eastern portion referred to as Prickend, later named West Chislehurst, and the central area surrounding the common with outlying areas consisting of farms and family estates.

The Saxons named the area Ciselhyrst 'the wood on a stony hill'. Hasted describes the name as being self-evident 'From the numerous trees which grew amid the gravelly soil of the neighbourhood and waved in primeval grandeur over the rocky brow of the hill'. By the eighteenth century it had altered to Chesilhurst. Hasted also records 'A number of elegant villas with gardens and plantations beautifully disposed around the common, being for the most part inhabited by persons of fortune and distinction'. Many great houses with extensive grounds were the residences of judges, bankers, East India Directors, Lord Mayors and wealthy merchants.

The poor soil is probably the reason the commons are still in existence, consistency being mainly of sandy gravelly soil which overlies an earlier geological strata. Chalk is to be found 135 feet below the surface of the highest point. It was the advent of enclosures in 1759 which enabled the building of the workhouse. This island site later housed St Michael's Orphanage and is now private residences.

From a record of a meeting at the Bull's Head in 1776 the jurors stated on oath that 'Any person who should dig turf, make any encroachment or permit hogs to root up the soil of the commons did infringe the rights of the Lord of the Manor and the inhabitants of the Parish of Chislehurst'. The Lord of the Manor did, however, have the right to cut and sell trees, underwood, bracken, turf, peat and gorse, in fact anything growing on the common land. The area was exploited for gravel and minerals due to the demand from the rising industrialisation of North West Kent. This removal caused the formation of the ponds we now see and enjoy, Prickend Pond, the Rush Pond and the Overflow. At the turn of the century there were also ponds by the Tiger's Head, at the foot of Red Hill near the Library and at the corner of Kemnal Road. This pond was known locally as Websters after the family of that name who lived at Woodlands, now Roehampton Drive.

Areas of surface peat were removed altering the appearance of the commons. From time to time fires burned down gorse, sometimes smouldering for days underground, destroying the roots. One such fire in 1870 raged on St Paul's Cray Common for nearly a fortnight, the depth of peat being considerable and the area consisting mostly of heathers. The effect of this fire was remarkable. Some time afterwards an abundant growth of young birch trees appeared and in time became a thick wood. The birch are, even now, in the majority amongst the other trees in that area of the common.

General neglect was prevalent and the dumping of rubbish had taken their toll of the area. A public-spirited body of men, amongst them Mr H. Travers Hawes, Mr Nettleton Balme, Mr E.L. Beckwith and Mr Watts (Watts Lane) formed a preservation society which caused an Act of Parliament to be passed in 1880 which allowed the commons to be administered by a board of Conservators, sixteen in number. Great care has been taken over the years to insure their independence from any local authority. The sand deed was purchased from the Lord of the Manor in 1898 for £350. With the sale of this deed he lost all previous rights, only retaining the allowance to sport over the common and to have access to his estate. This small lane leading to one of the Scadbury Lodges still remains from St Paul's Cray Road.

The 1880 Act defined the Board of Conservators to consist of one person appointed in writing by the Lord of the Manor, eight elected by the Vestry of the Parish of Chislehurst and seven elected by the Vestry of the Parish of St Paul's Cray, four of whom shall be land owners or resident occupiers of property frontaging St Paul's Cray. All roads across the common were deemed to be common land and no road was to be wider than 40 feet including footways. Bye-laws helped to prevent encroachments, deposits of rubbish, cutting of herbage and damage to trees and shrubs. Notice boards were erected to this effect. The removal of ice from ponds was forbidden as many people stored ice underground for refrigeration purposes. A clerk was to be appointed to deal with the clerical and executive work.

A few varied details from the Minutes of Conservators' Meetings —

May 12th 1896 Permission given to Chislehurst cycling club to hold a bicycle race on the Cricket ground.

March 11th 1902 The usual arrangements for coconut shies etc on Easter Monday to be allowed in spite of the prevelance of smallpox in London.

October 17th 1910 Erection of red triangle motor sign was agreed.

July 21st 1900 Resolved no further licences to be granted for the letting of donkeys for riding on the commons except for Bank Holidays.

In 1918 three thousand birch trees were felled on St Paul's Cray Common for the price of 1s 3d each.

In order to appreciate Chislehurst at this particular time it is necessary to recall some of the relevant historical facts and worthy residents to whom the village had borne witness.

William Camden, the famous Elizabethan historian and antiquarian, supposedly lived the last fourteen years of his life at Camden Place. He evacuated from London in order to escape the plague which was virulent at the time. Lower Camden, Camden Park Road, Camden Close and Camden Grove were all named after this illustrious man. The original estate also took in the areas of Lubbock Road, Wilderness Road and spacious lands out towards Red Hill. The property did not, however, carry his name until one hundred years after his death. He died in 1623 and was buried in Poets Corner at Westminster Abbey. Sir Thomas and Lady Walsingham were at that time in residence at Scadbury Manor and were neighbours of William Camden.

Several other notables owned Camden Place, amongst them Lord Chief Justice Pratt who took the title Baron Camden. After lying empty for some years because of the unpleasant connection with the murdered Mr and Mrs Bonar, a Mr Strode purchased and improved the house. Some of the fittings were reputed to be of the finest French craftsmanship of the eighteenth century and originally came from a hunting lodge belonging to the Bourbon family. The drawing-room possessed an elaborate mantlepiece of Dresden china and the tapestries were known to have fetched enormous prices when sold on the death of Mr Strode. It was ironic that many of the rooms had firebacks displaying armorial bearings of France in view of the next occupant of the house.

Napoleon III formed an acquaintance with Mr Strode in the 1840's and when in 1870 came his fall from power after the Franco Prussian War, Mr Strode offered his home to the Emperor. Although the Emperor continued to scheme and plot nothing became of his intrigues and he died in 1873 after some years of ill health.

His funeral was attended by the Prince of Wales and was a sombre spectacle. A huge procession, led by a deputation of French workmen from Paris, crossed the common from Camden Place to St Mary's Church in Crown Lane. Behind the hearse walked his only son, the Prince Imperial, and the Murat Princes, Lord Sydney and Lord Sheffield represented Queen

The Prince Imperial, at one time in love with a local girl

The Memorial in Petts Wood to William Willett, the inventor of daylight saving.

Prince Imperial Memorial

Victoria. There were officers of the Imperial Household and generals of the French and Italian Armies in full dress uniform streaming across the common on a mild day in January. Throughout the ceremony the funeral bell tolled from St Nicholas Church in respect of the dead leader. The Empress stayed on in Camden Place with her son who was to meet a tragic end in South Africa in 1879. His funeral procession was also magnificent and Queen Victoria stayed at Camden Place to console the distraught Empress, one of several visits she made to the imperial family.

On the common opposite Camden Place the people of Chislehurst erected a memorial to the popular Prince in the shape of a Celtic cross. This granite monument is decorated with golden bees and violets, the emblems of the House of Bonaparte, and can still be seen on its original site.

Some part of the Camden estate was sold to Sir William Willett, the well known builder and the inventor of daylight saving. He loved fresh air and sunshine and regretted the lost hours of daylight when sleeping in bed. Following in his father's business he designed quality houses in Mayfair, South Kensington, Belsize Park, Regent's Park, Sloane Square and in Sussex at Hove. Priority in the design was given for the admission of light. Willett acquired the Camden Park estate in 1890 intending to develop the whole area. Problems arose over access across common land and only Camden Park Road and Wilderness Road were laid out. The upper part of Camden Park Road was developed, Willett's distinctive style of architecture being easily recognisable. Sir William himself lived at The Cedars facing the cricket ground. The handsome red brick building at the junction of Lubbock Road and Lower Camden were his stables housing some fine mounts.

The Chislehurst Golf Club was formed in 1894 and was formally opened by Arthur Balfour, Camden House being utilised as the Clubhouse. An unusually fine painting was made of the house by James Tisot, the renowned French painter. Apparently it was a favourite visiting place of his and the painting has been exhibited from time to time.

Scadbury, recently acquired by the London Borough of Bromley, has known many august 'Lords of the Manor' in its long history since the thirteenth century and beyond. In 1424 it was bought by Thomas Walsingham, a London merchant, and remained in his family until 1657. His great grandson, Edmund, was knighted at the battle of Flodden and served Henry VIII as Lieutenant of the Tower of London for many years. His nephew, Sir Francis Walsingham, Queen Elizabeth's famous secretary, is said to have been born at Scadbury. His daughter married Sir Philip Sidney, the renowned poet and scholar, who died of wounds whilst fighting in the Netherlands in 1586. Later she married the ill-fated Robert Devereux, Earl of Essex, who was beheaded on the orders of the Queen.

The Walsinghams were followed by Sir Richard Betteson and after 73 years the Manor passed by marriage and purchase to Colonel Selwyn. His

The Stocks at Scadbury

The Moat Hall, Scadbury. The reconstruction by Hugh Marsham-Townshend.

daughter married Thomas Townshend in 1751 in whose family ownership it remained until the death of the Honorable John Marsham Townshend in 1975.

The Hon. Thomas Townshend, 1701 – 1780, pulled down the ancient manor house intending to rebuild on a grander scale. With the sudden death of his wife he lost interest and purchased Frognal which was the seat of his descendants until 1921. During these intervening years Scadbury was run by a bailiff.

The son of Albinia and Thomas Townshend was created the First Lord Sydney in 1783 and held the office of colonial secretary. Six days after Captain A. Phillips landed at Botany Bay in 1788 the future city of Sydney was founded and named after the Colonial Secretary, Lord Sydney. He suggested the colonisation of New South Wales. It was from that time onwards for 70 years that England took the unprecedented step of transporting thousands of convicts to the penal settlement which was set up at Botany Bay. There is also another Sydney city in Nova Scotia which is named for the same Lord Sydney.

The third and last Lord Sydney, created Earl by Queen Victoria, died in 1890 and was buried at Chislehurst. A recumbent figure of this famous man lies over his tomb in the Scadbury Chapel at St Nicholas Church. Having no issue the title became extinct and his half-sister's son, the Rt Hon Robert Marsham, inherited the Manor of Chislehurst and Scadbury on condition he added the name of Townshend to his own.

The Frognal estate was taken over as a hospital for the wounded during the Great War and it was here early plastic surgery was pioneered. Many had reason to be grateful for a patient rebuilding of a damaged face or disfigured hands. Later it became a hospital for convalescent soldiers and it was a common sight to see men in 'hospital blue' walking in the grounds of the hospital. Eventually it was named Queen Mary's Hospital with which we are all familiar, and consisted of long rows of wooden huts. The remains of the mansion were used as a nurses' home and later for offices. Even now it can be seen alongside the modern hospital which has been built to replace the old.

After the First World War the Townshend family returned to Scadbury, to the plain Victorian mansion built near the historic remains of the old house.

Hugh Marsham Townshend became interested in restoring the old manor house but unfortunately no contemporary illustrations of the old house existed. The house was known to have been of multi-period construction, some early medieval work with many later additions. The lower part of the house was brick and the upper storey of timber. Sir Hugh consolidated the footings by adding further courses of bricks which in some ways merely confused the issue, making it difficult to discern the old from the new. The adjacent Kiln Field and Chalk Pit Field indicate the original building materials were probably obtained locally.

Bickley Hall, at one time owned by Mr Wythes who was responsible for the construction of the water arch at the summit of Summer Hill. Bickley Hall later became a school.

Awaiting the mail train at Chislehurst Station

During the excavation of the moat and foundations large cracks were revealed which could have been the reason for the demolition in 1752. It was Sir Hugh's interest in the original building which caused his curiosity to be aroused when Manor Farm was dismantled in 1936 in what is now Cray Avenue. He was convinced the ancient timbers, which included a medieval crown post roof, had come from the old manor hall at Scadbury which had stood on the moated site until the eighteenth century. These remains were re-erected at ground level and tiled over, thus making an impressive crown post roof for posterity. However, in later years the remains suffered two disastrous fires, were deemed unsafe and pulled down. It was a great tragedy that most of the old records which would now be so informative were lost in the fires.

Chislehurst Station was once sited at the foot of the Old Hill, this being at that time the main road to Bromley. My Wythes of Bickley Hall built a Water Tower in 1860. It was of imitation German half-timbered style and was placed at the entrance to his estate. He was determined to keep his property private so intended to fit the tower with gates and the private estate he hoped to build would be amply supplied with water from the tower. This proved impossible due to an ancient right of way which led through the area. It was never necessary to put the water tower to practical use as there was already an ample supply of water available. This unusual building straddled the Bromley Road at the summit of Summer Hill. It never had the gates fitted and traffic was always allowed through. Two families lived in this unique arch which provided a single width road for traffic and a separate path for pedestrians.

The gradient of Summer Hill was easier than that of the Old Hill and this new road soon became the best and most frequented route to the railway. A request was put to the Southern Railway to move the station to its present site.

The new station was huge by today's standards, especially in view of the small population it served. It was plainly built of red brick with heavy iron girders and excessively long platforms, all encased with massive brick walls. There were two entrances, one on the Bickley side for goods which were raised and lowered to the platforms by lifts, and the other entrance which passengers use today. Full-time staff manned two newspaper and magazine stalls and waiting rooms on each platform provided a welcoming coal fire in the grates. Outside coach and horses plied for hire. Coastal trains made special unscheduled stops at Chislehurst when someone important wished to alight. They were greeted on the platform by the station-master resplendent in frock coat, pin-striped trousers and a black silk hat. Mr Lord, the station-master, drew a heavy gold watch from his waistcoat pocket, checked the time of the train and signalled for its departure. The station-master's house was situated on the Bickley side of the bridge and is now a private house.

Afternoon tea at Chislehurst Caves

Beneath Summer and Old Hills lie a labyrinth of man made tunnels carved from chalk. These excavations are approximately twelve feet in height and width and were dug in pre-Roman times. The caves were thought to be excavated for the purpose of lime burning and a kiln for this use once existed on Old Hill. During the Great War the caves were used to store ammunition for which they were considered one hundred per cent safe. Between the wars the caves were open to the public and at one time mushroom growing was tried out.

The last war brought thousands of bombed out people to shelter in those inhospitable subterranean caverns. Before electricity was installed hundreds of precariously perched candles were the only form of lighting, casting long shadows and creating an eerie atmosphere. Some made the caves their permanent home and tried to make them more homelike with strips of carpet on the floor and curtains to create an illusion of privacy. Others used the caves as an air raid shelter, arriving by train at dusk and returning at dawn to see what remained of their homes.

The magnificent mansion of Foxbury in Kemnal Road was the home of the Tiarks family, of Schroder Bank renown, and was built in 1876. The estate covered many acres and encompassed several farms and former estates, including Homewood in Perry Street and a large portion of land belonging to Kemnal Manor. There were lakes with ornamental water fowl and waterfalls cascading over rocks, fountains spraying iridescent water into shimmering pools and landscape gardens ablaze with alpines. There were shrubberies and arbours, summer houses, formal gardens and long weedfree gravel drives.

In summer the Sunday School children had a picnic in this fairytale garden. They ate jam sandwiches and sticky buns and drank lemonade and ginger pop. Games were organised and races run; grazed knees were bandaged and small children comforted and catechisms forgotten until the following Sunday.

Partridge and pheasants abounded in the woods and gamekeepers made certain there were plenty for the shoots which were organised with beaters and dogs.

At this time the Tiarks owned land on both sides of Kemnal Road and beyond the South Lodge gate the lakes could clearly be seen from the road. The walls dividing up the fields were of west country stone and transported at great cost from Cornwall. Mr Limes, the head gardener, lived at the North Lodge and would pass the time of day with me as I walked to the main London Road to pick up the bus for the city, as did Canon F.H. Murray many years before me.

In the 1920s and thirties polo was played on the fields where Middlesex and St Bartholomew's Hospital now play rugby and cricket. There was much entertaining at the big house and national celebrities were often to be seen arriving and leaving through the lodge gates. Foxbury mansion is now owned by the Woolwich Equitable Building Society.

STORIES

JOHN BUCHAN
Stories

Introduced and selected by
Giles Foden

London
The Folio Society
2008

'A Captain of Salvation' and 'A Journey of Little Profit' first appeared in *The Yellow Book* in January 1896 and April 1896 respectively; 'Politics and the May-Fly' first appeared in *Chamber's Journal* in May 1896; 'Streams of Water in the South' first appeared in *Grey Weather* in 1899; 'The Watcher by the Threshold', 'Fountainblue', 'The Grove of Ashtaroth' and 'Space' first appeared in *Blackwood's Magazine* (the former in *The Atlantic Monthly* at the same time) in December 1900, August 1901, June 1910 and May 1911 respectively; ' "Divus" Johnston' first appeared in *The Golden Hynde* in December 1913; 'Basilissa' and 'Fullcircle' first appeared in *Blackwood's Magazine* (the latter in *The Atlantic Monthly* at the same time) in April 1914 and January 1920 respectively; 'The Loathly Opposite', 'Ship to Tarshish' (originally entitled 'Ships to Tarshish'), 'Tendebant Manus', 'The Last Crusade', 'Sing a Song of Sixpence' and 'The Wind in the Portico' first appeared in *Pall Mall Magazine* in October 1927, November 1927, December 1927, January 1928 (serially), February 1928 and March 1928 respectively; 'The Strange Adventures of Mr Andrew Hawthorn' first appeared in Cynthia Asquith's *The Silver Ship* in 1932.

First published by The Folio Society Ltd 2008
The Folio Society Ltd
44 Eagle Street, London WC1R 4FS
www.foliosociety.com

This edition follows the text of the three-volume *Complete Short Stories* published by Thistle Publishing in 1996, with minor emendations.

Second printing 2009

Set in Goudy at The Folio Society.
Printed on Abbey Wove paper by Martins the Printers Ltd,
Berwick upon Tweed. Bound at Hunter & Foulis, Edinburgh,
in cloth, blocked with a design by the artist.

CONTENTS

ILLUSTRATIONS

vii

INTRODUCTION

These stories were published between 1896 and 1932. London's Stock Market and clubland feature in a couple of them, but their true terrain is the Scottish moor – or its analogues in Alpine peak, African savannah and Canadian tundra. John Buchan's primary concern in them is to examine how individuals end up in such places, and what others say about the space left behind. Why do we actively seek jeopardy? Why light out for perilous wilderness, treacherous mountain, stormy ocean? These are the questions asked by Buchan's short stories.

If there were such a thing as a prose of departure, then this book would be its best exemplum. Such a category, however, might obscure with too much fine literary feeling the male principle of striving to escape settled home life which is one of the things going on in these tales. For yes, it is mostly men round here. Or, more to the point, somewhere else. Not here. Doing their duty, maybe, in their own way, but not usually at the kitchen table.

Buchan himself always loved walking, regularly covering thirty miles in one day. He knew the Highlands well, enjoying fishing and stalking. He knew even better the remoter spots of the Border hills, whose semi-nomadic shepherds made a great impression on him as a young man. But despite the aggressively male environment of his stories, whether it be club or camp, Buchan took his home life with him. After his marriage to Susan Grosvenor in 1907, they visited Scotland together nearly every year for a summer holiday.

Some things don't need too much explanation. A good deal of these stories are simple testaments to their author's love of the outdoors. The weather plays a large role. So does hunting and fly-fishing, recalling similar episodes in *John Macnab* (1925), Buchan's best-selling novel recounting how three powerful men try to poach two stags and a salmon from a Scottish estate.

Yet while it is mainly the relation between men and landscapes which attracts Buchan's pen, too much can be made of this. It is the skill of his characterisation and the clarity of his writing which put him in the front rank of British short-story writers. He is not just a landscape painter. The vividness of the scenes, the freshness of the style, the penetrating shrewdness of the psychology – this is why Buchan continues to appeal to a large popular audience. He does so despite the passionate disagreements about gender, class and Empire to which his work nowadays often gives rise.

Another sign of Buchan's literary virtue is the sheer complexity of some of the narrative structures on display here. Sometimes there are as many as three sets of interlocking narrators. Very often there is more than one occasion or jumping-off point from which the tale is told. Characters recur, interrupt each other's narration, are referred to in asides.

As a consequence of this technique, Buchan could include many of these tales in *The Runagates Club* (1928). His last collection of stories, it brought together disparate material under the guise of fantastic tales told by classic Buchan characters familiar from the novels – Lord Lamancha, Sandy Arbuthnot, Sir Edward Leithen and others – over lunch or after dinner at their club. Many of the narrating individuals have bit parts or interpolating roles in tales other than those they narrate. So the historian Martin Peckwether tells 'Fullcircle' (although the narrator in the original version reproduced here is called Jardine) but has an interpolating role in 'Tendebant Manus'.

Probably the most important character in this respect is Sir Edward Leithen, Border Scot, London-based barrister and MP. One of the powerful men who takes up the poaching challenge in *John Macnab*, he is said by Susan Buchan to have been the closest of Buchan's characters to that of the author himself. He is the linchpin of Buchan's world.

Leithen is often up in Scotland taking a rest from hard work, but he has nothing on Buchan himself in this respect. Buchan's own life is like a morality tale promoting personal industry. His literary output comprised thirty novels and more than sixty non-fiction books. Little read today, the non-fiction books, including biographies of Walter Scott and Cromwell and a massive history of the First World War, contain some of his best work. Yet despite the pride he took in it, and the success it brought him, writing formed only a small part of John Buchan's achievements.

Born in Perth in 1875, he was the son of a minister of the Free Kirk who preached in the Gorbals. He was educated at Hutcheson's Grammar School and at Glasgow University, in whose magazine he published his first short story, 'On Cademuir Hill' (1894). He won a scholarship to Brasenose College, Oxford, where he was awarded a first in Greats and wrote his first two historical novels, *Sir Quixote of the Moors* (1895) and *John Burnet of Barns* (1898).

After Oxford Buchan studied for the Bar, combining journalism and legal work until 1901 when he took a job as a civil servant in South Africa, arriving there in the wake of the Anglo-Boer War. By 1903, he was back in London, producing a copious stream of journalism, stories and full-length books. Buchan continued to work as a barrister at this time, specialising in tax work and publishing a textbook on the subject. In 1907, he also became a director of the publishing firm Thomas Nelson.

In the First World War, he was a correspondent for *The Times* and a staff officer at General Haig's headquarters. He later worked in intelligence and propaganda, before being appointed Director of the Ministry of Information. During this period too, he published some of his greatest novels, including *The Thirty-Nine Steps* (1915) and *Greenmantle* (1916), both of which sold in vast quantities.

After the war, Buchan became deputy chairman of Reuters, the news agency. In 1920, he bought a rambling Oxfordshire manor house, Elsfield, versions of which would feature in various stories and novels. In 1927, Buchan won the seat for the Scottish Universities as a Tory MP, all the while continuing his prodigious literary output. Honours flowed in middle age. He was made Baron Tweedsmuir of Elsfield and a Lord High Commissioner to the General Assembly of the Church of Scotland. In 1935, Buchan was appointed Governor-General of Canada. He died in 1940 in Montreal from a cerebral stroke, leaving behind him the brooding *Sick Heart River* (1941), in which Leithen is killed off.

As Andrew Lownie – Buchan's biographer, and the person responsible for unearthing and collecting many of Buchan's more elusive stories – has noted, Buchan's method of publication of stories changed during the First World War. Before the war, he tended to write short stories and publish them in magazines ad hoc, only collecting them in book form when he had amassed enough. After the war, he wrote stories expressly intended to be collected in books and then sold first serial rights at the time of book publication.

Structurally, these stories owe a good deal to fairy- and folk-tales in their use of traditional situations, motifs and patterns. They also often spring from a quotation or a Biblical reference or from Buchan's wealth of classical learning. Another notable aspect of the stories is Buchan's smooth use of Scots dialect and idiom.

Thematically, there is much play with 'the gods of the Pagans'. Buchan is fascinated by the survival of atavistic forces in the modern age. In a typical gambit, a kind of literary camouflage, positive primitivism is often used to fight negative atavism. Ancestral forces are themselves deployed against the family curse, and understanding old rituals becomes the best way of deflecting their deleterious effects. In such contexts, doing one's duty ostensibly means the triumph of courage over fear, civilised belief over barbaric superstition, fortitude over weak-mindedness. However, the way the stories themselves so often depend on the unknown for their power suggests something more complex may be taking place.

The story 'Basilissa', originally published in *Blackwood's Magazine* in 1914 and later transformed into the novel *The Dancing Floor* (1926), contains many of these currents. It is the tale of a young man, Vernon, who is haunted by a recurrent dream from boyhood of a house on an island in which something happens. He does not know quite what the thing is, only that he will be brought where he is needed at the appointed time, when fate will take a hand (as it often does in this writer's work).

Other common Buchan themes are the delicate balance of civilisation and anarchy and – in effect the same concern in microcosm – the relationship between personal will-power and sensuality. In 'A Captain of Salvation', the story of a man brought down by drink and 'evil living', then redeemed by the Salvation Army and his own strength of will, we see an individual representation of Buchan's general preoccupation with the fragility of ordered society: 'He simply *went under*, disappeared from the ranks of life into the seething, struggling, disordered crowd below.'

'A Captain of Salvation' was first published in 1896 in *The Yellow Book*, alongside contributions from George Gissing, Kenneth Grahame and H. G. Wells. Its hero's former life was one of reckless adventure throughout the Empire. Meeting Hilton, an old colleague in crime who tempts him to resume their activities, the Captain is subject to an internal struggle. The temptation is vouchsafed in the form of geographically expansive narratives, as Hilton reminds him of the pagan joy of picketing in the Drakensberg, sailing down the Irrawaddy, or sugar farming in Queensland.

This fine early story's concern with the ordered and the disordered prefigures many other instances later in Buchan's literary career. In 'Fountainblue' (1901), collected here, the Cabinet minister Maitland talks of the 'very narrow line between the warm room and the savage out-of-doors . . . You call it miles of rampart; I call the division a line, a thread, a sheet of glass.' The same sentiment is expressed in Buchan's novel *The Power House* (1916): 'You think that a wall as solid as the earth separates civilisation from barbarism. I tell you the division is a thread, a sheet of glass. A touch here, a push there, and you bring back the reign of Saturn.'

Buchan often in fact actively seems to be trying to do just that in these tales. Like his novels, they derive much of their power from flirtation with sin, the underworld or the occult. In one story he raises the devil directly. 'A Journey of Little Profit', also in *The Yellow Book* in 1896, tells the story of a young drover who does not sup with a long enough spoon. The lack of mastery over one's own passions identified in the shepherd seems to be linked in Buchan's mind with the eternal struggle between good and evil.

In Buchan's world-view, only the strongest men can contain that struggle, which is signified throughout his work by a religiously inflected dialectic between mastery and weakness. Mastery over one's own sensuality usually means the fulfilment of one's destiny and some great role in life. So the Salvation Captain has 'almost the power' of being a great leader, 'for in his masterful brow and firm mouth there were hints of extraordinary strength'. One of his companions, meanwhile, who does not have this strength, is depicted as having 'flopped on his knees beside the sofa and poured forth entreaties to his Master'.

As President of the Scottish History Society in later life, Buchan played a big role in preserving collections of folkloric records. In these stories we see him playing a similar kind of curatorial role. It is part of Buchan's genius to link the observed patterns of agricultural life under stress from industry and social change to a mythic past in which materialism played no role.

This is strongly evident in the story 'Streams of Water in the South' (1896). One of my own favourites, it may be that it was also one of the author's own since it is among the few stories to be included in both of his main short-story collections *Grey Weather* (1899) and *The Moon Endureth* (1912). As Lownie has pointed out, 'It exhibits certain parallels with Walter Scott's "Wandering Willie's Tale".' In his stories Buchan consciously imitated not just Scott but also R. L. Stevenson. He also, in a slightly different mode, paid homage to Joseph Conrad and Rudyard Kipling.

'Streams of Water in the South' is narrated part by a young man who seems close to Buchan himself, part by the shepherd Jock Rorison. The main character is Streams o' Water or Yeddie or Adam Logan, as he is variously known. Streams o' Water is a strange figure who appears out of nowhere in the Border hills to help drovers herding their sheep through torrential burns. He does so out of a mixture of pure generosity and a compulsion which is destinal or even curse-like.

The harshly realist ending is in sharp contrast to what we first hear about Streams o' Water. It begins in a 'romantic narration' of Rorison's which is listened to and described by the young Buchan figure. Then, 'the strange figure wrestling in the brown stream took fast hold on my mind, and I asked the shepherd for further tales.' By the time Yeddie appears again, he moves like a wraith between actuality, story and legend:

> So the shepherd talked, and as at evening we stood by his door we saw a figure moving into the gathering shadows. I knew it at once and did not need my friend's 'There gangs "Streams o' Water" ' to recognise it. Something wild and pathetic in the old man's face haunted me like a dream, and as the dusk swallowed him up, he seemed like some old Druid recalled of the gods to his ancient habitation of the moors.

Ancient habitations also feature in 'The Watcher by the Threshold' (1900), the title story of another collection of Buchan stories, published in 1902. Ladlaw, 'a cheery, good-humoured fellow, a great sportsman,' is transformed when believing himself possessed by the spirit of the surrounding moor, apparently the holy land of the ancient Picts. Ladlaw also exemplifies another common concern of many of these stories, which is the man who suffers a change in his life.

Sometimes it can be a happy change. In ' "Divus" Johnston' (1913), a sailor from the Glasgow suburbs finds himself being worshipped as a god somewhere in south-east Asia. But more usually the change is a sad one involving a sacrifice of some type. In 'Fountainblue', for example, the politician disappointed in love, Maitland, 'saw our indoor civilisation and his own destiny in so sharp a contrast that he could not choose but make the severance'. He throws off his glittering political career to go to Africa.

The special house or garden or other type of place is another preoccupation of Buchan's. In Scottish legend it might be a fairy glen. In his autobiography, Buchan himself described it as the sacred grove of the Greeks, 'a *temenos*, a place enchanted and consecrate'. One of its most powerful showings is in the story 'The Grove of Ashtaroth' (1910), in which the main character worships an ancient goddess in his garden.

The same idea is at work in 'The Wind in the Portico' (1928), in which a man builds a temple for Vaunus, a British god of the hills, who then takes revenge by burning his votary for trying to change the dedication of the temple. We also see the special place in 'Basilissa', 'The Watcher by the Threshold' and 'Fountainblue'.

Once again in the last-named there is a sense of an anti-materialist primitive remnant continuing to exert its power over the centuries: 'Fountainblue – the name rang witchingly in his ears. Fountainblue, the last home of the Good Folk, the last hold of the vanished kings, where the last wolf in Scotland was slain, and, as stories go, the last saint of the Great Ages taught the people – what had Fountainblue to do with his hard world of facts and figures?'

The themes of the special place and transformation of individuals come together most powerfully in 'Fullcircle' (1920), in which visitors to a house in the Midlands see it and its owners, the Giffens, become subject to successive changes. The story comes from house-hunting trips Buchan made with Susan in the Cotswolds in 1917 while looking for Elsfield. Loosely based on Sidney and Beatrice Webb, the Giffens start as psychologising socialists 'in revolt against everything and everybody with any ancestry'. They end, via a period as hunting and fishing members of squirearchy, as austere yet strangely sensual Catholics. The house, which contains a small chapel and was built by a Catholic aristocrat after the Restoration, has come 'full circle'. As the fascinated and part frightened narrator puts it, 'Some agency had been at work here, some agency other and more potent than the process of time.'

In 'The Loathly Opposite' (1927), the agency at work is a code-writer on the opposing German side in the First World War. Fans of Robert Harris's *Enigma* and those interested in the work at Bletchley Park in the subsequent war will be amused by how the cypher is broken. But as Lownie has pointed out, perhaps the real coup of the story is how it links decypheration with 'cracking the code' of the human mind.

'Ship to Tarshish' (1927) is one of Buchan's most technic-
ally well-achieved stories. It may not have the outlandish
elements we find in others, but its narrative of Jim Hallward,
a man who flees England to Canada out of 'funk' after a
financial crisis, then comes back – then goes again, this time
out of courage – encapsulates many of Buchan's themes, in
particular that of finding redemption through hard work.

'Ship to Tarshish' bears interesting comparison with
some of the other stories in this volume. In 'A Captain of
Salvation' the change in life is one way, though there are
temptations to reverse it; in ' "Divus" Johnston', the change
is reversed, but Johnston comes back from the East a much
richer man. In Hallward's case the change is reversed and
turned about once again, and the riches are those of the
spirit.

For sheer effect, the most powerful story in this volume
is 'Tendebant Manus' (1927). This story of spiritual companionship between brothers after one of them has died
is extraordinarily convincing. Partly it is the setting that
does this, the wonderful duck-shooting scene in which the
principal revelation is made. But the main reason for the
effectiveness of the story is the way the magic of it is not
determined by some external power but by the actual
workings of the human mind. Anyone who has ever been
bereaved will appreciate its power.

Both first published in *Pall Mall Magazine* in 1928, 'The
Last Crusade' and 'Sing a Song of Sixpence' are also very
effective. One a story of the emergent media industry owing
something to Buchan's time at Reuters, the other a strangely
toned, much anthologised tale of terrorism told by Leithen
himself, they are expressly concerned with the impact of
modernity. In terms of content, they look back to Joseph

Conrad's political short stories of the 1890s and forward not just to the thriller-writers of today but also to more avant-garde authors.

The last story in this volume, 'The Strange Adventures of Mr Andrew Hawthorn' (1932), is in many ways the comic counterpoint of 'Ship to Tarshish'. Another story about a man who dips out of life, it begins with a kind of explanation of the allure of this trope:

> Any disappearance is a romantic thing, especially if it be unexpected and inexplicable. To vanish from the common world and leave no trace, and to return with the same suddenness and mystery, satisfies the eternal human sense of wonder. That is why the old stories make so much of it. Tamlane and Kilmeny and Ogier the Dane retired to Fairy Land, and Oisin to the Land of the Ever Living, and no man knows the manner of their going or their return. The common world goes on, but they are far away in a magic universe of their own.

It is Buchan's ability to transport his readers to this magic universe which has produced so many devotees of his writing. I think he actively believed in that universe and for all his best efforts as a good Presbyterian could not stop his own mental recursion to the pagan.

In 'Space' (1910), which proceeds from his reading of the French physicist Henri Poincaré, he even tries to find a scientific basis for that recursion: 'How if Space is really full of things we cannot see and as yet do not know?' This tale of a doomed scientist told by Leithen to an unnamed narrator ends with the latter seeking refuge in solid, evidence-based reality:

We were now on the gravel of the drive, and I was feeling better. The thought of dinner warmed my heart and drove out the eeriness of the twilight glen. The hour between dog and wolf was passing. After all, there was a gross and jolly earth at hand for wise men who had a mind to comfort.

Leithen, however, fixes on 'the land of pure spirit'. The two positions are held in balance in Buchan's stories. One only needs begin reading them to be either taken into a separate world of the imagination or returned with a necessary bump to harsh physical reality. Many writers perform one or other of these services. Few are capable of doing both. Even rarer are those who, like John Buchan, can do both at the same time.

GILES FODEN

A Captain of Salvation

Nor is it any matter of sorrow to us that the gods of the Pagans are no more. For whatsoever virtue was theirs is embodied in our most blessed faith. For whereas Apollo was the most noble of men in appearance and seemed to his devotees the incarnation (if I may use so sacred a word in a profane sense) of the beauty of the male, we have learned to apprehend a higher beauty of the Spirit, as in our blessed Saints. And whereas Jupiter was the king of the world, we have another and more excellent King, even God the Father, the Holy Trinity. And whereas Mars was the god of war, the strongest and most warlike of beings, we have the great soldier of our cause, even the Captain of our Salvation. And whereas the most lovely of women was Venus, beautiful alike in spirit and body, to wit our Blessed Lady. So it is seen that whatever delights are carnal and of the flesh, such are met by greater delights of Christ and His Church.

An Extract from the writings of Donisarius, a Monk of Padua

The Salvation Captain sat in his room at the close of a windy March day. It had been a time of storm and sun, blustering showers and flying scuds of wind. The spring was at the threshold with its unrest and promise; it was the season of turmoil and disquietude in Nature, and turmoil and disquietude in those whose ears are open to her piping. Even there, in a three-pair back, in the odoriferous lands of Limehouse, the spring penetrated with scarcely diminished vigour. Dust had been whistling in the narrow streets; the leaden sky, filled with vanishing spaces of blue,

I

had made the dull brick seem doubly sordid; and the sudden fresh gusts had caused the heavy sickening smells of stale food and unwholesome lodging to seem by contrast more hateful than words.

The Captain was a man of some forty years, tall, with a face deeply marked with weather and evil living. An air of super-induced gravity served only to accentuate the original. His countenance was a sort of epitome of life, full of traces of passion and nobler impulse, with now and then a shadow of refinement and a passing glimpse of breeding. His history had been of that kind which we would call striking, were it not so common. A gentleman born, a scholar after a fashion, with a full experience of the better side of civilisation, he had begun life as well as one can nowadays. For some time things had gone well; then came the utter and irretrievable ruin. A temptation which meets many men in their career met him, and he was overthrown. His name disappeared from the books of his clubs, people spoke of him in a whisper, his friends were crushed with shame. As for the man himself, he took it otherwise. He simply *went under*, disappeared from the ranks of life into the seething, struggling, disordered crowd below. He, if anything, rather enjoyed the change, for there was in him something of that brutality which is a necessary part of the natures of great leaders of men and great scoundrels. The accidents of his environment had made him the latter; he had almost the power of proving the former, for in his masterful brow and firm mouth there were hints of extraordinary strength. His history after his downfall was as picturesque a record as needs be. Years of wandering and fighting, sin and cruelty, generosity and meanness followed. There were few trades and few parts of the earth in which he had not tried his luck.

Then there had come a violent change. Somewhere on the face of the globe he had met a man and heard words; and the direction of his life veered round of a sudden to the opposite. Culture, family ties, social bonds had been of no avail to wean him from his headstrong impulses. An ignorant man, speaking plainly some strong sentences which are unintelligible to three-fourths of the world, had worked the change; and spring found him already two years a servant in that body of men and women who had first sought to teach him the way of life.

These two years had been years of struggle, which only a man who has lived such a life can hope to enter upon. A nature which has run riot for two decades is not cabined and confined at a moment's notice. He had been a wanderer like Cain, and the very dwelling in houses had its hardships for him. But in this matter even his former vice came to aid him. He had been proud and self-willed before in his conflict with virtue. He would be proud and self-willed now in his fight with evil. To his comrades and to himself he said that only the grace of God kept him from wrong; in his inmost heart he felt that the grace of God was only an elegant name for his own pride of will.

As he sat now in that unlovely place, he felt sick of his surroundings and unnaturally restive. The day had been a trying one for him. In the morning he had gone West on some money-collecting errand, one which his soul loathed, performed only as an exercise in resignation. It was a bitter experience for him to pass along Piccadilly in his shabby uniform, the badge in the eyes of most people of half-crazy weakness. He had passed restaurants and eating-houses, and his hunger had pained him, for at home he lived on the barest. He had seen crowds of well-dressed men and

3

JOHN BUCHAN STORIES

women, some of whom he dimly recognised, who had no
time even to glance at the insignificant wayfarer. Old ungodly longings after luxury had come to disturb him. He
had striven to banish them from his mind, and had muttered to himself many texts of Scripture and spoken many
catchword prayers, for the fiend was hard to exorcise.

The afternoon had been something worse, for he had
been deputed to go to a little meeting in Poplar, a gathering of factory-girls and mechanics who met there to talk of
the furtherance of Christ's kingdom. On his way the spirit
of spring had been at work in him. The whistling of the
wind among the crazy chimneys, the occasional sharp gust
from the river, the strong smell of a tan-yard, even the
rough working-dress of the men he passed, recalled to him
the roughness and vigour of his old life. In the forenoon
his memories had been of the fashion and luxury of his
youth; in the afternoon they were of his world-wide wanderings, their hardships and delights. When he came to
the stuffy upper room where the meeting was held, his
state of mind was far from the meek resignation which he
sought to cultivate. A sort of angry unrest held him, which
he struggled with till his whole nature was in a ferment.
The meeting did not tend to soothe him. Brother followed
sister in aimless remarks, seething with false sentiment
and sickly enthusiasm, till the strong man was near to disgust. The things which he thought he loved most dearly,
of a sudden became loathsome. The hysterical fervours of
the girls, which only yesterday he would have been ready
to call 'love for the Lord', seemed now perilously near
absurdity. The loud 'Amens' and 'Hallelujahs' of the men
jarred, not on his good taste (that had long gone under),
but on his sense of the ludicrous. He found himself more

4

than once admitting the unregenerate thought, 'What wretched nonsense is this? When men are living and dying, fighting and making love all around, when the glorious earth is calling with a hundred voices, what fools and children they are to babble in this way!' But this ordeal went by. He was able to make some conventional remarks at the end, which his hearers treasured as 'precious and true', and he left the place with the shamefaced feeling that for the first time in his new life he had acted a part.

It was about five in the evening ere he reached his room and sat down to his meal. There was half a stale loaf, a pot of cheap tea, and some of that extraordinary compound which the humorous grocers of the East call butter. He was hungry and ate without difficulty, but such fragments of aesthetic liking as he still possessed rose against it. He looked around his room. The table was common deal, supported by three legs and a bit of an old clothes-prop. On the horsehair sofa among the dusty tidies was his Bible, one or two publications of the Army, two bundles of the *War Cry*, some hymn-books, and – strange relic of the past – a battered Gaboriau. On the mantelpiece was a little Burmese idol, which acted as a watch-stand, some hideous photographs framed in black, and a china Duke of Wellington. Near it was his bed, ill-made and dingy, and at the bottom an old sea-trunk. On the top lay one relic of gentility, which had escaped the wreck of his fortunes, a silver-backed hair-brush.

The place filled him with violent repugnance. A smell of rich, greasy fish came upstairs to his nostrils; outside a woman was crying; and two children sprawled and giggled beside his door. This certainly was a wretched hole, and his life was hard almost beyond words. He solemnly reviewed

5

his recent existence. On the one side he set down the evils
– bad pay, severe and painful work, poor lodgings, poor
food and dismal company. Something stopped him just as
he was about to set down the other. 'Oh,' he cried, 'is the
love of Jesus nothing that I think like that?' And he began
to pray rapidly, 'Lord, I believe, forgive my unbelief.'

For a little he sat in his chair looking straight before
him. It would be impossible to put down in words the
peculiar hardness of his struggle. For he had to fight with
his memory and his inclinations, both of which are to a
certain extent independent of the will; and he did this not
by sheer strength of resolution, but by fixing his thought
upon an abstraction and attempting to clothe it in warm,
lovable attributes. He thought upon the countless mercies
of God towards him, as his creed showed them; and so
strong was the man that in a little he had gotten the
victory.

By-and-by he got up and put on his overcoat, thin
and patched, and called so only by courtesy. He suddenly
remembered his work, how he was engaged that night to
lead a crusade through some of the worst streets by the
river. Such a crusade was the romantic description by certain imaginative Salvationists of a procession of some dozen
men and women with tambourines and concertinas, singing
hymns, and sowing the good seed broadcast in the shape
of vociferous invitations to mercy and pardon. He hailed
it as a sort of anodyne to his pain. There was small time for
morbid recollection and introspection if one were engaged
in leading a crew of excited followers in places where they
were by no means sure of a favourable reception.

There was a noise without on the stairs, then a rap at
the door, and Brother Leather entered, whom Whitechapel

and the Mile End Road knew for the most vigilant of soldiers and violent of exhorters.

'Are you strong in the Lord, Captain?' he asked. 'For tonight we're goin' to the stronghold of Satan. It haint no use a invitin' and invitin'. It haint no good 'nless you compel them to come in. And by the 'elp of God we 'opes to do it. Sister Stokes, she has her tamb'rine, and there's five concertinies from Gray Street, and Brother Clover's been prayin' all day for a great outpourin' of blessin'. "The fields are wite unto th' 'arvest," ' he quoted.

The Captain rose hastily. 'Then hadn't we better be going?' he said. 'We're to start at seven, and it's half-past six already.'

'Let's have a word of prayer fust,' said the other; and straightway, in defiance of all supposed rules of precedence, this strange private soldier flopped on his knees beside the sofa and poured forth entreaties to his Master. This done he arose, and along with the Captain went down the dingy stairway to the door, and out into the narrow darkening street. The newly-lit gas lamps sent a flicker on the men's faces – the one flabby, soft and weak, but with eyes like coals of fire; the other as strong as steel, but listless and uneager. As they passed, a few ragged street-boys cried the old phrase of derision, 'I love Jesus', at the sight of the caps and the red-banded coats. Here again the one smiled as if he had heard the highest praise, while the other glanced angrily through the gloom as if he would fain rend the urchins, as the bears did the children who mocked Elisha.

At last they turned down a stone-paved passage and came into a little room lined with texts which represented the headquarters of the Army in the district. Sitting on the benches or leaning against the wall were a dozen or so of men and women, all wearing the familiar badge, save one man who had come in his working corduroys, and one girl in a black waterproof. The faces of the men were thin and eager, telling of many sacrifices cheerfully made for their cause, of spare dinners, and nights spent out o' bed, of heart-searchings and painful self-communings, of fervent pray-ing and violent speaking. Thin were the women too, thin and weary, with eyes in which utter lassitude strove against enthusiasm, and backs which ached as they rested. They had come from their labours, as seamstresses and milliners, as shop-girls and laundry-maids, and, instead of enjoying a well-won rest, were devoting their few hours of freedom to the furtherance of an ideal which many clever men have derided. Verily it is well for the world that abstract truth is not the measure of right and wrong, of joy and sorrow.

The Captain gave a few directions to the band and then proceeded to business. They were silent men and women in private life. The world was far too grave a mat-ter for them to talk idly. It was only in the streets that speech came thick and fast; here they were as silent as sphinxes – sphinxes a little tired, not with sitting but with going to and fro on the earth.

'Where are we going?' asked one woman.

The Captain considered for a minute ere he replied. 'Down by the Mordon Wharves,' he said, 'then up Blind Street and Gray Alley to Juke's Buildings, where we can stop and speak. You know the place, friend Leather?'

'Do I know my own dwellin'?' asked the man thus addressed in a surprised tone. 'Wy, I've lived there off an' on for twenty year, and I could tell some tyles o' the plyce as would make yer that keen you couldn't wait a minute but must be off doin' Christ's work.'

8

'We'll be off now,' said the Captain, who had no desire for his assistant's reminiscences. 'I'll go first with the flag and the rest of you can come in rank. See that you sing out well, for the Lord has much need of singing in these barren lands.' The desultory band clattered down the wooden stair into the street.

Once here the Captain raised the hymn. It was 'Oh, haven't I been happy since I met the Lord?', some rhapsodical words set to a popular music-hall air. To the chance hearer who hailed from more civilised places the thing must have seemed little better than a blasphemous parody. But all element of farce was absent from the hearts of the grim-faced men and women; and the scene as it lay, the squalid street with its filth stirred by the March wind, the high shifting sky overhead, the flicker and glare of the street lamps as each gust jostled them, the irregular singing, the marching amid the laughs or silent scorn of the bystanders – all this formed a picture which had in it more of the elements of the tragic or the noble than the ludicrous.

And the heart of the man at the head of the little procession was the stage of a drama which had little of the comic about it. The street, the open air, had inflamed again the old longings. Something of the enthusiasm of his following had entered into his blood; but it was a perverted feeling, and instead of desiring earnestly the success of his mission, he longed madly, fiercely for forbidden things. In the short encounter in his room he had come off the victor; but it had only been a forced peace, and now the adversary was at him tooth and nail once more. The meeting with the others had roused in him a deep disgust. Heaven above, was it possible that he, the cock of his troop, the man whom all had respected after a fashion, as men will respect

9

a strong man, should be a bear-leader to fools! The shame of it took him of a sudden, and as he shouted the more loudly he felt his heart growing hot within him at the thought. But, strangely enough, his very pride came once more to help him. At the thought, 'Have I really come to care what men say and think about me?' the strong pride within him rose in revolt and restored him to himself.

But the quiet was to be of short duration. A hateful, bitter thought began to rise in him – 'What am I in the world but a man of no importance? And I might have been – oh, I might have been anything I chose! I made a mess of it at the beginning, but is it not possible for a man to right himself again with the world? Have I ever tried it? Instead of setting manfully to the task, I let myself drift, and this is what I have become. And I might have been so different. I might have been back at my old clubs with my old friends, married, maybe, to a pretty wife, with a house near the Park, and a place in the country with shooting and riding to hounds, and a devilish fine time of it. And here I must go on slaving and gabbling, doing a fool's work at a drainer's pay.' Then came a burst of sharp mental anguish, remorse, hate, evil craving. But it passed, and a flood of counter-thoughts came to oppose it. The Captain was still unregenerate in nature, as the phrase goes, but the leaven was working in him. The thought of all that he had gained – God's mercy, pardon for his sins, a sure hope of happiness hereafter, and a glorified ideal to live by – made him stop short in his regrets.

The hymn had just dragged itself out to its quavering close. Wheeling round, he turned a burning eye on his followers. 'Let us raise another, friends,' he cried; and began, 'The Devil and me we can't agree' – which the rest heartily joined in.

And now the little procession reached a new stage in its journey. The narrow street had grown still more restricted. Gin palaces poured broad splashes of garish light across the pavement. Slatternly women and brutal men lined the footpath, and in the kennels filthy little urchins grinned and quarrelled. Every now and then some well-dressed, rakish artiste, or lady of the half-world, pushed her way through the crowds, or a policeman, tall and silent, stalked among the disorderly. Vanity Fair and its denizens were everywhere, from the chattering hucksters to the leering blackguards and sleek traffickers in iniquity. If anything on earth can bring a ray of decency into such a place, then in God's name let it come, whether it be called sense or rant by stay-at-home philosophers.

The hymn-singing added one more element to the discordant noise. But there was in it a suggestion of better things, which was absent from the song of the streets. The obvious chords of the music in that place acquired an adventitious beauty, just as the song of a humble hedge-linnet is lovely amid the croaking of ravens and hooting of owls. The people on the pavement looked on with varying interest. To most it was an everyday exhibition of the unaccountable. Women laughed, and shrieked coarse railleries; some of the men threatened, others looked on in amused scorn; but there was no impulse to active violence. The thing was tolerated as yonder seller of cheap watchguards was borne; for it is an unwritten law in the slums, that folk may do their own pleasure, as long as they cease from interfering offensively with the enjoyment of others.

' 'Oo's the cove wi' the flag, Bill?' asked one woman. ' 'E haint so bad as the rest. Most loikely 'e's taken up the job to dodge the nick.'

'Dodge the nick yersel', Lizer,' said the man addressed. 'Wy, it's the chap's wye o' making his livin', a roarin' and a preachin' like that. S'help me, I'd rather cry "Welks" any dye than go about wi' sich a crew.'

A woman, garishly adorned, with a handsome flushed face, looked up at the Captain.

'Why, it's Jack,' she cried. 'Bless me if it ain't Jack. Jack, Jack, what are you after now, not coming to speak to me. Don't you mind Sal, your little Sal. I'm coming to yer, I ain't forgotten yer.' And she began to push her way into mid-street.

The Captain looked to the side, and his glance rested upon her face. It was as if the Devil and all his angels were upon him that night. Evil memories of his past life thronged thick and fast upon him. He had already met and resisted the world, and now the flesh had come to torment him. But here his armour was true and fast. This was a temptation which he had choked at the very outset of his reformation. He looked for one moment at her, and in the utter loathing and repugnance of that look, she fell back; and the next instant was left behind.

The little streets which radiate from the wharf known as Mordon's are so interlaced and crooked that to find one's way in them is more a matter of chance than good guiding even to the initiated. The houses are small and close, the residence of the very sweepings of the population; the shops are ship-chandlers and low eating-houses, pawnshops, emporia of cheap jewellery, and remnant drapers. At this hour of the night there is a blaze of dull gas-light on either side, and the proprietors of the places of custom stand at their doors inviting the bystanders to inspect their goods. This is the hotbed of legalised crime, the rendezvous of half the wickedness of the earth. Lascars, Spaniards, French-men jostle Irishmen, and Scotsmen, and the true-born Englishmen in these narrow purlieus. If a man disappears utterly from view you may be sure to find him somewhere in the network of alleys, for there it would be hard for the law to penetrate *incolis invitis*. It is a sort of Cave of Adullam on the one hand, to which the morally halt and maimed of all nations resort; and, on the other, a nursery of young vice and unformed devilry. Sailors straddled about the pavement, or stood in knots telling their tales in loud voices and plentiful oaths; every beershop was continually discharging its stream of filthy occupants, filthy and pros-perous. The element of squalor and misery was here far less in evidence. All the inhabitants seemed gorged and well clad, but their faces were stained with vice so horrible that poverty and tatters would have been a welcome relief.

The Salvation band penetrated into this Sodom with fear in the heart of each member. It was hard for the Gospel to strive with such seared and branded consciences. The repulsive, self-satisfied faces of the men, the smug coun-tenances of the women, made that little band seem hopeless and Quixotic in the extreme. The Captain felt it, too; but in him there was mingled another feeling. He thought of himself as a combatant entering the arena. He felt dimly that some great struggle was impending, some monstrous temptation, some subtle wile of the Evil One. The thought made him the more earnest. 'Sing up, men,' he cried, 'the Devil is strong in this place.'

It was the truth, and the proof awaited him. A man stepped out from among the bystanders and slapped his shoulder. The Captain started and looked. It was the Devil in person.

'Hullo, Jack!' said the newcomer. 'Good God, who'd have thought of seeing you here? Have you gone off your head now?'

The Captain shivered. He knew the speaker for one of his comrades of the old days, the most daring and jovial of them all. The two had been hand and glove in all manner of evil. They had loved each other like brothers, till the great change came over the one, which fixed a gulf between them for ever.

'You don't mean to tell me you've taken up with this infernal nonsense, Jack? No, I won't believe it. It's just another of your larks. You were always the one for originality.'

'Go away, Hilton,' said the Captain hoarsely, 'go away. I've done with you. I can't see you any more.'

'What the deuce has come over you, Jack? Not speak to me any more! Why, what foolery is this? You've gone and turned a regular old wife, bless me if you haven't. Oh, man, give it up. It's not worth it. Don't you remember the fun we've had in our time? Gad, Jack, when you and I stood behind yon big tree in Kaffraria with twenty yelling devils wanting our blood; don't you remember how I fell and you got over me, and, though you were bleeding like a pig, you kept them off till the Cape troopers came up? And when we were lost, doing picketing up in the Drakensberg, you mind how we chummed together for our last meal? And heavens! it was near our last. I feel that infernal giddiness still. And yet you tell me to go away.'

'Oh, Hilton,' said the Captain, 'come and be one of us. The Lord's willing to receive you, if you'll only come. I've got the blessing, and there's one waiting for you if you'll only take it.'

'Blessing be damned!' said the other with a laugh. 'What do I want with your blessing when there's life and the world to see? What's the good of poking round here, and crying about the love of Jesus and singing twaddle, and seeing nobody but old wives and white-faced shopmen, when you might be out on the open road, with the wind and the stars and the sun, and meet with men, and have your fling like a man. Don't you remember the days at Port Said, when the old Frenchman twanged his banjo and the girls danced and – hang it, don't you feel the smell of the sand and the heat in your nostrils, you old fool?'

'Oh, my God!' said the Captain, 'I do. Go away, Hilton. For God's sake, go away and leave me!'

'Can't you think', went on the other, 'of the long nights when we dropped down the Irrawaddy, of the whistle of the wind in the white sails, and the singing of the boatmen, and the sick-suck of the alligators among the reeds; and how we went ashore at the little village and got arrack from the natives, and made a holy sight of the place in the morning? It was worth it, though we got the sack for it, old man.'

The Captain made no answer. He was muttering something to himself. It might have been a prayer.

'And then there was that time when we were up country in Queensland, sugar farming in the bush, thinking a billy of tea the best thing on earth, and like to faint with the work and the heat. But, Jove, wasn't it fine to head off the cattle when you knew you might have a big bull's horn in your side every minute? And then at night to sit outside the huts and smoke pig-tail and tell stories that would make your hair rise! We were a queer lot, Jack, but we were men, *men*, do you hear?'

15

A flood of recollection came over the Captain, vehement, all-powerful. He felt the magic of the East, the wonder of the South, the glory of the North burning in his heart. The old wild voices were calling him, voices of land and sea, the tongues of the moon and the stars and the beasts of the field, the halcyon voices of paganism and nature which are still strong in the earth. Behind him rose the irregular notes of the hymn; at his side was the tempter, and in his own heart was the prince of the world, the master of pleasure, the great juggler of pain. In that man there was being fought the old fight, which began in the Garden, and will never end, the struggle between the hateful right and the delicious wrong.

'Oh man, come with me,' cried Hilton, 'I've got a berth down there in a ship which sails tomorrow, and we'll go out to our old place, where they'll be glad to get us, and we'll have a devilish good time. I can't be staying here, with muggy stinks, and white-faced people, and preaching and praying, and sloppy weather. Come on, and in a month we'll be seeing the old Coal-sack above us, and smelling the palms and the sea-water; and then, after that, there'll be the Bush, the pines and the gum-trees and the blue sky, and the hot, clear air, and rough-riding and adventure; and by God we'll live like gentlemen and fine fellows, and never come back to this cursed hole any more. Come on, and leave the psalm-singing.'

A spasm of convulsive pain, of exquisite agony, of heart-breaking struggle came over the Captain's face, stayed a moment, and passed. He turned round to his followers. 'Sing louder, lads,' he cried, 'we're fighting a good fight.' And then his voice broke down, and he stumbled blindly on, still clutching the flag.

A Journey of Little Profit

The Devil he sang, the Devil he played
High and fast and free.
And this was ever the song he made,
As it was told to me.
Oh, I am the king of the air and the ground,
And lord of the seasons' roll,
And I will give you a hundred pound,
If you will give me your soul!

from *The Ballad of Grey Weather*

The cattle market of Inverforth is, as all men know north of the Tweed, the greatest market of the kind in the land. For days in the late Autumn there is the lowing of oxen and the bleating of sheep among its high wooden pens, and in the rickety sale-rings the loud clamour of auctioneers and the talk of farmers. In the open yard where are the drovers and the butchers, a race always ungodly and law-despising, there is such a Babel of cries and curses as might wake the Seven Sleepers. From twenty different adjacent eating-houses comes the clatter of knives, where the country folk eat their dinner of beef and potatoes, with beer for sauce, and the collies grovel on the ground for stray morsels. Hither come a hundred types of men from the Highland cateran with scarce a word of English, and the shentleman-farmer of Inverness and Ross, to lowland graziers and city tradesmen, not to speak of blackguards of many nationalities and more professions.

17

It was there I first met Duncan Stewart of Clacham-harstan, in the Moor of Rannoch, and there I heard this story. He was an old man when I knew him, grizzled and wind-beaten; a prosperous man, too, with many herds like Jacob and much pasture. He had come down from the North with kyloes, and as he waited on the Englishmen with whom he had trysted, he sat with me through the long day and beguiled the time with many stories. He had been a drover in his youth, and had travelled on foot the length and breadth of Scotland; and his memory went back hale and vigorous to times which are now all but historical. This tale I heard among many others as we sat on a pen amid the smell of beasts and the jabber of Gaelic.

'When I was just turned of twenty-five I was a wild young lad as ever was heard of. I had taken to the droving for the love of a wild life, and a wild life I led. My father's heart would be broken long syne with my doings, and well for my mother that she was in her grave since I was six years old. I paid no heed to the ministrations of godly Mr Mac-dougall of the Isles, who bade me turn from the error of my ways, but went on my own evil course, making siller, for I was a braw lad at the work and a trusted, and knowing the inside of every public from the pier of Cromarty to the streets of York. I was a wild drinker, caring in my cups for neither God nor man, a great hand with the cards, and fond of the lasses past all telling. It makes me shameful to this day to think on my evil life when I was twenty-five.

'Well, it chanced that in the back of the month of September I found myself in the city of Edinburgh with a flock of fifty sheep which I had bought as a venture from a drunken bonnet-laird and was thinking of selling somewhere wast the country. They were braw beasts, Leicester every one of them, well-fed and dirt-cheap at the price I gave. So it was with a light heart that I drove them out of the town by the Merchiston Road along by the face of the Pentlands. Two or three friends came with me, all like myself for folly, but maybe a little bit poorer. Indeed, I cared little for them, and they valued me only for the whisky which I gave them to drink my health in at the parting. They left me on the near side of Colinton, and I went on my way alone.

'Now, if you'll be remembering the road, you will mind that at the place called Kirk Newton, just afore the road begins to twine over the Big Muir and almost at the head of the Water o' Leith, there is a verra fine public. Indeed, it would be no lee to call it the best public between Embro' and Glesca. The good wife, Lucky Craik by name, was an old friend of mine, for many a good gill of her prandy have I bought; so what would I be doing but just turning aside for refreshment? She met me at the door, verra pleased-like to see me, and soon I had my legs aneath her table and a basin of toddy on the board before me. And whom did I find in the same place but my old comrade Toshie Maclean from the backside of Glen-Lyon. Toshie and I were acquaintances so old that it did not behoove us to be parting quick. Forbye the day was chill without; and within the fire was grand and the crack of the best.

'Then Toshie and I got on quarrelling about the price of Lachlan Farawa's beasts that he sold at Falkirk; and, the drink having aye a bad effect on my temper, I was for giving him the lie and coming off in a great rage. It was about six o'clock in the evening and an hour to nightfall, so Mistress Craik comes in to try and keep me. "Losh, Duncan," says she, "ye'll never try and win ower the muir the nicht. It's mae than ten mile to Carnwath, and there's nocht atween it and this but whaups and heathery braes." But when I am roused I will be more obstinate than ten mules, so I would be going, though I knew not under Heaven where I was going till. I was too full of good liquor and good meat to be much worth at thinking, so I got my sheep on the road an a big bottle in my pouch and set off into the heather. I knew not what my purpose was, whether I thought to reach the shieling of Carnwath, or whether I expected some house of entertainment to spring up by the wayside. But my fool's mind was set on my purpose of getting some miles further in my journey ere the coming of darkness.

'For some time I jogged happily on, with my sheep running well before me and my dogs trotting at my heels. We left the trees behind and struck out on the proad grassy path which bands the moor like the waist-strap of a sword. It was most dreary and lonesome with never a house in view, only bogs and grey hillsides and ill-looking waters. It was stony, too, and this more than aught else caused my Dutch courage to fail me, for I soon fell wearied, since much whisky is bad travelling fare, and began to curse my folly. Had my pride no kept me back, I would have returned to Lucky Craik's; but I was like the devil, for stiff-neckedness and thought of nothing but to push on.

'I own that I was verra well tired and quite spiritless when I first saw the House. I had scarce been an hour on the way, and the light was not quite gone; but still it was geyan dark, and the place sprang somewhat suddenly on my sight. For, looking a little to the left, I saw over a little strip of grass a big square dwelling with many outhouses, half farm and half pleasure-house. This, I thought, is the verra place I have been seeking and made sure of finding; so whistling a gay tune, I drove my flock toward it.

'When I came to the gate of the court, I saw better of what sort was the building I had arrived at. There was a square yard with monstrous high walls, at the left of which was the main block of the house, and on the right what I took to be the byres and stables. The place looked ancient, and the stone in many places was crumbling away; but the style was of yesterday and in no way differing from that of a hundred steadings in the land. There were some kind of arms above the gateway, and a bit of an iron stanchion; and when I had my sheep inside of it, I saw that the court was all grown up with green grass. And what seemed queer in that dusky half-light was the want of sound. There was no neichering of horses, nor routing of kye, nor clack of hens, but all as still as the top of Ben Cruachan. It was warm and pleasant too, though the night was chill without.

'I had no sooner entered the place than a row of sheep-pens caught my eye, fixed against the wall in front. This I thought mighty convenient, so I made all haste to put my beasts into them; and finding that there was a good supply of hay within, I leff them easy in my mind, and turned about to look for the door of the house.

'To my wonder, when I found it, it was open wide to the wall; so, being confident with much whisky, I never took thought to knock, but walked boldly in. There's some careless folk here, thinks I to myself, and I much misdoubt if the man knows aught about farming. He'll maybe just be a town's body taking the air on the muirs.

'The place I entered upon was a hall, not like a muir-land farmhouse, but more fine than I had ever seen. It was

21

laid with a verra fine carpet, all red and blue and gay colours, and in the corner in a fireplace a great fire crackled. There were chairs, too, and a walth of old rusty arms on the walls, and all manner of whigmaleeries that folk think ornamental. But nobody was there, so I made for the stair-case which was at the further side, and went up it stoutly. I made scarce any noise so thickly was it carpeted, and I will own it kind of terrified me to be walking in such a place. But when a man has drunk well he is troubled not overmuckle with modesty or fear, so I e'en stepped out and soon came to a landing where was a door.

'Now, thinks I, at last I have won to the habitable parts of the house; so laying my finger on the sneck I lifted it and entered. And there before me was the finest room in all the world; indeed I abate not a jot of the phrase, for I cannot think of anything finer. It was hung with braw pic-tures and lined with big bookcases of oak well-filled with books in fine bindings. The furnishing seemed carved by a skilled hand, and the cushions and curtains were soft vel-vet. But the best thing was the table, which was covered with a clean white cloth and set with all kind of good meat and drink. The dishes were of silver and as bright as Loch Awe water in an April sun. Eh, but it was a braw braw sight for a drover! And there at the far end, with a great pottle of wine before him, sat the master.

'He rose as I entered, and I saw him to be dressed in the pink of town fashion, a man of maybe fifty years, but hale and well-looking, with a peaked beard and trimmed mous-tache and thick eyebrows. His eyes were slanted a thought, which is a thing I hate in any man, but his whole appear-ance was pleasing.

' "Mr Stewart?" says he courteously, looking at me. "Is it

Mr Duncan Stewart that I will be indebted to for the honour of this visit?"

'I stared at him blankly, for how did he ken my name?

' "That is my name," I said, "but who the tevil tell't you about it?"

' "Oh, my name is Stewart myself," says he, "and all Stewarts should be well acquaint."

' "True," said I, "though I don't mind your face before. But now I am here, I think you have a most gallant place, Mr Stewart."

' "Well enough. But how have you come to't? We've few visitors."

'So I told him where I had come from, and where I was going, and why I was forwandered at this time of night among the muirs. He listened keenly, and when I had finished, he says verra friendly-like, "Then you'll bide all night and take supper with me. It would never be doing to let one of the clan go away without breaking bread. Sit ye down, Mr Duncan."

'I sat down gladly enough, though I own that at first I did not half-like the whole business. There was something unchristian about the place, and for certain it was not seemly that the man's name should be the same as my own, and that he should be so well posted in my doings. But he seemed so well-disposed that my misgivings soon vanished.

'So I seated myself at the table opposite my entertainer. There was a place laid ready for me, and beside the knife and fork a long horn-handled spoon. I had never seen a spoon so long and queer, and I asked the man what it meant. "Oh," says he, "the broth in this house is very often hot, so we need a long spoon to sup it. It is a common enough thing, is it not?"

23

'I could answer nothing to this, though it did not seem to me sense, and I had an inkling of something I had heard about long spoons which I thought was not good; but my wits were not clear, as I have told you already. A serving man brought me a great bowl of soup and set it before me. I had hardly plunged spoon intil it, when Mr Stewart cries out from the other end: "Now, Mr Duncan, I call you to witness that you sit down to supper of your own accord. I've an ill name in these parts for compelling folk to take meat with me when they dinna want it. But you'll bear me witness that you're willing."

' "Yes, by God, I am that," I said, for the savoury smell of the broth was rising to my nostrils. The other smiled at this as if well-pleased.

'I have tasted many soups, but I swear there never was one like that. It was as if all the good things in the world were mixed thegether – whisky and kale and shortbread and cocky-leeky and honey and salmon. The taste of it was enough to make a body's heart loup with fair gratitude. The smell of it was like the spicy winds of Arabia, that you read about in the Bible, and when you had taken a spoonful you felt as happy as if you had sellt a hundred yowes at twice their reasonable worth. Oh, it was grand soup!

' "What Stewarts did you say you comed from?" I asked my entertainer.

' "Oh," he says, "I'm connected with them all, Athole Stewarts, Appin Stewarts, Rannoch Stewarts; and a' I've a heap o' land thereaways."

' "Whereabouts?" says I, wondering. "Is't at the Blair o' Athole, or along by Tummel side, or wast the Loch o' Rannoch, or on the Muir, or in Mamore?"

' "In all the places you name," says he.

' "Got damn," says I, "then what for do you not bide there instead of in these stinking lawlands?"

'At this he laughed softly to himself. "Why, for maybe the same reason as yoursel, Mr Duncan. You know the proverb, 'A' Stewarts are sib to the Deil'."

'I laughed loudly; "Oh, you've been a wild one, too, have you? Then you're not worse than mysel. I ken the inside of every public in the Cowgate and Cannongate, and there's no another drover on the road my match at fechting and drinking and dicing." And I started on a long shameless catalogue of my misdeeds. Mr Stewart meantime listened with a satisfied smirk on his face.

' "Yes, I've heard tell of you, Mr Duncan," he says. "But here's something more, and you'll doubtless be hungry."

'And now there was set on the table a round of beef garnished with pot-herbs, all most delicately fine to the taste. From a great cupboard were brought many bottles of wine, and in a massive silver bowl at the table's head were put whisky and lemons and sugar. I do not know well what I drank, but whatever it might be it was the best ever brewed. It made you scarce feel the earth round about you, and you were so happy you could scarce keep from singing. I wad give much siller to this day for the receipt.

'Now, the wine made me talk, and I began to boast of my own great qualities, the things I had done and the things I was going to do. I was a drover just now, but it was not long that I would be being a drover. I had bought a flock of my own, and would sell it for a hundred pounds, no less; with that I would buy a bigger one till I had made money enough to stock a farm; and then I would leave the road and spend my days in peace, seeing to my land and living in good company. Was not my father, I cried, own cousin, thrice removed, to the Macleans o' Duart, and my mother's uncle's wife a Rory of Balnacroy? And I am a scholar too, said I, for I was a matter of two years at Embro' College, and might have been roaring in the pulpit, if I hadna liked the drink and the lassies too well.

' "See," said I, "I will prove it to you"; and I rose from the table and went to one of the bookcases. There were all manner of books, Latin and Greek, poets and philosophers, but in the main, divinity. For there I saw Richard Baxter's *Call to the Unconverted*, and Thomas Boston of Ettrick's *Fourfold State*, not to speak of the *Sermons* of half a hundred auld ministers, and the *Hind Let Loose*, and many books of the covenanting folk.

' "Faith," I says, "you've a fine collection, Mr What's-your-name," for the wine had made me free in my talk. "There is many a minister and professor in the Kirk, I'll warrant, who has a less godly library. I begin to suspect you of piety, sir."

' "Does it not behoove us", he answered in an unctuous voice, "to mind the words of Holy Writ that evil communications corrupt good manners, and have an eye to our company? These are all the company I have, except when some stranger such as you honours me – with a visit."

'I had meantime been opening a book of plays, I think by the famous William Shakespeare, and I here broke into a loud laugh. "Ha, ha, Mr Stewart," I says, "here's a sentence I've lighted on which is hard on you. Listen! 'The Devil can quote Scripture to advantage.' "

'The other laughed long. "He who wrote that was a shrewd man," he said, "but I'll warrant if you'll open another volume, you'll find some quip on yourself."

'I did as I was bidden, and picked up a white-backed

book, and opening it at random, read: "There be many who spend their days in evil and wine-bibbing, in lusting and cheating, who think to mend while yet there is time; but the opportunity is to them for ever awanting, and they go down open-mouthed to the great fire."

' "Psa," I cried, "some wretched preaching book, I will have none of them. Good wine will be better than bad theology." So I sat down once more at the table.

' "You're a clever man, Mr Duncan," he says, "and a well-read one. I commend your spirit in breaking away from the bands of the Kirk and the college, though your father was so thrawn against you."

' "Enough of that," I said, "though I don't know who told you"; I was angry to hear my father spoken of, as though the grieving him was a thing to be proud of.

' "Oh, as you please," he says; "I was just going to say that I commended your spirit in sticking the knife into the man in the Pleasaunce, the time you had to hide for a month about the backs o' Leith."

' "How do you ken that?" I asked hotly, "you've heard more about me than ought to be repeated, let me tell you."

' "Don't be angry," he said sweetly; "I like you well for these things, and you mind the lassie in Athole that was so fond of you. You treated her well, did you not?"

'I made no answer, being too much surprised at his knowledge of things which I thought none knew but myself.

' "Oh yes, Mr Duncan. I could tell you what you were doing today, how you cheated Jock Gallowa out of six pounds, and sold a horse to the farmer of Haypath that was scarce fit to carry him home. And I know what you are meaning to do the morn at Glesca, and I wish you well of it."

' "I think you must be the Devil," I said blankly.

' "The same, at your service," said he, still smiling.

'I looked at him in terror, and even as I looked I kenned by something in his eyes and the twitch of his lips that he was speaking the truth.

' "And what place is this, you . . ." I stammered.

' "Call me Mr S.," he says gently, "and enjoy your stay while you are here and don't concern yourself about the lawing."

' "The lawing!" I cried in astonishment, "and is this a house of public entertainment?"

' "To be sure, else how is a poor man to live?"

' "Name it," said I, "and I will pay and be gone."

' "Well," said he, "I make it a habit to give a man his choice. In your case it will be your wealth or your chances hereafter, in plain English your flock or your—"

' "My immortal soul," I gasped.

' "Your soul," said Mr S., bowing, "though I think you call it by too flattering an adjective."

' "You damned thief," I roared, "you would entice a man into your accursed house and then strip him bare."

' "Hold hard," said he, "don't let us spoil our good fellowship by incivilities. And, mind you, I took you to witness to begin with that you sat down of your own accord."

' "So you did," said I, and could say no more.

' "Come, come," he says, "don't take it so bad. You may keep all your gear and yet part from here in safety. You've but to sign your name, which is no hard task to a college-bred man, and go on living as you live just now to the end. And let me tell you, Mr Duncan Stewart, that you should take it as a great obligement that I am willing to take your

28

bit soul instead of fifty sheep. There's no many would value it so high."

' "Maybe no, maybe no," I said sadly, "but it's all I have. D'ye no see that if I gave it up, there would be no chance left of mending? And I'm sure I do not want your company to all eternity."

' "Faith, that's uncivil," he says; "I was just about to say that we had had a very pleasant evening."

'I sat back in my chair very down-hearted. I must leave this place as poor as a kirk-mouse, and begin again with little but the clothes on my back. I was strongly tempted to sign the bit paper thing and have done with it all, but somehow I could not bring myself to do it. So at last I says to him: "Well, I've made up my mind. I'll give you my sheep, sorry though I be to lose them, and I hope I may never come near this place again as long as I live."

' "On the contrary," he said, "I hope often to have the pleasure of your company. And seeing that you've paid well for your lodging, I hope you'll make the best of it. Don't be sparing on the drink."

'I looked hard at him for a second. "You've an ill name, and an ill trade, but you're no a bad sort yoursel, and, do you ken, I like you."

' "I'm much obliged to you for the character," says he, "and I'll take your hand on't."

'So I filled up my glass and we set to, and such an evening I never mind of. We never got fou, but just in a fine good temper and very entertaining. The stories we told and the jokes we cracked are still a kind of memory with me, though I could not come over one of them. And then, when I got sleepy, I was shown to the brawest bedroom, all hung with pictures and looking-glasses, and with bed-clothes of the finest linen and a coverlet of silk. I bade Mr S. good-night, and my head was scarce on the pillow ere I was sound asleep.

'When I awoke the sun was just newly risen, and the frost of a September morning was on my clothes. I was lying among green braes with nothing near me but crying whaups and heathery hills, and my two dogs running round about and howling as they were mad.'

Politics and the May-Fly

The farmer of Clachlands was a Tory, stern and unbending. It was the tradition of his family, from his grandfather, who had been land-steward to Lord Manorwater, down to his father, who had once seconded a vote of confidence in the sitting member. Such traditions, he felt, were not to be lightly despised; things might change, empires might wax and wane, but his obligation continued; a sort of perverted *noblesse oblige* was the farmer's watchword in life; and by dint of much energy and bad language, he lived up to it.

As fate would have it, the Clachlands ploughman was a Radical of Radicals. He had imbibed his opinions early in life from a speaker on the green of Gledsmuir, and ever since, by the help of a weekly penny paper and an odd volume of Gladstone's speeches, had continued his education. Such opinions in a conservative countryside carry with them a reputation for either abnormal cleverness or abnormal folly. The fact that he was a keen fisher, a famed singer of songs, and the best judge of horses in the place, caused the verdict of his neighbours to incline to the former, and he passed for something of an oracle among his fellows. The blacksmith, who was the critic of the neighbourhood, summed up his character in a few words. 'Him,' said he, in a tone of mingled dislike and admiration, 'him! He would sweer white was black the morn, and dod! he would prove it tae.'

It so happened in the early summer, when the land was green and the trout plashed in the river, that Her Majesty's

Government saw fit to appeal to an intelligent country. Among a people whose politics fight hard with their religion for a monopoly of their interests, feeling ran high and brotherly kindness departed. Houses were divided against themselves. Men formerly of no consideration found themselves suddenly important, and discovered that their intellects and conscience, which they had hitherto valued at little, were things of serious interest to their betters. The lurid light of publicity was shed upon the lives of the rival candidates; men formerly accounted worthy and respectable were proved no better than white sepulchres; and each man was filled with a morbid concern for his fellow's character and beliefs.

The farmer of Clachlands called a meeting of his labourers in the great dusty barn, which had been the scene of many similar gatherings. His speech on the occasion was rigorous and to the point. 'Ye are a' my men,' he said, 'an' I'll see that ye vote richt. Y're uneddicated folk, and ken naething aboot the matter, sae ye just tak' my word for't, that the Tories are in the richt and vote accordingly. I've been a guid maister to ye, and it's shurely better to pleesure me, than a wheen leein' scoondrels whae tramp the country with leather bags and printit trash.'

Then arose from the back the ploughman, strong in his convictions. 'Listen to me, you men,' says he; 'just vote as ye think best. The maister's a guid maister, as he says, but he's nocht to dae wi' your votin'. It's what they ca' inteemedation to interfere wi' onybody in this matter. So mind that, an' vote for the workin'-man an' his richts.'

Then ensued a war of violent words.

'Is this a meetin' in my barn, or a pennywaddin?'

'Ca't what ye please. I canna let ye mislead the men.'

'Whae talks about misleadin'? Is't misleadin' to lead them richt?'

'The question,' said the ploughman solemnly, 'is what you ca' richt.'

'William Laverhope, if ye werena a guid plooman, ye wad gang post-haste oot o' here the morn.'

'I carena what ye say. I'll stand up for the richts o' thae men.'

'Men!' – this with deep scorn. 'I could mak' better men than thae wi' a stick oot o' the plantin'.'

'Ay, ye say that noo, an' the morn ye'll be ca'in' ilka yin o' them *Mister*, a' for their votes.'

The farmer left in dignified disgust, vanquished but still dangerous; the ploughman in triumph mingled with despair. For he knew that his fellow-labourers cared not a whit for politics, but would follow to the letter their master's bidding.

The next morning rose clear and fine. There had been a great rain for the past few days, and the burns were coming down broad and surly. The Clachlands Water was chafing by bank and bridge and threatening to enter the hay-field, and every little ditch and sheep-drain was carrying its tribute of peaty water to the greater flood. The farmer of Clachlands, as he looked over the landscape from the doorstep of his dwelling, marked the state of the weather and pondered over it.

He was not in a pleasant frame of mind that morning. He had been crossed by a ploughman, his servant. He liked the man, and so the obvious way of dealing with him – by making things uncomfortable or turning him off – was shut against him. But he burned to get the upper hand of him, and discomfit once for all one who had dared to

33

question his wisdom and good sense. If only he could get him to vote on the other side – but that was out of the question. If only he could keep him from voting – that was possible but unlikely. He might forcibly detain him, in which case he would lay himself open to the penalties of the law, and be nothing the gainer. For the victory which he desired was a moral one, not a triumph of force. He would like to circumvent him by cleverness, to score against him fairly and honourably on his own ground. But the thing was hard, and, as it seemed to him at the moment, impossible.

Suddenly, as he looked over the morning landscape, a thought struck him and made him slap his legs and chuckle hugely. He walked quickly up and down the gravelled walk. 'Losh, it's guid. I'll dae't. I'll dae't, if the weather juist hauds.'

His unseemly mirth was checked by the approach of someone who found the farmer engaged in the minute examination of gooseberry leaves. 'I'm concerned aboot thae busses,' he was saying; 'they've been ill lookit to, an' we'll no hae half a crop.' And he went off, still smiling, and spent a restless forenoon in the Gledsmuir market.

In the evening he met the ploughman, as he returned from the turnip-singling, with his hoe on his shoulder. The two men looked at one another with the air of those who know that all is not well between them. Then the farmer spoke with much humility.

'I maybe spoke rayther severe yestreen,' he said. 'I hope I didna hurt your feelings.'

'Na, na! No me!' said the ploughman airily.

'Because I've been thinking ower the matter, an' I admit that a man has a richt to his ain thochts. A'body should

34

hae principles an' stick to them,' said the farmer, with the manner of one making a recondite quotation.

'Ay,' he went on, 'I respect ye, William, for your consistency. Ye're an example to us a'.'

The other shuffled and looked unhappy. He and his master were on the best of terms, but these unnecessary compliments were not usual in their intercourse. He began to suspect, and the farmer, who saw his mistake, hastened to change the subject.

'Graund weather for the fishin',' said he.

'Oh, is it no?' said the other, roused to excited interest by this home topic. 'I tell ye by the morn they'll be takin' as they've never ta'en this 'ear. Doon in the big pool in the Clachlands Water, at the turn o' the turnip-field, there are twae or three pounders, and aiblins yin o' twae pund. I saw them mysel' when the water was low. It's ower big the noo, but when it gangs doon the morn, and gets the colour o' porter, I'se warrant I could whup them oot o' there wi' the flee.'

'D' ye say sae?' said the farmer, sweetly. 'Weel, it's a lang time since I tried the fishin', but I yince was keen on't. Come in bye, William; I've something ye micht like to see.'

From a corner he produced a rod, and handed it to the other. It was a very fine rod indeed, one which the owner had gained in a fishing competition many years before, and treasured accordingly. The ploughman examined it long and critically. Then he gave his verdict. 'It's the brawest rod I ever saw, wi' a fine hickory butt, an' guid greenhert tap and middle. It wad cast the sma'est flee, and haud the biggest troot.'

'Weel,' said the farmer, genially smiling, 'ye have a half-holiday the morn when ye gang to the poll. There'll be plenty o' time in the evening to try a cast wi't. I'll lend it ye for the day.'

The man's face brightened. 'I wad tak' it verra kindly,' he said, 'if ye wad. My ain yin is no muckle worth, and, as ye say, I'll hae time for a cast the morn's nicht.'

'Dinna mention it. Did I ever let ye see my flee-book? Here it is,' and he produced a thick flannel book from a drawer. 'There's a maist miscellaneous collection, for a' waters an' a' weathers. I got a heap o' them frae auld Lord Manorwater, when I was a laddie, and used to cairry his basket.'

But the ploughman heeded him not, being deep in the examination of its mysteries. Very gingerly he handled the tiny spiders and hackles, surveying them with the eye of a connoisseur.

'If there's anything there ye think at a' like the water, I'll be verra pleased if ye'll try't.'

The other was somewhat put out by this extreme friend-liness. At another time he would have refused shame-facedly, but now the love of sport was too strong in him. 'Ye're far ower guid,' he said; 'thae twae paitrick wings are the verra things I want, an' I dinna think I've ony at hame. I'm awfu' gratefu' to ye, an' I'll bring them back the morn's nicht.'

'Guid-e'en,' said the farmer, as he opened the door, 'an' I wish ye may hae a guid catch.' And he turned in again, smiling sardonically.

The next morning was like the last, save that a little wind had risen, which blew freshly from the west. White cloudlets drifted across the blue, and the air was as clear as spring-water. Down in the hollow the roaring torrent had sunk to a full, lipping stream, and the colour had changed from a turbid yellow to a clear, delicate brown. In the town of Gledsmuir, it was a day of wild excitement, and the quiet Clachlands road bustled with horses and men. The labourers in the field scarce stopped to look at the passers, for in the afternoon they too would have their chance, when they might journey to the town in all importance, and record their opinions of the late Government.

The ploughman of Clachlands spent a troubled fore-noon. His nightly dreams had been of landing great fish, and now his waking thoughts were of the same. Politics for the time were forgotten. This was the day which he had looked forward to for so long, when he was to have been busied in deciding doubtful voters, and breathing activity into the ranks of his cause. And lo! the day had come and found his thoughts elsewhere. For all such things are, at the best, of fleeting interest, and do not stir men otherwise than sentimentally; but the old kindly love of field-sports, the joy in the smell of the earth and the living air, lie very close to a man's heart. So this apostate, as he cleaned his turnip rows, was filled with the excitement of the sport, and had no thoughts above the memory of past exploits and the anticipation of greater to come.

Midday came, and with it his release. He roughly calcu-lated that he could go to the town, vote, and be back in two hours, and so have the evening clear for his fishing. There had never been such a day for the trout in his mem-ory, so cool and breezy and soft, nor had he ever seen so glorious a water. 'If ye dinna get a fou basket the nicht, an' a feed the morn, William Laverhope, your richt hand has forgot its cunning,' said he to himself.

He took the rod carefully out, put it together, and made trial casts on the green. He tied the flies on a cast and put

37

it ready for use in his own primitive fly-book, and then bestowed the whole in the breast-pocket of his coat. He had arrayed himself in his best, with a white rose in his button-hole, for it behoved a man to be well dressed on such an occasion as voting. But yet he did not start. Some fascination in the rod made him linger and try it again and again.

Then he resolutely laid it down and made to go. But something caught his eye – the swirl of the stream as it left the great pool at the hay-field, or the glimpse of still, gleaming water. The impulse was too strong to be resisted. There was time enough and to spare. The pool was on his way to the town, he would try one cast ere he started, just to see if the water was good. So, with rod on his shoulder, he set off.

Somewhere in the background a man, who had been watching his movements, turned away, laughing silently, and filling his pipe.

A great trout rose to the fly in the hay-field pool, and ran the line up-stream till he broke it. The ploughman swore deeply, and stamped on the ground with irritation. His blood was up, and he prepared for battle. Carefully, skilfully he fished, with every nerve on tension and ever-watchful eyes. Meanwhile, miles off in the town the bustle went on, but the eager fisherman by the river heeded it not.

Late in the evening, just at the darkening, a figure arrayed in Sunday clothes, but all wet and mud-stained, came up the road to the farm. Over his shoulder he carried a rod, and in one hand a long string of noble trout. But the expression on his face was not triumphant; a settled

38

melancholy overspread his countenance, and he groaned as he walked.

Mephistopheles stood by the garden-gate, smoking and surveying his fields. A well-satisfied smile hovered about his mouth, and his air was the air of one well at ease with the world.

'Weel, I see ye've had guid sport,' said he to the melancholy Faust. 'By-the-bye, I didna notice ye in the toun. And losh! man, what in the warld have ye dune to your guid claes?'

The other made no answer. Slowly he took the rod to pieces and strapped it up; he took the fly-book from his pocket; he selected two fish from the heap; and laid the whole before the farmer.

'There ye are,' said he, 'and I'm verra much obleeged to ye for your kindness.' But his tone was of desperation and not of gratitude; and his face, as he went onward, was a study in eloquence repressed.

39

Streams of Water in the South

As streams of water in the South,
Our bondage, Lord, recall.

Psalm CXXVI
Scots Metrical Version

I

It was at the ford of the Clachlands Water in a tempestuous August that I, an idle boy, first learned the hardships of the Lammas droving. The shepherd of the Redswirehead, my very good friend, and his three shaggy dogs, were working for their lives in an angry water. The path behind was thronged with scores of sheep bound for the Gledsmuir market, and beyond it was possible to discern through the mist the few dripping dozen which had made the passage. Between raged yards of brown foam coming down from murky hills, and the air echoed with the yelp of dogs and the perplexed cursing of men.

Before I knew, I was helping in the task, with water lapping round my waist and my arms filled with a terrified sheep. It was no light task, for though the water was no more than three feet deep it was swift and strong, and a kicking hogg is a sore burden. But this was the only road; the stream might rise higher at any moment; and somehow or other those bleating flocks had to be transferred to their fellows beyond. There were six men at the labour, six men and myself, and all were cross and wearied and heavy with water.

I made my passages side by side with my friend the shepherd, and thereby felt much elated. This was a man who had dwelt all his days in the wilds, and was familiar with torrents as with his own doorstep. Now and then a swimming dog would bark feebly as he was washed against us, and flatter his fool's heart that he was aiding the work. And so we wrought on, till by midday I was dead-beat, and could scarce stagger through the surf, while all the men had the same gasping faces. I saw the shepherd look with longing eye up the long green valley, and mutter disconsolately in his beard.

'Is the water rising?' I asked.

'It's no rising,' said he, 'but I likena the look o' yon big black clud upon Cairncraw. I doubt there's been a shoor up the muirs, and a shoor there means twae mair feet o' water in the Clachlands. God help Sandy Jamieson's lambs, if there is.'

'How many are left?' I asked.

'Three, fower – no abune a score and a half,' said he, running his eye over the lessened flocks. 'I maun try to tak twae at a time.'

So for ten minutes he struggled with a double burden, and panted painfully at each return. Then with a sudden swift look up-stream he broke off and stood up. 'Get ower the water, every yin o' ye, and leave the sheep,' he said, and to my wonder every man of the five obeyed his word.

And then I saw the reason of his command, for with a sudden swift leap forward the Clachlands rose, and flooded up to where I had stood an instant before high and dry.

'It's come,' said the shepherd in a tone of fate, 'and there's fifteen no ower yet, and Lord kens how they'll dae't. They'll hae to gang roond by Gledsmuir Brig, and that's twenty mile o' a differ. 'Deed, it's no like that Sandy Jamieson will get a guid price the morn for sic sair for-fochen beasts.'

Then with firmly gripped staff he marched stoutly into the tide till it ran hissing below his armpits. 'I could dae't alane,' he cried, 'but no wi' a burden. For, losh, if ye slip-pit, ye'd be in the Tod's Pool afore ye could draw breath.'

And so we waited with the great white droves and five angry men beyond, and the path blocked by a surging flood. For half an hour we waited, holding anxious consultation across the stream, when to us thus busied there entered a newcomer, a helper from the ends of the earth.

He was a man of something over middle size, but with a stoop forward that shortened him to something beneath it. His dress was ragged homespun, the cast-off clothes of some sportsman, and in his arms he bore a bundle of sticks and heather-roots which marked his calling. I knew him for a tramp who long had wandered in the place, but I could not account for the whole-voiced shout of greeting which met him as he stalked down the path. He lifted his eyes and looked solemnly and long at the scene. Then something of delight came into his eye, his face relaxed, and flinging down his burden he stripped his coat and came toward us.

'Come on, Yeddie, ye're sair needed,' said the shepherd, and I watched with amazement this grizzled, crooked man seize a sheep by the fleece and drag it to the water. Then he was in the midst, stepping warily, now up, now down the channel, but always nearing the farther bank. At last with a final struggle he landed his charge, and turned to journey back. Fifteen times did he cross that water, and at the end his mean figure had wholly changed. For now he was straighter and stronger, his eye flashed, and his voice, as he cried out to the drovers, had in it a tone of command. I marvelled at the transformation; and when at length he had donned once more his ragged coat and shouldered his bundle, I asked the shepherd his name.

'They ca' him Adam Logan,' said my friend, his face still bright with excitement, 'but maist folk ca' him "Streams o' Water".'

'Ay,' said I, 'and why "Streams of Water"?'

'Juist for the reason ye see,' said he.

Now I knew the shepherd's way, and I held my peace, for it was clear that his mind was revolving other matters, concerned most probably with the high subject of the morrow's prices. But in a little, as we crossed the moor toward his dwelling, his thoughts relaxed and he remembered my question. So he answered me thus –

'Oh, ay; as ye were sayin', he's a queer man, Yeddie – aye been; guid kens whaur he cam frae first, for he's been trampin' the countryside since ever I mind, and that's no yesterday. He maun be sixty year, and yet he's as fresh as ever. If onything, he's a thocht dafter in his ongaein's and mair silent-like. But ye'll hae heard tell o' him afore?'

I owned ignorance.

'Tut,' said he, 'ye ken nocht. But Yeddie had aye a queer crakin' for waters. He never gangs on the road. Wi' him it's juist up yae glen and doon anither, and aye keepin' by the burnside. He kens every water i' the warld, every bit sheuch and burnie frae Gallowa' to Berwick. And he kens the way o' spates the best I ever seen, and I've heard tell o' him fordin' waters when nae ither thing could leeve i' them. He can weyse and wark his road sae cunnin'ly on the stanes that the roughest flood, if it's no juist fair ower

43

his heid, canna upset him. Mony a sheep has he saved to me, and it's mony a guid drove wad never hae won to Gledsmuir market but for Yeddie.'

I listened with a boy's interest in any romantic narration. Somehow, the strange figure wrestling in the brown stream took fast hold on my mind, and I asked the shepherd for further tales.

'There's little mair to tell,' he said, 'for a gangrel life is nane o' the liveliest. But d'ye ken the langnebbit hill that cocks its tap abune the Clachlands heid? Weel, he's got a wee bit o' grund on the tap frae the Yerl, and there he's howkit a grave for himsel'. He's sworn me and twae-three ithers to bury him there, wherever he may dee. It's a queer fancy in the auld dotterel.'

So the shepherd talked, and as at evening we stood by his door we saw a figure moving into the gathering shadows. I knew it at once, and did not need my friend's 'There gangs "Streams o' Water" ' to recognise it. Something wild and pathetic in the old man's face haunted me like a dream, and as the dusk swallowed him up, he seemed like some old Druid recalled of the gods to his ancient habitation of the moors.

II

Two years passed, and April came with her suns and rains, and again the waters brimmed full in the valleys. Under the clear, shining sky the lambing went on, and the faint bleat of sheep brooded on the hills. In a land of young heather and green upland meads, of faint odours of moorburn, and hill-tops falling in clean ridges to the sky-line, the veriest St Anthony would not abide indoors; so I flung all else to the winds and went a-fishing.

At the first pool on the Callowa, where the great flood sweeps nobly round a ragged shoulder of hill, and spreads into broad deeps beneath a tangle of birches, I began my labours. The turf was still wet with dew and the young leaves gleamed in the glow of morning. Far up the stream rose the grim hills which hem the mosses and tarns of the tableland, whence flow the greater waters of the country-side. An ineffable freshness, as of the morning alike of the day and the seasons, filled the clear hill air, and the remote peaks gave the needed touch of intangible romance.

But as I fished, I came on a man sitting in a green dell, busy at the making of brooms. I knew his face and dress, for who could forget such eclectic raggedness? – and I remembered that day two years before when he first hobbled into my ken. Now, as I saw him there, I was capti-vated by the nameless mystery of his appearance. There was something startling to one accustomed to the lack-lustre gaze of town-bred folk, in the sight of an eye as keen and wild as a hawk's from sheer solitude and lonely travel-ling. He was so bent and scarred with weather that he seemed as much a part of that woodland place as the birks themselves, and the noise of his labours did not startle the birds that hopped on the branches.

Little by little I won his acquaintance – by a chance reminiscence, a single tale, the mention of a friend. Then he made me free of his knowledge, and my fishing fared well that day. He dragged me up little streams to sequestered pools, where I had astonishing success; and then back to some great swirl in the Callowa where he had seen mon-strous takes. And all the while he delighted me with his talk, of men and things, of weather and place, pitched high in his thin, old voice, and garnished with many tones of lingering sentiment. He spoke in a broad, slow Scots, with so quaint a lilt in his speech that one seemed to be in an elder time among people of a quieter life and a quainter kindliness.

Then by chance I asked him of a burn of which I had heard, and how it might be reached. I shall never forget the tone of his answer as his face grew eager and he poured forth his knowledge.

'Ye'll gang up the Knowe Burn, which comes doun into the Cauldshaw. It's a wee tricklin' thing, trowin' in and out o' pools i' the rock, and comin' doun out o' the side o' Caerfraun. Yince a merry-maiden bided there, I've heard folks say, and used to win the sheep frae the Cauldshaw herd, and bile them i' the muckle pool below the fa'. They say that there's a road to the Ill Place there, and when the Deil likit he sent up the lowe and garred the water faem and fizzle like an auld kettle. But if ye're gaun to the Colm Burn ye maun haud atower the rig o' the hill frae the Knowe heid, and ye'll come to it wimplin' among green brae faces. It's a bonny bit, lonesome but awfu' bonny, and there's mony braw trout in its siller flow.'

Then I remembered all I had heard of the old man's craze, and I humoured him.

'It's a fine countryside for burns,' I said.

'Ye may say that,' said he gladly, 'a weel-watered land. But a' this braw south country is the same. I've traivelled frae the Yeavering Hill in the Cheviots to the Caldons in Galloway, and it's a' the same. When I was young, I've seen me gang north to the Hielands and doun to the English lawlands, but now that I'm gettin' auld I maun bide i'

46

the yae place. There's no a burn in the South I dinna ken, and I never cam to the water I couldna ford.'

'No?' said I. 'I've seen you at the ford o' Clachlands in the Lammas floods.'

'Often I've been there,' he went on, speaking like one calling up vague memories. 'Yince, when Tam Rorison was drooned, honest man. Yince again, when the brigs were ta'en awa', and the Back House o' Clachlands had nae bread for a week. But oh, Clachlands is a bit easy water. But I've seen the muckle Aller come roarin' sae high that it washed awa' a sheepfauld that stood weel up on the hill. And I've seen this verra burn, this bonny clear Callowa, lyin' like a loch for miles i' the haugh. But I never heeds a spate, for if a man just kens the way o't it's a canny, hairmless thing. I couldna wish to dee better than just be happit i' the waters o' my ain countryside, when my legs fail and I'm ower auld for the trampin'.'

Something in that queer figure in the setting of the hills struck a note of curious pathos. And towards evening as we returned down the glen the note grew keener. A spring sunset of gold and crimson flamed in our backs and turned the pools to fire. Far off down the vale the plains and the sea gleamed half in shadow. Somehow in the fragrance and colour and the delectable crooning of the stream, the fantastic and the dim seemed tangible and present, and high sentiment revelled for once in my prosaic heart.

And still more in the breast of my companion. He stopped and sniffed the evening air, as he looked far over hill and dale and then back to the great hills above us. 'Yon's Crappel, and Caerdon, and the Laigh Law,' he said, lingering with relish over each name, 'and the Gled comes doun atween them. I haena been there for a twalmonth,

47

and I maun hae another glisk o't, for it's a braw place.' Some bitter thought seemed to seize him, and his mouth twitched. 'I'm an auld man,' he cried, 'and I canna see ye a' again. There's burns and mair burns in the high hills that I'll never win to.' Then he remembered my presence, and stopped. 'Ye maunna mind me,' he said huskily, 'but the sicht o' thae lang blue hills makes me daft, now that I've faun i' the vale o' years. Yince I was young and could get where I wantit, but now I am auld and maun bide i' the same bit. And I'm aye thinkin' o' the waters I've been to, and the green heichs and howes and the linns that I canna win to again. I maun e'en be content wi' the Callowa, which is as guid as the best.'

I left him wandering down by the streamside and telling his crazy meditations to himself.

III

A space of years elapsed ere I met him, for fate had carried me far from the upland valleys. But once again I was afoot on the white moor roads; and, as I swung along one autumn afternoon up the path which leads from the Glen of Callowa to the Gled, I saw a figure before me which I knew for my friend. When I overtook him, his appearance puzzled and troubled me. Age seemed to have come on him at a bound, and in the tottering figure and the stoop of weakness I had difficulty in recognising the hardy frame of the man as I had known him. Something, too, had come over his face. His brow was clouded, and the tan of weather stood out hard and cruel on a blanched cheek. His eye seemed both wilder and sicklier, and for the first time I saw him with none of the appurtenances of his trade.

He greeted me feebly and dully, and showed little wish to speak. He walked with slow, uncertain step, and his breath laboured with a new panting. Every now and then he would look at me sidewise, and in his feverish glance I could detect none of the free kindliness of old. The man was ill in body and mind.

I asked him how he had done since I saw him last.

'It's an ill world now,' he said in a slow, querulous voice. 'There's nae need for honest men, and nae leevin'. Folk dinna heed me ava now. They dinna buy my besoms, they winna let me bide a nicht in their byres, and they're no like the kind canty folk in the auld times. And a' the country-side is changin'. Doun by Goldieslaw they're makkin' a dam for takin' water to the toun, and they're thinkin' o' daein' the like wi' the Callowa. Guid help us, can they no let the works o' God alane? Is there nae room for them in the dirty lawlands that they maun file the hills wi' their biggins?'

I conceived dimly that the cause of his wrath was a scheme for waterworks at the border of the uplands, but I had less concern for this than his strangely feeble health.

'You are looking ill,' I said. 'What has come over you?'

'Oh, I canna last for aye,' he said mournfully. 'My auld body's about dune. I've warkit it ower sair when I had it, and it's gaun to fail on my hands. Sleepin' out o' wat nichts and gangin' lang wantin' meat are no the best ways for a long life'; and he smiled the ghost of a smile.

And then he fell to wild telling of the ruin of the place and the hardness of the people, and I saw that want and bare living had gone far to loosen his wits. I knew the countryside, and I recognised that change was only in his mind. A great pity seized me for this lonely figure toiling on in the bitterness of regret. I tried to comfort him, but my words were useless, for he took no heed of me; with bent head and faltering step he mumbled his sorrows to himself.

Then of a sudden we came to the crest of the ridge where the road dips from the hill-top to the sheltered valley. Sheer from the heather ran the white streak till it lost itself among the reddening rowans and the yellow birks of the wood. The land was rich in autumn colour, and the shining waters dipped and fell through a pageant of russet and gold. And all around hills huddled in silent spaces, long brown moors crowned with cairns, or steep fortresses of rock and shingle rising to foreheads of steel-like grey. The autumn blue faded in the far sky-line to white, and lent distance to the farther peaks. The hush of the wilderness, which is far different from the hush of death, brooded over the scene, and like faint music came the sound of a distant scythe-swing, and the tinkling whisper which is the flow of a hundred streams.

I am an old connoisseur in the beauties of the uplands, but I held my breath at the sight. And when I glanced at my companion, he too had raised his head, and stood with wide nostrils and gleaming eye revelling in this glimpse of Arcady. Then he found his voice, and the weakness and craziness seemed for one moment to leave him.

'It's my ain land,' he cried, 'and I'll never leave it. D'ye see yon lang broun hill wi' the cairn?' and he gripped my arm fiercely and directed my gaze. 'Yon's my bit. I howkit it richt on the verra tap, and ilka year I gang there to mak it neat and orderly. I've trystit wi' fower men in different pairishes, that whenever they hear o' my death, they'll cairry me up yonder and bury me there. And then I'll

never leave it, but lie still and quiet to the world's end. I'll
aye hae the sound o' water in my ear, for there's five burns
tak' their rise on that hillside, and on a' airts the glens gang
doun to the Gled and the Aller.'

Then his spirit failed him, his voice sank, and he was
almost the feeble gangrel once more. But not yet, for again
his eye swept the ring of hills, and he muttered to himself
names which I knew for streams, lingeringly, lovingly as of
old affections. 'Aller and Gled and Callowa,' he crooned,
'braw names, and Clachlands and Cauldshaw and the
Lanely Water. And I maunna forget the Stark and the Lin
and the bonny streams o' the Creran. And what mair? I
canna mind a' the burns, the Howe and the Hollies and the
Fawn and the links o' the Manor. What says the Psalmist
about them?

> As streams of water in the South,
> Our bondage, Lord, recall.

Ay, but yon's the name for them. "Streams o' water in the
South." '

As we went down the slopes to the darkening vale I heard
him crooning to himself in a high, quavering voice the single
distich; then in a little his weariness took him again, and he
plodded on with no thought save for his sorrows.

IV

The conclusion of this tale belongs not to me, but to the
shepherd of the Redswirehead, and I heard it from him in
his dwelling, as I stayed the night, belated on the darkening

moors. He told me it after supper in a flood of misty Doric, and his voice grew rough at times, and he poked viciously at the dying peat.

'In the last back-end I was at Gledfoot wi' sheep, and a weary job I had and sma' credit. Ye ken the place, a lang dreich shore wi' the wind swirlin' and bitin' to the bane, and the broun Gled water choked wi' Solloway sand. There was nae room in ony inn in the town, so I bude to try a bit public on the Harbour Walk, where sailor-folk and fisher-men feucht and drank, and nae dacent men frae the hills thocht o' gangin'. I was in a gey ill way, for I had sell't my beasts dooms cheap, and I thocht o' the lang miles hame in the wintry weather. So after a bite o' meat I gangs oot to get the air and clear my heid, which was a' rammled wi' the auction-ring.

'And whae did I find, sittin' on a bench at the door, but the auld man Yeddie? He was waur changed than ever. His lang hair was hingin' ower his broo, and his face was thin and white as a ghaist's. His claes fell loose about him, and he sat wi' his hand on his auld stick and his chin on his hand, hearin' nocht and glowerin' afore him. He never saw nor kenned me till I shook him by the shouthers, and cried him by his name.

' "Whae are ye?" says he, in a thin voice that gaed to my hert.

' "Ye ken me fine, ye auld fule," says I. "I'm Jock Rori-son o' the Redswirehead, whaur ye've stoppit often."

' "Redswirehead," he says, like a man in a dream. "Redswirehead! That's at the tap o' the Clachlands Burn as ye gang ower to the Dreichil."

' "And what are ye daein' here? It's no your countryside ava, and ye're no fit noo for lang trampin'."

' "No," says he, in the same weak voice and wi' nae fushion in him, "but they winna hae me up yonder noo. I'm ower auld and useless. Yince a'body was gled to see me, and wad keep me as lang's I wantit, and had aye a guid word at meeting and pairting. Noo it's a' changed, and my wark's dune."

'I saw fine that the man was daft, but what answer could I gie to his havers? Folk in the Callowa glens are as kind as afore, but ill weather and auld age had put queer notions intil his heid. Forbye, he was seeck, seeck unto death, and I saw mair in his ee than I likit to think.

' "Come in-by and get some meat, man," I said. "Ye're famishin' wi' cauld and hunger."

' "I canna eat," he says, and his voice never changed. "It's lang since I had a bite, for I'm no hungry. But I'm awfu' thirsty. I cam here yestreen, and I can get nae water to drink like the water in the hills. I maun be settin' out back the morn, if the Lord spares me."

'I mindit fine that the body wad tak nae drink like an honest man, but maun aye draibble wi' burn water, and noo he had got the thing on the brain. I never spak a word, for the maitter was bye ony mortal's aid.

'For lang he sat quiet. Then he lifts his heid and looks awa ower the grey sea. A licht for a moment cam intil his een.

' "Whatna big water's yon?" he said, wi' his puir mind aye rinnin' on waters.

' "That's the Solloway," says I.

' "The Solloway," says he; "it's a big water, and it wad be an ill job to ford it."

' "Nae man ever fordit it," I said.

' "But I never yet cam to the water I couldna ford," says

he. "But what's that queer smell i' the air? Something snell and cauld and unfreendly."

' "That's the salt, for we're at the sea here, the mighty ocean."

'He keepit repeatin' the word ower in his mouth. "The salt, the salt! I've heard tell o' it afore, but I dinna like it. It's terrible cauld."

'By this time an on-ding o' rain was coming up frae the water, and I bade the man come indoors to the fire. He followed me, as biddable as a sheep, draggin' his legs like yin far gone in seeckness. I set him by the fire, and put whisky at his elbow, but he wadna touch it.

' "I've nae need o' it," said he. "I'm fine and warm"; and he sits staring at the fire, aye comin' ower again and again, "The Solloway, the Solloway. It's a guid name and a muckle water." But sune I gaed to my bed, being heavy wi' sleep, for I had traivelled for twae days.

'The next morn I was up at six and oot to see the weather. It was a' changed. The muckle tides lay lang and still as our ain Loch o' the Lee, and far ayont I saw the big blue hills o' England shine bricht and clear. I thankit Providence for the day, for it was better to tak the lang miles back in the sun than in a blast o' rain.

'But as I lookit I saw folk comin' up frae the beach cairryin' something atween them. My hert gied a loup, and "Some puir, drooned sailor body," says I to mysel', "whae has perished in yesterday's storm." But as they cam nearer I got a glisk which made me run like daft, and lang ere I was up on them I saw it was Yeddie.

'He lay drippin' and white, wi' his puir auld hair lyin' back frae his broo and the duds clingin' to his legs. But oot

54

o' the face there had gane a' the seeckness and weariness. His een were stelled as if he had been lookin' forrit to something, and his lips were set like a man on a lang errand. And mair, his stick was grippit sae firm in his hand that nae man could lowse it, so they e'en let it be.

'Then they tell't me the tale o't, how at the earliest licht they had seen him wanderin' alang the sands, juist as they were putting out their boats to sea. They wondered and watched him, till of a sudden he turned to the water and wadit in, keeping straucht on till he was oot o' sicht. They rowed a' their pith to the place, but they were ower late. Yince they saw his heid appear abune water, still wi' his face to the other side; and then they got his body, for the tide was rinnin' low in the mornin'.

'We brocht him up to the house and laid him there till the folk i' the town had heard o' the business. Syne the procurator-fiscal came and certifeed the death, and the rest was left to me. I got a wooden coffin made and put him in it, juist as he was, wi' his staff in his hand and his auld duds about him. I mindit o' my sworn word, for I was yin o' the four that had promised, and I settled to dae his bidding. It was saxteen miles to the hills, and yin and twenty to the lanely tap whaur he had howkit his grave. But I never heedit it. I'm a strong man, weel used to the walkin', and my hert was sair for the auld body. Now that he had gotten deliverance from his affliction, it was for me to leave him in the place he wantit. Forbye, he wasna muckle heavier than a bairn.

'It was a long road, a sair road, but I did it, and by seven o'clock I was at the edge o' the muirlands. There was a braw mune, and a' the glens and taps stood out as clear as midday. Bit by bit, for I was gey tired, I warstled ower the rigs and up the cleuchs to the Gled-head; syne up the stany Gled-cleuch to the lang grey hill which they ca' the Hurlybackit. By ten I had come to the cairn, and black i' the mune I saw the grave. So there I buried him, and though I'm no a releegious man, I couldna help sayin' ower him the guid words o' the Psalmist –

> As streams of water in the South,
> Our bondage, Lord, recall.'

So if you go from the Gled to the Aller, and keep far over the north side of the Muckle Muneraw, you will come in time to a stony ridge which ends in a cairn. There you will see the whole hill country of the south, a hundred lochs, a myriad streams, and a forest of hill-tops. There on the very crest lies the old man, in the heart of his own land, at the fountain-head of his many waters. If you listen you will hear a noise as of a swaying of trees or a ripple on the sea. It is the sound of the rising of burns, which, innumerable and unnumbered, flow thence to the silent glens for evermore.

The Watcher by the Threshold

A chill evening in the early October of the year 189– found me driving in a dogcart through the belts of antique woodland which form the lowland limits of the hilly parish of More. The Highland express, which brought me from the north, took me no farther than Perth. Thence it had been a slow journey in a disjointed local train, till I emerged on the platform at Morefoot, with a bleak prospect of pot stalks, coal heaps, certain sour corn lands, and far to the west a line of moor where the sun was setting. A neat groom and a respectable trap took the edge off my discomfort, and soon I had forgotten my sacrifice and found eyes for the darkening landscape. We were driving through a land of thick woods, cut at rare intervals by old long-frequented highways. The More, which at Morefoot is an open sewer, became a sullen woodland stream, where the brown leaves of the season drifted. At times we would pass an ancient lodge, and through a gap in the trees would come a glimpse of chipped crowstep gable. The names of such houses, as told me by my companion, were all famous. This one had been the home of a drunken Jacobite laird, and a king of north country Medmenham. Unholy revels had waked the old halls, and the devil had been toasted at many a hell-fire dinner. The next was the property of a great Scots law family, and there the old Lord of Session, who built the place, in his frouzy wig and carpet slippers, had laid down the canons of Taste for his day and society. The whole country had the air of faded and bygone gentility. The mossy roadside walls had stood for two hundred years; the few wayside houses were toll bars or defunct hostelries. The names, too, were great: Scots baronial with a smack of France – Chatelray and Riverslaw, Black Holm and Fountainblue. The place had a cunning charm, mystery dwelt in every cranny, and yet it did not please me. The earth smelt heavy and raw; the roads were red underfoot; all was old, sorrowful and uncanny. Compared with the fresh Highland glen I had left, where wind and sun and flying showers were never absent, all was chilly and dull and dead. Even when the sun sent a shiver of crimson over the crests of certain firs, I felt no delight in the prospect. I admitted shamefacedly to myself that I was in a very bad temper.

I had been staying at Glenaicill with the Clanroydens, and for a week had found the proper pleasure in life. You know the house with its old rooms and gardens, and the miles of heather which defend it from the world. The shooting had been extraordinary for a wild place late in the season; for there are few partridges, and the woodcock are notoriously late. I had done respectably in my stalking, more than respectably on the river, and creditably on the moors. Moreover, there were pleasant people in the house – and there were the Clanroydens. I had had a hard year's work, sustained to the last moment of term, and a fortnight in Norway had been disastrous. It was therefore with real comfort that I had settled myself down for another ten days in Glenaicill, when all my plans were shattered by Sibyl's letter. Sibyl is my cousin and my very good friend, and in old days when I was briefless I had fallen in love with her many times. But she very sensibly chose otherwise, and married a man Ladlaw – Robert John Ladlaw, who had been at school with me. He was a cheery, good-humoured

fellow, a great sportsman, a justice of the peace, and deputy lieutenant for his county, and something of an antiquary
in a mild way. He had a box in Leicestershire to which he
went in the hunting season, but from February till October
he lived in his moorland home. The place was called the
House of More, and I had shot at it once or twice in recent
years. I remembered its loneliness and its comfort, the
charming diffident Sibyl, and Ladlaw's genial welcome.
And my recollections set me puzzling again over the letter
which that morning had broken into my comfort. 'You
promised us a visit this autumn,' Sibyl had written, 'and I
wish you would come as soon as you can.' So far common
politeness. But she had gone on to reveal the fact that
Ladlaw was ill; she did not know how, exactly, but something, she thought, about his heart. Then she had signed
herself my affectionate cousin, and then had come a short,
violent postscript, in which, as it were, the fences of convention had been laid low. 'For Heaven's sake, come and
see us,' she scrawled below. 'Bob is terribly ill, and I am
crazy. Come at once.' To cap it she finished with an after-
thought: 'Don't bother about bringing doctors. It is not
their business.'

She had assumed that I would come, and dutifully I set
out. I could not regret my decision, but I took leave to
upbraid my luck. The thought of Glenaicill, with the woodcock beginning to arrive and the Clanroydens imploring
me to stay, saddened my journey in the morning, and the
murky, coaly, midland country of the afternoon completed
my depression. The drive through the woodlands of More
failed to raise my spirits. I was anxious about Sibyl and
Ladlaw, and this accursed country had always given me a
certain eeriness on my first approaching it. You may call it

silly, but I have no nerves and am little susceptible to vague sentiment. It was sheer physical dislike of the rich deep soil, the woody and antique smells, the melancholy roads and trees, and the flavour of old mystery. I am aggressively healthy and wholly Philistine. I love clear outlines and strong colours, and More with its half tints and hazy distances depressed me miserably. Even when the road crept uphill and the trees ended, I found nothing to hearten me in the moorland which succeeded. It was genuine moorland, close on eight hundred feet above the sea, and through it ran this old grass-grown coach road. Low hills rose to the left, and to the right, after some miles of peat, flared the chimneys of pits and oil works. Straight in front the moor ran out into the horizon, and there in the centre was the last dying spark of the sun. The place was as still as the grave save for the crunch of our wheels on the grassy road, but the flaring lights to the north seemed to endow it with life. I have rarely had so keenly the feeling of movement in the inanimate world. It was an unquiet place, and I shivered nervously. Little gleams of loch came from the hollows, the burns were brown with peat, and every now and then there rose in the moor jags of sickening red stone. I remembered that Ladlaw had talked about the place as the old Manann, the holy land of the ancient races. I had paid little attention at the time, but now it struck me that the old peoples had been wise in their choice. There was something uncanny in this soil and air. Framed in dank mysterious woods and a country of coal and ironstone, at no great distance from the capital city, it was a sullen relic of a lost barbarism. Over the low hills lay a green pastoral country with bright streams and valleys, but here, in this peaty desert, there were few sheep and little cultivation. The

House of More was the only dwelling, and, save for the ragged village, the wilderness was given over to the wild things of the hills. The shooting was good, but the best shooting on earth would not persuade me to make my abode in such a place. Ladlaw was ill; well, I did not wonder. You can have uplands without air, moors that are not health-giving, and a country life which is more arduous than a townsman's. I shivered again, for I seemed to have passed in a few hours from the open noon to a kind of dank twilight.

We passed the village and entered the lodge gates. Here there were trees again – little innocent new-planted firs, which flourished ill. Some large plane trees grew near the house, and there were thickets upon thickets of the ugly elderberry. Even in the half darkness I could see that the lawns were trim and the flower beds respectable for the season; doubtless Sibyl looked after the gardeners. The oblong whitewashed house, more like a barrack than ever, opened suddenly on my sight, and I experienced my first sense of comfort since I left Glenaicill. Here I should find warmth and company; and sure enough, the hall door was wide open, and in the great flood of light which poured from it Sibyl stood to welcome me.

She ran down the steps as I dismounted, and, with a word to the groom, caught my arm and drew me into the shadow. 'Oh, Henry, it was so good of you to come. You mustn't let Bob think that you know he is ill. We don't talk about it. I'll tell you afterwards. I want you to cheer him up. Now we must go in, for he is in the hall expecting you.'

While I stood blinking in the light, Ladlaw came forward with outstretched hand and his usual cheery greeting. I looked at him and saw nothing unusual in his appearance; a little drawn at the lips, perhaps, and heavy below the eyes, but still fresh-coloured and healthy. It was Sibyl who showed change. She was very pale, her pretty eyes were deplorably mournful, and in place of her delightful shyness there were the self-confidence and composure of pain. I was honestly shocked, and as I dressed my heart was full of hard thoughts about Ladlaw. What could his illness mean? He seemed well and cheerful, while Sibyl was pale; and yet it was Sibyl who had written the postscript. As I warmed myself by the fire, I resolved that this particular family difficulty was my proper business.

The Ladlaws were waiting for me in the drawing-room. I noticed something new and strange in Sibyl's demeanour. She looked to her husband with a motherly, protective air, while Ladlaw, who had been the extreme of masculine independence, seemed to cling to his wife with a curious appealing fidelity. In conversation he did little more than echo her words. Till dinner was announced he spoke of the weather, the shooting, and Mabel Clanroyden. Then he did a queer thing; for when I was about to offer my arm to Sibyl he forestalled me, and clutching her right arm with his left hand led the way to the dining-room, leaving me to follow in some bewilderment.

I have rarely taken part in a more dismal meal. The House of More has a pretty Georgian panelling through most of the rooms, but in the dining-room the walls are level and painted a dull stone colour. Abraham offered up Isaac in a ghastly picture in front of me. Some photographs of the Quorn hung over the mantelpiece, and five or six drab ancestors filled up the remaining space. But one thing was new and startling. A great marble bust, a genuine antique, frowned on me from a pedestal. The

head was in the late Roman style, clearly of some emperor, and in its commonplace environment the great brows, the massive neck and the mysterious solemn lips had a surprising effect. I nodded toward the thing, and asked what it represented.

Ladlaw grunted something which I took for 'Justinian', but he never raised his eyes from his plate. By accident I caught Sibyl's glance. She looked toward the bust, and laid a finger on her lips.

The meal grew more doleful as it advanced. Sibyl scarcely touched a dish, but her husband ate ravenously of everything. He was a strong, thickset man, with a square kindly face burned brown by the sun. Now he seemed to have suddenly coarsened. He gobbled with undignified haste, and his eye was extraordinarily vacant. A question made him start, and he would turn on me a face so strange and inert that I repented the interruption.

I asked him about the autumn's sport. He collected his wits with difficulty. He thought it had been good, on the whole, but he had shot badly. He had not been quite so fit as usual. No, he had had nobody staying with him. Sibyl had wanted to be alone. He was afraid the moor might have been undershot, but he would make a big day with keepers and farmers before the winter.

'Bob has done pretty well,' Sibyl said. 'He hasn't been out often, for the weather has been very bad here. You can have no idea, Henry, how horrible this moorland place of ours can be when it tries. It is one great sponge sometimes, with ugly red burns and mud to the ankles.'

'I don't think it's healthy,' said I.

Ladlaw lifted his face. 'Nor do I. I think it's intolerable, but I am so busy I can't get away.'

63

Once again I caught Sibyl's warning eye as I was about to question him on his business.

Clearly the man's brain had received a shock, and he was beginning to suffer from hallucinations. This could be the only explanation, for he had always led a temperate life. The distrait, wandering manner was the only sign of his malady, for otherwise he seemed normal and mediocre as ever. My heart grieved for Sibyl, alone with him in this wilderness.

Then he broke the silence. He lifted his head and looked nervously around till his eye fell on the Roman bust.

'Do you know that this countryside is the old Manann?' he said.

It was an odd turn to the conversation, but I was glad of a sign of intelligence. I answered that I had heard so.

'It's a queer name,' he said oracularly, 'but the thing it stood for was queerer, Manann, Manaw,' he repeated, rolling the words on his tongue. As he spoke, he glanced sharply, and, as it seemed to me, fearfully, at his left side.

The movement of his body made his napkin slip from his left knee and fall on the floor. It leaned against his leg, and he started from its touch as if he had been bitten by a snake. I have never seen a more sheer and transparent terror on a man's face. He got to his feet, his strong frame shaking like a rush. Sibyl ran round to his side, picked up the napkin and flung it on a sideboard. Then she stroked his hair as one would stroke a frightened horse. She called him by his old boy's name of Robin, and at her touch and voice he became quiet. But the particular course then in progress was removed, untasted.

In a few minutes he seemed to have forgotten his behaviour, for he took up the former conversation. For a time he spoke well and briskly. 'You lawyers', he said, 'understand only the dry framework of the past. You cannot conceive the rapture, which only the antiquary can feel, of constructing in every detail an old culture. Take this Manann. If I could explore the secret of these moors, I would write the world's greatest book. I would write of that prehistoric life when man was knit close to nature. I would describe the people who were brothers of the red earth and the red rock and the red streams of the hills. Oh, it would be horrible, but superb, tremendous! It would be more than a piece of history; it would be a new gospel, a new theory of life. It would kill materialism once and for all. Why, man, all the poets who have deified and personified nature would not do an eighth part of my work. I would show you the unknown, the hideous, shrieking mystery at the back of this simple nature. Men would see the profundity of the old crude faiths which they affect to despise. I would make a picture of our shaggy, sombre-eyed forefather, who heard strange things in the hill silences. I would show him brutal and terror-stricken, but wise, wise, God alone knows how wise! The Romans knew it, and they learned what they could from him, though he did not tell them much. But we have some of his blood in us, and we may go deeper. Manann! A queer land nowadays! I sometimes love it and sometimes hate it, but I always fear it. It is like that statue, inscrutable.'

I would have told him that he was talking mystical nonsense, but I had looked toward the bust, and my rudeness was checked on my lips. The moor might be a common piece of ugly waste land, but the statue was inscrutable – of that there was no doubt. I hate your cruel heavy-mouthed Roman busts; to me they have none of the beauty of life, and little of the interest of art. But my eyes were fastened on this as they had never before looked on marble. The oppression of the heavy woodlands, the mystery of the silent moor, seemed to be caught and held in this face. It was the intangible mystery of culture on the verge of savagery – a cruel, lustful wisdom, and yet a kind of bitter austerity which laughed at the game of life and stood aloof. There was no weakness in the heavy-veined brow and slumbrous eyelids. It was the face of one who had conquered the world, and found it dust and ashes; one who had eaten of the tree of the knowledge of good and evil, and scorned human wisdom. And at the same time, it was the face of one who knew uncanny things, a man who was the intimate of the half-world and the dim background of life. Why on earth I should connect the Roman grandee* with the moorland parish of More I cannot say, but the fact remains that there was that in the face which I knew had haunted me through the woodlands and bogs of the place – a sleepless, dismal, incoherent melancholy.

'I bought that at Colenzo's', Ladlaw said, 'because it took my fancy. It matches well with this place.'

I thought it matched very ill with his drab walls and Quorn photographs, but I held my peace.

'Do you know who it is?' he asked. 'It is the head of the greatest man the world has ever seen. You are a lawyer and know your Justinian.'

---

* I have identified the bust, which, when seen under other circumstances, had little power to affect me. It was a copy of the head of Justinian in the Tesci Museum at Venice, and several duplicates exist, dating apparently from the seventh century, and showing traces of Byzantine decadence in the scroll work on the hair. It is engraved in M. Delacroix's *Byzantium*, and, I think, in Windscheid's *Pandektenlehrbuch*.

The *Pandects* are scarcely part of the daily work of a common-law barrister. I had not looked into them since I left college.

'I know that he married an actress,' I said, 'and was a sort of all-round genius. He made law, and fought battles, and had rows with the Church. A curious man! And wasn't there some story about his selling his soul to the devil, and getting law in exchange? Rather a poor bargain!'

I chattered away, sillily enough, to dispel the gloom of that dinner table. The result of my words was unhappy. Ladlaw gasped and caught at his left side, as if in pain. Sibyl, with tragic eyes, had been making signs to me to hold my peace. Now she ran round to her husband's side and comforted him like a child. As she passed me, she managed to whisper in my ear to talk to her only, and let her husband alone.

For the rest of dinner I obeyed my orders to the letter. Ladlaw ate his food in gloomy silence, while I spoke to Sibyl of our relatives and friends, of London, Glenaicill, and any random subject. The poor girl was dismally forgetful, and her eye would wander to her husband with wifely anxiety. I remember being suddenly overcome by the comic aspect of it all. Here were we three fools alone in the dank upland: one of us sick and nervous, talking out-of-the-way nonsense about Manann and Justinian, gobbling his food and getting scared at his napkin; another gravely anxious; and myself at my wits' end for a solution. It was a Mad Tea-Party with a vengeance: Sibyl the melancholy little Dormouse, and Ladlaw the incomprehensible Hatter. I laughed aloud, but checked myself when I caught my cousin's eye. It was really no case for finding humour. Ladlaw was very ill, and Sibyl's face was getting deplorably thin.

I welcomed the end of that meal with unmannerly joy, for I wanted to speak seriously with my host. Sibyl told the butler to have the lamps lighted in the library. Then she leaned over toward me and spoke low and rapidly: 'I want you to talk with Bob. I'm sure you can do him good. You'll have to be very patient with him, and very gentle. Oh, please try to find out what is wrong with him. He won't tell me, and I can only guess.'

The butler returned with word that the library was ready to receive us, and Sibyl rose to go. Ladlaw half rose, protesting, making the most curious feeble clutches to his side. His wife quieted him. 'Henry will look after you, dear,' she said. 'You are going into the library to smoke.' Then she slipped from the room, and we were left alone.

He caught my arm fiercely with his left hand, and his grip nearly made me cry out. As we walked down the hall, I could feel his arm twitching from the elbow to the shoulder. Clearly he was in pain, and I set it down to some form of cardiac affection, which might possibly issue in paralysis.

I settled him in the biggest armchair, and took one of his cigars. The library is the pleasantest room in the house, and at night, when a peat fire burned on the old hearth and the great red curtains were drawn, it used to be the place for comfort and good talk. Now I noticed changes. Ladlaw's bookshelves had been filled with the Proceedings of antiquarian societies and many light-hearted works on sport. But now the Badminton library had been cleared out of a shelf where it stood most convenient to the hand, and its place taken by an old Leyden reprint of Justinian. There were books on Byzantine subjects of which I never dreamed he had heard the names; there were volumes of history and speculation, all of a slightly bizarre kind; and to crown everything, there were several bulky medical works with gaudily coloured plates. The old atmosphere of sport and travel had gone from the room with the medley of rods, whips and gun cases which used to cumber the tables. Now the place was moderately tidy and somewhat learned, and I did not like it.

Ladlaw refused to smoke, and sat for a little while in silence. Then of his own accord he broke the tension.

'It was devilish good of you to come, Harry. This is a lonely place for a man who is a bit seedy.'

'I thought you might be alone,' I said, 'so looked you up on my way down from Glenaicill. I'm sorry to find you feeling ill.'

'Do you notice it?' he asked sharply.

'It's tolerably patent,' I said. 'Have you seen a doctor?'

He said something uncomplimentary about doctors, and kept looking at me with his curious dull eyes.

I remarked the strange posture in which he sat, his head screwed round to his right shoulder, and his whole body a protest against something at his left hand.

'It looks like a heart,' I said. 'You seem to have pains in your left side.'

Again a spasm of fear. I went over to him and stood at the back of his chair.

'Now for goodness' sake, my dear fellow, tell me what is wrong. You're scaring Sibyl to death. It's lonely work for the poor girl, and I wish you would let me help you.'

He was lying back in his chair now, with his eyes half shut, and shivering like a frightened colt. The extraordinary change in one who had been the strongest of the strong kept me from realising his gravity. I put a hand on his shoulder, but he flung it off.

69

'For God's sake, sit down!' he said hoarsely. 'I'm going to tell you, but I'll never make you understand.'

I sat down promptly opposite him.

'It's the devil,' he said very solemnly.

I am afraid that I was rude enough to laugh. He took no notice, but sat, with the same tense, miserable air, staring over my head.

'Right,' said I. 'Then it is the devil. It's a new complaint, so it's as well I did not bring a doctor. How does it affect you?'

He made the old impotent clutch at the air with his left hand. I had the sense to become grave at once. Clearly this was some serious mental affection, some hallucination born of physical pain.

Then he began to talk in a low voice, very rapidly, with his head bent forward like a hunted animal's. I am not going to set down what he told me in his own words, for they were incoherent often, and there was much repetition. But I am going to write the gist of the odd story which took my sleep away on that autumn night, with such explanations and additions I think needful. The fire died down, the wind arose, the hour grew late, and still he went on in his mumbling recitative. I forgot to smoke, forgot my comfort – everything but the odd figure of my friend and his inconceivable romance. And the night before I had been in cheerful Glenaicill!

He had returned to the House of More, he said, in the latter part of May, and shortly after he fell ill. It was a trifling sickness – influenza or something – but he had never quite recovered. The rainy weather of June depressed him, and the extreme heat of July made him listless and weary. A

70

kind of insistent sleepiness hung over him, and he suffered much from nightmare. Toward the end of July his former health returned, but he was haunted with a curious oppression. He seemed to himself to have lost the art of being alone. There was a perpetual sound in his left ear, a kind of moving and rustling at his left side, which never left him by night or day. In addition, he had become the prey of nerves and an insensate dread of the unknown.

Ladlaw, as I have explained, was a commonplace man, with fair talents, a mediocre culture, honest instincts, and the beliefs and incredulities of his class. On abstract grounds, I should have declared him an unlikely man to be the victim of an hallucination. He had a kind of dull bourgeois rationalism, which used to find reasons for all things in heaven and earth. At first he controlled his dread with proverbs. He told himself it was the sequel of his illness or the light-headedness of summer heat on the moors. But it soon outgrew his comfort. It became a living second presence, an *alter ego* which dogged his footsteps. He grew acutely afraid of it. He dared not be alone for a moment, and clung to Sibyl's company despairingly. She went off for a week's visit in the beginning of August, and he endured for seven days the tortures of the lost. The malady advanced upon him with swift steps. The presence became more real daily. In the early dawning, in the twilight, and in the first hour of the morning it seemed at times to take a visible bodily form. A kind of amorphous featureless shadow would run from his side into the darkness, and he would sit palsied with terror. Sometimes, in lonely places, his footsteps sounded double, and something would brush elbows with him. Human society alone exorcised it. With Sibyl at his side he was happy; but as soon as she left him, the

71

thing came slinking back from the unknown to watch by him. Company might have saved him, but joined to his affliction was a crazy dread of his fellows. He would not leave his moorland home, but must bear his burden alone among the wild streams and mosses of that dismal place.

The 12th came, and he shot wretchedly, for his nerve had gone to pieces. He stood exhaustion badly, and became a dweller about the doors. But with this bodily inertness came an extraordinary intellectual revival. He read widely in a blundering way, and he speculated unceasingly. It was characteristic of the man that as soon as he left the paths of the prosaic he should seek his supernatural in a very concrete form. He assumed that he was haunted by the devil – the visible personal devil in whom our fathers believed. He waited hourly for the shape at his side to speak, but no words came. The Accuser of the Brethren in all but tangible form was his ever-present companion. He felt, he declared, the spirit of old evil entering subtly into his blood. He sold his soul many times over, and yet there was no possibility of resistance. It was a Visitation more undeserved than Job's, and a thousandfold more awful.

For a week or more he was tortured with a kind of religious mania. When a man of a healthy secular mind finds himself adrift on the terrible ocean of religious troubles he is peculiarly helpless, for he has not the most rudimentary knowledge of the winds and tides. It was useless to call up his old carelessness; he had suddenly dropped into a new world where old proverbs did not apply. And all the while, mind you, there was the shrinking terror of it – an intellect all alive to the torture and the most unceasing physical fear. For a little he was on the far edge of idiocy.

Then by accident it took a new form. While sitting with

Sibyl one day in the library, he began listlessly to turn over the leaves of an old book. He read a few pages, and found the hint to a story like his own. It was some French *Life of Justinian*, one of the unscholarly productions of last century, made up of stories from Procopius and tags of Roman law. Here was his own case written down in black and white; and the man had been a king of kings. This was a new comfort, and for a little – strange though it may seem – he took a sort of pride in his affliction. He worshipped the great Emperor, and read every scrap he could find on him, not excepting the *Pandects* and the *Digest*. He sent for the bust in the dining-room, paying a fabulous price. Then he settled himself to study his imperial prototype, and the study became an idolatry. As I have said, Ladlaw was a man of ordinary talents, and certainly of meagre imaginative power. And yet from the lies of the Secret History and the crudities of German legalists he had constructed a marvellous portrait of a man. Sitting there in the half-lighted room, he drew the picture: the quiet cold man with his inheritance of Dacian mysticism, holding the great world in fee, giving it law and religion, fighting its wars, building its churches, and yet all the while intent upon his own private work of making his peace with his soul – the churchman and warrior whom all the world worshipped, and yet one going through life with his lip quivering. He Watched by the Threshold ever at the left side. Sometimes at night, in the great Brazen Palace, warders heard the Emperor walking in the dark corridors, alone, and yet not alone; for once, when a servant entered with a lamp, he saw his master with a face as of another world, and something beside him which had no face or shape, but which he knew to be that hoary Evil which is older than the stars.

Crazy nonsense! I had to rub my eyes to assure myself that I was not sleeping. No! There was my friend with his suffering face, and it was the library of More.

And then he spoke of Theodora – actress, harlot, *dévote*, empress. For him the lady was but another part of the uttermost horror, a form of the shapeless thing at his side. I felt myself falling under the fascination. I have no nerves and little imagination, but in a flash I seemed to realise something of that awful featureless face, crouching ever at a man's hand, till darkness and loneliness come, and it rises to its mastery. I shivered as I looked at the man in the chair before me. These dull eyes of his were looking upon things I could not see, and I saw their terror. I realised that it was grim earnest for him. Nonsense or no, some devilish fancy had usurped the place of his sanity, and he was being slowly broken upon the wheel. And then, when his left hand twitched, I almost cried out. I had thought it comic before; now it seemed the last proof of tragedy.

He stopped, and I got up with loose knees and went to the window. Better the black night than the intangible horror within. I flung up the sash and looked out across the moor. There was no light; nothing but an inky darkness and the uncanny rustle of elder bushes. The sound chilled me, and I closed the window.

'The land is the old Manann,' Ladlaw was saying. 'We are beyond the pale here. Do you hear the wind?'

I forced myself back into sanity and looked at my watch. It was nearly one o'clock.

'What ghastly idiots we are!' I said. 'I am off to bed.'

Ladlaw looked at me helplessly. 'For God's sake, don't leave me alone!' he moaned. 'Get Sibyl.'

We went together back to the hall, while he kept the same feverish grasp on my arm. Someone was sleeping in a chair by the hall fire, and to my distress I recognised my hostess. The poor child must have been sadly wearied. She came forward with her anxious face.

'I'm afraid Bob has kept you very late, Henry,' she said. 'I hope you will sleep well. Breakfast at nine, you know.' And then I left them.

Over my bed there was a little picture, a reproduction of some Italian work, of Christ and the Demoniac. Some impulse made me hold my candle up to it. The madman's face was torn with passion and suffering, and his eye had the pained furtive expression which I had come to know. And by his left side there was a dim shape crouching.

I got into bed hastily, but not to sleep. I felt that my reason must be going. I had been pitchforked from our clear and cheerful modern life into the mists of old superstition. Old tragic stories of my Calvinist upbringing returned to haunt me. The man dwelt in by a devil was no new fancy, but I believed that science had docketed and analysed and explained the devil out of the world. I remembered my dabblings in the occult before I settled down to law – the story of Donisarius, the monk of Padua, the unholy legend of the Face of Proserpine, the tales of *succubi* and *incubi*, the Leannan Sith and the Hidden Presence. But here was something stranger still. I had stumbled upon that very possession which fifteen hundred years ago had made the monks of New Rome tremble and cross themselves. Some devilish occult force, lingering through the ages, had come to life after a long sleep. God knows what earthly connection there was between the splendid Emperor of the World and my prosaic

75

friend, or between the glittering shores of the Bosporus and this moorland parish! But the land was the old Manann! The spirit may have lingered in the earth and air, a deadly legacy from Pict and Roman. I had felt the uncanniness of the place; I had augured ill of it from the first. And then in sheer disgust I rose and splashed my face with cold water.

I lay down again, laughing miserably at my credulity. That I, the sober and rational, should believe in this crazy fable was too palpably absurd. I would steel my mind resolutely against such harebrained theories. It was a mere bodily ailment – liver out of order, weak heart, bad circulation, or something of that sort. At the worst it might be some affection of the brain, to be treated by a specialist. I vowed to myself that next morning the best doctor in Edinburgh should be brought to More.

The worst of it was that my duty compelled me to stand my ground. I foresaw the few remaining weeks of my holiday blighted. I should be tied to this moorland prison, a sort of keeper and nurse in one, tormented by silly fancies. It was a charming prospect, and the thought of Glenaicill and the woodcock made me bitter against Ladlaw. But there was no way out of it. I might do Ladlaw good, and I could not have Sibyl worn to death by his vagaries.

My ill nature comforted me, and I forgot the horror of the thing in its vexation. After that I think I fell asleep and dozed uneasily till morning. When I woke I was in a better frame of mind. The early sun had worked wonders with the moorland. The low hills stood out fresh-coloured and clear against a pale October sky; the elders sparkled with frost; the raw film of morn was rising from the little loch in tiny clouds. It was a cold, rousing day, and I dressed in good spirits and went down to breakfast.

I found Ladlaw looking ruddy and well; very different from the broken man I remembered of the night before. We were alone, for Sibyl was breakfasting in bed. I remarked on his ravenous appetite, and he smiled cheerily. He made two jokes during the meal; he laughed often, and I began to forget the events of the previous day. It seemed to me that I might still flee from More with a clear conscience. He had forgotten about his illness. When I touched distantly upon the matter he showed a blank face.

It might be that the affection had passed; on the other hand, it might return to him at the darkening. I had no means to decide. His manner was still a trifle distrait and peculiar, and I did not like the dullness in his eye. At any rate, I should spend the day in his company, and the evening would decide the question.

I proposed shooting, which he promptly vetoed. He was no good at walking, he said, and the birds were wild. This seriously limited the possible occupations. Fishing there was none, and hill-climbing was out of the question. He proposed a game at billiards, and I pointed to the glory of the morning. It would have been sacrilege to waste such sunshine in knocking balls about. Finally we agreed to drive somewhere and have lunch, and he ordered the dogcart.

In spite of all forebodings I enjoyed the day. We drove in the opposite direction from the woodland parts, right away across the moor to the coal country beyond. We lunched at the little mining town of Borrowmuir, in a small and noisy public house. The roads made bad going, the country was far from pretty, and yet the drive did not bore me. Ladlaw talked incessantly – talked as I had never heard man talk before. There was something indescribable in all he said, a different point of view, a lost groove of thought, a kind of innocence and archaic shrewdness in one. I can only give you a hint of it, by saying that it was like the mind of an early ancestor placed suddenly among modern surroundings. It was wise with a remote wisdom, and silly (now and then) with a quite antique and distant silliness.

I will give instances of both. He provided me with a theory of certain early fortifications, which must be true, which commends itself to the mind with overwhelming conviction, and yet which is so out of the way of common speculation that no man could have guessed it. I do not propose to set down the details, for I am working at it on my own account. Again, he told me the story of an old marriage custom, which till recently survived in this district – told it with full circumstantial detail and constant allusions to other customs which he could not possibly have known of. Now for the other side. He explained why well water is in winter warmer than a running stream, and this was his explanation: at the antipodes our winter is summer, consequently, the water of a well which comes through from the other side of the earth must be warm in winter and cold in summer, since in our summer it is winter there. You perceive what this is. It is no mere silliness, but a genuine effort of an early mind, which had just grasped the fact of the antipodes, to use it in explanation.

Gradually I was forced to the belief that it was not Ladlaw who was talking to me, but something speaking through him, something at once wiser and simpler. My old fear of the devil began to depart. This spirit, the exhalation, whatever it was, was ingenuous in its way, at least in its daylight aspect. For a moment I had an idea that it was a real reflex of Byzantine thought, and that by cross-examining I might make marvellous discoveries. The ardour of the scholar began to rise in me, and I asked a question about that much-debated point, the legal status of the *apocrisiarii*. To my vexation he gave no response. Clearly the intelligence of this familiar had its limits.

It was about three in the afternoon, and we had gone half of our homeward journey, when signs of the old terror began to appear. I was driving, and Ladlaw sat on my left. I noticed him growing nervous and silent, shivering at the flick of the whip, and turning halfway round toward me. Then he asked me to change places, and I had the unpleasant work of driving from the wrong side. After that I do not think he spoke once till we arrived at More, but sat huddled together, with the driving rug almost up to his chin – an eccentric figure of a man.

I foresaw another such night as the last, and I confess my heart sank. I had no stomach for more mysteries, and somehow with the approach of twilight the confidence of the day departed. The thing appeared in darker colours, and I found it in my mind to turn coward. Sibyl alone deterred me. I could not bear to think of her alone with this demented being. I remembered her shy timidity, her innocence. It was monstrous that the poor thing should be called on thus to fight alone with phantoms.

When we came to the House it was almost sunset. Ladlaw got out very carefully on the right side, and for a second stood by the horse. The sun was making our shadows long, and as I stood beyond him it seemed for a moment that his shadow was double. It may have been mere fancy, for I had not time to look twice. He was standing, as I have said, with his left side next the horse. Suddenly the harmless elderly cob fell into a very panic of fright, reared upright, and all but succeeded in killing its master. I was in time to pluck Ladlaw from under its feet, but the beast had become perfectly unmanageable, and we left a groom struggling to quiet it.

In the hall the butler gave me a telegram. It was from my clerk, summoning me back at once to an important consultation.

Here was a prompt removal of my scruples. There could be no question of my remaining, for the case was one of the first importance, which I had feared might break off my holiday. The consultation fell in vacation time to meet the convenience of certain people who were going abroad, and there was the most instant demand for my presence. I must go, and at once; and, as I hunted in the time-table, I found that in three hours' time a night train for the south would pass Borrowmuir which might be stopped by special wire.

But I had no pleasure in my freedom. I was in despair about Sibyl, and I hated myself for my cowardly relief. The dreary dining-room, the sinister bust, and Ladlaw crouching and quivering – the recollection, now that escape was before me, came back on my mind with the terror of a nightmare. My first thought was to persuade the Ladlaws to come away with me. I found them both in the drawing-room – Sibyl very fragile and pale, and her husband sitting as usual like a frightened child in the shadow of her skirts. A sight of him was enough to dispel my hope. The man was fatally ill, mentally, bodily; and who was I to attempt to minister to a mind diseased?

But Sibyl – she might be saved from the martyrdom. The servants would take care of him, and, if need be, a doctor might be got from Edinburgh to live in the house. So while he sat with vacant eyes staring into the twilight,

I tried to persuade Sibyl to think of herself. I am frankly a sun worshipper. I have no taste for arduous duty, and the quixotic is my abhorrence. I laboured to bring my cousin to this frame of mind. I told her that her first duty was to herself, and that this vigil of hers was beyond human endurance. But she had no ears for my arguments.

'While Bob is ill I must stay with him,' she said always in answer, and then she thanked me for my visit, till I felt a brute and a coward. I strove to quiet my conscience, but it told me always that I was fleeing from my duty; and then, when I was on the brink of a nobler resolution, a sudden overmastering terror would take hold of me, and I would listen hysterically for the sound of the dogcart on the gravel.

At last it came, and in a sort of fever I tried to say the conventional farewells. I shook hands with Ladlaw, and when I dropped his hand it fell numbly on his knee. Then I took my leave, muttering hoarse nonsense about having had a 'charming visit', and 'hoping soon to see them both in town'. As I backed to the door, I knocked over a lamp on a small table. It crashed on the floor and went out, and at the sound Ladlaw gave a curious childish cry. I turned like a coward, and ran across the hall to the front door, and scrambled into the dogcart.

The groom would have driven me sedately through the park, but I must have speed or go mad. I took the reins from him and put the horse into a canter. We swung through the gates and out into the moor road, for I could have no peace till the ghoulish elder world was exchanged for the homely ugliness of civilisation. Once only I looked back, and there against the sky line, with a solitary lit window, the House of More stood lonely in the red desert.

Fountainblue

I

Once upon a time, as the story-books say, a boy came over a ridge of hill, from which a shallow vale ran out into the sunset. It was a high, wind-blown country, where the pines had a crook in their backs and the rocks were scarred and bitten with winter storms. But below was the beginning of pastoral. Soft birch-woods, shady beeches, meadows where cattle had browsed for generations, fringed the little brown river as it twined to the sea. Farther, and the waves broke on white sands, the wonderful billows of the West which cannot bear to be silent. And between, in a garden wilderness, with the evening flaming in its windows, stood Fountainblue, my little four-square castle which guards the valley and the beaches.

The boy had torn his clothes, scratched his face, cut one finger deeply, and soaked himself with bog-water, but he whistled cheerfully and his eyes were happy. He had had an afternoon of adventure, startling emprises achieved in solitude; assuredly a day to remember and mark with a white stone. And the beginning had been most unpromising. After lunch he had been attired in his best raiment, and, in the misery of a broad white collar, despatched with his cousins to take tea with the small lady who domineered in Fountainblue. The prospect had pleased him greatly, the gardens fed his fancy, the hostess was an old confederate, and there were sure to be excellent things to eat. But his curious temper had arisen to torment him. On the way he quarrelled with his party, and in a moment found himself out of sympathy with the future. The enjoyment crept out of the prospect. He knew that he did not shine in society, he foresaw an afternoon when he would be left out in the cold and his hilarious cousins treated as the favoured guests. He reflected that tea was a short meal at the best, and that games on a lawn were a poor form of sport. Above all, he felt the torture of his collar and the straitness of his clothes. He pictured the dreary return in the twilight, when the afternoon, which had proved, after all, such a dismal failure, had come to a weary end. So, being a person of impulses, he mutinied at the gates of Fountainblue and made for the hills. He knew he should get into trouble, but trouble, he had long ago found out, was his destiny, and he scorned to avoid it. And now, having cast off the fear of God and man, he would for some short hours do exactly as he pleased.

Half-crying with regret for the delights he had forsworn, he ran over the moor to the craggy hills which had always been forbidden him. When he had climbed among the rocks awe fell upon the desolate little adventurer, and he bewailed his choice. But soon he found a blue hawk's nest, and the possession of a coveted egg inspired him to advance. By-and-by he had climbed so high that he could not return, but must needs scale Stob Ghabhar itself. With a quaking heart he achieved it, and then, in the pride of his heroism, he must venture down the Grey Correi where the wild goats lived. He saw a bearded ruffian, and pursued him with stones, stalking him cunningly till he was out of breath. Then he found odd little spleenwort ferns, which he pocketed, and high up in the rocks a friendly raven croaked his encouragement. And then, when the shadows lengthened, he set off cheerily homewards, hungry, triumphant and very weary.

All the way home he flattered his soul. In one afternoon he had been hunter and trapper, and what to him were girls' games and pleasant things to eat? He pictured himself the hardy outlaw, feeding on oatmeal and goat's-flesh, the terror and pride of his neighbourhood. Could the little mistress of Fountainblue but see him now, how she would despise his prosaic cousins! And then, as he descended on the highway, he fell in with his forsaken party.

For a wonder they were in good spirits – so good that they forgot to remind him, in their usual way, of the domestic terrors awaiting him. A man had been there who had told them stories and shown them tricks, and there had been coconut cake, and Sylvia had a new pony on which they had ridden races. The children were breathless with excitement, very much in love with each other as common sharers in past joys. And as they talked all the colour went out of his afternoon. The blue hawk's egg was cracked, and it looked a stupid, dingy object as it lay in his cap. His rare ferns were crumpled and withered, and who was to believe his stories of Stob Ghabhar and the Grey Correi? He had been a fool to barter ponies and tea and a man who knew tricks for the barren glories of following his own fancy. But at any rate he would show no sign. If he was to be an outlaw, he would carry his outlawry well; so with a catch in his voice and tears in his eyes he jeered at his inattentive companions, upbraiding himself all the while for his folly.

II

The sun was dipping behind Stob Ghabhar when Maitland drove over the ridge of hill, whence the moor-road dips to Fountainblue. Twenty long miles from the last outpost of railway to the western sea-loch, and twenty of the barest, steepest miles in the bleak north. And all the way he had been puzzling himself with the half-painful, half-pleasing memories of a childhood which to the lonely man still overtopped the present. Every wayside bush was the home of recollection. In every burn he had paddled and fished; here he had found the jack-snipe's nest, there he had hidden when the shepherds sought him for burning the heather in May. He lost for a little the burden of his years and cares, and lived again in that old fresh world which had no boundaries, where sleep and food were all his thought at night, and adventure the sole outlook of the morning. The western sea lay like a thin line of gold beyond the moorland, and down in the valley in a bower of trees lights began to twinkle from the little castle. The remote mountains, hiding deep corries and woods in their bosom, were blurred by twilight to a single wall of hazy purple, which shut off this fairy glen impenetrably from the world. Fountainblue – the name rang witchingly in his ears. Fountainblue, the last home of the Good Folk, the last hold of the vanished kings, where the last wolf in Scotland was slain, and, as stories go, the last saint of the Great Ages taught the people – what had Fountainblue to do with his hard world of facts and figures? The thought woke him to a sense of the present, and for a little he relished the paradox. He had left it long ago, an adventurous child; now he was returning with success behind him and a portion of life's good things his own. He was rich, very rich, and famous. Few men of forty had his power, and he had won it all in fair struggle with enemies and rivals and a niggardly world. He had been feared and hated, as he had been extravagantly admired; he had been rudely buffeted by fortune, and had met the blows with a fighter's joy. And out of it all something hard and austere had shaped itself, something very much a man, but a man with little heart and a lack of kindly human failings. He was master of himself in a curious degree, but the mastery absorbed his interests. Nor had he ever regretted it, when suddenly in this outlandish place the past swept over him, and he had a vision of a long avenue of vanished hopes. It pleased and disquieted him, and as the road dipped into the valley he remembered the prime cause of this mood of vagaries.

He had come up into the north with one purpose in view, he frankly told himself. The Etheridges were in Fountainblue, and ever since, eight months before, he had met Clara Etheridge, he had forgotten his ambitions. A casual neighbour at a dinner-party, a chance partner at a ball – and then he had to confess that this slim, dark, bright-eyed girl had broken in irrevocably upon his contentment. At first he hated it for a weakness, then he welcomed the weakness with feverish ecstasy. He did nothing by halves, so he sought her company eagerly, and, being a great man in his way, found things made easy for him. But the girl remained shy and distant, flattered doubtless by his attention, but watching him curiously as an intruder from an alien world. It was characteristic of the man that he never thought of a rival. His whole aim was to win her love; for rivalry with other men he had the contempt of a habitual conqueror. And so the uneasy wooing went on till the Etheridges left town, and he found himself a fortnight later with his work done and a visit before him to which he looked forward with all the vehemence of a nature whose strong point had always been its hope. As the road wound among the fir-trees, he tried to forecast the life at Fountainblue, and map out the future in his usual business-like way. But now the future refused to be thus shorn and parcelled: there was an unknown quantity in it which defied his efforts.

The house-party were sitting round the hall-fire when he entered. The high-roofed place, the flagged floor strewn with rugs, and the walls bright with the glow of fire on armour, gave him a boyish sense of comfort. Two men in knickerbockers were lounging on a settle, and at his entrance came forward to greet him. One was Sir Hugh Clanroyden, a follower of his own; the other he recognised as a lawyer named Durward. From the circle of women Miss Etheridge rose and welcomed him. Her mother was out, but would be back for dinner; meantime he should be shown his room. He noticed that her face was browner, her hair a little less neat, and there seemed something franker and kindlier in her smile. So in a very good humour he went to rid himself of the dust of the roads.

Durward watched him curiously, and then turned, laughing, to his companion, as the girl came back to her friends with a heightened colour in her cheeks.

'Romeo the second,' he said. 'We are going to be spectators of a comedy. And yet, heaven knows! Maitland is not cast for comedy.'

The other shook his head. 'It will never come off. I've known Clara Etheridge most of my life, and I would as soon think of marrying a dancing-girl to a bishop. She is a delightful person, and my very good friend, but how on earth is she ever to understand Maitland? And how on earth can he see anything in her? Besides, there's another man.'

Durward laughed. 'Despencer! I suppose he will be a serious rival with a woman; but imagine him Maitland's rival in anything else! He'd break him like a rotten stick in half an hour. I like little Despencer, and I don't care about Maitland; but all the same it is absurd to compare the two, except in love-making.'

'Lord, it will be comic,' and Clanroyden stretched his long legs and lay back on a cushion. The girls were still chattering beside the fire, and the twilight was fast darkening into evening.

'You dislike Maitland?' he asked, looking up. 'Now, I wonder why?'

Durward smiled comically at the ceiling. 'Oh, I know I oughtn't to. I know he's supposed to be a man's man, and that it's bad form for a man to say he dislikes him. But I'm honest enough to own to detesting him. I suppose he's great, but he's not great enough yet to compel one to fall down and worship him, and I hate greatness in the making. He goes through the world with his infernal arrogance and expects everybody to clear out of his way. I am told we live in an age of reason, but that fellow has burked reason. He never gives a reason for a thing he does, and if you try to argue he crushes you. He has killed good talk for ever with his confounded rudeness. All the little sophistries and conventions which make life tolerable are so much rubbish to him, and he shows it. The plague of him is that he can never make-believe. He is as hard as iron, and as fierce as the devil, and about as unpleasant. You may respect the sledge-hammer type, but it's confoundedly dull. Why, the man has not the imagination of a rabbit, except in his description of people he dislikes. I liked him when he said that Layden reminded him of a dissipated dove, because I disliked Layden; but when Freddy Alton played the fool and people forgave him, because he was a good sort, Maitland sent him about his business, saying he had no further use for weaklings. He is so abominably cold-blooded and implacable that everyone must fear him, and yet most people can afford to despise him. All the kind simple things of life are shut out of his knowledge. He has no nature, only a heart of stone and an iron will and a terribly subtle brain. Of course he is a great man – in a way, but at the best he is only half a man. And to think that he should have fallen in love, and be in danger of losing to Despencer! It's enough to make one forgive him.'

Clanroyden laughed. 'I can't think of Despencer. It's too absurd. But, seriously, I wish I saw Maitland well rid of this mood, married or cured. That sort of man doesn't take things easily.'

'It reminds one of Theocritus and the Cyclops in love. Who would have thought to see him up in this moorland place, running after a girl? He doesn't care for sport.'

'Do you know that he spent most of his childhood in this glen, and that he *is* keen about sport? He is too busy for many holidays, but he once went with Burton to the Caucasus, and Burton said the experience nearly killed him. He said that the fellow was tireless, and as mad and reckless as a boy with nothing to lose.'

'Well, that simply bears out what I say of him. He does not understand the meaning of sport. When he gets keen about anything he pursues it as carefully and relentlessly

89

as if it were something on the Stock Exchange. Now little Despencer is a genuine sportsman in his canary-like way. He loves the art of the thing and the being out of doors. Maitland, I don't suppose, ever thinks whether it is a ceiling or the sky above his august head. Despencer—'

But at the moment Clanroyden uncrossed his legs, bringing his right foot down heavily upon his companion's left. Durward looked up and saw a young man coming towards him, smiling.

The newcomer turned aside to say something to the girls round the fire, and then came and sat on an arm of the settle. He was a straight, elegant person, with a well-tanned, regular face, and very pleasant brown eyes.

'I've had such an afternoon,' he said. 'You never saw a place like Cairnlora. It's quite a little stone tower all alone in a fir-wood, and nothing else between the moor and the sea. It is furnished as barely as a prison, except for the chairs, which are priceless old Dutch things. Oh, and the silver at tea was the sort of thing that only Americans can buy nowadays. Mrs Etheridge is devoured with envy. But the wonder of the house is old Miss Elphinstone. She must be nearly seventy, and she looks forty-five, except for her hair. She speaks broad Scots, and she has the manners of a *marquise*. I would give a lot to have had Raeburn paint her. She reminded me of nothing so much as a hill-wind with her keen high-coloured old face. Yes, I have enjoyed the afternoon.'

'Jack has got a new enthusiasm,' said Durward. 'I wish I were like you to have a new one once a week. By the way, Maitland has arrived at last.'

'Really!' said Despencer. 'Oh, I forgot to tell you something which you would never have guessed. Miss Elphinstone is Maitland's aunt, and he was brought up a good deal at Cairnlora. He doesn't take his manners from her, but I suppose he gets his cleverness from that side of the family. She disapproves of him strongly, so of course I had to defend him. And what do you think she said? "He has betrayed his tradition. He has sold his birthright for a mess of pottage and I wish him joy of his bargain!" Nice one for your party, Hugh.'

Miss Etheridge had left the group at the fire and was standing at Despencer's side. She listened to him with a curious air of solicitude, like an affectionate sister. At the mention of Maitland's name Clanroyden had watched her narrowly, but her face did not change. And when Despencer asked, 'Where is the new arrival?' she talked of him with the utmost nonchalance.

Maitland came down to dinner, ravenously hungry and in high spirits. Nothing was changed in this house since he had stared at the pictures and imagined terrible things about the armour and broken teacups with childish impartiality. His own favourite seat was still there, where, hidden by a tapestry screen, he had quarrelled with Sylvia while their elders gossiped. This sudden flood of memories mellowed him towards the world. He was cordial to Despencer, forbore to think Durward a fool, and answered every one of Mr Etheridge's many questions. For the first time he felt the success of his life. The old house recalled his childhood, and the sight of Clanroyden, his devoted follower, reminded him of his power. Somehow the wearyful crying for the moon, which had always tortured him, was exchanged for a glow of comfort, a shade of complacency in his haggard soul . . . And then the sight of Clara dispelled his satisfaction.

Here in this cheerful homely party of friends he found himself out of place. On state occasions he could acquit himself with credit, for the man had a mind. He could make the world listen to him when he chose, and the choice was habitual. But now his loneliness claimed its lawful consequences, and he longed for the little friendly graces which he had so often despised. Despencer talked of scenery and weather with a tenderness to which this man, who loved nature as he loved little else, was an utter stranger. This elegant and appropriate sentiment would have worried him past endurance, if Miss Clara had not shared it. It was she who told some folk-tale about the Grey Correi with the prettiest hesitancy which showed her feeling. And then the talk drifted to books and people, flitting airily about their petty world. Maitland felt himself choked by their accomplishments. Most of the subjects were ones no sane man would trouble to think of, and yet here were men talking keenly about trifles and disputing with nimble-witted cleverness on the niceties of the trivial. Feeling miserably that he was the only silent one, he plunged desperately into the stream, found himself pulled up by Despencer and deftly turned. The event gave him the feeling of having been foiled by a kitten.

Angry with the world, angrier with his own angularity, he waited for the end of the meal. Times had not changed in this house since he had been saved by Sylvia from social disgrace. But when the women left the room he found life easier. His host talked of sport, and he could tell him more about Stob Ghabhar than any keeper. Despencer, victorious at dinner, now listened like a docile pupil. Durward asked a political question, and the answer came sharp and

definite. Despencer demurred gently, after his fashion.
'Well, but surely—' and a grimly smiling 'What do you
know about it?' closed the discussion. The old Maitland
had returned for the moment.

The night was mild and impenetrably dark, and the fall
of waters close at hand sounded like a remote echo. An
open hall-door showed that some of the party had gone
out to the garden, and the men followed at random. A
glimmer of white frocks betrayed the women on the lawn,
standing by the little river which slipped by cascade and
glide from the glen to the low pasture-lands. In the featureless dark there was no clue to locality. The place might
have been Berkshire or a suburban garden.

Suddenly the scream of some animal came from the near
thicket. The women started and asked what it was.

'It was a hill-fox,' said Maitland to Clara. 'They used to
keep me awake at nights on the hill. They come and bark
close to your ear and give you nightmare.'

The lady shivered. 'Thank Heaven for the indoors,' she
said. 'Now, if I had been the daughter of one of your old
Donalds of the Isles, I should have known that cry only
too well. Wild nature is an excellent background, but give
me civilisation in front.'

Maitland was looking into the wood. 'You will find it
creeps far into civilisation if you look for it. There is a very
narrow line between the warm room and the savage out-
of-doors.'

'There are miles of luxuries,' the girl cried, laughing.
'People who are born in the wrong country have to hunt
over half the world before they find their savagery. It is all
very tame, but I love the tameness. You may call yourself
primitive, Mr Maitland, but you are the most complex and

93

modern of us all. What would Donald of the Isles have said to politics and the Stock Exchange?'

They had strolled back to the house. 'Nevertheless I maintain my belief,' said the man. 'You call it miles of rampart; I call the division a line, a thread, a sheet of glass. But then, you see, you only know one side, and I only know the other.'

'What preposterous affectation!' the girl said, as with a pretty shiver she ran indoors. Maitland stood for a moment looking back at the darkness. Within the firelit hall, with its rugs and little tables and soft chairs, he had caught a glimpse of Despencer smoking a cigarette. As he looked towards the hills he heard the fox's bark a second time, and then somewhere from the black distance came a hawk's scream, hoarse, lonely and pitiless. The thought struck him that the sad elemental world of wood and mountain was far more truly his own than this cosy and elegant civilisation. And, oddly enough, the thought pained him.

III

The day following was wet and windy, when a fire was grateful, and the hills, shrouded in grey mist, had no attractions. The party read idly in armchairs during the morning, and in the afternoon Maitland and Clanroyden went down to the stream-mouth after sea-trout. So Despencer remained to talk to Clara, and, having played many games of picquet and grown heartily tired of each other, as tea-time approached they fell to desultory comments on their friends. Maitland was beginning to interest the girl in a new way. Formerly he had been a great person who was sensible enough to admire her, but something remote and unattractive, for whom friendship (much less love) was impossible. But now she had begun to feel his power, his manhood. The way in which other men spoke of him impressed her unconsciously, and she began to ask Despencer questions which were gall and wormwood to that young man. But he answered honestly, after his fashion.

'Isn't he very rich?' she asked. 'And I suppose he lives very plainly?'

'Rich as Croesus, and he sticks in his ugly rooms in the Albany because he never thinks enough about the thing to change. I've been in them once, and you never saw such a place. He's a maniac for fresh air, so they're large enough, but they're littered like a stable with odds and ends of belongings. He must have several thousand books, and yet he hasn't a decent binding among them. He hasn't a photograph of a single soul, and only one picture, which, I believe, was his father. But you never saw such a collection of whips and spurs and bits. It smells like a harness-room, and there you find Maitland, when by any chance he is at home, working half the night and up to the eyes in papers. I don't think the man has any expenses except food and rent, for he wears the same clothes for years. And he has given up horses.'

'Was he fond of horses?' Miss Clara asked.

'Oh, you had better ask him. I really can't tell you any more about him.'

'But how do his friends get on with him?'

'He has hardly any, but his acquaintances, who are all the world, say he is the one great man of the future. If you want to read what people think of him, you had better look at the "Monthly".'

Under cover of this one ungenerous word Despencer made his escape, for he hated the business, but made it the rule of his life 'never to crab a fellow'. Miss Clara promptly sought out the 'Monthly', and found twenty pages of super-fine analysis and bitter, grudging praise. She read it with interest, and then lay back in her chair and tried to fix her thoughts. It is only your unhealthy young woman who worships strength in the abstract, and the girl tried to determine whether she admired the man as a power or disliked him as a brute. She chose a compromise, and the feeling which survived was chiefly curiosity.

The result of the afternoon was that when the fishermen returned, and Maitland, in dry clothes, appeared for tea, she settled herself beside him and prepared to talk. Maitland, being healthily tired, was in an excellent temper, and he found himself enticed into what for him was a rare performance – talk about himself. They were sitting apart from the others, and, ere ever he knew, he was answering the girl's questions with an absent-minded frankness. In a little she had drawn from him the curious history of his life, which most men knew, but never from his own lips.

'I was at school for a year,' he said, 'and then my father died and our affairs went to pieces. I had to come back and go into an office, a sort of bank. I hated it, but it was good for me, for it taught me something, and my discontent made me ambitious. I had about eighty pounds a year, and I saved from that. I worked too at books incessantly, and by-and-by I got an Oxford scholarship, at an obscure college. I went up there, and found myself in a place where everyone seemed well off, while I was a pauper. However, it didn't trouble me much, for I had no ambition to play the fool. I only cared about two things – horses and meta-physics. I hated all games, which I thought only fit for children. I daresay it was foolish, but then you see I had had a queer upbringing. I managed to save a little money, and one vacation when I was wandering about in Norfolk, sleeping under haystacks and working in harvest-fields when my supplies ran down, I came across a farmer. He was a good fellow and a sort of sportsman, and I took a fancy to him. He had a colt to sell which I fancied more, for I saw it had blood in it. So I bought it for what seemed a huge sum to me in those days, but I kept it at his farm and I superintended its education. I broke it myself and taught it to jump, and by-and-by in my third year I brought it to Oxford and entered for the Grind on it. People laughed at me, but I knew my own business. The little boys who rode in the thing knew nothing about horses, and not one in ten could ride; so I entered and won. It was all I wanted, for I could sell my horse then, and the fellow who rode second bought it. It was decent of him, for I asked a big figure, and I think he had an idea of doing me a kindness. I made him my private secretary the other day.'

'You mean Lord Drapier?' she asked.

'Yes – Drapier. That gave me money to finish off and begin in town. Oh, and I had got a first in my schools. I knew very little about anything except metaphysics, and I never went to tutors. I suppose I knew a good deal more than the examiners in my own subject, and anyhow they felt obliged to give me my first after some grumbling. Then I came up to town with just sixty pounds in my pocket, but I had had the education of a gentleman.'

Maitland looked out of the window, and the sight of the mist-clad hills recalled him to himself. He wondered

97

why he was telling the girl this story, and he stopped suddenly.

'And what did you do in town?' she asked, with interest.

'I hung round and kept my eyes open. I nearly starved, for I put half my capital on a horse which I thought was safe, and lost it. By-and-by, quite by accident, I came across a curious fellow, Ransome – you probably have heard his name. I met him in some stables where he was buying a mare, and he took a liking to me. He made me his secretary, and then, because I liked hard work, he let me see his business. It was enormous, for the man was a genius after a fashion; and I slaved away in his office and down at the docks for about three years. He paid me just enough to keep body and soul together and cover them with clothes; but I didn't grumble, for I had a sort of idea that I was on my probation. And then my apprenticeship came to an end.'

'Yes,' said the girl.

'Yes; for you see Ransome was an odd character. He had a sort of genius for finance, and within his limits he was even a great administrator. But in everything else he was as simple as a child. His soul was idyllic: he loved green fields and Herrick and sheep. So it had always been his fancy to back out some day and retire with his huge fortune to some country place and live as he pleased. It seemed that he had been training me from the first day I went into the business, and now he cut the rope and left the whole enormous concern in my hands. I needed every atom of my wits, and the first years were a hard struggle. I became of course very rich; but I had to do more, I had to keep the thing at its old level. I had no natural turn for the work, and I had to acquire capacity by sheer grind. However, I managed it, and then, when I felt my position sure, I indulged myself with a hobby and went into politics.'

'You call it a hobby?'

'Certainly. The ordinary political career is simply a form of trifling. There's no trade on earth where a man has to fear so few able competitors. Of course it's very public and honourable and that sort of thing, and I like it; but sometimes it wearies me to death.'

The girl was looking at him with curious interest. 'Do you always get what you want?' she asked.

'Never,' he said.

'Then is your success all disappointment?'

'Oh, I generally get a bit of my ambitions, which is all one can hope for in this world.'

'I suppose your ambitions are not idyllic, like Mr Ransome's?'

He laughed. 'No, I suppose not. I never could stand your Corot meadows and ivied cottages and village church bells. But I am at home in this glen, or used to be.'

'You said that last night, and I thought it was affectation,' said the girl; 'but perhaps you are right. I'm not at home in this scenery, at any rate in this weather. Ugh, look at that mist driving and that spur of Stob Ghabhar! I really must go and sit by the fire.'

IV

The next day dawned clear and chill, with a little frost to whiten the heather; but by midday the sun had turned August to June, and sea and land drowsed in a mellow heat. Maitland was roused from his meditations with a

pipe on a garden-seat by the appearance of Miss Clara, her
eyes bright with news. He had taken her in to dinner the
night before, and for the first time in his life had found
himself talking easily to a woman. Her interest of the
afternoon had not departed; and Despencer in futile disgust shunned the drawing-room, his particular paradise,
and played billiards with Clanroyden in the spirit of an
unwilling martyr.

'We are going out in the yacht', Miss Clara cried, as she
emerged from the shadow of a fuchsia-hedge, 'to the Isles
of the Waves, away beyond the Seal's Headland. Do you
know the place, Mr Maitland?'

'Eilean na Cille? Yes. It used to be dangerous for currents, but a steam-yacht does not require to fear them.'

'Well, we'll be ready to start at twelve, and I must go in
to give orders about lunch.'

A little later she came out with a bundle of letters in
her hands. 'Here are your letters, Mr Maitland; but you
mustn't try to answer them, or you'll be late.' He put the
lot in his jacket pocket and looked up at the laughing girl.
'My work is six hundred miles behind me,' he said, 'and
today I have only the Eilean na Cille to think of.' And, as
she passed by, another name took the place of the Eilean,
and it seemed to him that at last he had found the link
which was to bind together the two natures – his boyhood
and his prime.

Out on the loch the sun was beating with that steady
August blaze which is more torrid than midsummer. But as
the yacht slipped between the horns of the land, it came
into a broken green sea with rollers to the north where the
tireless Atlantic fretted on the reefs. In a world of cool salt
winds and the golden weather of afternoon, with the cries

of tern and gull about the bows and the foam and ripple of green water in the wake, the party fell into a mood of supreme contentment. The restless Miss Clara was stricken into a figure of contemplation, which sat in the bows and watched the hazy blue horizon and the craggy mainland hills in silent delight. Maitland was revelling in the loss of his isolation. He had ceased to be alone, a leader, and for the moment felt himself one of the herd, a devotee of humble pleasures. His mind was blank, his eyes filled only with the sea, and the lady of his devotion, in that happy moment of romance, seemed to have come at last within the compass of his hopes.

The Islands of the Waves are low green ridges which rise little above the highest tide-mark. The grass is stiff with salt, the sparse heather and rushes are crooked with the winds, but there are innumerable little dells where a light wild scrub flourishes, and in one a spring of sweet water sends a tiny stream to the sea. The yacht's company came ashore in boats, and tea was made with a great bustle beside the well, while the men lay idly in the bent and smoked. All wind seemed to have died down, a soft, cool, airless peace like a June evening was abroad, and the heavy surging of the tides had sunk to a distant whisper. Maitland lifted his head, sniffed the air, and looked uneasily to the west, meeting the eye of one of the sailors engaged in the same scrutiny. He beckoned the man to him.

'What do you make of the weather?' he asked.

The sailor, an East-coast man from Arbroath, shook his head. 'It's owner lown a' of a sudden,' he said. 'It looks like mair wind nor we want, but I think it'll haud till the morn.'

Maitland nodded and lay down again. He smiled at the return of his old sea craft and weather-lore, on which he had prided himself in his boyhood; and when Miss Clara came up to him with tea she found him grinning vacantly at the sky.

'What a wonderful lull in the wind,' she said. 'When I was here last these were real isles of the waves, with spray flying over them and a great business to land. But now they might be the island in Fountainblue lake.'

'Did you ever hear of the Ocean Quiet?' he asked. 'I believe it to be a translation of a Gaelic word which is a synonym for death, but it is also a kind of natural phenomenon. Old people at Cairnlora used to talk of it. They said that sometimes fishermen far out at sea in blowing weather came into a place of extraordinary peace, where the whole world was utterly still and they could hear their own hearts beating.'

'What a pretty fancy!' said the girl.

'Yes; but it had its other side. The fishermen rarely came home alive, and if they did they were queer to the end of their days. Another name for the thing was the Breathing of God. It is an odd idea, the passing from the wholesome turmoil of nature to the uncanny place where God crushes you by His silence.'

'All the things to eat are down by the fire,' she said, laughing. 'Do you know, if you weren't what you are, people might think you a poet, Mr Maitland. I thought you cared for none of these things.'

'What things?' he asked. 'I don't care for poetry. I am merely repeating the nonsense I was brought up on. Shall I talk to you about politics?'

'Heaven forbid! And now I will tell you my own story about these isles. There is a hermit's cell on one of them and crosses, like Iona. The hermit lived alone all winter, and was fed by boats from the shore when the weather was calm. When one hermit died another took his place, and no one knew where he came from. Now one day a great lord in Scotland disappeared from his castle. He was the King's Warden of the Marches and the greatest soldier of his day, but he disappeared utterly out of men's sight, and people forgot about him. Long years after the Northmen in a great fleet came down upon these isles, and the little chiefs fled before them. But suddenly among them there appeared an old man, the hermit of the Wave Islands, who organised resistance and gathered a strong army. No one dared oppose him, and the quarrelsome petty chiefs forgot their quarrels under his banner, for he had the air of one born to command. At last he met the invaders in the valley of Fountainblue, and beat them so utterly that few escaped to their ships. He fell himself in the first charge, but not before his followers had heard his battle-cry of "Saint Bride", and known the Hermit of the Isles and the great King's Warden were the same.'

'That was a common enough thing in wild times. Men grew tired of murder and glory and waving banners, and wanted quiet to make their peace with their own souls. I should have thought the craving scarcely extinct yet.'

'Then here is your chance, Mr Maitland,' said the girl, laughing. 'A little trouble would make the hut habitable, and you could simply disappear, leaving no address to forward your letters to. Think of the sensation, "Disappearance of a Secretary of State", and the wild theories and the obituaries. Then some day when the land question became urgent on the mainland, you would turn up suddenly, settle it with extraordinary wisdom, and die after confiding your life-story to some country reporter. But I am afraid it would scarcely do, for you would be discovered by Scotland Yard, which would be ignominious.'

'It is a sound idea, but the old device is too crude. However, it could be managed differently. Some day, when civilisation grows oppressive, Miss Clara, I will remember your advice.'

The afternoon shadows were beginning to lengthen, and from the west a light sharp wind was crisping the sea. The yacht was getting up steam, and boats were coming ashore for the party. The deep blue waters were flushing rose-pink as the level westering sun smote them from the summit of a cloudbank. The stillness had gone, and the air was now full of sounds and colour. Miss Clara, with an eye on the trim yacht, declared her disapproval. 'It is an evening for the cutter,' she cried, and in spite of Mrs Etheridge's protests she gave orders for it to be made ready. Then the self-willed young woman looked round for company. 'Will you come, Mr Maitland?' she said. 'You can sail a boat, can't you? And Mr Despencer, I shall want you to talk to me when Mr Maitland is busy. We shall race the yacht, for we ought to be able to get through the Scart's Neck with this wind.'

'I am not sure if you are wise, Miss Clara,' and Maitland pulled down his brows as he looked to the west. 'It will be wind – in a very little, and you stand the chance of a wetting.'

'I don't mind. I want to get the full good of such an evening. You want to be near the water to understand one of our sunsets. I can be a barbarian too, you know.'

It was not for Maitland to grumble at this friendliness; so he followed her into the cutter with Despencer, who had no love for the orders but much for her who gave them.

He took the helm and steered, with directions from the lady, from his memory of the intricate coast. Despencer with many rugs looked to Miss Clara's comfort, and, having assured his own, was instantly entranced with the glories of the evening.

The boat tripped along for a little in a dazzle of light into the silvery grey of the open water. Far in front lay the narrow gut called the Scart's Neck, which was the by-way to the loch of Fountainblue. Then Maitland at the helm felt the sheets suddenly begin to strain, and, looking behind, saw that the Isles of the Waves were almost lost in the gloom, and that the roseate heavens were quickly darkening behind. The wind which he had feared was upon them; a few seconds more and it was sending the cutter staggering among billows. He could hardly make himself heard in the din, as he roared directions to Despencer about disposing of his person in another part of the boat. The girl with flushed face was laughing in pure joy of the storm. She caught a glimpse of Maitland's serious eye and looked over the gunwale at the threatening west. Then she too became quiet, and meekly sat down on the thwart to which he motioned her.

The gale made the Scart's Neck impossible, and the murky sky seemed to promise greater fury ere the morning. Twilight was falling, and the other entrance to the quiet loch meant the rounding of a headland and a difficult course through a little archipelago. It was the only way, for return was out of the question, and it seemed vain to risk the narrow chances of the short-cut. Maitland looked down at his two companions, and reflected with pleasure that he was the controller of their fates. He had sailed much as a boy, and he found in this moment of necessity that his old lore returned to him. He felt no mistrust of his powers: whatever the gale he could land them at Fountainblue, though it might take hours and involve much discomfort. He remembered the coast like his own name; he relished the grim rage of the elements, and he kept the cutter's head out to sea with a delight in the primeval conflict.

The last flickering rays of light, coming from the screen of cloud, illumined the girl's pale face, and the sight disquieted him. There was a hint of tragedy in this game. Despencer, nervously self-controlled, was reassuring Clara. Ploughing onward in the blackening night in a frail boat on a wind-threshed sea was no work for a girl. But it was Despencer who was comforting her! Well, it was his proper work. He was made for the business of talking soft things to women. Maitland, his face hard with spray, looked into the darkness with a kind of humour in his heart. And then, as the boat shore and dipped into the storm, its human occupants seemed to pass out of the picture, and it was only a shell tossed on great waters in the unfathomable night. The evening had come, moonless and starless, and Maitland steered as best he could by the deeper blackness which was the configuration of the shore. Something loomed up that he knew for the headland, and they were drifting in a quieter stretch of sea, with the breakers grumbling ahead from the little tangle of islands.

Suddenly he fell into one of the abstractions which had always dogged him through his strenuous life. His mind was clear, he chose his course with a certain precision, but the winds and waves had become to him echoes of echoes. Wet with spray and shifting his body constantly with the movement of the boat, it yet was all a phantasmal existence, while his thoughts were following an airy morrice in a fairyland world. The motto of his house, the canting motto of old reivers, danced in his brain – *Parmi ceu haut bois conduyrai m'amie* – 'Through the high wood I will conduct my love' – and in a land of green forests, dragon-haunted, he was piloting Clara robed in a quaint medieval gown, himself in speckless plate-armour. His fancy fled through a score of scenes, sometimes on a dark heath, or by a lonely river, or among great mountains, but always the lady and her protector. Clara, looking up from Despencer's side, saw his lips moving, noted that his eyes were glad, and for a moment hoped better things of their chances.

Then suddenly she was dumb with alarm, for the cutter heeled over, and but that Maitland woke to clear consciousness and swung the sheet loose, all would have been past. The adventure nerved him and quickened his senses. The boat seemed to move more violently than the wind drove her, and in the utter blackness he felt for the first time the grip of the waters. The ugly cruel monster had wakened, and was about to wreak its anger on the toy. And then he remembered the currents which raced round Eilean Righ and the scattered isles. Dim shapes loomed up, shapes strange and unfriendly, and he felt miserably that he was as helpless now as Despencer. To the left night had wholly shut out the coast; his one chance was to run for one of the isles and risk a landing. It would be a dreary waiting for the dawn, but safety had come before any comfort. And yet, he remembered, the little islands were rock-bound and unfriendly, and he was hurrying forward in the grip of a black current with a gale behind and unknown reefs before.

And then he seemed to remember something of this current which swept along the isles. In a little – so he recalled a boyish voyage in clear weather – they would come to a place where the sea ran swift and dark beside a kind of natural wharf. Here he had landed once upon a time, but it was a difficult enterprise, needing a quick and a far leap at the proper moment, for the stream ran very fast. But if this leap were missed there was still a chance. The isle was the great Eilean Righ, and the current swung round its southern end, and then, joining with another stream, turned up its far side, and for a moment washed the shore. But if this second chance were missed, then nothing remained but to fall into the great sea-going stream and be carried out to death in the wide Atlantic. He strained his eyes to the right for Eilean Righ. Something seemed to approach, as they bent under an access of the gale. They bore down upon it, and he struggled to keep the boat's head away, for at this pace to grate upon rock would mean upsetting. The sail was down, fluttering amidships like a captive bird, and the gaunt mast bowed with the wind. A horrible fascination, the inertia of nightmare, seized him. The motion was so swift and beautiful; why not go on and onward, listlessly? And then, conquering the weakness, he leaned forward and called to Clara. She caught his arm like a child, and he pulled her up beside him. Then he beckoned Despencer, and, shrieking against the din, told him to follow him when he jumped. Despencer nodded, his teeth chattering with cold and the novel business. Suddenly out of the darkness, a yard on their right, loomed a great flat rock along which the current raced like a mill-lade. The boat made to strike, but Maitland forced her nose out to sea, and then as the stern swung round he seized his chance. Holding Clara with his left arm he stood up, balanced himself for a moment on the gunwale, and jumped. He landed sprawling on his side on some wet seaweed, over which the sea was lipping, but undeniably on land. As he pulled himself up he had a vision of the cutter, dancing like a cork, vanishing down the current into the darkness.

Holding the girl in his arms he picked his way across the rock pools to the edge of the island heather. For a moment he thought Clara had fainted. She lay still and inert, her eyes shut, her hair falling foolishly over her brow. He sprinkled some water on her face, and she revived sufficiently to ask her whereabouts. He was crossing the island to find Despencer, but he did not tell her. 'You are safe,' he said, and he carried her over the rough ground as lightly as a child. An intense exhilaration had seized him. He ran over the flats and strode up the low hillocks with one thought possessing his brain. To save Despencer, that of course was the far-off aim on his mind's horizon, but all the foreground was filled with the lady. *Parmi ceu haut bois* – the old poetry of the world had penetrated to his heart. The black night and the wild wind and the sea were the ministrants of love. The hollow shams of life with their mincing conventions had departed, and in this savage out-world a man stood for a man. The girl's light tweed jacket was no match for this chill gale, so he stopped for a moment, took off his own shooting-coat and put it round her. And then, as he came over a little ridge, he was aware of a grumbling of waters and the sea.

The beach was hidden in a veil of surf which sprinkled the very edge of the bracken. Beyond, the dark waters were boiling like a caldron, for the tides in this little bay ran with the fury of a river in spate. A moon was beginning to struggle through the windy clouds, and surf, rock and wave began to shape themselves out of the night. Clara stood on the sand, a slim, desolate figure, and clung to Maitland's arm. She was still dazed with the storm and the baffling suddenness of change. Maitland, straining his eyes out to sea, was in a waking dream. With the lady no toil was too great, no darkness terrible; for her he would scale the blue air and plough the hills and do all the lover's feats of romance. And then suddenly he shook her hand roughly from his arm and ran forward, for he saw something coming down the tide.

Before he left the boat he had lowered the sail, and the cutter swung to the current, an odd amorphous thing, now heeling over with a sudden gust and now pulled back to balance by the strong grip of the water. A figure seemed to sit in the stern, making feeble efforts to steer. Maitland knew the coast and the ways of the sea. He ran through the surf-ring into the oily-black eddies, shouting to Despencer to come overboard. Soon he was not ten yards from the cutter's line, where the current made a turn towards the shore before it washed the iron rocks to the right. He found deep water, and in two strokes was in the grip of the tides and borne wildly towards the reef. He prepared himself for what was coming, raising his feet and turning his right shoulder to the front. And then with a shock he was pinned against the rock-wall, with the tides tugging at his legs, while his hands clung desperately to a shelf. Here he remained, yelling directions to the coming boat. Surf was in his eyes, so that at first he could not see, but at last in a dip of the waves he saw the cutter, a man's form in the stern, plunging not twenty yards away. Now was his chance or never, for while the tide would take a boat far from his present place of vantage, it would carry a lighter thing, such

as a man's body, in a circle nearer to the shore. He yelled again, and the world seemed to him quiet for a moment, while his voice echoed eerily in the void. Despencer must have heard it, for the next moment he saw him slip pluckily overboard, making the cutter heel desperately with his weight. And then – it seemed an age – a man, choking and struggling weakly, came down the current, and, pushing his right arm out against the rush of water, he had caught the swimmer by the collar and drawn him in to the side of the rock.

Then came the harder struggle. Maitland's left hand was numbing, and though he had a foothold, it was too slight to lean on with full weight. A second lassitude oppressed him, a supreme desire to slip into those racing tides and rest. He was in no panic about death, but he had the practical man's love of an accomplished task, and it nerved him to the extreme toil. Slowly by inches he drew himself up the edge of the reef, cherishing jealously each grip and foothold, with Despencer, half-choked and all but fainting, hanging heavily on his right arm. Blind with spray, sick with sea-water, and aching with his labours, he gripped at last the tangles of seaweed, which meant the flat surface, and with one final effort raised himself and Despencer to the top. There he lay for a few minutes with his head in a rock-pool till the first weariness had passed.

He staggered with his burden in his arms along the ragged reef to the strip of sand where Clara was weeping hysterically. The sight of her restored Maitland to vigour, the appeal of her lonely figure there in the wet brackens. She must think them all dead, he reflected, and herself desolate, for she could not have interpreted rightly his own wild rush into the waves. When she heard his voice she started, as if at a ghost, and then seeing his burden, ran towards him. 'Oh, he is dead!' she cried. 'Tell me! Tell me!' and she clasped the inert figure so that her arm crossed Maitland's. Despencer, stupefied and faint, was roused to consciousness by a woman's kisses on his cheek, and still more by his bearer abruptly laying him on the heather. Clara hung over him like a mother, calling him by soft names, pushing his hair from his brow, forgetful of her own wet and sorry plight. And meanwhile Maitland stood watching, while his palace of glass was being shivered about his ears.

Aforetime his arrogance had kept him from any thought of jealousy; now the time and place were too solemn for trifling, and facts were laid bare before him. Sentiment does not bloom readily in a hard nature, but if it once comes to flower it does not die without tears and agonies. The wearied man, who stood quietly beside the hysterical pair, had a moment of peculiar anguish. Then he conquered sentiment, as he had conquered all other feelings of whose vanity he was assured. He was now, as he was used to be, a man among children; and as a man he had his work. He bent over Clara. 'I know a hollow in the middle of the island', he said, 'where we can camp the night. I'll carry Despencer, for his ankle is twisted. Do you think you could try to walk?'

The girl followed obediently, her eyes only on her lover. Her trust in the other was infinite, her indifference to him impenetrable; while he, hopelessly conscious of his fate, saw in the slim dishevelled figure at his side the lost lady, the mistress for him of all romance and generous ambitions. The new springs in his life were choked; he had still his work, his power and, thank God, his courage; but the career which ran out to the horizon of his vision was black and loveless. And he held in his arms the thing which had frustrated him, the thing he had pulled out of the deep in peril of his body; and at the thought life for a moment seemed to be only a comic opera with tragedy to shift the scenes.

He found a cleft between two rocks with a soft floor of heather. There had been no rain, so the bracken was dry, and he gathered great armfuls and driftwood logs from the shore. Soon he had a respectable pile of timber, and then in the nick of the cleft he built a fire. His matches, being in his jacket pocket, had escaped the drenchings of salt water, and soon with a smoke and crackling and sweet scent of burning wood, a fire was going cheerily in the darkness. Then he made a couch of bracken, and laid there the still feeble Despencer. The man was more weak than ill; but for his ankle he was unhurt; and a little brandy would have brought him to himself. But this could not be provided, and Clara saw in his condition only the sign of mortal sickness. With haggard eyes she watched by him, easing his head, speaking soft kind words, forgetful of her own cold and soaking clothes. Maitland drew her gently to the fire, shook down the bracken to make a rest for her head, and left a pile of logs ready for use. 'I am going to the end of the island', he said, 'to light a fire for a signal. It is the only part which they can see on the mainland, and if they see the blaze they will come off for us as soon as it is light.' The pale girl listened obediently. This man was the master, and in his charge was the safety of her lover and herself.

Maitland turned his back upon the warm nook, and stumbled along the ridge to the northern extremity of the isle. It was not a quarter of a mile away, but the land was so

rough with gullies and crags that the journey took him
nearly an hour. Just off the extreme point was a flat rock,
sloping northward to a considerable height, a place from
which a beacon could penetrate far over the mainland. He
gathered brackens for kindling, and driftwood which former tides had heaped on the beach; and then with an
armful he splashed through the shallow surf to the rock.
Scrambling to the top, he found a corner where a fire
might be lit, a place conspicuous and yet sheltered. Here
he laid his kindling, and then in many wet journeys he
carried his stores of firewood from the mainland to the rock.
The lighting was nervous work, for he had few matches;
but at last the dampish wood had caught, and tongues of
flame shot up out of the smoke. Meantime the wind had
sunk lower, the breakers seemed to have been left behind,
and the eternal surge of the tides became the dominant
sound to the watcher by the beacon.

And then, it seemed to him, the great convulsions of
the night died away, and a curious peace came down upon
the waters. The fire leaped in the air, the one living thing
in a hushed and expectant world. It was not the quiet of
sleep but of a sudden cessation, like the lull after a great
flood or a snowslip. The tides still eddied and swayed, but
it was noiselessly; the world moved, yet without sound or
friction. The bitter wind which chilled his face and stirred
up the red embers was like a phantom blast, without the
roughness of a common gale. For a moment he seemed to
be set upon a high mountain with the world infinitely
remote beneath his feet. To all men there come moments
of loneliness of body, and to some few the mingled ecstasy
and grief of loneliness of soul. The child-tale of the Ocean
Quiet came back to him, the hour of the Breathing of God.

Surely the great silence was now upon the world. But it was an evil presage, for all who sailed into it were home-less wanderers for ever after. Ah well! He had always been a wanderer, and the last gleam of home had been left behind, where by the firelight in the cold cranny a girl was crooning over her lover.

His past, his monotonous, brilliant past, slipped by with the knotless speed of a vision. He saw a boy, haunted with dreams, chafing at present delights, clutching evermore at the faint things of fancy. He saw a man, playing with the counters which others played with, fighting at first for bare existence and then for power and the pride of life. Success came over his path like a false dawn, but he knew in his heart that he had never sought it. What was that remote ineffable thing he had followed? Here in the quiet of the shadowy waters he had the moment of self-revelation which comes to all, and hopes and dim desires seemed to stand out with the clearness of accomplished facts. There had always been something elect and secret at the back of his fiercest ambitions. The ordinary cares of men had been to him but little things to be played with; he had won by despising them; casting them from him, they had fallen into the hollow of his hand. And he had held them at little, finding his reward in his work, and in a certain alert-ness and freshness of spirit which he had always cherished. There is a story of island-born men who carry into inland places and the streets of cities the noise of sea-water in their ears, and hear continually the tern crying and the surf falling. So from his romantic boyhood this man had borne an arrogance towards the things of the world which had given him a contemptuous empire over a share of them. As he saw the panorama of his life no place or riches entered

into it, but only himself, the haggard, striving soul, growing in power, losing, perhaps, in wisdom. And then, at the
end of the way, Death, to shrivel the power to dust, and
with the might of his sunbeam to waken to life the forgotten world of the spirit.

In the hush he seemed to feel the wheel and the drift of
things, the cosmic order of nature. He forgot his weariness
and his plashing clothes as he put more wood on the beacon and dreamed into the night. The pitiless sea, infinite,
untamable, washing the Poles and hiding Earth's secrets in
her breast, spoke to him with a far-remembered voice. The
romance of the remote isles, the homes of his people,
floating still in a twilight of old story, rose out of the darkness. His life, with its routine and success, seemed in a
moment hollow, a child's game, unworthy of a man. The
little social round, the manipulation of half-truths, the
easy victories over fools – surely this was not the task for
him. He was a dreamer, but a dreamer with an iron hand;
he was scarcely in the prime of life; the world was wide
and his chances limitless. One castle of cards had already
been overthrown; the Ocean Quiet was undermining
another. He was sick of domesticity of every sort – of
town, of home, of civilisation. The sad elemental world
was his, the fury and the tenderness of nature, the peace of
the wilds which old folk had called the Breathing of God.
Parmi ceu haut bois conduyrai m'amie – this was still his
motto, to carry untarnished to the end an austere and
beautiful dream. His little ambitions had been but shreds
and echoes and shadows of this supreme reality. And his
love had been but another such simulacrum; for what he
had sought was no foolish, laughing girl, but the Immortal
Shepherdess, who, singing the old songs of youth, drives

her flocks to the hill in the first dewy dawn of the world.

Suddenly he started and turned his head. Day was breaking in a red windy sky, and somewhere a boat's oars were plashing in the sea. And then he realised for the first time that he was cold and starving and soaked to the bone.

V

Mr Henry Durward to Lady Claudia Etheridge

'. . . Things have happened, my dear Clo, since I last wrote; time has passed; tomorrow I leave this place and go to stalk with Drapier; and yet in the stress of departure I take time to answer the host of questions with which you assailed me. I am able to give you the best of news. You have won your bet. Your prophecy about the conduct of the "other Etheridge girl" has come out right. They are both here, as it happens, having come on from Fountainblue – both the hero and the heroine, I mean, of this most reasonable romance. You know Jack Despencer, one of the best people in the world, though a trifle given to chirping. But I don't think the grasshopper will become a burden to Miss Clara, for she likes that sort of thing. She must, for there is reason to believe that she refused for its sake the greatest match – I speak with all reverence – which this happy country could offer. I know you like Maitland as little as I do, but we agree in admiring the Colossus from a distance. Well, the Colossus has, so to speak, been laid low by a frivolous member of your sex. It is all a most romantic tale. Probably you have heard the gist of it, but here is the full and circumstantial account.

*

'We found Maitland beside the fire he had been feeding all night, and I shall never forget his figure alone in the dawn on that rock, drenched and dishevelled, but with his haggard white face set like a Crusader's. He took us to a kind of dell in the centre of the island, where we found Clara and Despencer shivering beside a dying fire. He had a twisted ankle and had got a bad scare, while she was perfectly composed, though she broke down when we got home. It must have been an awful business for both, but Maitland never seems to have turned a hair. I want to know two things. First, how in the presence of great danger he managed to get his dismissal from the lady – for get it he assuredly did, and Despencer at once appeared in the part of the successful lover; second, what part he played in the night's events. Clara remembered little, Despencer only knew that he had been pulled out of the sea, but over all Maitland seems to have brooded like a fate. As usual he told us nothing. It was always his way to give the world results and leave it to find out his methods for itself . . .

'Despencer overwhelmed him with gratitude. His new happiness made him in love with life, and he included Maitland in the general affection. The night's events seemed to have left their mark on the great man also. He was very quiet, forgot to be rude to anybody, and was kind to both Clara and Despencer. It is his way of acknowledging defeat, the great gentleman's way, for, say what we like about him, he is a tremendous gentleman, one of the last of the breed . . .

'And then he went away – two days later. Just before he went Hugh Clanroyden and myself were talking in the library, which has a window opening on a flower-garden.

Despencer was lying in an invalid's chair under a tree and Clara was reading to him. Maitland was saying good-bye, and he asked for Despencer. We told him that he was with Clara in the garden. He smiled one of those odd scarce smiles of his, and went out to them. When I saw his broad shoulders bending over the chair and the strong face looking down at the radiant Jack with his amiable good looks, confound it, Clo, I had to contrast the pair, and admit with Shakespeare the excellent foppery of the world. Well-a-day! "Smooth Jacob still robs homely Esau." And perhaps it is a good thing, for we are most of us Jacobs, and Esau is an uncomfortable fellow in our midst.

'A week later came the surprising, the astounding news that he had taken the African Governorship. A career ruined, everyone said, the finest chance in the world flung away; and then people speculated, and the story came out in bits, and there was only one explan-ation. It is the right one, as I think you will agree, but it points to some hidden weakness in that iron soul that he could be moved to fling over the ambitions of years because of a girl's choice. He will go and bury himself in the wilds, and our party will have to find another leader. Of course he will do his work well, but it is just as if I were to give up my chances of the Woolsack for a county-court judgeship. He will probably be killed, for he has a million enemies; he is perfectly fearless, and he does not under-stand the arts of compromise. It was a privilege, I shall always feel, to have known him. He was a great man, and yet – intellect, power, character, were at the mercy of a girl's caprice. As I write, I hear Clara's happy laugh below in the garden, probably at some witticism of the fortunate

Jack's. Upon which, with my usual pride in the obvious, I am driven to reflect that the weak things in life may confound the strong, and that, after all, the world is to the young . . .'

VI

Sir Hugh Clanroyden to Mr Henry Durward
some years later

'. . . I am writing this on board ship, as you will see from the heading, and shall post it when I get to the Cape. You have heard of my appointment, and I need not tell you how deep were my searchings of heart before I found courage to accept. Partly I felt that I had got my chance; partly I thought – an inconsequent feeling – that Maitland, if he had lived, would have been glad to see me in the place. But I am going to wear the Giant's Robe, and Heaven knows I have not the shoulders to fill it. Yet I am happy in thinking that I am in a small sense faithful to his memory.

'No further news, I suppose, has come of the manner of his death? Perhaps we shall never know, for it was on one of those Northern expeditions with a few men by which he held the frontier. I wonder if anyone will ever write fully the history of all that he did? It must have been a titanic work, but his methods were always so quiet that people accepted his results like a gift from Providence. He was given, one gathers, a practically free hand, and he made the country – four years' work of a man of genius. They wished to bring his body home, but he made them bury him where he fell – a characteristic last testament. And so he has gone out of the world into the world's history.

'I am still broken by his death, but, now that he is away, I begin to see him more clearly. Most people, I think, misunderstood him. I was one of his nearest friends, and I only knew bits of the man. For one thing – and I hate to use the vulgar word – he was the only aristocrat I ever heard of. Our classes are three-fourths of them of yesterday's growth, without the tradition, character, manner, or any trait of an aristocracy. And the few who are nominally of the blood have gone to seed in mind, or are spoilt by coarse marriages, or, worst of all, have the little trifling superior airs of incompetence. But he, he had the most transcendent breeding in mind and spirit. He had no need for self-assertion, for his most casual acquaintances put him at once in a different class from all other men. He had never a trace of a vulgar ideal; men's opinions, worldly honour, the common pleasures of life, were merely degrees of the infinitely small. And yet he was no bloodless mystic. If race means anything, he had it to perfection. Dreams and fancies to him were the realities, while facts were the shadows which he made dance as it pleased him.

'The truth is, that he was that rarest of mortals, the iron dreamer. He thought in aeons and cosmic cycles, and because of it he could do what he pleased in life. We call a man practical if he is struggling in the crowd with no knowledge of his whereabouts, and yet in our folly we deny the name to the clear-sighted man who can rule the crowd from above. And here I join issue with you and everybody else. You thought it was Miss Clara's refusal which sent him abroad and interrupted his career. I read the thing otherwise. His love for the girl was a mere accident, a survival of the domestic in an austere spirit. Something, I do not know what, showed him his true desires. She may have rejected him; he may never have spoken to her; in any case the renunciation had to come. You must remember that that visit to Fountainblue was the first that he had paid since his boyhood to his boyhood's home. Those revisitings have often a strange trick of self-revelation. I believe that in that night on the island he saw our indoor civilisation and his own destiny in so sharp a contrast that he could not choose but make the severance. He found work where there could be small hope of honour or reward, but many a chance for a hero. And I am sure that he was happy, and that it was the longed-for illumination that dawned on him with the bullet which pierced his heart.

'But, you will say, the fact remains that he was once in love with Miss Clara, and that she would have none of him. I do not deny it. He was never a favourite with women; but, thank heaven, I have better things to do than study their peculiarities . . .'

The Grove of Ashtaroth

We were sitting around the camp fire, some thirty miles north of a place called Taqui, when Lawson announced his intention of finding a home. He had spoken little the last day or two, and I had guessed that he had struck a vein of private reflection. I thought it might be a new mine or irrigation scheme, and I was surprised to find that it was a country-house.

'I don't think I shall go back to England,' he said, kicking a sputtering log into place. 'I don't see why I should. For business purposes I am far more useful to the firm in South Africa than in Throgmorton Street. I have no relations left except a third cousin, and I have never cared a rush for living in town. That beastly house of mine in Hill Street will fetch what I gave for it – Isaacson cabled about it the other day, offering for furniture and all. I don't want to go into Parliament, and I hate shooting little birds and tame deer. I am one of those fellows who are born Colonial at heart, and I don't see why I shouldn't arrange my life as I please. Besides, for ten years I have been falling in love with this country, and now I am up to the neck.'

He flung himself back in the camp-chair till the canvas creaked, and looked at me below his eyelids. I remember glancing at the lines of him, and thinking what a fine make of a man he was. In his untanned field-boots, breeches and grey shirt he looked the born wilderness-hunter, though less than two months before he had been driving down to the City every morning in the sombre regimentals of his class. Being a fair man, he was gloriously tanned, and there was a clear line at his shirt-collar to mark the limits of his sunburn. I had first known him years ago, when he was a broker's clerk working on half commission. Then he had gone to South Africa, and soon I heard he was a partner in a mining house which was doing wonders with some gold areas in the North. The next step was his return to London as the new millionaire – young, good-looking, wholesome in mind and body, and much sought after by the mothers of marriageable girls. We played polo together, and hunted a little in the season, but there were signs that he did not propose to become the conventional English gentleman. He refused to buy a place in the country, though half the Homes of England were at his disposal. He was a very busy man, he declared, and had not time to be a squire. Besides, every few months he used to rush out to South Africa. I saw that he was restless, for he was always badgering me to go big-game hunting with him in some remote part of the earth. There was that in his eyes, too, which marked him out from the ordinary blonde type of our countrymen. They were large and brown and mysterious, and the light of another race was in their odd depths.

To hint such a thing would have meant a breach of friendship, for Lawson was very proud of his birth. When he first made his fortune he had gone to the Heralds to dis-

cover his family, and those obliging gentlemen had provided a pedigree. It appeared that he was a scion of the
house of Lowson or Lowieson, an ancient and rather disreputable clan on the Scottish side of the Border. He took
a shooting in Teviotdale on the strength of it, and used
to commit lengthy Border ballads to memory. But I had
known his father, a financial journalist who never quite
succeeded, and I had heard of a grandfather who sold
antiques in a back street at Brighton. The latter, I think,
had not changed his name, and still frequented the syna-
gogue. The father was a progressive Christian, and the
mother had been a blonde Saxon from the Midlands. In
my mind there was no doubt, as I caught Lawson's heavy-
lidded eyes fixed on me. My friend was of a more ancient
race than the Lowsons of the Border.

'Where are you thinking of looking for your house?' I
asked. 'In Natal or in the Cape Peninsula? You might get
the Fishers' place if you paid a price.'

'The Fishers' place be hanged!' he said crossly. 'I don't
want any stuccoed overgrown Dutch farm. I might as well
be at Roehampton as in the Cape.'

He got up and walked to the far side of the fire, where a
lane ran down through thornscrub to a gully of the hills.
The moon was silvering the bush of the plains, forty miles
off and three thousand feet below us.

'I am going to live somewhere hereabouts,' he answered
at last.

I whistled. 'Then you've got to put your hand in your
pocket, old man. You'll have to make everything, including a map of the countryside.'

'I know,' he said; 'that's where the fun comes in. Hang
it all, why shouldn't I indulge my fancy? I'm uncommonly

125

well off, and I haven't chick or child to leave it to. Supposing I'm a hundred miles from a railhead, what about it? I'll make a motor-road and fix up a telephone. I'll grow most of my supplies, and start a colony to provide labour. When you come and stay with me, you'll get the best food and drink on earth, and sport that will make your mouth water. I'll put Lochleven trout in these streams – at six thousand feet you can do anything. We'll have a pack of hounds, too, and we can drive pig in the woods, and if we want big game there are the Mangwe flats at our feet. I tell you I'll make such a country-house as nobody ever dreamed of. A man will come plumb out of stark savagery into lawns and rose-gardens.' Lawson flung himself into his chair again and smiled dreamily at the fire.

'But why here, of all places?' I persisted. I was not feeling very well and did not care for the country.

'I can't quite explain. I think it's the sort of land I have always been looking for. I always fancied a house on a green plateau in a decent climate looking down on the tropics. I like heat and colour, you know, but I like hills too, and greenery, and the things that bring back Scotland. Give me a cross between Teviotdale and the Orinoco, and, by Gad! I think I've got it here.'

I watched my friend curiously, as with bright eyes and eager voice he talked of his new fad. The two races were very clear in him – the one desiring gorgeousness, the other athirst for the soothing spaces of the North. He began to plan out the house. He would get Adamson to design it, and it was to grow out of the landscape like a stone on the hillside. There would be wide verandahs and cool halls, but great fireplaces against winter time. It would all be very simple and fresh – 'clean as morning' was his odd phrase; but then another idea supervened, and he talked of bringing the Tintorets from Hill Street. 'I want it to be a civilised house, you know. No silly luxury, but the best pictures and china and books . . . I'll have all the furniture made after the old plain English models out of native woods. I don't want second-hand sticks in a new country. Yes, by Jove, the Tintorets are a great idea, and all those Ming pots I bought. I had meant to sell them, but I'll have them out here.'

He talked for a good hour of what he would do, and his dream grew richer as he talked, till by the time we went to bed he had sketched something liker a palace than a country-house. Lawson was by no means a luxurious man. At present he was well content with a Wolseley valise, and shaved cheerfully out of a tin mug. It struck me as odd that a man so simple in his habits should have so sumptuous a taste in bric-à-brac. I told myself, as I turned in, that the Saxon mother from the Midlands had done little to dilute the strong wine of the East.

It drizzled next morning when we inspanned, and I mounted my horse in a bad temper. I had some fever on me, I think, and I hated this lush yet frigid table-land, where all the winds on earth lay in wait for one's marrow. Lawson was, as usual, in great spirits. We were not hunting, but shifting our hunting-ground, so all morning we travelled fast to the north along the rim of the uplands.

At midday it cleared, and the afternoon was a pageant of pure colour. The wind sank to a low breeze; the sun lit the infinite green spaces, and kindled the wet forest to a jewelled coronal. Lawson gaspingly admired it all, as he cantered bareheaded up a bracken-clad slope. 'God's

country,' he said twenty times. 'I've found it.' Take a piece
of Saxon downland; put a stream in every hollow and a
patch of wood; and at the edge, where the cliffs at home
would fall to the sea, put a cloak of forest muffling the
scarp and dropping thousands of feet to the blue plains.
Take the diamond air of the Gornergrat, and the riot of
colour which you get by a West Highland lochside in late
September. Put flowers everywhere, the things we grow in
hothouses, geraniums like sun-shades and arums like trum-
pets. That will give you a notion of the countryside we were
in. I began to see that after all it was out of the common.

And just before sunset we came over a ridge and found
something better. It was a shallow glen, half a mile wide,
down which ran a blue-grey stream in linns like the Spean,
till at the edge of the plateau it leaped into the dim forest
in a snowy cascade. The opposite side ran up in gentle slopes
to a rocky knoll, from which the eye had a noble prospect
of the plains. All down the glen were little copses, half
moons of green edging some silvery shore of the burn, or delicate clusters of tall trees nodding on the hill brow. The
place so satisfied the eye that for the sheer wonder of its perfection we stopped and stared in silence for many minutes.

Then 'The House,' I said, and Lawson replied softly,
'The House!'

We rode slowly into the glen in the mulberry gloaming.
Our transport waggons were half an hour behind, so we had
time to explore. Lawson dismounted and plucked handfuls
of flowers from the water-meadows. He was singing to
himself all the time – an old French catch about *Cadet
Rousselle* and his *trois maisons*.

'Who owns it?' I asked.

'My firm, as like as not. We have miles of land about

128

here. But whoever the man is, he has got to sell. Here I build my tabernacle, old man. Here, and nowhere else!'

In the very centre of the glen, in a loop of the stream, was one copse which even in that half light struck me as different from the others. It was of tall, slim, fairy-like trees, the kind of wood the monks painted in old missals. No, I rejected the thought. It was no Christian wood. It was not a copse, but a 'grove' – one such as Diana may have flitted through in the moonlight. It was small, forty or fifty yards in diameter, and there was a dark something at the heart of it which for a second I thought was a house.

We turned between the slender trees, and – was it fancy? – an odd tremor went through me. I felt as if I were penetrating the *temenos* of some strange and lovely divinity, the goddess of this pleasant vale. There was a spell in the air, it seemed, and an odd dead silence.

Suddenly my horse started at a flutter of light wings. A flock of doves rose from the branches, and I saw the burnished green of their plumes against the opal sky. Lawson did not seem to notice them. I saw his keen eyes staring at the centre of the grove and what stood there.

It was a little conical tower, ancient and lichened, but, so far as I could judge, quite flawless. You know the famous Conical Temple at Zimbabwe, of which prints are in every guide-book. This was of the same type, but a thousand-fold more perfect. It stood about thirty feet high, of solid masonry, without door or window or cranny, as shapely as when it first came from the hands of the old builders. Again I had the sense of breaking in on a sanctuary. What right had I, a common vulgar modern, to be looking at this fair thing, among these delicate trees, which some white goddess had once taken for her shrine?

Lawson broke in on my absorption. 'Let's get out of this,' he said hoarsely, and he took my horse's bridle (he had left his own beast at the edge) and led him back to the open. But I noticed that his eyes were always turning back, and that his hand trembled.

'That settles it,' I said after supper. 'What do you want with your mediaeval Venetians and your Chinese pots now? You will have the finest antique in the world in your garden – a temple as old as time, and in a land which they say has no history. You had the right inspiration this time.'

I think I have said that Lawson had hungry eyes. In his enthusiasm they used to glow and brighten; but now, as he sat looking down at the olive shades of the glen, they seemed ravenous in their fire. He had hardly spoken a word since we left the wood.

'Where can I read about those things?' he asked, and I gave him the names of books.

Then, an hour later, he asked me who were the builders. I told him the little I knew about Phoenician and Sabaean wanderings, and the ritual of Sidon and Tyre. He repeated some names to himself and went soon to bed.

As I turned in, I had one last look over the glen, which lay ivory and black in the moon. I seemed to hear a faint echo of wings, and to see over the little grove a cloud of light visitants. 'The Doves of Ashtaroth have come back,' I said to myself. 'It is a good omen. They accept the new tenant.' But as I fell asleep I had a sudden thought that I was saying something rather terrible.

Three years later, pretty nearly to a day, I came back to see what Lawson had made of his hobby. He had bidden me often to Welgevonden, as he chose to call it – though I do not know why he should have fixed a Dutch name to a countryside where Boer never trod. At the last there had been some confusion about dates, and I wired the time of my arrival, and set off without an answer. A motor met me at the queer little wayside station of Taqui, and after many miles on a doubtful highway I came to the gates of the park, and a road on which it was a delight to move. Three years had wrought little difference in the landscape. Lawson had done some planting – conifers and flowering shrubs and such-like – but wisely he had resolved that Nature had for the most part forestalled him. All the same, he must have spent a mint of money. The drive could not have been beaten in England, and fringes of mown turf on either hand had been pared out of the lush meadows. When we came over the edge of the hill and looked down on the secret glen, I could not repress a cry of pleasure. The house stood on the farther ridge, the view-point of the whole neighbourhood; and its brown timbers and white rough-cast walls melted into the hillside as if it had been there from the beginning of things. The vale below was ordered in lawns and gardens. A blue lake received the rapids of the stream, and its banks were a maze of green shades and glorious masses of blossom. I noticed, too, that the little grove we had explored on our first visit stood alone in a big stretch of lawn, so that its perfection might be clearly seen. Lawson had excellent taste, or he had had the best advice.

The butler told me that his master was expected home shortly, and took me into the library for tea. Lawson had left his Tintorets and Ming pots at home after all. It was a long, low room, panelled in teak half-way up the walls, and the shelves held a multitude of fine bindings. There were good rugs on the parquet floor, but no ornaments anywhere, save three. On the carved mantelpiece stood two of the old soapstone birds which they used to find at Zimbabwe, and between, on an ebony stand, a half moon of alabaster, curiously carved with zodiacal figures. My host had altered his scheme of furnishing; but I approved the change.

He came in about half-past six, after I had consumed two cigars and all but fallen asleep. Three years make a difference in most men, but I was not prepared for the change in Lawson. For one thing, he had grown fat. In place of the lean young man I had known, I saw a heavy, flaccid being, who shuffled in his gait, and seemed tired and listless. His sunburn had gone, and his face was as pasty as a city clerk's. He had been walking, and wore shapeless flannel clothes, which hung loose even on his enlarged figure. And the worst of it was, that he did not seem over-pleased to see me. He murmured something about my journey, and then flung himself into an arm-chair and looked out of the window.

I asked him if he had been ill.

'Ill! No!' he said crossly. 'Nothing of the kind. I'm perfectly well.'

'You don't look as fit as this place should make you. What do you do with yourself? Is the shooting as good as you hoped?'

He did not answer, but I thought I heard him mutter something like 'shooting be damned'.

Then I tried the subject of the house. I praised it extravagantly, but with conviction. 'There can be no place like it in the world,' I said.

He turned his eyes on me at last, and I saw that they were as deep and restless as ever. With his pallid face they made him look curiously Semitic. I had been right in my theory about his ancestry.

'Yes,' he said slowly, 'there is no place like it – in the world.'

Then he pulled himself to his feet. 'I'm going to change,' he said. 'Dinner is at eight. Ring for Travers, and he'll show you your room.'

I dressed in a noble bedroom, with an outlook over the garden-vale and the escarpment to the far line of the plains, now blue and saffron in the sunset. I dressed in an ill temper, for I was seriously offended with Lawson, and also seriously alarmed. He was either very unwell or going out of his mind, and it was clear, too, that he would resent any anxiety on his account. I ransacked my memory for rumours, but found none. I had heard nothing of him except that he had been extraordinarily successful in his speculations, and that from his hill-top he directed his firm's operations with uncommon skill. If Lawson was sick or mad, nobody knew of it.

Dinner was a trying ceremony. Lawson, who used to be rather particular in his dress, appeared in a kind of smoking suit with a flannel collar. He spoke scarcely a word to me, but cursed the servants with a brutality which left me aghast. A wretched footman in his nervousness spilt some sauce over his sleeve. Lawson dashed the dish from his hand, and volleyed abuse with a sort of epileptic fury. Also he, who had been the most abstemious of men, swallowed disgusting quantities of champagne and old brandy.

He had given up smoking, and half an hour after we left the dining-room he announced his intention of going to bed. I watched him as he waddled upstairs with a feeling of angry bewilderment. Then I went to the library and lit a pipe. I would leave first thing in the morning – on that I was determined. But as I sat gazing at the moon of alabaster and the soapstone birds my anger evaporated, and concern took its place. I remembered what a fine fellow Lawson had been, what good times we had had together. I remembered especially that evening when we had found this valley and given rein to our fancies. What horrid alchemy in the place had turned a gentleman into a brute? I thought of drink and drugs and madness and insomnia, but I could fit none of them into my conception of my friend. I did not consciously rescind my resolve to depart, but I had a notion that I would not act on it.

The sleepy butler met me as I went to bed. 'Mr Lawson's room is at the end of your corridor, sir,' he said. 'He don't sleep over well, so you may hear him stirring in the night. At what hour would you like breakfast, sir? Mr Lawson mostly has his in bed.'

My room opened from the great corridor, which ran the full length of the front of the house. So far as I could make out, Lawson was three rooms off, a vacant bedroom and his servant's room being between us. I felt tired and cross, and tumbled into bed as fast as possible. Usually I sleep well, but now I was soon conscious that my drowsiness was wearing off and that I was in for a restless night. I got up and laved my face, turned the pillows, thought of sheep coming over a hill and clouds crossing the sky; but none of the old devices were any use. After about an hour of make-believe I surrendered myself to facts, and, lying on my back, stared at the white ceiling and the patches of moonshine on the walls.

It certainly was an amazing night. I got up, put on a dressing-gown, and drew a chair to the window. The moon was almost at its full, and the whole plateau swam in a radiance of ivory and silver. The banks of the stream were black, but the lake had a great belt of light athwart it, which made it seem like a horizon, and the rim of land beyond it like a contorted cloud. Far to the right I saw the delicate outlines of the little wood which I had come to think of as the Grove of Ashtaroth. I listened. There was not a sound in the air. The land seemed to sleep peacefully beneath the moon, and yet I had a sense that the peace was an illusion. The place was feverishly restless.

I could have given no reason for my impression, but there it was. Something was stirring in the wide moonlit landscape under its deep mask of silence. I felt as I had felt on the evening three years ago when I had ridden into the grove. I did not think that the influence, whatever it was, was maleficent. I only knew that it was very strange, and kept me wakeful.

By-and-by I bethought me of a book. There was no lamp in the corridor save the moon, but the whole house was bright as I slipped down the great staircase and over the hall to the library. I switched on the lights and then switched them off. They seemed a profanation, and I did not need them.

I found a French novel, but the place held me and I stayed. I sat down in an arm-chair before the fireplace and the stone birds. Very odd those gawky things, like prehistoric Great Auks, looked in the moonlight. I remember that the alabaster moon shimmered like translucent pearl, and I fell to wondering about its history. Had the old Sabaeans used such a jewel in their rites in the Grove of Ashtaroth?

Then I heard footsteps pass the window. A great house like this would have a watchman, but these quick shuffling footsteps were surely not the dull plod of a servant. They passed on to the grass and died away. I began to think of getting back to my room.

In the corridor I noticed that Lawson's door was ajar, and that a light had been left burning. I had the unpardonable curiosity to peep in. The room was empty, and the bed had not been slept in. Now I knew whose were the footsteps outside the library window.

I lit a reading-lamp and tried to interest myself in *La Cruelle Enigme*. But my wits were restless, and I could not keep my eyes on the page. I flung the book aside and sat down again by the window. The feeling came over me that I was sitting in a box at some play. The glen was a huge stage, and at any moment the players might appear on it. My attention was strung as high as if I had been waiting for the advent of some world-famous actress. But nothing came. Only the shadows shifted and lengthened as the moon moved across the sky.

Then quite suddenly the restlessness left me, and at the same moment the silence was broken by the crow of a cock and the rustling of trees in a light wind. I felt very sleepy, and was turning to bed when again I heard footsteps without. From the window I could see a figure moving across the garden towards the house. It was Lawson, got up in the sort of towel dressing-gown that one wears on board ship. He was walking slowly and painfully, as if very weary. I did not see his face, but the man's whole air was that of extreme fatigue and dejection.

I tumbled into bed and slept profoundly till long after daylight.

The man who valeted me was Lawson's own servant. As he was laying out my clothes I asked after the health of his master, and was told that he had slept ill and would not rise till late. Then the man, an anxious-faced Englishman, gave me some information on his own account. Mr Lawson was having one of his bad turns. It would pass away in a day or two, but till it had gone he was fit for nothing. He advised me to see Mr Jobson, the factor, who would look to my entertainment in his master's absence.

Jobson arrived before luncheon, and the sight of him was the first satisfactory thing about Welgevonden. He was a big, gruff Scot from Roxburghshire, engaged, no doubt, by Lawson as a duty to his Border ancestry. He had short grizzled whiskers, a weatherworn face and a shrewd, calm blue eye. I knew now why the place was in such perfect order.

We began with sport, and Jobson explained what I could have in the way of fishing and shooting. His exposition was brief and business-like, and all the while I could see his eye searching me. It was clear that he had much to say on other matters than sport.

I told him that I had come here with Lawson three years before, when he chose the site. Jobson continued to regard me curiously. 'I've heard tell of ye from Mr Lawson. Ye're an old friend of his, I understand.'

'The oldest,' I said. 'And I am sorry to find that the place does not agree with him. Why it doesn't I cannot imagine, for you look fit enough. Has he been seedy for long?'

'It comes and goes,' said Mr Jobson. 'Maybe once a month he has a bad turn. But on the whole it agrees with him badly. He's no' the man he was when I first came here.'

Jobson was looking at me very seriously and frankly. I risked a question.

'What do you suppose is the matter?'

He did not reply at once, but leaned forward and tapped my knee.

'I think it's something that doctors canna cure. Look at me, sir. I've always been counted a sensible man, but if I told you what was in my head you would think me daft. But I have one word for you. Bide till tonight is past and then speir your question. Maybe you and me will be agreed.'

The factor rose to go. As he left the room he flung me back a remark over his shoulder – 'Read the eleventh chapter of the First Book of Kings.'

After luncheon I went for a walk. First I mounted to the crown of the hill and feasted my eyes on the unequalled loveliness of the view. I saw the far hills in Portuguese territory, a hundred miles away, lifting up thin blue fingers into the sky. The wind blew light and fresh, and the place was fragrant with a thousand delicate scents. Then I descended to the vale, and followed the stream up through the garden. Poinsettias and oleanders were blazing in coverts, and there was a paradise of tinted water-lilies in the slacker reaches. I saw good trout rise at the fly, but I did not think about fishing. I was searching my memory for a recollection which would not come. By-and-by I found myself beyond the garden, where the lawns ran to the fringe of Ashtaroth's Grove.

It was like something I remembered in an old Italian picture. Only, as my memory drew it, it should have been peopled with strange figures – nymphs dancing on the sward, and a prick-eared faun peeping from the covert. In the warm afternoon sunlight it stood, ineffably gracious and beautiful, tantalising with a sense of some deep hidden loveliness. Very reverently I walked between the slim trees, to where the little conical tower stood half in sun and half in shadow. Then I noticed something new. Round the tower ran a narrow path, worn in the grass by human feet. There had been no such path on my first visit, for I remembered the grass growing tall to the edge of the stone. Had the Kaffirs made a shrine of it, or were there other and stranger votaries?

When I returned to the house I found Travers with a message for me. Mr Lawson was still in bed, but he would like me to go to him. I found my friend sitting up and drinking strong tea – a bad thing, I should have thought, for a man in his condition. I remember that I looked over the room for some sign of the pernicious habit of which I believed him a victim. But the place was fresh and clean, with the windows wide open, and, though I could not have given my reasons, I was convinced that drugs or drink had nothing to do with the sickness.

He received me more civilly, but I was shocked by his looks. There were great bags below his eyes, and his skin had the wrinkled puffy appearance of a man in dropsy. His voice, too, was reedy and thin. Only his great eyes burned with some feverish life.

'I am a shocking bad host,' he said, 'but I'm going to be still more inhospitable. I want you to go away. I hate anybody here when I'm off colour.'

'Nonsense, I said; 'you want looking after. I want to know about this sickness. Have you had a doctor?'

He smiled wearily. 'Doctors are no earthly use to me. There's nothing much the matter, I tell you. I'll be all right in a day or two, and then you can come back. I want you to go off with Jobson and hunt in the plains till the end of the week. It will be better fun for you, and I'll feel less guilty.'

Of course I pooh-poohed the idea, and Lawson got angry. 'Damn it, man,' he cried, 'why do you force yourself on me when I don't want you? I tell you your presence here makes me worse. In a week I'll be as right as the mail, and then I'll be thankful for you. But get away now; get away, I tell you.'

I saw that he was fretting himself into a passion. 'All right,' I said soothingly; 'Jobson and I will go off hunting. But I am horribly anxious about you, old man.'

He lay back on his pillows. 'You needn't trouble. I only want a little rest. Jobson will make all arrangements, and Travers will get you anything you want. Goodbye.'

I saw it was useless to stay longer, so I left the room. Outside I found the anxious-faced servant. 'Look here,' I said, 'Mr Lawson thinks I ought to go, but I mean to stay. Tell him I'm gone if he asks you. And for Heaven's sake keep him in bed.'

The man promised, and I thought I saw some relief in his face.

I went to the library, and on the way remembered Jobson's remark about First Kings. With some searching I found a Bible and turned up the passage. It was a long screed about the misdeeds of Solomon, and I read it through without enlightenment. I began to re-read it, and a word suddenly caught my attention –

For Solomon went after Ashtaroth, the goddess of the Zidonians.

That was all, but it was like a key to a cipher. Instantly there flashed over my mind all that I had heard or read of that strange ritual which seduced Israel to sin. I saw a sun-burnt land and a people vowed to the stern service of Jehovah. But I saw, too, eyes turning from the austere sac-rifice to lonely hill-top groves and towers and images, where dwelt some subtle and evil mystery. I saw the fierce prophets, scourging the votaries with rods, and a nation penitent before the Lord; but always the backsliding again, and the hankering after forbidden joys. Ashtaroth was the old god-dess of the East. Was it not possible that in all Semitic blood there remained, transmitted through the dim gener-ations, some craving for her spell? I thought of the grand-father in the back street at Brighton and of those burning eyes upstairs.

As I sat and mused my glance fell on the inscrutable stone birds. They knew all those old secrets of joy and ter-ror. And that moon of alabaster! Some dark priest had worn it on his forehead when he worshipped, like Ahab, 'all the host of Heaven'. And then I honestly began to be afraid. I a prosaic, modern Christian gentleman, a half-believer in casual faiths, was in the presence of some hoary mystery of sin far older than creeds or Christendom. There was fear in my heart – a kind of uneasy disgust, and above all a nervous eerie disquiet. Now I wanted to go away, and yet I was ashamed of the cowardly thought. I pictured Ashtaroth's Grove with sheer horror. What tragedy was in the air? What secret awaited twilight? For the night was coming, the night of the Full Moon, the season of ecstasy and sacrifice.

I do not know how I got through that evening. I was disinclined for dinner, so I had a cutlet in the library and sat smoking till my tongue ached. But as the hours passed a more manly resolution grew up in my mind. I owed it to old friendship to stand by Lawson in this extremity. I could not interfere – God knows, his reason seemed already rocking – but I could be at hand in case my chance came. I determined not to undress, but to watch through the night. I had a bath, and changed into light flannels and slippers. Then I took up my position in a corner of the library close to the window, so that I could not fail to hear Lawson's footsteps if he passed.

Fortunately I left the lights unlit, for as I waited I grew drowsy, and fell asleep. When I woke the moon had risen, and I knew from the feel of the air that the hour was late. I sat very still, straining my ears, and as I listened I caught the sound of steps. They were crossing the hall stealthily, and nearing the library door. I huddled into my corner as Lawson entered.

He wore the same towel dressing-gown, and he moved swiftly and silently as if in a trance. I watched him take the alabaster moon from the mantelpiece and drop it in his pocket. A glimpse of white skin showed that the gown was his only clothing. Then he moved past me to the window, opened it, and went out.

Without any conscious purpose I rose and followed, kicking off my slippers that I might go quietly. He was running, running fast, across the lawns in the direction of the grove – an odd shapeless antic in the moonlight. I stopped, for there was no cover, and I feared for his reason if he saw me. When I looked again he had disappeared among the trees.

I saw nothing for it but to crawl, so on my belly I wormed my way over the dripping sward. There was a ridiculous suggestion of deer-stalking about the game which tickled me and dispelled my uneasiness. Almost I persuaded myself

I was tracking an ordinary sleep-walker. The lawns were broader than I imagined, and it seemed an age before I reached the edge of the grove. The world was so still that I appeared to be making a most ghastly amount of noise. I remember that once I heard a rustling in the air, and looked up to see the green doves circling about the treetops.

There was no sign of Lawson. On the edge of the grove I think that all my assurance vanished. I could see between the trunks to the little tower, but it was quiet as the grave, save for the wings above. Once more there came over me the unbearable sense of anticipation I had felt the night before. My nerves tingled with mingled expectation and dread. I did not think that any harm would come to me, for the powers of the air seemed not malignant. But I knew them for powers, and felt awed and abased. I was in the presence of the 'host of Heaven', and I was no stern Israelit-ish prophet to prevail against them.

I must have lain for hours waiting in that spectral place, my eyes riveted on the tower and its golden cap of moonshine. I remember that my head felt void and light, as if my spirit were becoming disembodied and leaving its dew-drenched sheath far below. But the most curious sensation was of something drawing me to the tower, something mild and kindly and rather feeble, for there was some other and stronger force keeping me back. I yearned to move nearer, but I could not drag my limbs an inch. There was a spell somewhere which I could not break. I do not think I was in any way frightened now. The starry influence was playing tricks with me, but my mind was half asleep. Only I never took my eyes from the little tower. I think I could not, if I had wanted to.

Then suddenly from the shadows came Lawson. He was

stark-naked, and he wore, bound across his brow, the half moon of alabaster. He had something, too, in his hand – something which glittered.

He ran round the tower, crooning to himself, and flinging wild arms to the skies. Sometimes the crooning changed to a shrill cry of passion, such as a maenad may have uttered in the train of Bacchus. I could make out no words, but the sound told its own tale. He was absorbed in some infernal ecstasy. And as he ran, he drew his right hand across his breast and arms, and I saw that it held a knife.

I grew sick with disgust – not terror, but honest physical loathing. Lawson, gashing his fat body, affected me with an overpowering repugnance. I wanted to go forward and stop him, and I wanted, too, to be a hundred miles away. And the result was that I stayed still. I believe my own will held me there, but I doubt if in any case I could have moved my legs.

The dance grew swifter and fiercer. I saw the blood dripping from Lawson's body, and his face ghastly white above his scarred breast. And then suddenly the horror left me; my head swam; and for one second – one brief second – I seemed to peer into a new world. A strange passion surged up in my heart. I seemed to see the earth peopled with forms – not human, scarcely divine, but more desirable than man or god. The calm face of Nature broke up for me into wrinkles of wild knowledge. I saw the things which brush against the soul in dreams, and found them lovely. There seemed no cruelty in the knife or the blood. It was a delicate mystery of worship, as wholesome as the morning song of birds. I do not know how the Semites found Ashtaroth's ritual; to them it may well have been more rapt and passionate than it seemed to me. For I saw

in it only the sweet simplicity of Nature, and all riddles of lust and terror soothed away as a child's nightmares are calmed by a mother. I found my legs able to move, and I think I took two steps through the dusk towards the tower.

And then it all ended. A cock crew, and the homely noises of earth were renewed. While I stood dazed and shivering, Lawson plunged through the grove towards me. The impetus carried him to the edge, and he fell fainting just outside the shade.

My wits and common-sense came back to me with my bodily strength. I got my friend on my back, and staggered with him towards the house. I was afraid in real earnest now, and what frightened me most was the thought that I had not been afraid sooner. I had come very near the 'abomination of the Zidonians'.

At the door I found the scared valet waiting. He had apparently done this sort of thing before.

'Your master has been sleep-walking, and has had a fall,' I said. 'We must get him to bed at once.'

We bathed the wounds as he lay in a deep stupor, and I dressed them as well as I could. The only danger lay in his utter exhaustion, for happily the gashes were not serious, and no artery had been touched. Sleep and rest would make him well, for he had the constitution of a strong man. I was leaving the room when he opened his eyes and spoke. He did not recognise me, but I noticed that his face had lost its strangeness, and was once more that of the friend I had known. Then I suddenly bethought me of an old hunting remedy which he and I always carried on our expeditions. It is a pill made up from an ancient Portuguese prescription. One is an excellent specific for fever. Two are invaluable if you are lost in the bush, for they send a man for many hours into a deep sleep, which prevents suffering and madness, till help comes. Three give a painless death. I went to my room and found the little box in my jewel-case. Lawson swallowed two, and turned wearily on his side. I bade his man let him sleep till he woke, and went off in search of food.

I had business on hand which would not wait. By seven, Jobson, who had been sent for, was waiting for me in the library. I knew by his grim face that here I had a very good substitute for a prophet of the Lord.

'You were right,' I said. 'I have read the eleventh chapter of First Kings, and I have spent such a night as I pray God I shall never spend again.'

'I thought you would,' he replied. 'I've had the same experience myself.'

'The grove?' I said.

'Ay, the wud,' was the answer in broad Scots.

I wanted to see how much he understood.

'Mr Lawson's family is from the Scotch Border?'

'Ay. I understand they come off Borthwick Water side,' he replied, but I saw by his eyes that he knew what I meant.

'Mr Lawson is my oldest friend,' I went on, 'and I am going to take measures to cure him. For what I am going to do I take the sole responsibility. I will make that plain to your master. But if I am to succeed I want your help. Will you give it to me? It sounds like madness, and you are a sensible man and may like to keep out of it. I leave it to your discretion.'

Jobson looked me straight in the face. 'Have no fear for me,' he said; 'there is an unholy thing in that place, and if

146

I have the strength in me I will destroy it. He has been a good master to me, and forbye, I am a believing Christian. So say on, sir.'

There was no mistaking the air. I had found my Tishbite.

'I want men,' I said, 'as many as we can get.'

Jobson mused. 'The Kaffirs will no' gang near the place, but there's some thirty white men on the tobacco farm. They'll do your will, if you give them an indemnity in writing.'

'Good,' said I. 'Then we will take our instructions from the only authority which meets the case. We will follow the example of King Josiah.' I turned up the twenty-third chapter of Second Kings, and read:

'And the high places that were before Jerusalem, which were on the right hand of the Mount of Corruption, which Solomon the king of Israel had builded for Ashtaroth the abomination of the Zidonians . . . did the king defile.

And he brake in pieces the images, and cut down the groves, and filled their places with the bones of men.

Moreover the altar that was at Beth-el, and the high place which Jeroboam the son of Nebat, who made Israel to sin, had made, both that altar and the high place he brake down, and burned the high place, and stamped it small to powder, and burned the grove.'

Jobson nodded. 'It'll need dinnymite. But I've plenty of yon down at the workshops. I'll be off to collect the lads.'

Before nine the men had assembled at Jobson's house. They were a hardy lot of young farmers from home, who took their instructions docilely from the masterful factor.

147

On my orders they had brought their shot-guns. We armed them with spades and woodmen's axes, and one man wheeled some coils of rope in a hand-cart.

In the clear, windless air of morning the grove, set amid its lawns, looked too innocent and exquisite for ill. I had a pang of regret that a thing so fair should suffer; nay, if I had come alone, I think I might have repented. But the men were there, and the grim-faced Jobson was waiting for orders. I placed the guns, and sent beaters to the far side. I told them that every dove must be shot.

It was only a small flock, and we killed fifteen at the first drive. The poor birds flew over the glen to another spinney, but we brought them back over the guns and seven fell. Four more were got in the trees, and the last I killed myself with a long shot. In half an hour there was a pile of little green bodies on the sward.

Then we went to work to cut down the trees. The slim stems were an easy task to a good woodman, and one after another they toppled to the ground. And meantime, as I watched, I became conscious of a strange emotion.

It was as if someone were pleading with me. A gentle voice, not threatening, but pleading – something too fine for the sensual ear, but touching inner chords of the spirit. So tenuous it was and distant that I could think of no personality behind it. Rather it was the viewless, bodiless grace of this delectable vale, some old exquisite divinity of the groves. There was the heart of all sorrow in it, and the soul of all loveliness. It seemed a woman's voice, some lost lady who had brought nothing but goodness unrepaid to the world. And what the voice told me was that I was destroying her last shelter.

That was the pathos of it – the voice was homeless. As

the axes flashed in the sunlight and the wood grew thin, that gentle spirit was pleading with me for mercy and a brief respite. It seemed to be telling of a world for centuries grown coarse and pitiless, of long sad wanderings, of hardly won shelter, and a peace which was the little all she sought from men. There was nothing terrible in it, no thought of wrongdoing. The spell which to Semitic blood held the mystery of evil, was to me, of the Northern race, only delicate and rare and beautiful. Jobson and the rest did not feel it; I with my finer senses caught nothing but the hopeless sadness of it. That which had stirred the passion in Lawson was only wringing my heart. It was almost too pitiful to bear. As the trees crashed down and the men wiped the sweat from their brows, I seemed to myself like the murderer of fair women and innocent children. I remember that the tears were running over my cheeks. More than once I opened my mouth to countermand the work, but the face of Jobson, that grim Tishbite, held me back. I knew now what gave the Prophets of the Lord their mastery, and I knew also why the people sometimes stoned them.

The last tree fell, and the little tower stood like a ravished shrine, stripped of all defence against the world. I heard Jobson's voice speaking. 'We'd better blast that stane thing now. We'll trench on four sides and lay the dinnymite. Ye're no' looking weel, sir. Ye'd better go and sit down on the brae-face.'

I went up the hillside and lay down. Below me, in the waste of shorn trunks, men were running about, and I saw the mining begin. It all seemed like an aimless dream in which I had no part. The voice of that homeless goddess was still pleading. It was the innocence of it that tortured me. Even so must a merciful Inquisitor have suffered from the plea of some fair girl with the aureole of death on her hair. I knew I was killing rare and unrecoverable beauty. As I sat dazed and heartsick, the whole loveliness of Nature seemed to plead for its divinity. The sun in the heavens, the mellow lines of upland, the blue mystery of the far plains, were all part of that soft voice. I felt bitter scorn for myself. I was guilty of blood; nay, I was guilty of the sin against light which knows no forgiveness. I was murdering innocent gentleness, and there would be no peace on earth for me. Yet I sat helpless. The power of a sterner will constrained me. And all the while the voice was growing fainter and dying away into unutterable sorrow.

Suddenly a great flame sprang to heaven, and a pall of smoke. I heard men crying out, and fragments of stone fell around the ruins of the grove. When the air cleared, the little tower had gone out of sight.

The voice had ceased and there seemed to me to be a bereaved silence in the world. The shock moved me to my feet, and I ran down the slope to where Jobson stood rubbing his eyes.

'That's done the job. Now we maun get up the tree roots. We've no time to howk. We'll just dinnymite the feck o' them.'

The work of destruction went on, but I was coming back to my senses. I forced myself to be practical and reasonable. I thought of the night's experience and Lawson's haggard eyes, and I screwed myself into a determination to see the thing through. I had done the deed; it was my business to make it complete. A text in Jeremiah came into my head: '*Their children remember their altars and their groves by the green trees upon the high hills.*' I would see to it that this grove should be utterly forgotten.

We blasted the tree roots, and, yoking oxen, dragged the debris into a great heap. Then the men set to work with their spades, and roughly levelled the ground. I was getting back to my old self, and Jobson's spirit was becoming mine.

'There is one thing more,' I told him. 'Get ready a couple of ploughs. We will improve upon King Josiah.' My brain was a medley of Scripture precedents, and I was determined that no safeguard should be wanting.

We yoked the oxen again and drove the ploughs over the site of the grove. It was rough ploughing, for the place was thick with bits of stone from the tower, but the slow Afrikander oxen plodded on, and sometime in the afternoon the work was finished. Then I sent down to the farm for bags of rock-salt, such as they use for cattle. Jobson and I took a sack apiece, and walked up and down the furrows, sowing them with salt.

The last act was to set fire to the pile of tree-trunks. They burned well, and on the top we flung the bodies of the green doves. The birds of Ashtaroth had an honourable pyre.

Then I dismissed the much-perplexed men, and gravely shook hands with Jobson. Black with dust and smoke I went back to the house, where I bade Travers pack my bags and order the motor. I found Lawson's servant, and heard from him that his master was sleeping peacefully. I gave some directions, and then went to wash and change.

Before I left I wrote a line to Lawson. I began by transcribing the verses from the twenty-third chapter of Second Kings. I told him what I had done, and my reason. 'I take the whole responsibility upon myself,' I wrote. 'No man in the place had anything to do with it but me. I acted as I did for the sake of our old friendship, and you will believe it was no easy task for me. I hope you will understand. Whenever you are able to see me send me word, and I will come back and settle with you. But I think you will realise that I have saved your soul.'

The afternoon was merging into twilight as I left the house on the road to Taqui. The great fire, where the grove had been, was still blazing fiercely, and the smoke made a cloud over the upper glen, and filled all the air with a soft violet haze. I knew that I had done well for my friend, and that he would come to his senses and be grateful. My mind was at ease on that score, and in something like comfort I faced the future. But as the car reached the ridge I looked back to the vale I had outraged. The moon was rising and silvering the smoke, and through the gaps I could see the tongues of fire. Somehow, I know not why, the lake, the stream, the garden-coverts, even the green slopes of hill, wore an air of loneliness and desecration.

And then my heartache returned, and I knew that I had driven something lovely and adorable from its last refuge on earth.

Space

J'ai dit que nous pourrions concevoir, vivant dans notre monde, des êtres pensants dont le tableau de distribution serait à quatre dimensions et qui par conséquent penseraient dans l'hyperespace. Il n'est pas certain toutefois que de pareils êtres, en admettant qu'ils y naissent, pourraient y vivre et s'y défendre contre les mille dangers dont ils y seraient assaillis.

H. POINCARÉ: *Science et Méthode*

Le silence éternel de ces espaces infinis m'effraie.

PASCAL

Leithen told me this story one evening in early September as we sat beside the pony track which gropes its way from Glenaicill up the Correi na Sidhe. I had arrived that afternoon from the south, while he had been taking an off-day from a week's stalking, so we had walked up the glen together after tea to get the news of the forest. A rifle was out on the Correi na Sidhe beat, and a thin spire of smoke had risen from the top of Sgurr Dearg to show that a stag had been killed at the burn-head. The lumpish hill pony with its deer-saddle had gone up the Correi in a gillie's charge, while we followed at leisure, picking our way among the loose granite rocks and the patches of wet bogland. The track climbed high on one of the ridges of Sgurr Dearg, till it hung over a caldron of green glen with the Alt-na-Sidhe churning in its linn a thousand feet below. It was a breathless evening, I remember, with a pale-blue sky just clearing from the haze of the day. West-wind weather may make the North, even in September, no bad imitation of the Tropics, and I sincerely pitied the man who all these stifling hours had been toiling on the screes of Sgurr Dearg. By and by we sat down on a bank of heather, and idly watched the trough swimming at our feet. The clatter of the pony's hoofs grew fainter, the drone of bees had gone, even the midges seemed to have forgotten their calling. No place on earth can be so deathly still as a deer-forest early in the season before the stags have begun roaring, for there are no sheep with their homely noises, and only the rare croak of a raven breaks the silence. The hillside was far from sheer – one could have walked down with a little care – but something in the shape of the hollow and the remote gleam of white water gave it an air of extraordinary depth and space. There was a shimmer left from the day's heat, which invested bracken and rock and scree with a curious airy unreality. One could almost have believed that the eye had tricked the mind, that all was mirage, that five yards from the path the solid earth fell away into nothingness. I have a bad head, and instinctively I drew farther back into the heather. Leithen's eyes were looking vacantly before him.

'Did you ever know Hollond?' he asked.

Then he laughed shortly. 'I don't know why I asked that, but somehow this place reminded me of Hollond. That glimmering hollow looks as if it were the beginning of eternity. It must be eerie to live with the feeling always on one.'

Leithen seemed disinclined for further exercise. He lit a pipe and smoked quietly for a little. 'Odd that you didn't know Hollond. You must have heard his name. I thought you amused yourself with metaphysics.'

Then I remembered. There had been an erratic genius who had written some articles in *Mind* on that dreary subject, the mathematical conception of infinity. Men had praised them to me, but I confess I never quite understood their argument. 'Wasn't he some sort of mathematical professor?' I asked.

'He was, and, in his own way, a tremendous swell. He wrote a book on Number, which has translations in every European language. He is dead now, and the Royal Society founded a medal in his honour. But I wasn't thinking of that side of him.'

It was the time and place for a story, for the pony would not be back for an hour. So I asked Leithen about the other side of Hollond which was recalled to him by Correi na Sidhe. He seemed a little unwilling to speak . . .

'I wonder if you will understand it. You ought to, of course, better than me, for you know something of philosophy. But it took me a long time to get the hang of it, and I can't give you any kind of explanation. He was my fag at Eton, and when I began to get on at the Bar I was able to advise him on one or two private matters, so that he rather fancied my legal ability. He came to me with his story because he had to tell someone, and he wouldn't trust a colleague. He said he didn't want a scientist to know, for scientists were either pledged to their own theories and wouldn't understand, or, if they understood, would get ahead of him in his researches. He wanted a lawyer, he said, who was accustomed to weighing evidence. That was good sense, for evidence must always be judged by the same laws, and I suppose in the long-run the most abstruse business comes down to a fairly simple deduction from certain data. Anyhow, that was the way he used to talk, and I listened to him, for I liked the man, and had an enormous respect for his brains. At Eton he sluiced down all the mathematics they could give him, and he was an astonishing swell at Cambridge. He was a simple fellow, too, and talked no more jargon than he could help. I used to climb with him in the Alps now and then, and you would never have guessed that he had any thoughts beyond getting up steep rocks.

'It was at Chamonix, I remember, that I first got a hint of the matter that was filling his mind. We had been taking an off-day, and were sitting in the hotel garden, watching the Aiguilles getting purple in the twilight. Chamonix always makes me choke a little – it is so crushed in by those great snow masses. I said something about it – said I liked open spaces like the Gornergrat or the Bel Alp better. He asked me why: if it was the difference of the air, or merely the wider horizon? I said it was the sense of not being crowded, of living in an empty world. He repeated the word "empty" and laughed.

' "By 'empty' you mean", he said, "where things don't knock up against you?"

'I told him No. I mean just empty, void, nothing but blank ether.

' "You don't knock up against things here, and the air is as good as you want. It can't be the lack of ordinary emptiness you feel."

'I agreed that the word needed explaining. "I suppose it is mental restlessness," I said. "I like to feel that for a tremendous distance there is nothing round me. Why, I don't know. Some men are built the other way and have a terror of space."

'He said that that was better. "It is a personal fancy, and depends on your *knowing* that there is nothing between you and the top of the Dent Blanche. And you know because your eyes tell you there is nothing. Even if you were blind, you might have a sort of sense about adjacent matter. Blind men often have it. But in any case, whether got from instinct or sight, the *knowledge* is what matters."

'Hollond was embarking on a Socratic dialogue in which I could see little point. I told him so, and he laughed.

' "I am not sure that I am very clear myself. But yes – there *is* a point. Supposing you knew – not by sight or by instinct, but by sheer intellectual knowledge, as I know the truth of a mathematical proposition – that what we call empty space was full, crammed. Not with lumps of what we call matter like hills and houses, but with things as real – as real to the mind. Would you still feel crowded?"

' "No," I said, "I don't think so. It is only what we call matter that signifies. It would be just as well not to feel crowded by the other thing, for there would be no escape from it. But what are you getting at? Do you mean atoms or electric currents or what?"

'He said he wasn't thinking about that sort of thing, and began to talk of another subject.

'Next night, when we were pigging it at the Géant *cabane*, he started again on the same tack. He asked me how I accounted for the fact that animals could find their way back over great tracts of unknown country. I said I supposed it was the homing instinct.

' "Rubbish, man," he said. "That's only another name for the puzzle, not an explanation. There must be some reason for it. They must *know* something that we cannot understand. Tie a cat in a bag and take it fifty miles by train and it will make its way home. That cat has some clue that we haven't."

157

'I was tired and sleepy, and told him that I did not care a rush about the psychology of cats. But he was not to be snubbed, and went on talking.

' "How if Space is really full of things we cannot see and as yet do not know? How if all animals and some savages have a cell in their brain or a nerve which responds to the invisible world? How if all Space be full of these landmarks, not material in our sense, but quite real? A dog barks at nothing, a wild beast makes an aimless circuit. Why? Perhaps because Space is made up of corridors and alleys, ways to travel and things to shun? For all we know, to a greater intelligence than ours the top of Mont Blanc may be as crowded as Piccadilly Circus."

'But at that point I fell asleep and left Hollond to repeat his questions to a guide who knew no English and a snoring porter.

'Six months later, one foggy January afternoon, Hollond rang me up at the Temple and proposed to come to see me that night after dinner. I thought he wanted to talk Alpine shop, but he turned up in Duke Street about nine with a kit-bag full of papers. He was an odd fellow to look at – a yellowish face with the skin stretched tight on the cheek-bones, clean shaven, a sharp chin which he kept poking forward, and deep-set, greyish eyes. He was a hard fellow too, always in pretty good condition, which was remarkable considering how he slaved for nine months out of the twelve. He had a quiet, slow-spoken manner, but that night I saw that he was considerably excited.

'He said that he had come to me because we were old friends. He proposed to tell me a tremendous secret. "I must get another mind to work on it or I'll go crazy. I don't want a scientist. I want a plain man."

'Then he fixed me with a look like a tragic actor's. "Do you remember that talk we had in August at Chamonix – about Space? I daresay you thought I was playing the fool. So I was in a sense, but I was feeling my way towards something which has been in my mind for ten years. Now I have got it, and you must hear about it. You may take my word that it's a pretty startling discovery."

'I lit a pipe and told him to go ahead, warning him that I knew about as much science as the dust-man.

'I am bound to say that it took me a long time to understand what he meant. He began by saying that everybody thought of Space as an "empty homogeneous medium". "Never mind at present what the ultimate constituents of that medium are. We take it as a finished product, and we think of it as mere extension, something without any quality at all. That is the view of civilised man. You will find all the philosophers taking it for granted. Yes, but every living thing does not take that view. An animal, for instance. It feels a kind of quality in Space. It can find its way over new country, because it perceives certain landmarks, not necessarily material, but perceptible, or if you like intelligible. Take an Australian savage. He has the same power, and, I believe, for the same reason. He is conscious of intelligible landmarks."

' "You mean what people call a sense of direction," I put in.

' "Yes, but what in Heaven's name is a sense of direction? The phrase explains nothing. However incoherent the mind of the animal or the savage may be, it is there somewhere, working on some data. I've been all through the psychological and anthropological side of the business, and after you eliminate clues from sight and hearing and smell and half-conscious memory there remains a solid lump of the inexplicable."

'Hollond's eye had kindled, and he sat doubled up in his chair, dominating me with a finger.

' "Here, then, is a power which man is civilising himself out of. Call it anything you like, but you must admit that it is a power. Don't you see that it is a perception of another kind of reality that we are leaving behind us? . . . Well, you know the way nature works. The wheel comes full circle, and what we think we have lost we regain in a higher form. So for a long time I have been wondering whether the civilised mind could not recreate for itself this lost gift, the gift of seeing the quality of Space. I mean that I wondered whether the scientific modern brain could not get to the stage of realising that Space is not an empty homogeneous medium, but full of intricate differences, intelligible and real, though not with our common reality."

'I found all this very puzzling, and he had to repeat it several times before I got a glimpse of what he was talking about.

' "I've wondered for a long time," he went on, "but now, quite suddenly, I have begun to know." He stopped and asked me abruptly if I knew much about mathematics.

' "It's a pity," he said, "but the main point is not technical, though I wish you could appreciate the beauty of some of my proofs." Then he began to tell me about his last six months' work. I should have mentioned that he was a brilliant physicist besides other things. All Hollond's tastes were on the borderlands of sciences, where mathematics fades into metaphysics and physics merges in the abstrusest kind of mathematics. Well, it seems he had been working for years at the ultimate problem of matter, and especially of that rarefied matter we call ether or space. I forget what his view was – atoms or molecules or electric waves. If he ever told me I have forgotten, but I'm not certain that I ever knew. However, the point was that these ultimate constituents were dynamic and mobile, not a mere passive medium but a medium in constant movement and change. He claimed to have discovered – by ordinary inductive experiment – that the constituents of ether possessed certain functions, and moved in certain figures obedient to certain mathematical laws. Space, I gathered, was perpetually "forming fours" in some fancy way.

'Here he left his physics and became the mathematician. Among his mathematical discoveries had been certain curves or figures or something whose behaviour involved a new dimension. I gathered that this wasn't the ordinary Fourth Dimension that people talk of, but that fourth-dimensional inwardness or involution was part of it. The explanation lay in the pile of manuscripts he left with me, but though I tried honestly I couldn't get the hang of it. My mathematics stopped with desperate finality just as he got into his subject.

'His point was that the constituents of Space moved according to these new mathematical figures of his. They were always changing, but the principles of their change were as fixed as the law of gravitation. Therefore, if you once grasped these principles you knew the contents of the void. What do you make of that?'

I said that it seemed to me a reasonable enough argument, but that it got one very little way forward. 'A man', I said, 'might know the contents of Space and the laws of their arrangement and yet be unable to see anything more than his fellows. It is a purely academic knowledge. His mind knows it as the result of many deductions, but his senses perceive nothing.'

Leithen laughed. 'Just what I said to Hollond. He asked the opinion of my legal mind. I said I could not pronounce on his argument, but that I could point out that he had established no *trait d'union* between the intellect which understood and the senses which perceived. It was like a blind man with immense knowledge but no eyes, and therefore no peg to hang his knowledge on and make it useful. He had not explained his savage or his cat. "Hang it, man," I said, "before you can appreciate the existence of your Spacial forms you have to go through elaborate experiments and deductions. You can't be doing that every minute. Therefore you don't get any nearer to the *use* of the sense you say that man once possessed, though you can explain it a bit." '

'What did he say?' I asked.

'The funny thing was that he never seemed to see my difficulty. When I kept bringing him back to it he shied off with a new wild theory of perception. He argued that the mind can live in a world of realities without any sensuous stimulus to connect them with the world of our ordinary life. Of course that wasn't my point. I supposed that this world of Space was real enough to him, but I wanted to know how he got there. He never answered me. He was the typical Cambridge man, you know – dogmatic about uncertainties, but curiously diffident about the obvious. He laboured to get me to understand the notion of his mathematical forms, which I was quite willing to take on trust from him. Some queer things he said, too. He took our feeling about Left and Right as an example of our instinct for the quality of Space. But when I objected that Left and

Right varied with each object, and only existed in connection with some definite material thing, he said that that was exactly what he meant. It was an example of the mobility of the Spacial forms. Do you see any sense in that?'

I shook my head. It seemed to me pure craziness.

'And then he tried to show me what he called the "involution of Space", by taking two points on a piece of paper. The points were a foot away when the paper was flat, but they coincided when it was doubled up. He said that there were no gaps between the figures, for the medium was continuous, and he took as an illustration the loops on a cord. You are to think of a cord always looping and unlooping itself according to certain mathematical laws. Oh, I tell you, I gave up trying to follow him. And he was so desperately in earnest all the time. By his account Space was a sort of mathematical pandemonium.'

Leithen stopped to refill his pipe, and I mused upon the ironic fate which had compelled a mathematical genius to make his sole confidant of a philistine lawyer, and induced that lawyer to repeat it confusedly to an ignoramus at twilight on a Scotch hill. As told by Leithen it was a very halting tale.

'But there was one thing I could see very clearly,' Leithen went on, 'and that was Hollond's own case. This crowded world of Space was perfectly real to him. How he had got to it I do not know. Perhaps his mind, dwelling constantly on the problem, had unsealed some atrophied cell and restored the old instinct. Anyhow, he was living his daily life with a foot in each world.

'He often came to see me, and after the first hectic discussions he didn't talk much. There was no noticeable

163

change in him – a little more abstracted perhaps. He would walk in the street or come into a room with a quick look round him, and sometimes for no earthly reason he would swerve. Did you ever watch a cat crossing a room? It sidles along by the furniture and walks over an open space of carpet as if it were picking its way among obstacles. Well, Hollond behaved like that, but he had always been counted a little odd, and nobody noticed it but me.

'I knew better than to chaff him, and we had stopped argument, so that there wasn't much to be said. But sometimes he would give me news about his experiences. The whole thing was perfectly clear and scientific and above-board, and nothing creepy about it. You know how I hate the washy supernatural stuff they give us nowadays. Hollond was well and fit, with an appetite like a hunter. But as he talked, sometimes – well, you know I haven't much in the way of nerves or imagination – but I used to get a little eerie. Used to feel the solid earth dissolving round me. It was the opposite of vertigo, if you understand me – a sense of airy realities crowding in on you – crowding the mind, that is, not the body.

'I gathered from Hollond that he was always conscious of corridors and halls and alleys in Space, shifting, but shifting according to inexorable laws. I never could get quite clear as to what this consciousness was like. When I asked he used to look puzzled and worried and helpless. I made out from him that one landmark involved a sequence, and once given a bearing from an object you could keep the direction without a mistake. He told me he could easily, if he wanted, go in a dirigible from the top of Mont Blanc to the top of Snowdon in the thickest fog and without a compass, if he were given the proper angle to start from. I confess I didn't follow that myself. Material objects had nothing to do with the Spacial forms, for a table or a bed in our world might be placed across a corridor of Space. The forms played their game independent of our kind of reality. But the worst of it was, that if you kept your mind too much in one world you were apt to forget about the other, and Hollond was always barking his shins on stones and chairs and things.

'He told me all this quite simply and frankly. Remember, his mind and no other part of him lived in his new world. He said it gave him an odd sense of detachment to sit in a room among people, and to know that nothing there but himself had any relation at all to the infinite strange world of Space that flowed around them. He would listen, he said, to a great man talking, with one eye on the cat on the rug, thinking to himself how much more the cat knew than the man.'

'How long was it before he went mad?' I asked.

It was a foolish question, and made Leithen cross. 'He never went mad in your sense. My dear fellow, you're very much wrong if you think there was anything pathological about him – then. The man was brilliantly sane. His mind was as keen as a keen sword. I couldn't understand him, but I could judge of his sanity right enough.'

I asked if it made him happy or miserable.

'At first I think it made him uncomfortable. He was restless because he knew too much and too little. The unknown pressed in on his mind, as bad air weighs on the lungs. Then it lightened, and he accepted the new world in the same sober practical way that he took other things. I think that the free exercise of his mind in a pure medium gave him a feeling of extraordinary power and ease. His

165

eyes used to sparkle when he talked. And another odd thing he told me. He was a keen rock-climber, but, curiously enough, he had never a very good head. Dizzy heights always worried him, though he managed to keep hold on himself. But now all that had gone. The sense of the fullness of Space made him as happy – happier, I believe – with his legs dangling into eternity, as sitting before his own study fire.

'I remember saying that it was all rather like the mediaeval wizards who made their spells by means of numbers and figures.

'He caught me up at once. "Not numbers," he said. "Number has no place in Nature. It is an invention of the human mind to atone for a bad memory. But figures are a different matter. All the mysteries of the world are in them, and the old magicians knew that at least, if they knew no more."

'He had only one grievance. He complained that it was terribly lonely. "It is the Desolation", he would quote, "spoken of by Daniel the prophet." He would spend hours travelling those eerie shifting corridors of Space with no hint of another human soul. How could there be? It was a world of pure reason, where human personality had no place. What puzzled me was why he should feel the absence of this. One wouldn't, you know, in an intricate problem of geometry or a game of chess. I asked him, but he didn't understand the question. I puzzled over it a good deal, for it seemed to me that if Hollond felt lonely, there must be more in this world of his than we imagined. I began to wonder if there was any truth in fads like psychical research. Also, I was not so sure that he was as normal as I had thought: it looked as if his nerves might be going bad.

'Oddly enough, Hollond was getting on the same track himself. He had discovered, so he said, that in sleep everybody now and then lived in this new world of his. You know how one dreams of triangular railway platforms with trains running simultaneously down all three sides and not colliding. Well, this sort of cantrip was "common form", as we say at the Bar, in Hollond's Space, and he was very curious about the why and wherefore of Sleep. He began to haunt psychological laboratories, where they experiment with the charwoman and the odd man, and he used to go up to Cambridge for séances. It was a foreign atmosphere to him, and I don't think he was very happy in it. He found so many charlatans that he used to get angry, and declare he would be better employed at Mothers' Meetings!'

From far up the glen came the sound of the pony's hoofs. The stag had been loaded up, and the gillies were returning. Leithen looked at his watch. 'We'd better wait and see the beast,' he said.

'. . . Well, nothing happened for more than a year. Then one evening in May he burst into my rooms in high excitement. You understand quite clearly that there was no suspicion of horror or fright or anything unpleasant about this world he had discovered. It was simply a series of interesting and difficult problems. All this time Hollond had been rather extra well and cheery. But when he came in I thought I noticed a different look in his eyes, something puzzled and diffident and apprehensive.

' "There's a queer performance going on in the other world," he said. "It's unbelievable. I never dreamed of such a thing. I – I don't quite know how to put it, and I don't know how to explain it, but – but I am becoming aware that there are other beings – other minds – moving in Space besides mine."

'I suppose I ought to have realised then that things were beginning to go wrong. But it was very difficult, he was so rational and anxious to make it all clear. I asked him how he knew. There could, of course, on his own showing be no *change* in that world, for the forms of Space moved and existed under inexorable laws. He said he found his own mind failing him at points. There would come over him a sense of fear – intellectual fear – and weakness, a sense of something else, quite alien to Space, thwarting him. Of course he could only describe his impressions very lamely, for they were purely of the mind, and he had no material peg to hang them on, so that I could realise them. But the gist of it was that he had been gradually becoming conscious of what he called "Presences" in his world. They had no effect on Space – did not leave foot-prints in its corridors, for instance – but they affected his mind. There was some mysterious contact established between him and them. I asked him if the affection was unpleasant, and he said "No, not exactly." But I could see a hint of fear in his eyes.

'Think of it. Try to realise what intellectual fear is. I can't, but it is conceivable. To you and me fear implies pain to ourselves or some other, and such pain is always in the last resort pain of the flesh. Consider it carefully and you will see that it is so. But imagine fear so sublimated and transmuted as to be the tension of pure spirit. I can't realise it, but I think it possible. I don't pretend to understand how Hollond got to know about these Presences. But there was no doubt about the fact. He was positive, and he wasn't in the least mad – not in our sense. In that very month he published his book on Number, and gave a German professor who attacked it a most tremendous public trouncing.

'I know what you are going to say – that the fancy was a weakening of the mind from within. I admit I should have thought of that, but he looked so confoundedly sane and able that it seemed ridiculous. He kept asking me my opinion, as a lawyer, on the facts he offered. It was the oddest case ever put before me, but I did my best for him. I dropped all my own views of sense and nonsense. I told him that, taking all that he had told me as fact, the Presences might be either ordinary minds traversing Space in sleep; or minds such as his which had independently captured the sense of Space's quality; or, finally, the spirits of just men made perfect, behaving as psychical researchers think they do. It was a ridiculous task to set a prosaic man, and I wasn't quite serious. But Holland was serious enough.

'He admitted that all three explanations were conceivable, but he was very doubtful about the first. The projection of the spirit into Space during sleep, he thought, was a faint and feeble thing, and these were powerful Presences. With the second and the third he was rather impressed. I suppose I should have seen what was happening and tried to stop it; at least, looking back that seems to have been my duty. But it was difficult to think that anything was wrong with Holland; indeed, the odd thing is that all this time the idea of madness never entered my head. I rather backed him up. Somehow the thing took my fancy, though I thought it moonshine at the bottom of my heart. I enlarged on the pioneering before him. "Think", I told him, "what may be waiting for you. You may discover the meaning of Spirit. You may open up a new world, as rich as the old one, but imperishable. You may prove to mankind their immortality and deliver them for ever from the fear of death. Why, man, you are picking at the lock of all the world's mysteries."

'But Hollond did not cheer up. He seemed strangely languid and dispirited. "That is all true enough," he said, "if you are right, if your alternatives are exhaustive. But suppose they are something else, something . . ." What that "something" might be he had apparently no idea, and very soon he went away.

'He said another thing before he left. He asked me if I ever read poetry, and I said, "Not often". Nor did he: but he had picked up a little book somewhere and found a man who knew about the Presences. I think his name was Traherne, one of the seventeenth-century fellows. He quoted a verse which stuck to my fly-paper memory. It ran something like this:

> Within the region of the air,
> Compassed about with Heavens fair,
> Great tracts of lands there may be found,
> Where many numerous hosts,
> In those far distant coasts,
> For other great and glorious ends
> Inhabit, my yet unknown friends.

Hollond was positive he did not mean angels or anything of the sort. I told him that Traherne evidently took a cheerful view of them. He admitted that, but added: "He had religion, you see. He believed that everything was for the best. I am not a man of faith, and can only take comfort from what I understand. I'm in the dark, I tell you . . ."

'Next week I was busy with the Chilian Arbitration case, and saw nobody for a couple of months. Then one evening I ran against Hollond on the Embankment, and thought him looking horribly ill. He walked back with me to my rooms, and hardly uttered one word all the way. I gave him a stiff whisky-and-soda, which he gulped down absent-mindedly. There was that strained, hunted look in his eyes that you see in a frightened animal's. He was always lean, but now he had fallen away to skin and bone.

' "I can't stay long," he told me, "for I'm off to the Alps tomorrow and I have a lot to do." Before then he used to plunge readily into his story, but now he seemed shy about beginning. Indeed, I had to ask him a question.

' "Things are difficult," he said hesitatingly, "and rather distressing. Do you know, Leithen, I think you were wrong about – about what I spoke to you of. You said there must be one of three explanations. I am beginning to think that there is a fourth . . ."

'He stopped for a second or two, then suddenly leaned forward and gripped my knee so fiercely that I cried out. "That world is the Desolation," he said in a choking voice, "and perhaps I am getting near the Abomination of the Desolation that the old prophet spoke of. I tell you, man, I am on the edge of a terror, a terror", he almost screamed, "that no mortal can think of and live."

'You can imagine that I was considerably startled. It was lightning out of a clear sky. How the devil could one associate horror with mathematics? I don't see it yet . . . At any rate, I— You may be sure I cursed my folly for ever pretending to take him seriously. The only way would have been to have laughed him out of it at the start. And yet I couldn't, you know – it was too real and reasonable.

Anyhow, I tried a firm tone now, and told him the whole thing was arrant raving bosh. I bade him be a man and pull himself together. I made him dine with me, and took him home, and got him into a better state of mind before he went to bed. Next morning I saw him off at Charing Cross, very haggard still, but better. He promised to write to me pretty often . . .'

The pony, with a great eleven-pointer lurching athwart its back, was abreast of us, and from the autumn mist came the sound of soft Highland voices. Leithen and I got up to go, when we heard that the rifle had made direct for the Lodge by a short cut past the Sanctuary. In the wake of the gillies we descended the Correi road into a glen all swimming with dim purple shadows. The pony minced and boggled; the stag's antlers stood out sharp on the rise against a patch of sky, looking like a skeleton tree. Then we dropped into a covert of birches and emerged on the white glen highway.

Leithen's story had bored and puzzled me at the start, but now it had somehow gripped my fancy. Space a domain of endless corridors and Presences moving in them! The world was not quite the same as an hour ago. It was the hour, as the French say, 'between dog and wolf', when the mind is disposed to marvels. I thought of my stalking on the morrow, and was miserably conscious that I would miss my stag. Those airy forms would get in the way. Confound Leithen and his yarns!

'I want to hear the end of your story,' I told him, as the lights of the Lodge showed half a mile distant.

'The end was a tragedy,' he said slowly. 'I don't much care to talk about it. But how was I to know? I couldn't see the nerve going. You see I couldn't believe it was all non-sense. If I could I might have seen. But I still think there was something in it – up to a point. Oh, I agree he went mad in the end. It is the only explanation. Something must have snapped in that fine brain, and he saw the little bit more which we call madness. Thank God, you and I are prosaic fellows . . .

'I was going out to Chamonix myself a week later. But before I started I got a post-card from Hollond, the only word from him. He had printed my name and address, and on the other side had scribbled six words – "*I know at last – God's mercy. – H.G.H.*" The handwriting was like a sick man of ninety. I knew that things must be pretty bad with my friend.

'I got to Chamonix in time for his funeral. An ordinary climbing accident – you probably read about it in the papers. The Press talked about the toll which the Alps took from intellectuals – the usual rot. There was an inquiry, but the facts were quite simple. The body was only recognised by the clothes. He had fallen several thousand feet.

'It seems that he had climbed for a few days with one of the Kronigs and Dupont, and they had done some hair-raising things on the Aiguilles. Dupont told me that they had found a new route up the Montanvert side of the Charmoz. He said that Hollond climbed like a "*diable fou*", and if you know Dupont's standard of madness you will see that the pace must have been pretty hot. "But monsieur was sick," he added; "his eyes were not good. And I and Franz, we were grieved for him and a little afraid. We were glad when he left us."

'He dismissed the guides two days before his death. The next day he spent in the hotel, getting his affairs straight.

173

He left everything in perfect order, but not a line to a soul, not even to his sister. The following day he set out alone about three in the morning for the Grepon. He took the road up the Nantillons glacier to the Col, and then he must have climbed the Mummery crack by himself. After that he left the ordinary route and tried a new traverse across the Mer de Glace face. Somewhere near the top he fell, and next day a party going to the Dent du Requin found him on the rocks thousands of feet below.

'He had slipped in attempting the most foolhardy course on earth, and there was a lot of talk about the dangers of guideless climbing. But I guessed the truth, and I am sure Dupont knew, though he held his tongue . . .'

We were now on the gravel of the drive, and I was feeling better. The thought of dinner warmed my heart and drove out the eeriness of the twilight glen. The hour between dog and wolf was passing. After all, there was a gross and jolly earth at hand for wise men who had a mind to comfort.

Leithen, I saw, did not share my mood. He looked glum and puzzled, as if his tale had aroused grim memories. He finished it at the Lodge door.

'. . . For, of course, he had gone out that day to die. He had seen the something more, the little bit too much, which plucks a man from his moorings. He had gone so far into the land of pure spirit that he must needs go further and shed the fleshly envelope that cumbered him. God send that he found rest! I believe that he chose the steepest cliff in the Alps for a purpose. He wanted to be unrecognisable. He was a brave man and a good citizen. I think he hoped that those who found him might not see the look in his eyes.'

174

'Divus' Johnston

In deorum numerum relatus est non ore modo decernentium sed et persuasione vulgi.

SUETONIUS

We were discussing the vagaries of ambition, and decided that most of the old prizes that humanity contended for had had their gilt rubbed off. Kingdoms, for example, which younger sons used to set out to conquer. It was agreed that nowadays there was a great deal of drudgery and very little fun in being a king.

'Besides, it can't be done,' Leithen put in. 'The Sarawak case. Sovereignty over territory can only be acquired by a British subject on behalf of His Majesty.'

There was far more real power, someone argued, in the profession of prophet. Mass-persuasion was never such a force as today. Sandy Arbuthnot, who had known Gandhi and admired him, gave us a picture of that strange popular leader – ascetic, genius, dreamer, child. 'For a little,' he said, 'Gandhi had more absolute sway over a bigger lump of humanity than anybody except Lenin.'

'I once knew Lenin,' said Fulleylove, the traveller, and we all turned to him.

'It must have been more than twenty years ago,' he explained. 'I was working at the British Museum and lived in lodgings in Bloomsbury, and he had a room at the top of the house. Ilyitch was the name we knew him by. He was a little, beetle-browed chap, with a pale face and the most

175

amazing sleepy black eyes, which would suddenly twinkle and blaze as some thought passed through his mind. He was very pleasant and good-humoured, and would spend hours playing with the landlady's children. I remember I once took him down with me for a day into the country, and he was the merriest little grig . . . Did I realise how big he was? No, I cannot say I did. He was the ordinary Marxist, and he wanted to resurrect Russia by hydraulics and electrification. He seemed to be a funny compound of visionary and *terre-à-terre* scientist. But I realised that he could lay a spell on his countrymen. I have been to Russian meetings with him – I talk Russian, you know – and it was astounding the way he could make his audience look at him like hungry sheep. He gave me the impression of utter courage and candour, and a kind of demoniac simplicity . . . No, I never met him again, but oddly enough I was in Moscow during his funeral. Russian geographers were interesting themselves in the line of the old silk-route to Cathay, and I was there by request to advise them. I had not a very comfortable time, but everybody was very civil to me. So I saw Lenin's funeral, and unless you saw that you can have no notion of his power. A great black bier like an altar, and hundreds and thousands of people weeping and worshipping – yes, worshipping.'

'The successful prophet becomes a kind of god,' said Lamancha. 'Have you ever known a god, Sandy? . . . No more have I. But there is one living today somewhere in Scotland. Johnston is his name. I once met a very particular friend of his. I will tell you the story, and you can believe it or not as you like.'

I had this narrative – he said – from my friend Mr Peter Thomson of 'Jessieville', Maxwell Avenue, Strathbungo, whom I believe to be a man incapable of mendacity, or, indeed, of imagination. He is a prosperous and retired ship's captain, dwelling in the suburbs of Glasgow, who plays two rounds of golf every day of the week, and goes twice every Sunday to a pink, new church. You may often see his ample figure, splendidly habited in broadcloth and finished off with one of those square felt hats which are the Scottish emblem of respectability, moving sedately by Mrs Thomson's side down the avenue of 'Balmorals' and 'Bellevues' where dwell the aristocracy of Strathbungo. It was not there that I met him, however, but in a Clyde steamboat going round the Mull, where I spent a comfortless night on my way to a Highland fishing. It was blowing what he called 'wee bit o' wind', and I could not face the odorous bunks which opened on the dining-room. Seated abaft the funnel, in an atmosphere of ham-and-eggs, bilge and fresh western breezes, he revealed his heart to me, and this I found in it.

'About the age of forty' – said Mr Thomson – 'I was captain of the steamer *Archibald McKelvie*, 1,700 tons burthen, belonging to Brock, Rattray and Linklater of Greenock. We were principally engaged in the China trade, but made odd trips into the Malay Archipelago and once or twice to Australia. She was a handy bit boat, and I'll not deny that I had many mercies vouchsafed to me when I was her skipper. I raked in a bit of salvage now and then, and my trading commission, paid regularly into the British Linen Bank at Maryhill, was mounting up to a fairish sum. I had no objection to Eastern parts, for I had a good constitution and had outgrown the daftnesses of youth. The berth suited me well, I had a decent lot for ship's company, and

I would gladly have looked forward to spending the rest of my days by the *Archibald McKelvie*.

'Providence, however, thought otherwise, for He was preparing a judgment against that ship like the kind you read about in books. We were five days out from Singapore, shaping our course for the Philippines, where the Americans were then fighting, when we ran into a queer lown sea. Not a breath of air came out of the sky; if you kindled a match the flame wouldna leap, but smouldered like touchwood; and every man's body ran with sweat like a mill-lade. I kenned fine we were in for the terrors of hell, but I hadna any kind of notion how terrible hell could be. First came a wind that whipped away my funnel, like a potato-peeling. We ran before it, and it was like the swee-gee we used to play at when we were laddies. One moment the muckle sea would get up on its hinder end and look at you, and the next you were looking at it as if you were on top of Ben Lomond looking down on Luss. Presently I saw land in a gap of the waters, a land with great blood-red mountains, and, thinks I to myself, if we keep up the pace this boat of mine will not be hindered from ending two or three miles inland in somebody's kail-yard. I was just wondering how we would get the *Archibald McKelvie* back to her native element when she saved me the trouble; for she ran dunt on some kind of a rock, and went straight to the bottom.

'I was the only man saved alive, and if you ask me how it happened I don't know. I felt myself choking in a whirlpool; then I was flung through the air and brought down with a smack into deep waters; then I was in the air again, and this time I landed amongst sand and tree-trunks and got a bash on the head which dozened my senses.

178

'When I came to it was morning, and the storm had abated. I was lying about half-way up a beach of fine white sand, for the wave that had carried me landwards in its flow had brought me some of the road back in its ebb. All round me was a sort of free-coup – trees knocked to matchwood, dead fish, and birds and beasts, and some boards which I jaloused came from the *Archibald McKelvie*. I had a big bump on my head, but otherwise I was well and clear in my wits, though empty in the stomach and very dowie in the heart. For I knew something about the islands, of which I supposed this to be one. They were either barren wastes, with neither food nor water, or else they were inhabited by the bloodiest cannibals of the archipelago. It looked as if my choice lay between having nothing to eat and being eaten myself.

'I got up, and, after returning thanks to my Maker, went for a walk in the woods. They were full of queer painted birds, and it was an awful job climbing in and out of the fallen trees. By and by I came into an open bit with a burn where I slockened my thirst. It cheered me up, and I was just beginning to think that this was not such a bad island, and looking to see if I could find anything in the nature of coconuts, when I heard a whistle like a steam-siren. It was some sort of signal, for the next I knew I was in the grip of a dozen savages, my arms and feet were lashed together, and I was being carried swiftly through the forest.

'It was a rough journey, and the discomfort of that heathen handling kept me from reflecting upon my desperate position. After nearly three hours we stopped, and I saw that we had come to a city. The streets were not much to look at, and the houses were mud and thatch, but on a hillock in the middle stood a muckle temple not unlike a

Chinese pagoda. There was a man blowing a horn, and a lot of folk shouting, but I paid no attention, for I was sore troubled with the cramp in my left leg. They took me into one of the huts and made signs that I was to have it for my lodging. They brought me water to wash, and a very respectable dinner, which included a hen and a vegetable not unlike greens. Then they left me to myself, and I lay down and slept for a round of the clock.

'I was three days in that hut. I had plenty to eat and the folk were very civil, but they wouldn't let me outbye and there was no window to look out of. I couldna make up my mind what they wanted with me. I was a prisoner, but they did not behave as if they bore any malice, and I might have thought I was an honoured guest, but for the guards at the door. Time hung heavy on my hands, for I had nothing to read and no light to read by. I said over all the chapters of the Bible and all the Scots songs I could remember, and I tried to make a poem about my adventures, but I stuck at the fifth line, for I couldna find a rhyme to McKelvie.

'On the fourth morning I was awakened by the most deafening din. I saw through the door that the streets were full of folk in holiday clothes, most of them with flowers in their hair and carrying palm branches in their hands. It was like something out of a Bible picture book. After I had my breakfast four lads in long white gowns arrived, and in spite of all my protests they made a bonny spectacle of me. They took off my clothes, me blushing with shame, and rubbed me with a kind of oil that smelt of cinnamon. Then they shaved my chin, and painted on my forehead a mark like a freemason's. Then they put on me a kind of white nightgown with a red sash round the middle, and they wouldna be hindered from clapping on my head a great wreath of hothouse flowers, as if I was a funeral.

'And then like a thunder-clap I realised my horrible position. *I was a funeral.* I was to be offered up as a sacrifice to some heathen god – an awful fate for a Free-kirk elder in the prime of life.

'I was so paralytic with terror I never tried to resist. Indeed, it would have done me little good, for outside there were, maybe, two hundred savages, armed and drilled like soldiers. I was put into a sort of palanquin, and my bearers started at a trot with me up the hill to the temple, the whole population of the city running alongside, and singing songs about their god. I was sick with fear, and I durstna look up, for I did not know what awesome sight awaited me.

'At last I got my courage back. "Peter," I says to myself, "be a man. Remember your sainted Covenanting fore-fathers. You have been chosen to testify for your religion, though it's no likely that yon savages will understand what you say." So I shut my jaw and resolved before I died to make a declaration of my religious principles, and to loosen some of the heathen's teeth with my fists.

'We stopped at the temple door and I was led through a court and into a muckle great place like a barn, with bats flying about the ceiling. Here there were nearly three thousand heathens sitting on their hunkers. They sang a hymn when they saw me, and I was just getting ready for action when my bearers carried me into another place, which I took to be the Holy of Holies. It was about half the size of the first, and at the end of it was a great curtain of leopards' skins hanging from roof to floor. My bearers set me in the middle of the room, and then rolled about on their stomachs in adoration before the curtain. After a bit they finished their prayers and crawled out backwards, and I was left alone in that fearsome place.

'It was the worst experience of my life. I believed that behind the skins there was a horrible idol, and that at any moment a priest with a knife would slip in to cut my throat. You may crack about courage, but I tell you that a man who can wait without a quiver on his murderers in the middle of a gloomy kirk is more than human. I am not ashamed to confess that the sweat ran over my brow, and my teeth were knocking in my head.

'But nothing happened. Nothing, except that as I sat there I began to notice a most remarkable smell. At first I thought the place was on fire. Then I thought it was the kind of stink called incense that they make in Popish kirks, for I once wandered into a cathedral in Santiago. But neither guess was right, and then I put my thumb on the proper description. It was nothing but the smell of the third-class carriages on the Coatbridge train on a Saturday night after a football match – the smell of plug tobacco smoked in clay pipes that were no just very clean. My eyes were getting accustomed to the light, and I found the place no that dark; and as I looked round to see what caused the smell, I spied something like smoke coming from beyond the top of the curtain.

'I noticed another thing. There was a hole in the curtain, about six feet from the floor, and at that hole as I watched I saw an eye. My heart stood still, for, thinks I, that'll be the priest of Baal who presently will stick a knife into me. It was long ere I could screw up courage to look again, but I did it. And then I saw that the eye was not that of a savage, which would be black and blood-shot. It was a blue eye, and, as I looked, it winked at me.

182

'And then a voice spoke out from behind the curtain, and this was what it said. It said, "God-sake, Peter, is that you? And how did ye leave them a' at Maryhill?"

'And from behind the curtain walked a muckle man, dressed in a pink blanket, a great red-headed man, with a clay pipe in his mouth. It was the god of the savages, and who do ye think it was? A man Johnston, who used to bide in the same close as me in Glasgow . . .'

Mr Thomson's emotion overcame him, and he accepted a stiff drink from my flask. Wiping away a tear, which may have been of sentiment or of mirth, he continued:

'You may imagine that I was joyful and surprised to see him, and he, so to speak, fell on my neck like the father of the Prodigal Son. He hadna seen a Scotch face for four years. He raked up one or two high priests and gave instructions, and soon I was comfortably lodged in a part of the temple close to his own rooms. Eh, man, it was a noble sight to see Johnston and the priests. He was a big, red-haired fellow, six feet four, and as strong as a stot, with a voice like a north-easter, and yon natives fair crawled like caterpillars in his presence. I never saw a man with such a natural talent for being a god. You would have thought he had been bred to the job all his days, and yet I minded him keeping a grocer's shop in the Dalmarnock Road.

'That night he told me his story. It seemed that he had got a post in Shanghai in a trading house, and was coming out to it in one of those God-forgotten German tramps that defile the China seas. Like me, he fell in with a hurricane, and, like me, his ship was doomed. He was a powerful swimmer, and managed to keep afloat until he found some drifting wreckage, and after the wind had

183

gone down he paddled ashore. There he was captured by the savages, and taken, like me, to their city. They were going to sacrifice him, but one chief, wiser than the rest, called attention to his size and strength, and pointed out that they were at war with their neighbours, and that a big man would be of more use in the fighting line than on an altar in the temple.

'So off went Johnston to the wars. He was a bonny fighter, and very soon they made him captain of the royal bodyguard, and a fortnight later the general commanding-in-chief over the whole army. He said he had never enjoyed himself so much in his life, and when he got back from his battles the whole population of the city used to meet him with songs and flowers. Then an old priest found an ancient prophecy about a Red God who would come out of the sea and lead the people to victory. Very soon there was a strong party for making Johnston a god, and when, with the help of a few sticks of trade dynamite, he had blown up the capital of the other side and brought back his army in triumph with a prisoner apiece, popular feeling could not be restrained. Johnston was hailed as divine. He hadna much grip of the language, and couldna explain the situation, so he thought it best to submit.

' "Mind you," he said to me, "I've been a good god to these poor blind ignorant folk." He had stopped the worst of their habits and put down human sacrifices, and got a sort of town council appointed to keep the city clean, and he had made the army the most efficient thing ever heard of in the islands. And now he was preparing to leave. This was what they expected, for the prophecy had said that the Red God, after being the saviour of his people, would depart as he had come across the sea. So, under his directions, they had built him a kind of boat with which he hoped to reach Singapore. He had got together a consider-able fortune, too, chiefly in rubies, for as a god he had plenty of opportunities of acquiring wealth honestly. He said there was a sort of greengrocer's and butcher's shop before his altar every morning, and he got one of the priests, who had some business notions, to sell off the goods for him.

'There was just one thing that bothered Mr Johnston. He was a good Christian man and had been an elder in a kirk in the Cowcaddens, and he was much in doubt whether he had not committed a mortal sin in accepting the worship of these heathen islanders. Often I argued it out with him, but I did not seem able to comfort him rightly. "Ye see," he used to say to me, "if I have broken anything, it's the spirit and no the letter of the command-ment. I havena set up a graven image, for ye canna call me a graven image."

'I mind that I quoted to him the conduct of Naaman, who was allowed to bow in the house of Rimmon, but he would not have it. "No, no," he cried, "that has nothing to do with the point. It's no a question of my bowing in the house of Rimmon. I'm auld Rimmon himself." '

'That's a strange story, Mr Thomson,' I said. 'Is it true?'

'True as death. But you havena heard the end of it. We got away, and by-and-by we reached Singapore, and in course of time our native land. Johnston, he was a very rich man now, and I didna go without my portion; so the loss of the *Archibald McKelvie* turned out the best piece of luck in my life. I bought a share in Brock's Line, but nothing would content Johnston but that he must be a gentleman. He got a big estate in Annandale, where all the Johnstons came from long ago, and one way and another he has spent an awful siller on it. Land will swallow up money quicker than the sea.'

'And what about his conscience?' I asked.

'It's keeping quieter,' said Mr Thomson. 'He takes a great interest in Foreign Missions, to which he subscribes largely, and they tell me that he has given the funds to build several new kirks. Oh yes, and he's just been adopted as a prospective Liberal candidate. I had a letter from him no further back than yesterday. It's about his political career, as he calls it. He told me, what didna need telling, that I must never mention a word about his past. "If discretion was necessary before," he says, "it's far more necessary now, for how could the Party of Progress have any confidence in a man if they heard he had once been a god?" '

Basilissa

When Vernon was a very little boy he was the sleepiest of mortals, but in the spring he had seasons of bad dreams, and breakfast became an idle meal. Mrs Ganthony, greatly concerned, sent for Dr Moreton from Axby, and homely remedies were prescribed.

'It is the spring fever,' said the old man. 'It gives the gout to me and nightmares to this baby; it brings lads and lasses together, and scatters young men about the world. An antique complaint, Mrs Ganthony. But it will right itself, never fear. *Ver non semper viret.*' Chuckling at his ancient joke, the doctor mounted his horse, leaving the nurse only half comforted. 'What fidgets me', she told the housekeeper, 'is the way his lordship holds his tongue. For usual he'll shout as lusty as a whelp. But now I finds him in the morning with his eyes like moons and his skin white and shiny, and never a cheep has he given the whole blessed night, with me laying next door, and it open, and a light sleeper at all times, Mrs Wace, ma'am.'

Every year the dreams came, generally – for his springs were spent at Severns – in the big new night-nursery at the top of the west wing, which his parents had built not long before their death. It had three windows looking over the moorish flats which run up to the Lancashire fells, and from one window, by craning your neck, you could catch a glimpse of the sea. It was all hung, too, with a Chinese paper whereon pink and green parrots squatted in wonderful blue trees, and there seemed generally to be a wood fire burning. Vernon's recollections of his childish nightmare are hazy. He always found himself in a room different from the nursery and bigger, but with the same smell of wood smoke. People came and went, such as his nurse, the butler, Simon the head-keeper, Uncle Appleby his guardian, Cousin Jennifer, the old woman who sold oranges in Axby, and a host of others. Nobody hindered them from going away, and they seemed to be pleading with him to come too. There was danger in the place; something was going to happen in that big room, and if by that time he was not gone there would be mischief. But it was quite clear to him that he could not go. He must stop there, with the wood smoke in his nostrils, and await the advent of a terrible Something. But he was never quite sure of the nature of the compulsion. He had a notion that if he made a rush for the door at Uncle Appleby's heels he would be allowed to escape, but that somehow he would be behaving badly. Anyhow, the place put him into a sweat of fright, and Mrs Ganthony looked darkly at him in the morning.

Vernon was nine before this odd spring dream began to take definite shape – at least he thinks he must have been about that age. The dream-stage was emptying. There was nobody in the room now but himself, and he saw its details a little more clearly. It was not any apartment in the modern magnificence of Severns. Rather it looked like one of the big old panelled chambers which the boy remembered from visits to Midland country-houses, where he had arrived after dark and had been put to sleep in a great bed in a place lit with dancing firelight. In the morning it had looked only an ordinary big room, but at that hour of the evening it had seemed an enchanted citadel.

The dream-room was not unlike these, for there was the scent of a wood fire and there were dancing shadows, but he could not see clearly the walls or the ceiling, and there was no bed. In one corner was a door which led to the outer world, and through this he knew that he might on no account pass. Another door faced him, and he knew that he had only to turn the handle and enter it. But he did not want to, for he understood quite clearly what was beyond. There was another room like the first one, but he knew nothing about it, except that opposite the entrance another door led out of it. Beyond was a third chamber, and so on interminably. There seemed to the boy no end to this fantastic suite. He thought of it as a great snake of masonry, winding up hill and down dale away to the fells or the sea. Yes, but there was an end. Somewhere far away in one of the rooms was a terror waiting on him, or, as he feared, coming towards him. Even now it might be flitting from room to room, every minute bringing its soft tread nearer to the chamber of the wood fire.

About this time of life the dream was an unmitigated horror. Once it came while he was ill with a childish fever, and it sent his temperature up to a point which brought Dr Moreton galloping from Axby. In his waking hours he did not, as a rule, remember it clearly; but during the fever, asleep and awake, that sinuous building, one room thick, with each room opening from the other, was never away from his thoughts. It fretted him to think that outside were the cheerful moors where he hunted for plovers' eggs, and that only a thin wall of stone kept him from pleasant homely things. The thought used to comfort him for a moment when he was awake, but in the dream it never came near him. Asleep, the whole world seemed one suite of rooms, and he, a forlorn little prisoner, doomed to wait grimly on the slow coming through the many doors of a Fear which transcended word and thought.

He was a silent, self-absorbed boy, and though the fact of his nightmares was patent to the little household, the details remained locked in his heart. Not even to Uncle Appleby would he tell them when that gentleman, hurriedly kind, came down to visit his convalescent ward. His illness made Vernon grow, and he shot up into a lanky, leggy boy – weakly, too, till the hills tautened his sinews again. His Greek blood – his grandmother had been a Karolides – had given him a face curiously like the young Byron, with a finely-cut brow and nostrils, and hauteur in the full lips. But Vernon had no Byronic pallor, for his upland home kept him sunburnt and weather-beaten, and below his straight Greek brows shone a pair of grey and steadfast and very English eyes.

He was about fifteen – so he thinks – when he made the great discovery. The dream had become almost a custom now. It came in April at Severns during the Easter holidays – a night's discomfort (it was now scarcely more) in the rush and glory of the spring fishing. There was a moment of the old wild heart-fluttering; but a boy's fancy is quickly dulled, and the endless corridors were now more of a prison than a witch's ante-chamber. By this time, with the help of his diary, he had fixed the date of the dream: it came regularly on the night of the first Monday of April. Now the year I speak of he had been on a long expedition into the hills, and had stridden homewards at a steady four miles an hour among the gleams and shadows of an April twilight. He was alone at Severns, so he had his supper in the big library, where afterwards he sat watching the leaping flames in the open stone hearth. He was very weary, and sleep fell upon him in his chair. He found himself in the wood-smoke chamber, and before him the door leading to the unknown. But it was no indefinite fear that lay beyond. He knew clearly – though how he knew he could not tell – that each year the Something came one room nearer, and was even now but ten rooms off. In ten years his own door would open, and then –

He woke in the small hours, chilled and mazed, but with a curious new assurance in his heart. Hitherto the nightmare had left him in gross terror, unable to endure the prospect of its recurrence, till the kindly forgetfulness of youth had soothed him. But now, though his nerves were tense with fright, he perceived that there was a limit to the mystery. Some day it must declare itself, and fight on equal terms. As he thought over the matter in the next few days he had the sense of being forewarned and prepared for some great test of courage. The notion exhilarated as much as it frightened him. Late at night, or on soft, dripping days, or at any moment of lessened vitality, he would bitterly wish that he had been born an ordinary mortal. But on a keen morning of frost, when he rubbed himself warm after a cold tub, or at high noon of summer, the adventure of the dream almost pleased him. Unconsciously he braced himself to a harder discipline. His fitness, moral and physical, became his chief interest, for reasons which would have been unintelligible to his friends and more so to his masters. He passed through school an aloof and splendid figure, magnificently athletic, with a brain as well as a perfect body – a good fellow in everybody's opinion, but a grave one. He had no intimates, and never shared the secret of the spring dream. For some reason which he could not tell, he would have burned his hand off rather than breathe a hint of it. Pure terror absolves from all conventions and demands a confidant, so terror, I think, must have largely departed from the nightmare as he grew older. Fear, indeed, remained, and awe and disquiet, but these are human things, whereas terror is of hell.

Had he told anyone, he would no doubt have become self-conscious and felt acutely his difference from other people. As it was, he was an ordinary schoolboy, much beloved, and, except at odd moments, unaware of any brooding destiny. As he grew up and his ambition awoke, the moments when he remembered the dream were apt to be disagreeable, for a boy's ambitions are strictly conventional and his soul revolts at the abnormal. By the time he was ready for the University he wanted above all things to run the mile a second faster than anyone else, and had vague hopes of exploring wild countries. For most of the year he lived with these hopes and was happy; then came April, and for a short season he was groping in dark places. Before and after each dream he was in a mood of exasperation; but when it came he plunged into a different atmosphere, and felt the quiver of fear and the quick thrill of expectation. One year, in the unsettled moods of nineteen, he made an attempt to avoid it. He and three others were on a walking tour in Brittany in gusty spring weather, and came late one evening to an inn by an estuary where seagulls clattered about the windows. Youth-like they ordered a great and foolish feast, and sat all night round a bowl of punch, while school songs and 'John Peel' contended with the dirling of the gale. At daylight they took the road again, without having closed an eye, and Vernon told himself that he was rid of his incubus. He wondered at the time why he was not more cheerful. Next April he was at Severns, reading hard, and on the first Monday of the month he went to bed with scarcely a thought of what that night used to mean. The dream did not fail him. Once more he was in the chamber with the wood fire; once again he was peering at the door and wondering with tremulous heart what lay beyond. For the Something had come nearer by two rooms, and was now only five doors away. He wrote in his diary at that time some lines from Keats' 'Indian Maid's Song':

> I would deceive her,
> And so leave her,
> But ah! she is so constant and so kind.

And there is a mark of exclamation against the 'she', as if he found some irony in it.

From that day the boy in him died. The dream would not suffer itself to be forgotten. It moulded his character and determined his plans like the vow of the young Hannibal at the altar. He had forgotten now either to fear or to hope; the thing was part of him, like his vigorous young body, his slow kindliness, his patient courage. He left Oxford at twenty-two with a prodigious reputation which his remarkable athletic record by no means explained. All men liked him, but no one knew him; he had a thousand acquaintances and a hundred friends, but no comrade. There was a sense of brooding power about him which attracted and repelled his little world. No one forecast any special career for him; indeed, it seemed almost disrespectful to condescend upon such details. It was not what Vernon would do that fired the imagination of his fellows, but what they dimly conceived that he already was. I remember my first sight of him about that time, a tall young man in his corner of a club smoking-room, with a head like Apollo's and eyes which received much but gave nothing. I guessed at once that he had foreign blood in him, not from any oddness of colouring or feature but from his silken reserve. We of the North are angular in our silences; we have not learned the art of gracious reticence.

His twenty-third April was spent in a hut on the Line, somewhere between the sources of the Congo and the Nile, in the trans-African expedition when Waldemar found the new variety of okapi. The following April I was in his company in a tent far up on the shoulder of a Kashmir mountain. On the first Monday of the month we had had a heavy day after ovis, and that night I was asleep almost before my weary limbs were tucked into my kaross. I knew nothing of Vernon's dream, but next morning I remember that I remarked a certain heaviness of eye, and wondered idly if the frame of this Greek divinity was as tough as it was shapely.

Next year Vernon left England early in March. He had resolved to visit again his grandmother's country and to indulge his passion for cruising in new waters.

His twenty ton yawl was sent as deck cargo to Patras, while he followed by way of Venice. He brought one man with him from Wyvenhoe, a lean gypsy lad called Martell, and for his other hand he found an Epirote at Corfu, who bore a string of names that began with Constantine. From Patras with a west wind they made good sailing up the Gulf of Corinth, and, passing through the Canal, came in the last days of March to the Piraeus. In that place of polyglot speech, whistling engines and the odour of gas-works, they delayed only for water and supplies, and presently had rounded Sunium, and were beating up the Euripus with the Attic hills rising sharp and clear in the spring sunlight. Vernon had no plan. It was a joy to him to be alone with the racing seas and the dancing winds, to scud past little headlands, pink and white with blossom, or to lie of a night in some hidden bay beneath the thymy crags. It was his habit on his journeys to discard the clothes of civilisation. In a blue jersey and old corduroy trousers, bare-headed and barefooted, he steered his craft and waited on the passing of the hours. Like an acolyte before the temple gate, he believed himself to be on the threshold of a new life.

Trouble began under the snows of Pelion as they turned the north end of Euboea. On the morning of the first Monday in April the light west winds died away, and scirocco blew harshly from the south. By midday it was half a gale, and in those yeasty shallow seas with an iron coast on the port the prospect looked doubtful. The nearest harbour was twenty miles distant, and as no one of the crew had been there before it was a question if they could make it by nightfall. With the evening the gale increased, and Constantine advised a retreat from the maze of rocky islands to the safer deeps of the Aegean. It was a hard night for the three, and there was no chance of sleep. More by luck than skill they escaped the butt of Skiathos, and the first light found them far to the east among the long seas of the North Aegean, well on the way to Lemnos. By eight o'clock the gale had blown itself out, and three soaked and chilly mortals relaxed their vigil. Soon bacon was frizzling on the cuddy-stove, and hot coffee and dry clothes restored them to comfort.

The sky cleared, and in bright sunlight, with the dregs of the gale behind him, Vernon stood in for the mainland, where the white crest of Olympus hung in the northern heavens. In the late afternoon they came into a little bay carved from the side of a high mountain. The slopes were gay with flowers, yellow and white and scarlet, and the young green of crops showed in the clearings. Among the thyme a flock of goats was browsing, shepherded by a little girl in a saffron skirt, who sang shrilly in snatches. Midway in the bay and just above the anchorage rose a great white building, which showed to seaward a blank white wall pierced with a few narrow windows. At first sight Vernon took it for a monastery, but a look through the glasses convinced him that its purpose was not religious. Once it had been fortified, and even now a broad causeway ran between it and the sea, which looked as if it had once held guns. The architecture was a jumble, showing here the enriched Gothic of Venice and there the straight lines and round arches of the East. It had once, he conjectured, been the hold of some Venetian sea-king, then the palace of a Turkish conqueror, and now was, perhaps, the homely manor-house of this pleasant domain.

A fishing-boat was putting out from the shore. He hailed its occupant and asked who owned the castle.

The man crossed himself and spat overboard. 'Basilissa,' he said, and turned his eyes seaward.

Vernon called Constantine from the bows and asked him what the word might mean. The Epirote crossed himself also before he spoke. 'It is the Lady of the Land,' he said, in a hushed voice. 'It is the great witch who is the Devil's bride. In old days in spring they made sacrifice to her, but they say her power is dying now. In my country we do not speak her name, but elsewhere they call her "Queen".' The man's bluff sailorly assurance had disappeared, and as Vernon stared at him in bewilderment he stammered and averted his eyes.

By supper-time he had recovered himself, and the weather-beaten three made such a meal as befits those who have faced danger together. Afterwards Vernon, as was his custom, sat alone in the stern, smoking and thinking his thoughts. He wrote up his diary with a ship's lantern beside him, while overhead the starless velvet sky seemed to hang low and soft like an awning. Little fires burned on the shore at which folk were cooking food – he could hear their voices, and from the keep one single lit window made an eye in the night.

He had leisure now for the thought which had all day been at the back of his mind. The night had passed and there had been no dream. The adventure for which he had prepared himself had vanished into the Aegean tides. He told himself that it was a relief, that an old folly was over, but he knew in his heart that he was bitterly disappointed. The fates had prepared the stage and rung up the curtain without providing the play. He had been fooled, and somehow the zest and savour of life had gone from him. No man can be strung high and then find his preparation idle without suffering a cruel recoil.

As he scribbled idly in his diary he found some trouble about dates. Down in his bunk was a sheaf of Greek papers bought at the Piraeus and still unlooked at. He fetched them up and turned them over with a growing mystification. There was something very odd about the business. One gets hazy about dates at sea, but he could have sworn that he had made no mistake. Yet here it was down in black and white, for there was no question about the number of days since he left the Piraeus. The day was not

197

Tuesday, as he had believed, but Monday, the first Monday of April.

He stood up with a beating heart and that sense of unseen hands which comes to all men once or twice in their lives. The night was yet to come, and with it the end of the dream. Suddenly he was glad, absurdly glad, he could almost have wept with the joy of it. And then he was conscious for the first time of the strangeness of the place in which he had anchored. The night was dark over him like a shell, enclosing the half-moon of bay and its one lit dwelling. The great hills, unseen but felt, ran up to snows, warding it off from a profane world. His nerves tingled with a joyful anticipation. Something, some wonderful thing, was coming to him out of the darkness.

Under an impulse for which he could give no reason, he called Constantine and gave his orders. Let him be ready to sail at any moment – a possible thing, for there was a light breeze off shore. Also let the yacht's dinghy be ready in case he wanted it. Then Vernon sat himself down again in the stern beside the lantern, and waited . . .

He was dreaming, and did not hear the sound of oars or the grating of a boat alongside. Suddenly he found a face looking at him in the ring of lamplight – an old bearded face curiously wrinkled. The eyes, which were grave and penetrating, scanned him for a second or two, and then a voice spoke –

'Will the Signor come with me? There is work for him to do this night.'

Vernon rose obediently. He had waited for this call these many years, and he was there to answer it. He went below and put a loaded revolver in his trouser-pocket, and then dropped over the yacht's side into a cockleshell of a boat. The messenger took the oars and rowed for the point of light on shore.

A middle-aged woman stood on a rock above the tide, holding a small lantern. In its thin flicker he made out a person with the air and dress of a French maid. She cast one glance at Vernon, and then turned wearily to the other. 'Fool, Mitri!' she said. 'You have brought a peasant.'

'Nay,' said the old man, 'he is no peasant. He is a Signor, and as I judge, a man of his hands.'

The woman passed the light of her lantern over Vernon's form and face. 'His dress is a peasant's, but such clothes may be a nobleman's whim. I have heard it of the English.'

'I am English,' said Vernon in French.

She turned on him with a quick movement of relief.

'You are English and a gentleman? But I know nothing of you, only that you have come out of the sea. Up in the House we women are alone, and my mistress has death to face, or a worse than death. We have no claim on you, and if you give us your service it means danger – ah, what danger! The boat is waiting. You have time to go back and go away and forget that you have seen this accursed place. But, O Monsieur, if you hope for Heaven and have pity on a defenceless angel, you will not leave us.'

'I am ready,' said Vernon.

'God's mercy,' she sighed, and, seizing his arm, drew him up the steep causeway, while the old man went ahead with the lantern. Now and then she cast anxious glances to the right where the little fires of the fishers twinkled along the shore. Then came a point when the three entered a narrow uphill road, where rocky steps had been cut in a tamarisk thicket. She spoke low in French to Vernon's ear –

'My mistress is the last of her line, you figure; a girl with a wild estate and a father long dead. She is good and gracious, as I who have tended her can witness, but she is young and cannot govern the wolves who are the men of these parts. They have a long hatred of her house, and now they have rumoured it that she is a witch and blights the crops and slays the children. No one will look at her; the priest – for they are all in the plot – signs himself and crosses the road; the little ones run screaming to their mothers. Once, twice, they have cursed our threshold and made the blood mark on the door. For two years we have been prisoners in the House, and only Mitri is true. They name her Basilissa, meaning the Queen of Hell, whom the ancients called Proserpine. There is no babe but will faint with fright if it casts eyes on her, and she as mild and innocent as Mother Mary . . .'

The woman stopped at a little door in a high wall of masonry. 'Nay, wait and hear me out. It is better that you hear the tale from me than from her. Mitri has the gossip of the place through his daughter's husband, and the word has gone round to burn the witch out. The winter in the hills has been cruel, and they blame their sorrow on her. The dark of the moon in April is the time fixed, for they say that a witch has power only in moonlight. This is the night, and down on the shore the fishers are gathered. The men from the hills are in the higher woods.'

'Have they a leader?' Vernon asked.

'A leader?' her voice echoed shrilly. 'But that is the worst of our terrors. There is one Vlastos, a lord in the mountains, who saw my mistress a year ago as she looked from the balcony at the Swallow-singing, and was filled with a passion for her. He has persecuted her since with his desires.

He is a king among these savages, being himself a very wolf in man's flesh. We have denied him, but he persists, and this night he announces that he comes for an answer. He offers to save her if she will trust him, but what is the honour of his kind? He is like a brute out of a cave. It were better for my lady to go to God in the fire than to meet all Hell in his arms. But this night we must choose, unless you prove a saviour.'

'Did you see my boat anchor in the bay?' Vernon asked, though he already knew the answer.

'But no,' she said. 'We live only to the landward side of the House. My lady told me that God would send a man to our aid. And I bade Mitri fetch him.'

The door was unlocked and the three climbed a staircase which seemed to follow the wall of a round tower. Presently they came into a stone hall with curious hangings like the old banners in a church. From the open flame of the lantern another was kindled, and the light showed a desolate place with crumbling mosaics on the floor and plaster dropping from the cornices. Through another corridor they went, where the air blew warmer and there was that indefinable scent which comes from human habitation. Then came a door which the woman held open for Vernon to enter. 'Wait there, Monsieur,' she said. 'My mistress will come to you.'

It was his own room, where annually he had waited with a fluttering heart since he was a child at Severns. A fire of wood – some resinous thing like juniper – burned on the hearth, and spirals of blue smoke escaped the stone chimney and filled the air with their pungent fragrance. On a Spanish cabinet stood an antique silver lamp, and there was a great blue Chinese vase filled with spring flowers.

Soft Turcoman rugs covered the wooden floor – Vernon noted every detail for never before had he been able to see his room clearly. A woman had lived here, for an embroidery frame lay on a table and there were silken cushions on the low divans. And facing him in the other wall there was a door.

In the old days he had regarded it with vague terror in his soul. Now he looked at it with the hungry gladness with which a traveller sees again the familiar objects of home. The hour of his destiny had struck. The thing for which he had trained himself in body and spirit was about to reveal itself in that doorway . . .

It opened, and a girl entered. She was tall and very slim, and moved with the free grace of a boy. She trod the floor like one walking in spring meadows. Her little head on the flower-like neck was bent sideways as if she were listening, and her eyes had the strange disquieting innocence of a child's. Yet she was a grown woman, nobly made, and lithe and supple as Artemis herself when she ranged with her maidens through the moonlit glades. Her face had the delicate pallor of pure health, and above it the masses of dark hair were bound with a thin gold circlet. She wore a gown of some soft white stuff, and had thrown over it a cloak of russet furs.

For a second – or so it seemed to Vernon – she looked at him as he stood tense and expectant like a runner at the start. Then the hesitation fled from her face. She ran to him with the confidence of a child who has waited long for the coming of a friend and has grown lonely and fearful. She gave him both her hands and in her tall pride looked him full in the eyes. 'You have come,' she sighed happily. 'I did not doubt it. They told me there was no help,

202

but, you see, they did not know about you. That was my own secret. The Monster had nearly gobbled me, Perseus, but of course you could not come quicker. And now you will take me away with you? See, I am ready. And Elise will come too, and old Mitri, for they could not live without me. We must hurry, for the Monster is very near.'

In that high moment of romance, when young love had burst upon him like spring, Vernon retained his odd discipline of soul. The adventure of the dream could not be satisfied by flight, even though his companion was a goddess.

'We will go, Andromeda, but not yet. I have something to say to the Monster.'

She broke into a ripple of laughter. 'Yes, that is the better way. Mitri will admit him alone, and he will think to find us women. But you will be here and you will speak to him.' Then her eyes grew solemn. 'He is very cruel, Perseus, and he is full of evil. He may devour us both. Let us be gone before he comes.'

It was Vernon's turn to laugh. At the moment no enterprise seemed too formidable, and a price must be paid for this far-away princess. And even as he laughed the noise of a great bell clanged through the house.

Mitri stole in with a scared face, and it was from Vernon that he took his orders. 'Speak them fair, but let one man enter and no more. Bring him here, and see that the gate is barred behind him. After that make ready for the road.' Then to the girl: 'Take off your cloak and wait here as if you were expecting him. I will stand behind the screen. Have no fear, for I will have him covered, and I will shoot him like a dog if he lays a finger on you.'

From the shelter of the screen Vernon saw the door open and a man enter. He was a big fellow of the common mountain type, gorgeously dressed in a uniform of white and crimson, with boots of yellow untanned leather, and a beltful of weapons. He was handsome in a coarse way, but his slanting eyes and the heavy lips scarcely hidden by the curling moustaches were ugly and sinister. He smiled, showing his white teeth, and spoke hurriedly in the guttural Greek of the north. The girl shivered at the sound of his voice, and to the watcher it seemed like Pan pursuing one of Dian's nymphs.

'You have no choice, my Queen,' he was saying. 'I have a hundred men at the gate who will do my bidding, and protect you against these fools of villagers till you are safe with me at Louko. But if you refuse me I cannot hold the people. They will burn the place over your head, and by tomorrow's morn these walls will be smouldering ashes with your fair body in the midst of them.'

Then his wooing became rougher. The satyr awoke in his passionate eyes. 'Nay, you are mine, whether you will it or not. I and my folk will carry you off when the trouble begins. Take your choice, my girl, whether you will go with a good grace, or trussed up behind a servant. We have rough ways in the hills with ungracious wenches.'

'I am going away,' she whispered, 'but not with you!'

The man laughed. 'Have you fetched down friend Michael and his angels to help you? By Saint John the Hunter, I would I had a rival. I would carve him prettily for the sake of your sweet flesh.'

Vernon kicked aside the screen. 'You will have your chance,' he said. 'I am ready.'

Vlastos stepped back with his hand at his belt. 'Who in the devil's name are you?' he asked.

'One who would dispute the lady with you,' said Vernon.

The man had recovered his confidence. 'I know nothing of you or whence you come, but tonight I am merciful. I give you ten seconds to disappear. If not, I will spit you, my fine cock, and you will roast in this oven.'

'Nevertheless the lady goes with me,' said Vernon, smiling.

Vlastos plucked a whistle from his belt, but before it reached his mouth he was looking into the barrel of Vernon's revolver. 'Pitch that thing on the floor,' came the command. 'Not there! Behind me! Off with that belt and give it to the lady. Quick, my friend.'

The dancing grey eyes dominated the sombre black ones. Vlastos flung down the whistle, and slowly removed the belt with its silver-mounted pistols and its brace of knives.

'Put up your weapon', he muttered, 'and fight me for her, as a man should.'

'I ask nothing better,' said Vernon, and he laid his revolver in the girl's lap.

He had expected a fight with fists, and was not prepared for what followed. Vlastos sprang at him like a wild beast and clasped him round the waist. He was swung off his feet in a grip that seemed more than human. For a second or two he swayed to and fro, recovered himself, and by a back-heel stroke forced his assailant to relax a little. Then, locked together in the middle of the room, the struggle began. Dimly out of a corner of his eye he saw the girl pick up the silver lamp and stand by the door holding it high.

Vernon had learned the rudiments of wrestling among the dalesmen of the North, but now he was dealing with one who followed no ordinary methods. It was a contest of sheer physical power. Vlastos was a stone or two heavier, and had an uncommon length of arm; but he was clumsily made, and flabby from gross living. Vernon was spare and hard and clean, but he lacked one advantage – he had never striven with a man save in friendly games, and the other was bred to kill. For a minute or two they swayed and stumbled, while Vernon strove for the old Westmorland 'inside click'. Every second brought him nearer to it, while the other's face was pressed close to his shoulder.

Suddenly he felt a sharp pain. Teeth met in his flesh, and there was the jar and shiver of a torn muscle. The thing sickened him, and his grip slackened. In a moment Vlastos had swung him over in a strangle-hold, and had his neck bent almost to breaking.

On the sickness followed a revulsion of fierce anger. He was contending not with a man, but with some shaggy beast from the thicket. The passion brought out the extra power which is dormant in us all against the last extremity. Two years before he had been mauled by a leopard on the Congo, and had clutched its throat with his hand and torn the life out. Such and no other was his antagonist. He was fighting with one who knew no code, and would gouge his eyes if he got the chance. The fear which had sickened him was driven out by fury. This wolf should go the way of other wolves who dared to strive with man.

By a mighty effort he got his right arm free, and though his own neck was in torture, he forced Vlastos' chin upward. It was a struggle of sheer endurance, till with a snarl the other slackened his pressure. Vernon slipped from his grasp, gave back a step, and then leaped for the under-grip. He seemed possessed with unholy strength, for the barrel of the man gave in his embrace. A rib cracked, and as they swayed to the breast-stroke, he felt the breath of his opponent coming in harsh gasps. It was the end, for with a twist which unlocked his arms he swung him high, and hurled him towards the fireplace. The head crashed on the stone hearth, and the man lay stunned among the blue jets of wood smoke.

Vernon turned dizzily to the girl. She stood, statue-like, with the lamp in her hand, and beside her huddled Mitri and Elise.

'Bring ropes,' he cried to the servants. 'We will truss up this beast. The other wolves will find him and learn a lesson.' He bound his legs and arms and laid him on a divan.

The fire of battle was still in his eyes, but it faded when they fell upon the pale girl. A great pity and tenderness filled him. She swayed to his arms, and her head dropped on his shoulder. He picked her up like a child, and followed the servants to the sea-stair.

But first he found Vlastos' whistle, and blew it shrilly. The answer was a furious hammering at the castle door . . .

Far out at sea, in the small hours, the yacht sped eastward with a favouring wind. Behind in the vault of night at a great distance shone a point of brightness, which flickered and fell as if from some mighty fire.

The two sat in the stern in that first rapture of comradeship which has no words to fit it. Her head lay in the crook of his arm, and she sighed happily, like one awakened to a summer's dawn from a night of ill dreams. At last he spoke.

'Do you know that I have been looking for you for twenty years?'

She nestled closer to him.

'And I', she said, 'have been waiting on you from the beginning of the world.'

Fullcircle

Between the Windrush and the Colne
I found a little house of stone –
A little wicked house of stone.

The October day was brightening toward late afternoon
when Leithen and I climbed the hill above the stream and
came in sight of the house. All morning a haze with the
sheen of pearl in it had lain on the folds of downland, and
the vision of far horizons, which is the glory of Cotswold,
had been veiled, so that every valley seemed as a place
enclosed and set apart. But now a glow had come into the
air, and for a little the autumn lawns stole the tints of summer. The gold of sunshine was warm on the grasses, and
only the riot of colour in the berry-laden edges of the fields
and the slender woodlands told of the failing year.

We were looking into a green cup of the hills, and it was
all a garden. A little place, bounded by slopes that defined
its graciousness with no hint of barrier, so that a dweller
there, though his view was but half a mile on any side,
would yet have the sense of dwelling on uplands and com-
manding the world. Round the top edge ran an old wall of
stones, beyond which the October bracken flamed to the
skyline. Inside were folds of ancient pasture, with here and
there a thorn-bush, falling to rose gardens and, on one side,
to the smooth sward of a terrace above a tiny lake.

At the heart of it stood the house like a jewel well-set.
It was a miniature, but by the hand of a master. The style

was late seventeenth century, when an agreeable classic convention had opened up to sunlight and comfort the dark magnificence of the Tudor fashion. The place had the spacious air of a great mansion, and was furnished in every detail with a fine scrupulousness. Only when the eye measured its proportions with the woods and the hillside did the mind perceive that it was a small dwelling.

The stone of Cotswold takes curiously the colour of the weather. Under thunderclouds it will be as dark as basalt; on a grey day it will be grey like lava but in sunshine it absorbs the sun. At the moment the little house was pale gold, like honey.

Leithen swung a long leg across the stile.

'Pretty good, isn't it?' he said. 'It's pure, authentic Sir Christopher Wren. The name is worthy of it, too. It is called Fullcircle.'

He told me its story. It had been built after the Restoration by the Carteron family, whose wide domains ran into these hills. The Lord Carteron of the day was a friend of the Merry Monarch; but it was not as a sanctuary for orgies that he built the house. Perhaps he was tired of the gloomy splendour of Minster Carteron, and wanted a home of his own and not of his ancestors' choosing. He had an elegant taste in letters, as we can learn from his neat imitations of Martial, his pretty *Bucolics* and the more than respectable Latin hexameters of his *Ars Vivendi*. Being a great nobleman, he had the best skill of the day to construct his hermitage, and thither he would retire for months at a time, with like-minded friends, to a world of books and gardens. He seems to have had no ill-wishers; contemporary memoirs speak of him charitably and Dryden spared him four lines of encomium. 'A selfish old dog,' Leithen called him.

'He had the good sense to eschew politics and enjoy life. His soul is in that little house. He only did one rash thing in his career – he anticipated the King, his master, by some years in turning Papist.'

I asked about its later history.

'After his death it passed to a younger branch of the Carterons. It left them in the eighteenth century, and the Applebys got it. They were a jovial lot of hunting squires and let the library go to the dogs. Old Colonel Appleby was still alive when I came to Borrowby. Something went wrong in his inside when he was nearly seventy, and the doctors knocked him off liquor. Not that he drank too much, though he did himself well. That finished the poor old boy. He told me that it revealed to him the amazing truth that during a long and, as he hoped, publicly useful life he had never been quite sober. He was a good fellow and I missed him when he died. The place went to a remote cousin called Giffen.'

Leithen's eyes as they scanned the prospect, seemed amused.

'Julian and Ursula Giffen – I dare say you know the names. They always hunt in couples, and write books about sociology and advanced ethics and psychics – books called either "The New This or That" or "The Truth about Something or Other". You know the sort of thing. They're deep in all the pseudo-sciences. They're decent souls, but you can guess the type. I came across them in a case I had at the Old Bailey – defending a ruffian who was charged with murder. I hadn't a doubt he deserved hanging on twenty counts, but there wasn't enough evidence to convict him on this one. Dodderidge was at his worst – it was just before they induced him to retire – and his handling of the jury was a masterpiece of misdirection. Of course, there was a shindy. The thing was a scandal, and it stirred up all the humanitarians till the murderer was almost forgotten in the iniquities of old Dodderidge. You must remember the case. It filled the papers for weeks. Well, it was in that connection that I fell in with the Giffens. I got rather to like them, and I've been to see them at their house in Hampstead. Golly, what a place! Not a chair fit to sit down on, and colours that made you want to howl. I never met people whose heads were so full of feathers.'

I said something about that being an odd *milieu* for him.

'Oh, I like human beings, all kinds. It's my profession to study them, for without that the practice of the law would be a dismal affair. There are hordes of people like the Giffens – only not so good, for they really have hearts of gold. They are the rootless stuff in the world today. In revolt against everything and everybody with any ancestry. A kind of innocent self-righteousness – wanting to be the people with whom wisdom begins and ends. They are mostly sensitive and tender-hearted, but they wear themselves out in an eternal dissidence. Can't build, you know, for they object to all tools, but very ready to crab. They scorn any form of Christianity, but they'll walk miles to patronise some wretched sect that has the merit of being brand new. "Pioneers" they call themselves – funny little unclad people adventuring into the cold desert with no maps. Giffen once described himself and his friends to me as "forward-looking", but that, of course, is just what they are not. To tackle the future you must have a firm grip of the past, and for them, the past is only a pathological curiosity. They're up to their necks in the mud of the present – but good, after a fashion; and innocent – sordidly innocent. Fate was in an ironical mood when she saddled them with that wicked little house.'

'Wicked' did not seem to me to be a fair word. It sat honey-coloured among its gardens with the meekness of a dove.

The sound of a bicycle on the road behind made us turn round, and Leithen advanced to meet a dismounting rider.

He was a tallish fellow, some forty years old, perhaps, with one of those fluffy blond beards that have never been shaved. Short-sighted, of course, and wore glasses. Biscuit-coloured knickerbockers and stockings clad his lean limbs.

Leithen introduced me. 'We are walking to Borrowby and stopped to admire your house. Could we have just a glimpse inside? I want Jardine to see the staircase.'

Mr Giffen was very willing. 'I've been over to Clyston to send a telegram. We have some friends for the weekend who might interest you. Won't you stay to tea?'

He had a gentle, formal courtesy about him, and his voice had the facile intonations of one who loves to talk. He led us through a little gate, and along a shorn green walk among the bracken, to a postern which gave entrance to the garden. Here, though it was October, there was still a bright show of roses, and the jet of water from the leaden Cupid dripped noiselessly among fallen petals. And then we stood before the doorway above which the old Carteron had inscribed a line of Horace.

I have never seen anything quite like the little hall. There were two, indeed, separated by a staircase of a wood that looked like olive. Both were paved with black-and-white marble, and the inner was oval in shape, with a gallery supported on slender walnut pillars. It was all in miniature, but it had a spaciousness which no mere size could give. Also it seemed to be permeated by the quintessence of sunlight. Its air was of long-descended, confident, equable happiness.

There were voices on the terrace beyond the hall. Giffen led us into a little room on the left. 'You remember the house in Colonel Appleby's time, Leithen. This was the chapel. It had always been the chapel. You see the change we have made – I beg your pardon, Mr Jardine. You're not by any chance a Roman Catholic?'

The room had a white panelling and, on two sides, deep windows. At one end was a fine Italian shrine of marble, and the floor was mosaic, blue and white, in a quaint Byzantine pattern. There was the same air of sunny cheerfulness as in the rest of the house. No mystery could find a lodgement here. It might have been a chapel for three centuries, but the place was pagan. The Giffens' changes were no sort of desecration. A green baize table filled most of the floor, surrounded by chairs like a committee room. On new rawwood shelves were files of papers and stacks of blue-books and those desiccated works into which reformers of society torture the English tongue. Two typewriters stood on a side table.

'It is our workroom,' Giffen explained. 'We hold our Sunday moots here. Ursula thinks that a weekend is wasted unless it produces some piece of real work. Often a quite valuable committee has its beginning here. We try to make our home a refuge for busy workers, where they need not idle but can work under happy conditions.'

' "A college situate in a clearer air," ' Leithen quoted.

But Giffen did not respond except with a smile; he had probably never heard of Lord Falkland.

A woman entered the room, a woman who might have been pretty if she had taken a little pains. Her reddish hair was drawn tightly back and dressed in a hard knot, and her clothes were horribly incongruous in a remote manor-house. She had bright eager eyes, like a bird, and hands that fluttered nervously. She greeted Leithen with warmth.

'We have settled down marvellously,' she told him. 'Julian and I feel as if we had always lived here, and our life has arranged itself so perfectly. My mothers' cottages in the village will soon be ready, and the Club is to be opened next week. Julian and I will carry on the classes ourselves for the first winter. Next year we hope to have a really fine programme. And then it is so pleasant to be able to entertain one's friends. Won't you stay to tea? Dr Swope is here, and Mary Elliston, and Mr Percy Blaker – you know, the Member of Parliament. Must you hurry off? I'm so sorry. What do you think of our workroom? It was utterly terrible when we first came here – a sort of decayed chapel, like a withered tuberose. We have let the air of heaven into it.'

I observed that I had never seen a house so full of space and light.

'Ah, you notice that? It is a curiously happy place to live in. Sometimes I'm almost afraid to feel so light-hearted. But we look on ourselves as only trustees. It is a trust we have to administer for the common good. You know, it's a house on which you can lay your own impress. I can imagine places which dominate the dwellers, but Fullcircle is plastic, and we can make it our own as much as if we had planned and built it. That's our chief piece of good fortune.'

We took our leave, for we had no desire for the company of Dr Swope and Mr Percy Blaker. When we reached the highway we halted and looked back on the little jewel. Shafts of the westering sun now caught the stone and turned the honey to ripe gold. Thin spires of amethyst smoke rose into the still air. I thought of the well-meaning, restless couple inside its walls, and somehow they seemed out of the picture. They simply did not matter. The house was the thing, for I had never met in inanimate stone such an air of gentle masterfulness. It had a personality of its own, clean-cut and secure, like a high-born old dame among the females of profiteers. And Mrs Giffen claimed to have given it her impress!

That night, in the library at Borrowby, Leithen discoursed of the Restoration. Borrowby, of which, by the expenditure of much care and a good deal of money, he had made a civilised dwelling, is a Tudor manor of the Cotswold type, with its high-pitched narrow roofs and tall stone chimneys, rising sheer from the meadows with something of the massiveness of a Border keep.

He nodded toward the linen-fold panelling and the great carved chimney-piece.

'In this kind of house you have the mystery of the elder England. What was Raleigh's phrase? "High thoughts and divine contemplations." The people who built this sort of thing lived close to another world, and thought bravely of death. It doesn't matter who they were – Crusaders or Elizabethans or Puritans – they all had poetry in them and the heroic and a great unworldliness. They had marvellous spirits, and plenty of joys and triumphs; but they had also their hours of black gloom. Their lives were like our weather – storm and sun. One thing they never feared – death. He walked too near them all their days to be a bogey.

'But the Restoration was a sharp break. It brought paganism into England; paganism and the art of life. No people have ever known better the secret of bland happiness.

Look at Fullcircle. There are no dark corners there. The man that built it knew all there was to be known about how to live. The trouble was that they did not know how to die. That was the one shadow on the glass. So they provided for it in a pagan way. They tried magic. They never became true Catholics – they were always pagan to the end, but they smuggled a priest into their lives. He was a kind of insurance premium against unwelcome mystery.'

It was not till nearly two years later that I saw the Giffens again. The May-fly season was about at its close, and I had snatched a day on a certain limpid Cotswold river. There was another man on the same beat, fishing from the opposite bank, and I watched him with some anxiety, for a duffer would have spoiled my day. To my relief I recognised Giffen. With him it was easy to come to terms, and presently the water was parcelled out between us.

We foregathered for luncheon, and I stood watching while he neatly stalked, rose and landed a trout. I confessed to some surprise – first that Giffen should be a fisherman at all, for it was not in keeping with my old notion of him; and second, that he should cast such a workmanlike line. As we lunched together, I observed several changes. He had shaved his fluffy beard, and his face was notably less lean, and had the clear even sunburn of the countryman. His clothes, too, were different. They also were workmanlike, and looked as if they belonged to him – he no longer wore the uneasy knickerbockers of the Sunday golfer.

'I'm desperately keen,' he told me. 'You see it's only my second May-fly season, and last year I was no better than a beginner. I wish I had known long ago what good fun fishing was. Isn't this a blessed place?' And he looked up through the canopy of flowering chestnuts to the June sky.

'I'm glad you've taken to sport,' I said, 'even if you only come here for the weekends. Sport lets you into the secrets of the countryside.'

'Oh, we don't go much to London now,' was his answer. 'We sold our Hampstead house a year ago. I can't think how I ever could stick that place. Ursula takes the same view. I wouldn't leave Oxfordshire just now for a thousand pounds. Do you smell the hawthorn? Last week this meadow was scented like Paradise. D'you know, Leithen's a queer fellow?'

I asked why.

'He once told me that this countryside in June made him sad. He said it was too perfect a thing for fallen humanity. I call that morbid. Do you see any sense in it?'

I knew what Leithen meant, but it would have taken too long to explain.

'I feel warm and good and happy here,' he went on. 'I used to talk about living close to nature. Rot! I didn't know what nature meant. Now—' He broke off. 'By Jove, there's a kingfisher. That is only the second I've seen this year. They're getting uncommon with us.'

'With us.' I liked the phrase. He was becoming a true countryman.

We had a good day – not extravagantly successful, but satisfactory – and he persuaded me to come home with him to Fullcircle for the night, explaining that I could catch an early train next morning at the junction. So we extricated a little two-seater from the midst of a clump of lilacs, and drove through four miles of sweet-scented dusk, with nightingales shouting in every thicket.

I changed into a suit of his flannels in a room looking out on the little lake where trout were rising, and I remember that I whistled from pure light-heartedness. In that adorable house one seemed to be still breathing the air of the spring meadows.

Dinner was my first big surprise. It was admirable – plain, but perfectly cooked, and with that excellence of basic material which is the glory of a well-appointed country house. There was wine, too, which I am certain was a new thing. Giffen gave me a bottle of sound claret, and afterwards some more than decent port. My second surprise was my hostess. Her clothes, like her husband's, must have changed, for I did not notice what she was wearing, and I had noticed it only too clearly the last time we met. More remarkable still was the difference in her face. For the first time I realised that she was a pretty woman. The contours had softened and rounded, and there was a charming well-being in her eyes, very different from the old restlessness. She looked content, infinitely content.

I asked about her mothers' cottages. She laughed cheerfully.

'I gave them up after the first year. They didn't mix well with the village people. I'm quite ready to admit my mistake, and it was the wrong kind of charity. The Londoners didn't like it – felt lonesome and sighed for the fried-fish shop; and the village women were shy of them – afraid of infectious complaints, you know. Julian and I have decided that our business is to look after our own people.'

It may have been malicious, but I said something about the wonderful scheme of village education.

'Another relic of Cockneyism,' laughed the lady, but Giffen looked a trifle shy.

'I gave it up because it didn't seem worth while. What is the use of spoiling a perfectly wholesome scheme of life by introducing unnecessary complications? Medicine is no good unless a man is sick, and these people are not sick. Education is the only cure for certain diseases the modern world has engendered, but if you don't find the disease, the remedy is superfluous. The fact is, I hadn't the face to go on with the thing. I wanted to be taught rather than to teach. There's a whole world round me of which I know very little, and my first business is to get to understand it. Any village poacher can teach me more of the things that matter than I have to tell him.'

'Besides, we have so much to do,' his wife added. 'There's the house and the garden and the home farm and the property. It isn't large, but it takes a lot of looking after.'

The dining-room was long and low-ceilinged, and had a white panelling in bold relief. Through the deep windows came odours of the garden and a faint tinkle of water. The dusk was deepening and the engravings in their rosewood frames were dim, but sufficient light remained to reveal the picture above the fireplace. It showed a middle-aged man in the clothes of the later Stuarts. The plump tapering fingers of one hand held a book; the other was hidden in the folds of a flowered waistcoat. The long curled wig framed a delicate face with something of the grace of youth left to it. There were quizzical lines about the mouth, and the eyes smiled pleasantly yet very wisely. It was the face of a man I should have liked to dine with. He must have been the best of company.

Giffen answered my question.

'That's the Lord Carteron who built the house. No – no relation. Our people were the Applebys, who came in 1753.

We've both fallen so deep in love with Fullcircle that we wanted to see the man who conceived it. I had some trouble getting it. It came out of the Minster Carteron sale, and I had to give a Jew dealer twice what he paid for it. It's a jolly thing to live with.'

It was indeed a curiously charming picture. I found my eyes straying to it till the dusk obscured the features. It was the face of one wholly at home in a suave world, learned in all the urbanities. A good friend, I thought, the old lord must have been, and a superlative companion. I could imagine neat Horatian tags coming ripely from his lips. Not a strong face, but somehow a dominating one. The portrait of the long-dead gentleman had still the atmosphere of life. Giffen raised his glass of port to him as we rose from table, as if to salute a comrade.

We moved to the room across the hall which had once been the Giffens' workroom, the cradle of earnest committees and weighty memoranda. This was my third surprise. Baize-covered table and raw-wood shelves had disappeared. The place was now half smoking-room, half library. On the walls hung a fine collection of coloured sporting prints, and below them were ranged low Hepplewhite bookcases. The lamplight glowed on the ivory walls, and the room, like everything else in the house, was radiant.

Above the mantelpiece was a stag's head – a fair eleven-pointer.

Giffen nodded proudly toward it. 'I got that last year at Machray. My first stag.'

There was a little table with an array of magazines and weekly papers. Some amusement must have been visible in my face, as I caught sight of various light-hearted sporting journals, for he laughed apologetically. 'You mustn't think that Ursula and I take in that stuff for ourselves. It amuses our guests, you know.'

I dared say it did, but I was convinced that the guests were no longer Dr Swope and Mr Percy Blaker.

One of my many failings is that I can never enter a room containing books without scanning the titles. Giffen's collection won my hearty approval. There were the very few novelists I can read myself – Miss Austen and Sir Walter and the admirable Marryat; there was a shelf full of memoirs, and a good deal of seventeenth- and eighteenth-century poetry; there was a set of the classics in fine editions, Bodonis and Baskervilles and such like; there was much county history and one or two valuable old Herbals and Itineraries. I was certain that two years earlier Giffen would have had no use for literature except some muddy Russian oddments, and I am positive that he would not have known the name of Surtees. Yet there stood the tall octavos recording the unedifying careers of Mr Jorrocks, Mr Facey Romford and Mr Soapy Sponge.

I was a little bewildered as I stretched my legs in a very deep armchair. Suddenly I had a strong impression of looking on at a play. My hosts seemed to be automata, moving docilely at the orders of a masterful stage manager, and yet with no sense of bondage. And as I looked on, they faded off the scene, and there was only one personality – that house so serene and secure, smiling at our modern antics, but weaving all the while an iron spell around its lovers.

For a second I felt an oppression as of something to be resisted. But no. There was no oppression. The house was too well-bred and disdainful to seek to captivate. Only those who fell in love with it could know its mastery, for all love exacts a price. It was far more than a thing of stone

221

and lime: it was a creed, an art, a scheme of life – older than any Carteron, older than England. Somewhere far back in time, in Rome, in Attica, or in an Aegean island, there must have been such places; and then they called them temples, and gods dwelt in them.

I was roused by Giffen's voice discoursing of his books. 'I've been rubbing up my classics again,' he was saying. 'Queer thing, but ever since I left Cambridge I have been out of the mood for them. And I'm shockingly ill-read in English literature. I wish I had more time for reading, for it means a lot to me.'

'There is such an embarrassment of riches here,' said his wife. 'The days are far too short for all there is to do. Even when there is nobody staying in the house I find every hour occupied. It's delicious to be busy over things one really cares for.'

'All the same I wish I could do more reading,' said Giffen. 'I've never wanted to so much before.'

'But you come in tired from shooting and sleep sound till dinner,' said the lady, laying an affectionate hand on his shoulder.

They were happy people, and I like happiness. Self-absorbed, perhaps, but I prefer selfishness in the ordinary way of things. We are most of us selfish dogs, and altruism makes us uncomfortable. But I had somehow in my mind a shade of uneasiness, for I was the witness of a transformation too swift and violent to be wholly natural. Years, no doubt, turn our eyes inward and abate our heroics, but not a trifle of two or three. Some agency had been at work here, some agency other and more potent than the process of time. The thing fascinated and partly frightened me. For the Giffens – though I scarcely dared to admit it – had deteriorated. They were far pleasanter people, I liked them infinitely better, I hoped to see them often again. I detested the type they used to represent, and shunned it like the plague. They were wise now, and mellow, and most agreeable human beings. But some virtue had gone out of them. An uncomfortable virtue, no doubt, but still a virtue; something generous and adventurous. In the earlier time, their faces had had a sort of wistful kindness. Now they had geniality – which is not the same thing.

What was the agency of this miracle? It was all around me: the ivory panelling, the olive-wood staircase, the lovely pillared hall.

I got up to go to bed with a kind of awe on me. As Mrs Giffen lit my candle, she saw my eyes wandering among the gracious shadows.

'Isn't it wonderful', she said, 'to have found a house which fits us like a glove? No! Closer. Fits us as a bearskin fits the bear. It has taken our impress like wax.'

Somehow I didn't think that impress had come from the Giffens' side.

A November afternoon found Leithen and myself jogging homeward from a run with the Heythrop. It had been a wretched day. Twice we had found and lost, and then a deluge had set in which scattered the field. I had taken a hearty toss into a swamp, and got as wet as a man may be, but the steady downpour soon reduced everyone to a like condition. When we turned toward Borrowby the rain ceased, and an icy wind blew out of the east which partially dried our sopping clothes. All the grace had faded from the Cotswold valleys. The streams were brown torrents, the meadows lagoons, the ridges bleak and grey, and a sky of scurrying clouds cast leaden shadows. It was a matter of ten miles to Borrowby; we had long ago emptied our flasks, and I longed for something hot to take the chill out of my bones.

'Let's look in at Fullcircle,' said Leithen, as we came out on the highroad from a muddy lane. 'We'll make the Giffens give us tea. You'll find changes there.'

I asked what changes, but he only smiled and told me to wait and see.

My mind was busy with surmises as we rode up the avenue. I thought of drink or drugs, and promptly discarded the notion. Fullcircle was, above all things, decorous and wholesome. Leithen could not mean the change in the Giffens' ways which had so impressed me a year before, for he and I had long ago discussed that. I was still puzzling over his words when we found ourselves in the inner hall, with the Giffens making a hospitable fuss over us.

The place was more delectable than ever. Outside was a dark November day, yet the little house seemed to be transfused with sunshine. I do not know by what art the old builders had planned it; but the airy pilasters, the perfect lines of the ceiling, the soft colouring of the wood seemed to lay open the house to a clear sky. Logs burned brightly on the massive steel andirons, and the scent and the fine blue smoke of them strengthened the illusion of summer.

Mrs Giffen would have us change into dry things, but Leithen pleaded a waiting dinner at Borrowby. The two of us stood by the fireplace, drinking tea, the warmth drawing out a cloud of vapour from our clothes to mingle with the wood smoke. Giffen lounged in an armchair and his wife sat by the tea-table. I was looking for the changes of which Leithen had spoken.

I did not find them in Giffen. He was much as I remembered him on the June night when I had slept here – a trifle fuller in the face, perhaps, a little more placid about the mouth and eyes. He looked a man completely content with life. His smile came readily, and his easy laugh. Was it my fancy, or had he acquired a look of the picture in the dining-room? I nearly made an errand to go and see it. It seemed to me that his mouth had now something of the portrait's delicate complacence. Lely would have found him a fit subject, though he might have boggled at his lean hands.

But his wife! Ah, there the changes were unmistakable. She was comely now rather than pretty, and the contours of her face had grown heavier. The eagerness had gone from her eyes and left only comfort and good humour. There was a suspicion, ever so slight, of rouge and powder. She had a string of good pearls – the first time I had seen her wear jewels. The hand that poured out the tea was plump, shapely and well cared for. I was looking at a most satisfactory mistress of a country house, who would see that nothing was lacking to the part.

She talked more and laughed oftener. Her voice had an airy lightness which would have made the silliest prattle charming.

'We are going to fill the house with young people and give a ball at Christmas,' she announced. 'This hall is simply clamouring to be danced in. You must come, both of you. Promise me. And, Mr Leithen, it would be very nice if you brought a party from Borrowby. Young men, please. We are overstocked with girls in these parts. We must do something to make the country cheerful in winter-time.'

I observed that no season could make Fullcircle other than cheerful.

225

'How nice of you!' she cried. 'To praise a house is to praise the householders, for a dwelling is just what its inmates make it. Borrowby is you, Mr Leithen, and Full-circle us.'

'Shall we exchange?' Leithen asked.

She made a mouth. 'Borrowby would crush me, but it suits a Gothic survival like you. Do you think you would be happy here?'

'Happy?' said Leithen thoughtfully. 'Happy? Yes, un-doubtedly. But it might be bad for my soul. There's just time for a pipe, Giffen, and then we must be off.'

I was filling my pipe as we crossed the outer hall, and was about to enter the smoking-room that I so well remembered, when Giffen laid a hand on my arm.

'We don't smoke there now,' he said hastily.

He opened the door and I looked in. The place had suffered its third metamorphosis. The marble shrine which I had noticed on my first visit had been brought back, and the blue mosaic pavement and the ivory walls were bare. At the eastern end stood a little altar, with, above it, a copy of a Correggio Madonna.

A faint smell of incense hung in the air, and the fragrance of hot-house flowers. It was a chapel, but, I swear, it was a more pagan place than when it had been workroom or smoking-room.

Giffen gently shut the door. 'Perhaps you may not have heard, but some months ago my wife became a Catholic. It is a good thing for women, I think. It gives them a regular ritual for their lives. So we restored the chapel, which had always been there in the days of the Carterons and the Applebys.'

'And you?' I asked.

He shrugged his shoulders.

'I don't bother much about that sort of thing. But I propose to follow suit. It will please Ursula and do no harm to anybody.'

We halted on the brow of the hill and looked back on the garden valley. Leithen's laugh, as he gazed, had more awe than mirth in it.

'That wicked little house! I'm going to hunt up every scrap I can find about old Tom Carteron. He must have been an uncommon clever fellow. He's still alive down there and making people do as he did. In that kind of place you may expel the priest and sweep it and garnish it, but he always returns.'

The wrack was lifting before the wind, and a shaft of late watery sun fell on the grey walls. It seemed to me that the little house wore an air of gentle triumph.

The Loathly Opposite

How loathly opposite I stood
To his unnatural purpose.

King Lear

Burminster had been to a Guildhall dinner the night
before, which had been attended by many – to him –
unfamiliar celebrities. He had seen for the first time in the
flesh people whom he had long known by reputation, and
he declared that in every case the picture he had formed of
them had been cruelly shattered. An eminent poet, he
said, had looked like a starting-price bookmaker, and a
financier of world-wide fame had been exactly like the
music-master at his preparatory school. Wherefore Burminster made the profound deduction that things were never
what they seemed.

'That's only because you have a feeble imagination,'
said Sandy Arbuthnot. 'If you had really understood Tim-
son's poetry you would have realised that it went with
close-cropped red hair and a fat body, and you should have
known that Macintyre [this was the financier] had the
music-and-metaphysics type of mind. That's why he puzzles
the City so. If you understand a man's work well enough
you can guess pretty accurately what he'll look like. I don't
mean the colour of his eyes and his hair, but the general
atmosphere of him.'

It was Sandy's agreeable habit to fling an occasional
paradox at the table with the view of starting an argument.

228

This time he stirred up Pugh, who had come to the War Office from the Indian Staff Corps. Pugh had been a great figure in Secret Service work in the East, but he did not look the part, for he had the air of a polo-playing cavalry subaltern. The skin was stretched as tight over his cheekbones as over the knuckles of a clenched fist, and was so dark that it had the appearance of beaten bronze. He had black hair, rather beady black eyes, and the hooky nose which in the Celt often goes with that colouring. He was himself a very good refutation of Sandy's theory.

'I don't agree,' Pugh said. 'At least not as a general principle. One piece of humanity whose work I studied with the microscope for two aching years upset all my notions when I came to meet it.'

Then he told us this story.

'When I was brought to England in November '17 and given a "hush" department on three floors of an eighteenth-century house in a back street, I had a good deal to learn about my business. That I learned it in reasonable time was due to the extraordinarily fine staff that I found provided for me. Not one of them was a regular soldier. They were all educated men – they had to be in that job – but they came out of every sort of environment. One of the best was a Shetland laird, another was an Admiralty Court KC, and I had besides a metallurgical chemist, a golf champion, a leader-writer, a popular dramatist, several actuaries and an East-end curate. None of them thought of anything but his job, and at the end of the war, when some ass proposed to make them OBEs, there was a very fair imitation of a riot. A more loyal crowd never existed, and they accepted me as their chief as unquestioningly as if I had been with them since 1914.

'To the war in the ordinary sense they scarcely gave a thought. You found the same thing in a lot of other behind-the-lines departments, and I daresay it was a good thing – it kept their nerves quiet and their minds concentrated. After all our business was only to decode and decypher German messages; we had nothing to do with the use which was made of them. It was a curious little nest, and when the Armistice came my people were flabbergasted – they hadn't realised that their job was bound up with the war.

'The one who most interested me was my second-in-command, Philip Channell. He was a man of forty-three, about five-foot-four in height, weighing, I fancy, under nine stone, and almost as blind as an owl. He was good enough at papers with his double glasses, but he could hardly recognise you three yards off. He had been a professor at some Midland college – mathematics or physics, I think – and as soon as the war began he had tried to enlist. Of course they wouldn't have him – he was about E5 in any physical classification, besides being well over age – but he would take no refusal, and presently he worried his way into the Government service. Fortunately he found a job which he could do superlatively well, for I do not believe there was a man alive with more natural genius for cryptography.

'I don't know if any of you have ever given your mind to that heart-breaking subject. Anyhow you know that secret writing falls under two heads – codes and cyphers, and that codes are combinations of words and cyphers of numerals. I remember how one used to be told that no code or cypher which was practically useful was really undiscoverable, and in a sense that is true, especially of codes. A system of communication which is in constant use must obviously not be too intricate, and a working code, if you get long enough for the job, can generally be read. That is why a code is periodically changed by the users. There are rules in worrying out the permutations and combinations of letters in most codes, for human ingenuity seems to run in certain channels, and a man who has been a long time at the business gets surprisingly clever at it. You begin by finding out a little bit, and then empirically building up the rules of decoding, till in a week or two you get the whole thing. Then, when you are happily engaged in reading enemy messages, the code is changed suddenly, and you have to start again from the beginning . . . You can make a code, of course, that it is simply impossible to read except by accident – the key to which is a page of some book, for example – but fortunately that kind is not of much general use.

'Well, we got on pretty well with the codes, and read the intercepted enemy messages, cables and wireless, with considerable ease and precision. It was mostly diplomatic stuff, and not very important. The more valuable stuff was in cypher, and that was another pair of shoes. With a code you can build up the interpretation by degrees, but with a cypher you either know it or you don't – there are no half-way houses. A cypher, since it deals with numbers, is a horrible field for mathematical ingenuity. Once you have written out the letters of a message in numerals there are many means by which you can lock it and double-lock it. The two main devices, as you know, are transposition and substitution, and there is no limit to the ways one or other or both can be used. There is nothing to prevent a cypher having a double meaning, produced by two different methods, and, as a practical question, you have to decide which meaning is intended. By way of an extra complication, too, the message, when decyphered, may turn out to

231

be itself in a difficult code. I can tell you our job wasn't exactly a rest cure.'

Burminster, looking puzzled, inquired as to the locking of cyphers.

'It would take too long to explain. Roughly, you write out a message horizontally in numerals; then you pour it into vertical columns, the number and order of which are determined by a key word; then you write out the contents of the columns horizontally, following the lines across. To unlock it you have to have the key word, so as to put it back into the vertical columns, and then into the original horizontal form.'

Burminster cried out like one in pain. 'It can't be done. Don't tell me that any human brain could solve such an acrostic.'

'It was frequently done,' said Pugh.

'By you?'

'Lord bless you, not by me. I can't do a simple crossword puzzle. By my people.'

'Give me the trenches,' said Burminster in a hollow voice. 'Give me the trenches any day. Do you seriously mean to tell me that you could sit down before a muddle of numbers and travel back the way they had been muddled to an original that made sense?'

'I couldn't, but Channell could – in most cases. You see, we didn't begin entirely in the dark. We already knew the kind of intricacies that the enemy favoured, and the way we worked was by trying a variety of clues till we hit on the right one.'

'Well, I'm blessed! Go on about your man Channell.'

'This isn't Channell's story,' said Pugh. 'He only comes into it accidentally . . . There was one cypher which always defeated us, a cypher used between the German General Staff and their forces in the East. It was a locked cypher, and Channell had given more time to it than to any dozen of the others, for it put him on his mettle. But he confessed himself absolutely beaten. He wouldn't admit that it was insoluble, but he declared that he would need a bit of real luck to solve it. I asked him what kind of luck, and he said a mistake and a repetition. That, he said, might give him a chance of establishing equations.

'We called this particular cypher "PY", and we hated it poisonously. We felt like pygmies battering at the base of a high stone tower. Dislike of the thing soon became dislike of the man who had conceived it. Channell and I used to – I won't say amuse, for it was too dashed serious – but torment ourselves by trying to picture the fellow who owned the brain that was responsible for PY. We had a pretty complete dossier of the German Intelligence Staff, but of course we couldn't know who was responsible for this particular cypher. We knew no more than his code name, Reinmar, with which he signed the simpler messages to the East, and Channell, who was a romantic little chap for all his science, had got it into his head that it was a woman. He used to describe her to me as if he had seen her – a she-devil, young, beautiful, with a much-painted white face, and eyes like a cobra's. I fancy he read a rather low class of novel in his off-time.

'My picture was different. At first I thought of the histrionic type of scientist, the "ruthless brain" type, with a high forehead and a jaw puckered like a chimpanzee. But that didn't seem to work, and I settled on a picture of a first-class *Generalstabsoffizier*, as handsome as Falkenhayn, trained to the last decimal, absolutely passionless, with a mind that worked with the relentless precision of a fine machine. We all of us at the time suffered from the bogey of this kind of German, and, when things were going badly, as in March '18, I couldn't sleep for hating him. The infernal fellow was so water-tight and armour-plated, a Goliath who scorned the pebbles from our feeble slings.

'Well, to make a long story short, there came a moment in September '18 when PY was about the most important thing in the world. It mattered enormously what Germany was doing in Syria, and we knew that it was all in PY. Every morning a pile of the intercepted German wireless messages lay on Channell's table, which were as meaningless to him as a child's scrawl. I was prodded by my chiefs and in turn I prodded Channell. We had a week to find the key to the cypher, after which things must go on without us, and if we had failed to make anything of it in eighteen months of quiet work, it didn't seem likely that we would succeed in seven feverish days. Channell nearly went off his head with overwork and anxiety. I used to visit his dingy little room and find him fairly grizzled and shrunken with fatigue.

'This isn't a story about him, though there is a good story which I may tell you another time. As a matter of fact we won on the post. PY made a mistake. One morning we got a long message dated *en clair*, then a very short message, and then a third message almost the same as the first. The second must mean "Your message of today's date unintelligible, please repeat", the regular formula. This gave us a translation of a bit of the cypher. Even that would not have brought it out, and for twelve hours Channell was on the verge of lunacy, till it occurred to him that Reinmar might have signed the long message with his name, as we used to do sometimes in cases of extreme urgency. He was right, and, within three hours of the last moment Operations could give us, we had the whole thing pat. As I have said, that is a story worth telling, but it is not this one.

'We both finished the war too tired to think of much except that the darned thing was over. But Reinmar had been so long our unseen but constantly pictured opponent that we kept up a certain interest in him. We would like to have seen how he took the licking, for he must have known that we had licked him. Mostly when you lick a man at a game you rather like him, but I didn't like Reinmar. In fact I made him a sort of compost of everything I had ever disliked in a German. Channell stuck to his she-devil theory, but I was pretty certain that he was a youngish man with an intellectual arrogance which his country's débâcle would in no way lessen. He would never acknowledge defeat. It was highly improbable that I should ever find out who he was, but I felt that if I did, and met him face to face, my dislike would be abundantly justified.

'As you know, for a year or two after the Armistice I was a pretty sick man. Most of us were. We hadn't the fillip of getting back to civilised comforts, like the men in the trenches. We had always been comfortable enough in body, but our minds were fagged out, and there is no easy cure for that. My digestion went nobly to pieces, and I endured a miserable space of lying in bed and living on milk and olive-oil. After that I went back to work, but the darned thing always returned, and every leech had a different regime to advise. I tried them all – dry meals, a snack every two hours, lemon juice, sour milk, starvation, knocking off tobacco – but nothing got me more than half-way out of the trough. I was a burden to myself and a nuisance to others, dragging my wing through life, with a constant pain in my tummy.

'More than one doctor advised an operation, but I was chary about that, for I had seen several of my friends operated on for the same mischief and left as sick as before. Then a man told me about a German fellow called Christoph, who was said to be very good at handling my trouble. The best hand at diagnosis in the world, my informant said – no fads – treated every case on its merits – a really original mind. Dr Christoph had a modest Kurhaus at a place called Rosensee in the Sächsische Schweiz. By this time I was getting pretty desperate, so I packed a bag and set off for Rosensee.

'It was a quiet little town at the mouth of a narrow valley, tucked in under wooded hills, a clean fresh place with open channels of running water in the streets. There was a big church with an onion spire, a Catholic seminary, and a small tanning industry. The Kurhaus was half-way up a hill, and I felt better as soon as I saw my bedroom, with its bare scrubbed floors and its wide verandah looking up into a forest glade. I felt still better when I saw Dr Christoph. He was a small man with a grizzled beard, a high forehead, and a limp, rather like what I imagine the Apostle Paul must have been. He looked wise, as wise as an old owl. His English was atrocious, but even when he found that I talked German fairly well he didn't expand in speech. He would deliver no opinion of any kind until he had had me at least a week under observation; but somehow I felt comforted, for I concluded that a first-class brain had got to work on me.

'The other patients were mostly Germans with a sprinkling of Spaniards, but to my delight I found Channell. He also had been having a thin time since we parted. Nerves were his trouble – general nervous debility and perpetual insomnia, and his college had given him six months' leave of absence to try to get well. The poor chap was as lean as a sparrow, and he had the large dull eyes and the dry lips of the sleepless. He had arrived a week before me, and like me was under observation. But his vetting was different from mine, for he was a mental case, and Dr Christoph used to devote hours to trying to unriddle his nervous tangles. "He is a good man for a German," said Channell, "but he is on the wrong tack. There's nothing wrong with my mind. I wish he'd stick to violet rays and massage, instead of asking me silly questions about my great-grandmother."

'Channell and I used to go for invalidish walks in the woods, and we naturally talked about the years we had worked together. He was living mainly in the past, for the war had been the great thing in his life, and his professorial duties seemed trivial by comparison. As we tramped among the withered bracken and heather his mind was always harking back to the dingy little room where he had smoked cheap cigarettes and worked fourteen hours out of the twenty-four. In particular he was as eagerly curious about our old antagonist, Reinmar, as he had been in 1918. He was more positive than ever that she was a woman, and I believe that one of the reasons that had induced him to try a cure in Germany was a vague hope that he might get on her track. I had almost forgotten about the thing, and I was amused by Channell in the part of the untiring sleuth-hound.

' "You won't find her in the Kurhaus," I said. "Perhaps she is in some old Schloss in the neighbourhood, waiting for you like the Sleeping Beauty."

237

' "I'm serious," he said plaintively. "It is purely a matter of intellectual curiosity, but I confess I would give a great deal to see her face to face. After I leave here, I thought of going to Berlin to make some inquiries. But I'm handicapped for I know nobody and I have no credentials. Why don't you, who have a large acquaintance and far more authority, take the thing up?"

'I told him that my interest in the matter had flagged and that I wasn't keen on digging into the past, but I promised to give him a line to our Military Attaché if he thought of going to Berlin. I rather discouraged him from letting his mind dwell too much on events in the war. I said that he ought to try to bolt the door on all that had contributed to his present breakdown.

' "That is not Dr Christoph's opinion," he said emphatically. "He encourages me to talk about it. You see, with me it is a purely intellectual interest. I have no emotion in the matter. I feel quite friendly towards Reinmar, whoever she may be. It is, if you like, a piece of romance. I haven't had so many romantic events in my life that I want to forget this."

' "Have you told Dr Christoph about Reinmar?" I asked.

' "Yes," he said, "and he was mildly interested. You know the way he looks at you with his solemn grey eyes. I doubt if he quite understood what I meant, for a little provincial doctor, even though he is a genius in his own line, is not likely to know much about the ways of the Great General Staff . . . I had to tell him, for I have to tell him all my dreams, and lately I have taken to dreaming about Reinmar."

' "What's she like?" I asked.

' "Oh, a most remarkable figure. Very beautiful, but uncanny. She has long fair hair down to her knees."

'Of course I laughed. "You're mixing her up with the Valkyries," I said. "Lord, it would be an awkward business if you met that she-dragon in the flesh."

'But he was quite solemn about it, and declared that his waking picture of her was not in the least like his dreams. He rather agreed with my nonsense about the old Schloss. He thought that she was probably some penniless grandee, living solitary in a moated grange, with nothing now to exercise her marvellous brain on, and eating her heart out with regret and shame. He drew so attractive a character of her that I began to think that Channell was in love with a being of his own creation, till he ended with, "But all the same she's utterly damnable. She must be, you know."

'After a fortnight I began to feel a different man. Dr Christoph thought that he had got on the track of the mischief, and certainly, with his deep massage and a few simple drugs, I had more internal comfort than I had known for three years. He was so pleased with my progress that he refused to treat me as an invalid. He encouraged me to take long walks into the hills, and presently he arranged for me to go out roebuck-shooting with some of the local junkers.

'I used to start before daybreak on the chilly November mornings and drive to the top of one of the ridges, where I would meet a collection of sportsmen and beaters, shepherded by a fellow in a green uniform. We lined out along the ridge, and the beaters, assisted by a marvellous collection of dogs, including the sporting dachshund, drove the roe towards us. It wasn't very cleverly managed, for the deer generally broke back, and it was chilly waiting in the first hours with a powdering of snow on the ground and the fir boughs heavy with frost crystals. But later, when the sun grew stronger, it was a very pleasant mode of spending a day. There was not much of a bag, but whenever a roe or a capercailzie fell all the guns would assemble and drink little glasses of *Kirschwasser*. I had been lent a rifle, one of those appalling contraptions which are double-barrelled shot-guns and rifles in one, and to transpose from one form to the other requires a mathematical calculation. The rifle had a hair trigger too, and when I first used it I was nearly the death of a respectable Saxon peasant.

'We all ate our midday meal together and in the evening, before going home, we had coffee and cakes in one or other of the farms. The party was an odd mixture, big farmers and small squires, an hotel-keeper or two, a local doctor, and a couple of lawyers from the town. At first they were a little shy of me, but presently they thawed, and after the first day we were good friends. They spoke quite frankly about the war, in which every one of them had had a share, and with a great deal of dignity and good sense.

'I learned to walk in Sikkim, and the little Saxon hills seemed to me inconsiderable. But they were too much for most of the guns, and instead of going straight up or down a slope they always chose a circuit, which gave them an easy gradient. One evening, when we were separating as usual, the beaters taking a short cut and the guns a circuit, I felt that I wanted exercise, so I raced the beaters downhill, beat them soundly, and had the better part of an hour to wait for my companions, before we adjourned to the farm for refreshment. The beaters must have talked about my pace, for as we walked away one of the guns, a lawyer called Meissen, asked me why I was visiting Rosensee at a time of year when few foreigners came. I said I was staying with Dr Christoph.

' "Is he then a private friend of yours?" he asked.

'I told him No, that I had come to his Kurhaus for treatment, being sick. His eyes expressed polite scepticism. He was not prepared to regard as an invalid a man who went down a hill like an avalanche.

'But, as we walked in the frosty dusk, he was led to speak of Dr Christoph, of whom he had no personal knowledge, and I learned how little honour a prophet may have in his own country. Rosensee scarcely knew him, except as a doctor who had an inexplicable attraction for foreign patients. Meissen was curious about his methods and the exact diseases in which he specialised. "Perhaps he may yet save me a journey to Homburg?" he laughed. "It is well to have a skilled physician at one's doorstep. The doctor is something of a hermit, and except for his patients does not appear to welcome his kind. Yet he is a good man, beyond doubt, and there are those who say that in the war he was a hero."

'This surprised me, for I could not imagine Dr Christoph in any fighting capacity, apart from the fact that he must have been too old. I thought that Meissen might refer to work in the base hospitals. But he was positive; Dr Christoph had been in the trenches; the limping leg was a war wound.

'I had had very little talk with the doctor, owing to my case being free from nervous complications. He would say a word to me morning and evening about my diet, and pass the time of day when we met, but it was not till the very eve of my departure that we had anything like a real conversation. He sent a message that he wanted to see me for not less than one hour, and he arrived with a batch of notes from which he delivered a kind of lecture on my case. Then I realised what an immense amount of care and solid thought he had expended on me. He had decided that his diagnosis was right – my rapid improvement suggested that – but it was necessary for some time to observe a simple regime, and to keep an eye on certain symptoms. So he took a sheet of notepaper from the table and in his small precise hand wrote down for me a few plain commandments.

'There was something about him, the honest eyes, the mouth which looked as if it had been often compressed in suffering, the air of grave goodwill, which I found curiously attractive. I wished that I had been a mental case like Channell, and had had more of his society. I detained him in talk, and he seemed not unwilling. By and by we drifted to the war and it turned out that Meissen was right.

'Dr Christoph had gone as medical officer in November '14 to the Ypres Salient with a Saxon regiment, and had spent the winter there. In '15 he had been in Champagne, and in the early months of '16 at Verdun, till he was invalided with rheumatic fever. That is to say, he had had about seventeen months of consecutive fighting in the worst areas with scarcely a holiday. A pretty good record for a frail little middle-aged man!

'His family was then at Stuttgart, his wife and one little boy. He took a long time to recover from the fever, and after that was put on home duty. "Till the war was almost over," he said, "almost over, but not quite. There was just time for me to go back to the front and get my foolish leg hurt." I must tell you that whenever he mentioned his war experience it was with a comical deprecating smile, as if he agreed with anyone who might think that gravity like this should have remained in bed.

'I assumed that this home duty was medical, until he said something about getting rusty in his professional work. Then it appeared that it had been some job connected with Intelligence. "I am reputed to have a little talent for mathematics," he said. "No. I am no mathematical scholar, but, if you understand me, I have a certain mathematical aptitude. My mind has always moved happily among numbers. Therefore I was set to construct and to interpret cyphers, a strange interlude in the noise of war. I sat in a little room and excluded the world, and for a little I was happy."

'He went on to speak of the enclave of peace in which he had found himself, and as I listened to his gentle monotonous voice, I had a sudden inspiration.

'I took a sheet of notepaper from the stand, scribbled the word *Reinmar* on it, and shoved it towards him. I had a notion, you see, that I might surprise him into helping Channell's researches.

'But it was I who got the big surprise. He stopped thunderstruck, as soon as his eye caught the word, blushed scarlet over every inch of face and bald forehead, seemed to have difficulty in swallowing, and then gasped. "How did you know?"

'I hadn't known, and now that I did, the knowledge left me speechless. This was the loathly opposite for which Channell and I had nursed our hatred. When I came out of my stupefaction I found that he had recovered his balance and was speaking slowly and distinctly, as if he were making a formal confession.

' "You were among my opponents . . . that interests me deeply . . . I often wondered . . . You beat me in the end. You are aware of that?"

'I nodded. "Only because you made a slip," I said.

243

' "Yes, I made a slip. I was to blame – very gravely to blame, for I let my private grief cloud my mind."

'He seemed to hesitate, as if he were loath to stir something very tragic in his memory.

' "I think I will tell you," he said at last. "I have often wished – it is a childish wish – to justify my failure to those who profited by it. My chiefs understood, of course, but my opponents could not. In that month when I failed I was in deep sorrow. I had a little son – his name was Reinmar – you remember that I took that name for my code signature?"

'His eyes were looking beyond me into some vision of the past.

' "He was, as you say, my mascot. He was all my family, and I adored him. But in those days food was not plentiful. We were no worse off than many million Germans, but the child was frail. In the last summer of the war he developed phthisis due to malnutrition, and in September he died. Then I failed my country, for with him some virtue seemed to depart from my mind. You see, my work was, so to speak, his also, as my name was his, and when he left me he took my power with him . . . So I stumbled. The rest is known to you."

'He sat staring beyond me, so small and lonely, that I could have howled. I remember putting my hand on his shoulder, and stammering some platitude about being sorry. We sat quite still for a minute or two, and then I remembered Channell. Channell must have poured his views of Reinmar into Dr Christoph's ear. I asked him if Channell knew.

'A flicker of a smile crossed his face.

' "Indeed no. And I will exact from you a promise never to breathe to him what I have told you. He is my patient,

and I must first consider his case. At present he thinks that
Reinmar is a wicked and beautiful lady whom he may
some day meet. That is romance, and it is good for him to
think so . . . If he were told the truth, he would be pitiful,
and in Herr Channell's condition it is important that he
should not be vexed with such emotions as pity." '

Ship to Tarshish

Now the word of the Lord came unto Jonah the son of Amittai, saying, Arise, go to Nineveh . . . But Jonah . . . found a ship going to Tarshish: so he paid the fare thereof, and went down into it, to go with them unto Tarshish from the presence of the Lord.

Jonah I. i–iii

The talk one evening turned on the metaphysics of courage. It is a subject which most men are a little shy of discussing. They will heartily applaud a friend's pluck, but it is curious how rarely they will label a man a coward. Perhaps the reason is that we are all odd mixtures of strength and weakness, brave in certain things, timid in others; and since each is apt to remember his private funks more vividly than the things about which he is bold, we are chary about dogmatising.

Lamancha propounded the thesis that everybody had a yellow streak in them. We all, he said, at times shirk unpleasant duties, and invent an honourable explanation, which we know to be a lie.

Sandy Arbuthnot observed that the most temerarious deeds were often done by people who had begun by funking, and then, in the shame of the rebound, did a good deal more than those who had no qualms. 'The man who says I go not, and afterwards repents and goes, generally travels the devil of a long way.'

'Like Jonah,' said Lamancha, 'who didn't like the job allotted him, and took ship to Tarshish to get away from it, and then repented and went like a raging lion to Nineveh.'

Collatt, who had been a sailor and one of the Q-boat heroes in the war, demurred. 'I wonder if Nineveh was as unpleasant as the whale's belly,' he said. Then he told us a story in illustration, not as one would have expected, out of his wild sea memories, but from his experience in the City, where he was now a bill-broker.

I got to know Jim Hallward first when he had just come down from the University. He was a tall, slim, fair-haired lad, with a soft voice and the kind of manners which make the ordinary man feel a lout. Eton and Christ Church had polished him till he fairly glistened. His clothes were sober works of art, and he was the cleanest thing you ever saw – always seemed to have just shaved and bathed after a couple of hours' hard exercise. We all liked him, for he was a companionable soul and had no frills, but in the City he was about as useless as a lily in a quickset hedge. Somebody called him an 'apolaustic epicene', which sounded accurate, though I don't know what the words mean. He used to come down to business about eleven o'clock and leave at four – earlier in summer, when he played polo at Hurlingham.

This lotus-eating existence lasted for two years. His father was the head of Hallwards, the merchant-bankers, who had been in existence since before the Napoleonic wars. It was an old-fashioned private firm with a tremendous reputation, but for some years it had been dropping a little out of the front rank. It had very few of the big issues, and, though reckoned as solid as the Bank of England, it had hardly kept pace with new developments. But just about the time Jim came down from Oxford his father seemed to get a new lease of life. Hallwards suddenly became ultra-progressive, took in a new manager from one of the big joint-stock banks, and launched out into business which before it would not have touched with the end of a barge-pole. I fancy the old man wanted to pull up the firm before he died, so as to leave a good thing to his only child.

In this new activity Jim can't have been of much use. His other engagements did not leave him a great deal of time to master the complicated affairs of a house like Hallwards. He spoke of his City connection with a certain distaste. The set he had got into were mostly eldest sons with political ambitions, and if Jim had any serious inclination it was towards Parliament, which he proposed to enter in a year or two. For the rest he played polo, and hunted, and did a little steeplechasing, and danced assiduously. Dancing was about the only thing he did really well, for he was only a moderate horseman and his politics were not to be taken seriously. So he was the complete *flâneur*, agreeable, popular, beautifully mannered, highly ornamental, and the most useless creature on earth. You see, he had slacked at school, and had just scraped through college, and had never done a real piece of work in his life.

In the autumn of 192–, whispers began to circulate about Hallwards. It seemed that they were doing a very risky class of business, and people shrugged their shoulders. But no one was prepared for the almighty crash which came at the beginning of the New Year. The firm had been trying to get control of a colonial railway, and for this purpose was quietly buying up the ordinary stock. But an American group, with unlimited capital, was out on the same tack, and the result was that the price was forced up, and Hallwards were foolish enough to go on buying. They borrowed up to the limit of their capacity, and called a halt too late. If the thing had been known in time the City might have made an effort to keep the famous old firm on its legs, but it all came like a thunderclap. Hallwards went down, the American group got their railway stock at a knockout price, and old Mr Hallward, who had been ailing for some months, had a stroke of paralysis and died.

I was desperately sorry for Jim. The foundations of his world were upset, and he hadn't a notion what to do about it. You see, he didn't know the rudiments of the business, and couldn't be made to understand it. He went about in a dream, with staring, unseeing eyes, like a puzzled child. At first he screwed himself up to a sort of effort. He had many friends who would help, he thought, and he made various suggestions, all of a bottomless futility. Very soon he found that his Mayfair popularity was no sort of asset to him. He must have realised that people were beginning to turn a colder eye on a pauper than on an eligible young man, and his overtures were probably met with curt refusals. Anyhow, in a week he had given up hope. He felt himself a criminal and behaved as such. He saw nobody but his solicitors, and when he met a friend in the street he turned and ran. A perfectly unreasonable sense of disgrace took possession of him, and there was a moment when I was afraid he might put an end to himself.

This went on for the better part of a month, while I and one or two others were trying to save something from the smash. We put up a fund and bought some of the wreck-age, with the idea of getting together a little company to nurse it. It was important to do something, for though Jim was an only child and his mother was dead, there were various elderly female relatives who had their incomes from Hallwards. The firm had been much respected and old Hallward had been popular, and Jim had no enemies. There is a good deal of camaraderie in the City, and a lot of us were willing to combine and keep Jim going. We were all ready to help him, if he would only sit down and put his back into the job.

But that was just what Jim would not do. He had got a horror of the City, and felt a pariah whenever he met anybody who knew about the crash. He had eyes like a hunted hare's, and one couldn't get any sense out of him. I don't think he minded the change in his comforts – the end of polo and hunting and politics, and the prospect of cheap lodgings and long office hours. I believe he welcomed all that as a kind of atonement. It was the disgrace of the thing that came between him and his sleep. He knew only enough of the City to have picked up a wrong notion of its standards, and imagined that everybody was pointing a finger at him as a fool, and possibly a crook.

It was very little use reasoning with him. I pointed out that the right thing for him to do was to shoulder the burden and retrieve his father's credit. He laughed bitterly.

'Much good I'd be at that,' he said. 'You know I'm a baby in business, though you're too polite to tell me so.'

'You can have a try,' I said. 'We'll all lend you a hand.'

It was no use. References to his father and the firm's ancient prestige and his old great-aunts only made him shiver. You could see that his misery made him blind to argument. Then I began to lose my temper. I told him that it was his duty as a man to face the music. I asked him what else he proposed to do.

He said he meant to go to Canada and start life anew. He would probably change his name. I got out of patience with his silliness.

'You're offered a chance here to make good,' I told him. 'In Canada you'll have to find your chance, and how in God's name are you going to do it? You haven't been bred the right way to succeed in the Dominions. You'll probably starve.'

'Quite likely,' was his dismal answer. 'I'll make my book for that. I don't mind anything so long as I'm in a place where nobody knows me.'

'Remember, you are running away,' I said, 'running away from what I consider your plain duty. You can't expect to win out if you begin by funking.'

'I know – I know,' he wailed. 'I am a coward.'

I said no more, for when a man is willing to admit that he is a coward his nerves have got the better of his reason.

Well, the upshot was that Jim sailed for Canada with a little short of two hundred pounds in his pocket – what was left of his last allowance. He could have had plenty of introductions, but he wouldn't take them. He seemed to be determined to bury himself, and I daresay, too, he got a morbid satisfaction out of discomfort. He had still the absurd notion of disgrace, and felt that any handicap he laid on himself was a kind of atonement.

He reached Montreal in the filthy weeks when the spring thaw begins – the worst sample of weather to be found on the globe. Jim had not procured any special outfit, and he landed with a kit consisting of two smart tweed suits, a suit of flannels, riding breeches and knickerbockers – the remnants of his London wardrobe. It wasn't quite the rig for a poor man to go looking for a job in. He had travelled steerage, and, as might have been expected from one in his condition, had not made friends, but he had struck up a tepid acquaintanceship with an Irishman who was employed in a lumber business. The fellow was friendly, and was struck by Jim's obvious air of education and good breeding, so, when he heard that he wanted work, he suggested that a clerkship might be got in his firm.

Jim applied, and was taken on as the clerk in charge of timber-cutting rights in Eastern Quebec. The work was purely mechanical, and simply meant keeping a record of numbered lots, checking them off on the map, and filling in the details in the register as they came to hand. But it required accuracy and strict attention, and Jim had little of either. Besides, he wrote the vile fist which is the special privilege of our public schools. He held down the job for a fortnight and then was fired.

He had found cheap lodgings in a boarding-house down east, and trudged the two miles in the slush to his office. His fellow-lodgers were willing enough to be friendly – clerks and shop-boys and typists and newspaper reporters most of them. Jim wasn't a snob, but he was rapidly becoming a hermit, for all his nerves were exposed and he shrank from his fellows. His shyness was considered English swank, and the others invented nicknames for him and sniggered when he appeared. Luckily he was too miserable to pay much attention. He had no interest in their games, their visits to the movies and to cheap dance-halls, and their precocious sweethearting. He could not get the hang of their knowing commercial jargon. They set him down as a snob, and he shrank from them as barbarians.

But there was one lodger, a sub-editor on a paper which I shall call the *Evening Hawk*, who saw a little farther than the rest. He realised that Jim was an educated man – a 'scholar' he called it, and he managed to get part of his confidence. So when Jim lost his lumber job he was offered a billet on the *Hawk*. There was no superfluity of men of his type in local journalism, and the editor thought it might give tone to his paper to have someone on the staff who could write decent English and keep them from making howlers about Europe. The *Hawk* was a lively, up-to-date production, very much Americanised in its traditions and its literary style, but it had just acquired some political influence and it hankered after more.

But Jim was no sort of success in journalism. He was tried out in a variety of jobs – as reporter, special correspondent, sub-editor – but he failed to give satisfaction in any. To begin with he had no news-sense. Not many things interested him in his present frame of mind, and he had no notion what would interest the *Hawk*'s readers. He couldn't compose snappy headlines, and it made him sick to try. His writing was no doubt a great deal more correct than that of his colleagues, but it was dull as ditch-water. To add to everything else he was desperately casual. It was not that he meant to be slack, but that he had no stimulus to make him concentrate his attention, and he was about the worst sub-editor, I fancy, in the history of the press.

Summer came, and sleet and icy winds gave place to dust and heat. Jim tramped the grilling streets, one vast ache of homesickness. He had to stick to his tweeds, for his flannel suit had got lost in his journeys between boarding-houses, and, as he mopped his brow in the airless newspaper rooms smelling of printers' ink and shaken by the great presses, he thought of green lawns at Hurlingham, and cool backwaters of the Isis, and clipped yew hedges in old gardens, and a pleasant club window overlooking St James's Street. He hungered for fresh air, but when on a Sunday morning he went for a long walk, he found no pleasure in the adjacent countryside. It all seemed dusty and tousled and unhomely. He wasn't complaining, for it seemed to him part of a rightful expiation, but he was very lonely and miserable.

I have said that he had landed with a couple of hundred pounds, and this he had managed to keep pretty well intact. One day at a quick-luncheon counter he got into talk with a man called McNee, a Manitoban who had fought in the war, and knew something about horses. McNee, like Jim, did not take happily to town life, and was very sick of his job with an automobile company, and looking about for a better. There was not much in common between the two men, except a dislike of Montreal, for I picture McNee as a rough diamond, an active enterprising fellow meant by Providence for a backwoods-man. He had heard of a big dam somewhere down in the Gaspé district, which was being constructed in connection with a pulp scheme. He knew one of the foremen, and believed that money might be made by anyone who could put up a little capital and run a store in the construction camp. He told Jim that it was a fine wild country with plenty of game in the woods, and that, besides making money easily, a storekeeper could have a white man's life. But every bit of a thousand dollars capital would be needed, and he could only lay his hands on a couple of hundred. To Jim in his stuffy lodging-house the scheme offered a blessed escape. He wanted to make money, he wanted fresh air and trees and running water, for your Englishman, though town-bred, always hankers after the country. So he gave up his job on the *Hawk*, just when it was about to give him up, and started out with McNee.

The place was his first disappointment. It was an ugly clearing in an interminable forest of dull spruces, which ran without a break to New Brunswick. However far you walked there was nothing to see except the low muffled hills and the monotonous green of the firs. The partners were given a big shack for their store, and made their sleeping quarters in one end of it. For stock they had laid in a quantity of tinned goods, tobacco, shirts and socks and boots, and a variety of musical instruments. But they found that most of their stuff was unmarketable, since the men were well fed and clothed by the company, and after a week their store had become a rough kind of café, selling hot-dogs, and ice cream and soft drinks. McNee was immensely proud of it and ornamented the walls with 'ideal faces' from the American magazines. He was a born restaurant keeper, if he had got his chance, but unfortunately there was not much profit in coco-cola and gingerade.

In about a fortnight the place became half eating-house, half club, where the workmen gathered of an evening to play cards. McNee was in his element, but Jim was no more use than a sick pup. He didn't understand the lingo, and his shyness and absorption made him as unpopular as in the Montreal boarding-houses. He saw his little capital slipping away, and there was no compensation in the way of a pleasant life. He tried to imitate McNee's air of hearty bonhomie, and miserably failed. His partner was a good fellow, and stood up for him when an irate navvy consigned him to perdition as a 'God-darned London dude', and Jim's own good temper and sense of only getting what he deserved did something to protect him. But he soon realised that he was a ghastly failure, and this knowledge prevented him expostulating with the other for his obvious shortcomings. For McNee soon became too much of a social success. Gaspé was not 'dry', and there was more than soft drinks consumed in the store, especially by the joint proprietor and his friend the foreman. Also McNee was a bit of a gambler and was perpetually borrowing small sums from capital to meet his losses.

Now and then Jim took a holiday, and tramped all of a long summer day. The country around being only partially surveyed, there was no map to be had, and he repeatedly lost himself. Once he struck a lumber camp and was given pork and beans by cheerful French-Canadians whose *patois* he could not follow. Once he had almost a happy day, when he saw his first moose. But generally he came back from stifling encounters with cedar swamps and *bois brûlé*, weary but unrefreshed. He was not in the frame of mind to get much comfort out of the Canadian wilds, for he was always sore with longing for a different kind of landscape.

The river on which the camp lay was the famous Maouchi, and twelve miles down on the St Lawrence shore was a big fishing-lodge owned by a rich New Yorker. Jim used to see members of the party – young men in marvellous knickerbockers and young women in jumpers like Joseph's coat, and he hid himself at the sight of them. Occasionally a big roadster would pass the store, conveying fishermen to some of the upper lakes. Once, when he was feeling specially dispirited after a long hot day, a car stopped at the door, and two people descended. They came into the store, and the young man asked for lemonade, declaring that their tongues were hanging out of their mouths. Happily McNee was there to serve them, while

Jim sheltered behind the curtain of the sleeping-room. He knew them both. One was a subaltern in the cavalry with whom he had played bridge in the club, the other was a girl whom he had danced with. Their workmanlike English clothes, their quiet clear English voices gave him a bad dose of homesickness. They were returning, he reflected, to hot baths and cool clean clothes and delicate food and civilised talk . . . For a moment he sickened at the sour stale effluvia of the eating-house, and the rank smell of the pork which McNee had been frying. Then he cursed himself for a fool and a child.

In the fall the work on the dam was shut down, and the store was closed. The partners couldn't remove their unsaleable goods, so the whole stock was sold at junk prices among the nearest villages. Jim found himself with about three hundred dollars in the world, and the long Canadian winter to get through. The fall on the other side of the Atlantic is the pick of the year, and the beauty of the flaming hillsides did a little to revive his spirits. McNee wanted to get back to Manitoba, where he had heard of a job, and Jim decided that he would try Toronto, which was supposed to be rather more healthy for Englishmen than the other cities. So the two travelled west together, and Jim insisted on paying McNee's fare to Winnipeg, thereby leaving himself a hundred and fifty dollars or so on which to face the world.

Toronto is the friendliest place on earth for the man who knows how to make himself at home there. There were plenty to help him if he had looked for them, for nowhere will you find more warm-hearted people to the square mile. But Jim's shyness and prickliness put him outside the pale. He made no effort to advertise the few assets he had, he was desperately uncommunicative, and his self-absorption was not unnaturally taken for 'side'. Also he made the mistake of letting himself get a little too far down in the social scale. His clothes had become very shabby, and his boots were bad; when the first snows came in November he bought himself a thick overcoat, and that left him no money to supplement the rest of his wardrobe, so that by Christmas he was a very good imitation of a tramp.

He tried journalism first, but as he gave no information about himself except that he had been for a few weeks on the Montreal *Hawk*, he had some difficulty in getting a job. At last he got work on a weekly rag simply because he had some notion of grammar. It lasted exactly a fortnight. Then he tried tutoring, and spent some of his last dollars on advertising; he had several nibbles, but always fell down at the interviews. One kind of parent jibbed at his superior manners, another at his inferior clothes. After that he jolted from one temporary job to another – a book-canvasser, an extra hand in a dry-goods-store in the Christmas week, where the counter hid the deficiencies of his raiment, a temporary clerk during a municipal election, a packer in a fancy-stationery business, and finally a porter in a third-class hotel. His employment was not continuous, and between jobs he must have nearly starved. He had begun in the ordinary cheap boarding-house, but, before he found quarters in the attic of the hotel he worked at, he had sunk to a pretty squalid kind of doss-house.

The physical discomfort was bad enough. He tramped the streets ill-clad and half-fed, and saw prosperous people in furs, and cheerful young parties, and fire-lit, book-lined rooms. But the spiritual trouble was worse. Sometimes, when things were very bad, he was fortunate enough to have his thoughts narrowed down to the obtaining of food and warmth. But at other times he would be tormented by a feeling that his misfortunes were deserved, and that Fate with a heavy hand was belabouring him because he was a coward. His trouble was no longer the idiotic sense of guilt about his father's bankruptcy; it was a much more rational penitence, for he was beginning to realise that I had been right, and that he had behaved badly in running away from a plain duty. At first he choked down the thought, but all that miserable winter it grew upon him. His disasters were a direct visitation of the Almighty on one who had shown the white feather. He came to have an almost mystical feeling about it. He felt that he was branded like Cain, so that everybody knew that he had funked, and yet he realised that a rotten morbid pride ironly prevented him from retracing his steps.

The second spring found him thin from bad feeding and with a nasty cough. He had the sense to see that a summer in that hotel would be the end of him, so, although he was in the depths of hopelessness, the instinct of self-preservation drove him to make a move. He wanted to get into the country, but it was impossible to get work on a farm from Toronto, and he had no money to pay for railway fares. In the end he was taken on as a navvy on a bit of railway construction work in the wilds of northern Ontario. He was given the price of his ticket and ten dollars' advance on his wages to get an outfit, and one day late in April he found himself dumped at a railhead on a blue lake, with firs, firs, as far as the eye could reach. But it was spring-time, the mating wildfowl were calling, the land was greening, and Jim drew long breaths of sweet air and felt that he was not going to die just yet.

But the camp was a roughish place, and he had no McNee to protect him. There was every kind of roughneck and deadbeat there, and Jim was a bad mixer. He was an obvious softy and new chum and a natural butt, and, since he was being tortured all the time by his conscience, his good nature and humble-mindedness were not so proof as they had been in Gaspé. His poor physical condition made him a bad workman, and he came in for a good deal of abuse as a slacker from the huskies who wrought beside him. The section boss was an Irishman called Malone with a tongue like a whiplash, and he found plenty of opportunities for practising his gift on Jim. But he was a just man, and after a bit of rough-tonguing he saw that Jim was very white about the gills and told him to show his hands. Not being accustomed to the pick, these were one mass of sores. Malone cross-examined him, found that he had been at college, and took him off construction and put him in charge of stores.

There he had an easier life, but he was more than ever the butt of the mess shack and the sleeping quarters. His crime was not only speaking with an English accent and looking like Little Willie, but being supposed to be a favourite of the boss. By and by the ragging became unbearable, and after his mug of coffee had been three times struck out of his hand at one meal, Jim lost his temper and hit out. In the fight which followed he was ridiculously outclassed. He had been fairly good at games, but he had never boxed since his private school, and it is well for Jim's kind of man to think twice before he takes on a fellow who has all his life earned his living by his muscles. But he stood up pluckily, and took a good deal of punishment before he was knocked out, and he showed no ill-will afterwards. The incident considerably improved his position. Malone, who heard of it, asked him where in God's name he had been brought up that he couldn't use his hands better, but didn't appear ill-pleased. The fight had another consequence. It gave him just a suspicion of self-confidence, and helped him on his way to the decision to which he was slowly being compelled.

A week later he was sent a hundred miles into the forest to take supplies to an advance survey party. It was something of a compliment that Malone should have picked him for the job, but Jim did not realise that. His brain was beating like a pendulum on his private trouble – that he had run away, that all his misfortunes were the punishment for his cowardice, and that, though he confessed his fault, he could not make his shrinking flesh go back. He saw England as an Eden indeed, but with angels and flaming swords at every gate. He pictured the lifted eyebrows and the shrugged shoulders as he crept into a clerk's job, with not only his father's shame on his head, but the added disgrace of his own flight. It had seemed impossible a year ago to stay on in London, but now it was a thousandfold more impossible to go home.

Yet the thought gave him no peace by day or night. He had six men in his outfit, two of them half-breeds, and the journey was partly by canoe – with heavy portages – and partly on foot with the stores in pack loads. It rained in torrents, the river was in flood, and the first day they made a bare twenty miles. The half-breeds were tough old customers, but the other four were not much to bank on, and on the third day, when they had to hump their packs and foot it on a bad trail through swampy woods in a cloud of flies, they decided that they had had enough. There was a new gold area just opened not so far away, and they announced that they intended to help themselves to what they wanted from the stores and then make a bee-line for the mines. They were an ugly type of tough, and had physically the upper hand of Jim and his half-breeds.

It was a nasty situation, and it shook Jim out of his private vexations. He spoke them fair, and proposed to make camp and rest for a day to talk it out. Privately he sent one of the half-breeds ahead to the survey party for help, while he kept his ruffians in play. Happily he had some whisky with him and he had them drinking and playing cards, which took him well into the afternoon. Then they discovered the half-breed's absence, and wouldn't believe Jim's yarn that he had gone off to find fresh meat. His only chance was to bluff high, and, since he didn't much care what happened to him, he succeeded. He went to bed that night with a tough beside him who had announced his intention of putting a bullet through his head if there was any dirty work. Sometime after midnight his messenger arrived with help, and fortunately his bedside-companion's bullet went wide. The stores, a bit depleted, were safely delivered, and when Jim got back to his base he received a solid cursing from his boss for his defective stewardship. But Malone concluded with one of his rare compliments. 'You'll train on, sonny,' he said. 'There's guts in you for all your goo-goo face.'

That episode put an end to Jim's indecision. His time in Canada had been one long chapter of black disasters, and he was confident that they were sent to him as a punishment. His last adventure had somehow screwed up his manhood. He hated Canada like poison, but the thought of going back to England made him green with apprehension. Yet he was clear that he must do it or never have a moment's peace. So he wrote to me and told me that for a year he had been considering things, and had come to the conclusion that he had behaved like a cad. He was coming back to get into any kind of harness I directed, and would I advance him thirty pounds for his journey?

Now the little company we had put together to nurse the wreckage of Hallwards had been doing rather well. One or two things had unexpectedly turned up trumps. There was enough money to keep the maiden aunts going, and it looked as if there would be a good deal presently for Jim. He had gone off leaving no address, so I had had no means of communicating with him. I cabled him a hundred pounds, and told him to come along.

One afternoon near the end of June he turned up in my office. He had crossed the Atlantic steerage, and his clothes were those of a docker who has been months out of work. The first thing he did was to plank eighty pounds on my desk. 'You sent me too much,' he said. 'I don't want to owe more than is necessary. You can stop the twenty quid out of my wages.'

At first sight I thought him very little changed in face. He was incredibly lean and tanned and his hair wanted cutting, but he had the same shy, hunted eyes as the boy who had bolted a year before. He did not seem to have won any self-confidence, except that the set of his mouth was a little firmer.

'I want to start work at once,' he said. 'I've come home to make atonement.'

It took me a long time to make him understand the position of affairs – that he could count even now on a respectable income, and that, if he put his back into it, Hallwards might once again become a power in the City.

263

'I was only waiting for you to come back,' I said, 'to revive the old name. Hallwards has a better sound than the Anglo-Orient Company.'

'But I can't touch a penny,' he said. 'What about the people who suffered through the bankruptcy?'

'There were very few,' I told him. 'None of the widow-and-orphan business. The banks were amply secured. The chief sufferers were your aunts and yourself, and that's going to be all right now.'

He listened with wide eyes, and slowly bewilderment gave place to relief, and relief to rapture. 'The first thing you've got to do', I said, 'is to go to your tailor and get some clothes. You'd better put up at an hotel till you can find a flat. I'll see about your club membership. If you want to play polo I'll lend you a couple of ponies. Come and dine with me tonight and tell me your story.'

'My God!' he murmured. 'Do you realise that for a year I've been on my uppers? That's my story.'

The rest of that summer Jim walked about in a happy mystification. Once he was decently dressed, I could see that Canada had improved him. He was better-looking, tougher, manlier; his shyness was now wariness and he had got a new and sounder code of values. He worked like a beaver in the office, and, though he was curiously slow and obtuse about some things, I began to see that he had his father's brains, and something, too, that old Hallward had never had, a sensitive, subtle imagination. For the rest he enjoyed himself. He came in for the end of the polo season, and he was welcomed back to his old set as if nothing had happened.

Then I ceased to see much of him. I had been over-working badly and needed a long holiday, so I went off to a

Scotch deer-forest in the middle of August and did not return till the beginning of October. Jim stuck tight to the office; he said that he had had all the holidays he wanted for a year or two.

On the second day after my return he came into my room and said that he wanted to speak to me privately. He wished, he said, that nothing should be done about the restoring the name of Hallwards. He would like the Anglo-Orient to go on just as it was before he returned, and he did not want the directorship which had been arranged.

'Why in the world?' I asked in amazement.

'Because I am going away. And I may be away for quite a time.'

When I found words, and that took some time, I asked if he had grown tired of England.

'Bless you, no! I love it better than any place on earth. The autumn scents are beginning, and London is snugging down for its blessed cosy winter, and the hunting will soon be starting, and last Sunday I heard the old cock pheasants shouting—'

'Where are you going? Canada?'

He nodded.

'Have you fallen in love with it?'

'I hate it worse than hell,' he said solemnly, and proceeded to say things which in the interest of Imperial good feeling I refrain from repeating.

'Then you must be mad!'

'No,' he said, 'I'm quite sane. It's very simple, and I've thought it all out. You know I ran away from my duty eighteen months ago. Well, I was punished for it. I was a howling failure in Canada . . . I haven't told you half . . . I pretty well starved . . . I couldn't hold down any job . . . I was

265

simply a waif and a laughing stock. And I loathed it – my God, how I loathed it! But I couldn't come back – the very thought of facing London gave me a sick pain. It took me a year to screw up my courage to do what I knew was my manifest duty. Well, I turned up, as you know.'

'Then that's all right, isn't it?' I observed obtusely. 'You find London better than you thought?'

'I find it Paradise,' and he smiled sadly. 'But it's a Paradise I haven't deserved. You see, I made a failure in Canada and I can't let it go at that. I hate the very name of the place and most of the people in it . . . Oh, I daresay there is nothing wrong with it, but one always hates a place where one has been a fool . . . I have got to go back and make good. I shall take two hundred pounds, just what I had when I first started out.'

I only stared, and he went on: 'I funked once, and that may be forgiven. But a man who funks twice is a coward. I funk Canada like the devil, and that is why I am going back. There was a man there – only one man – who said I had guts. I'm going to prove to that whole damned Dominion that I have guts, but principally I've got to prove it to myself . . . After that I'll come back to you, and we'll talk business.'

I could say nothing: indeed I didn't want to say anything. Jim was showing a kind of courage several grades ahead of old Jonah's. He had returned to Nineveh and found that it had no terrors, and was now going back to Tarshish, whales and all.

Tendebant Manus

Send not on your soul before
To dive from that beguiling shore,
And let not yet the swimmer leave
His clothes upon the sands of eve.

A. E. HOUSMAN

One night we were discussing Souldern, who had died a week before and whose memorial service had been held that morning in St Margaret's. He had come on amazingly in Parliament, one of those sudden rises which were common in the immediate post-war years, when the older reputations were being questioned and the younger men were too busy making a livelihood to have time for hobbies. His speeches, his membership of a commission where he had shown both originality and courage, and his reputed refusal, on very honourable grounds, of a place in the Cabinet, had given him in the popular mind a flavour of mystery and distinction. The papers had devoted a good deal of space to him, and there was a general feeling that his death – the result of a motor smash – was a bigger loss to the country than his actual achievement warranted.

'I never met him,' Palliser-Yeates said. 'But I was at school with his minor. You remember Reggie Souldern, Charles? An uncommon good fellow – makings of a fine soldier, too – disappeared with most of his battalion in March '18, and was never heard of again. Body committed to the pleasant land of France but exact spot unknown – rather like a burial at sea.'

'I knew George Souldern well enough,' said Lamancha, whom he addressed. 'I sat in the House with him for two years before the war. That is to say, I knew as much of him as anybody did, but there was very little you could lay hold of. He used to be a fussy, ineffective chap, very fertile in ideas which he never thought out, and always starting hares that he wouldn't hunt. But just lately he seems to have had a call, and he looked as if he might have a career. Rotten luck that a sharp corner and a lout of a motor-cyclist should have put an end to it.'

He turned to his neighbour. 'Wasn't he a relation of yours, Sir Arthur?'

The man addressed was the oldest member of the Club and by far the most distinguished. Sir Arthur Warcliff had been a figure of note when most of us were in our cradles. He began life in the Sappers, and before he was thirty had been in command of a troublesome little Somaliland expedition; then he had governed a variety of places with such success that he was seriously spoken of for India. In the war he would have liked to have returned back to soldiering, but they used him as the Cabinet handy-man, and he had all the worst diplomatic and administrative jobs to tackle. You see, he was a master of detail and had to translate the generalities of policy into action. He had never, as the jargon goes, got his personality over the footlights, so he was only a name to the public – but a tremendous name, of which every party spoke respectfully. He had retired now, and lived alone with his motherless boy. Usually, for all his sixty-five years, he seemed a contemporary, for he was curiously young at heart, but every now and then we looked at his wise, worn face, realised what he had been and was, and sat at his feet.

'Yes,' he said in reply to Lamancha. 'George Souldern was my wife's cousin, and I knew him well for the last twenty years. Since the war I knew him better, and in the past eighteen months I was, I think, his only intimate friend.'

'Was he a really big man?' Sandy Arbuthnot asked. 'I don't take much stock in his profession – but I thought – just for a moment – in that Irish row – that I got a glimpse of something rather out of the ordinary.'

'He had first-class brains.'

Sandy laughed. 'That doesn't get you very far,' he said. The phrase 'first-class brains' had acquired at the time a flavour of comedy.

'No. It doesn't. If you had asked me the question six years ago I should have said that George was a brilliant failure. Immensely clever in his way, really well educated – which very few of us are – laborious as a beaver, but futile. The hare that is always being passed by every kind of tortoise. He had everything in his favour, but nothing ever came out as he wanted it. I only knew him after he came down from Oxford, but I believe that at the University he was a nonpareil.'

'I was up with him,' said Peckwether, the historian. 'Oh, yes, he was a big enough figure there. He was head of Winchester, and senior scholar of Balliol, and took two Firsts and several University prizes in his stride. He must have sat up all night, for he never appeared to work – you see, it was his pose to do things easily – a variety of the Grand Manner. He was a most disquieting undergraduate. In his political speeches he had the air of having just left a Cabinet meeting.'

'Was he popular?' someone asked.

'Not a bit,' said Peckwether. 'And for all his successes we didn't believe in him. He was too worldly-wise – what we used to call "banausic" – too bent on getting on. We felt that he had all his goods in the shop window, and that there was no margin to him.'

Sir Arthur smiled. 'A young man's contemporaries are pretty shrewd judges. When I met him first I felt the same thing. He wasn't a prig, and he had a sense of humour, and he had plenty of ordinary decent feeling. But he was the kind of man who could never forget himself and throw his cap over the moon. One couldn't warm to him . . . But, unlike you, I thought he would succeed. The one thing lacking was money, and within two years he had remedied that. He married a rich wife; the lady died, but the fortune remained. I believe it was an honest love match, and for a long time he was heart-broken, and when he recovered he buried himself in work. You would have said that something was bound to happen. Young, rich, healthy, incredibly industrious, able, presentable – you would have said that any constituency would have welcomed him, that his party would have jumped at him, that he would have been a prodigious success.

'But he wasn't. He made a bad candidate, and had to stand three times before he got into the House. And there he made no kind of impression, though he spoke conscientiously and always on matters he knew about. He wrote a book on the meaning of colonial nationalism – fluent, well expressed, sensible, even in parts eloquent, but somehow it wasn't read. He was always making speeches at public dinners and at the annual meetings of different kinds of associations, but it didn't seem to signify what he said, and he was scarcely reported. There was no conspiracy of silence to keep him down, for people rather liked him. He simply seemed to have no clear boundary lines and to be imperfectly detached from the surrounding atmosphere. I could never understand why.'

'Lack of personality,' said Lamancha. 'I remember feeling that.'

'Yes, but what is personality? He had the things that make it – brains and purpose. One liked him – was impressed by his attainments, but, if you understand me, one wasn't impressed by the man . . . It wasn't ordinary lack of confidence, for on occasion he could be aggressive. It was the lack of a continuity of confidence – in himself and in other things. He didn't *believe* enough. That was why, as you said, he was always starting hares that he wouldn't hunt. Some excellent and unanswerable reason would occur to him why he should slack off. He was what I believe you call a good party man and always voted orthodoxly, but, after four years in the House, instead of being a leader he was rapidly becoming a mere cog in the machine. He didn't seem to be able to make himself count.

'That was his position eight years ago, and it was not far from a tragedy. He was as able as any man in the Cabinet, but he lacked the demonic force which even stupid people sometimes possess. I can only describe him in paradoxes. He was at once conceited and shy, inordinately ambitious and miserably conscious that he never got the value of his abilities out of life . . . Then came the war.'

'He served, didn't he?' Leithen asked. 'I remember running across him at GHQ.'

'You may call it serving, if you mean that he was never out of uniform for four years. But he didn't fight. I wanted him to. I thought a line battalion might make a man of

271

him, but he shrank from the notion. It wasn't lack of courage – I satisfied myself of that. But he hadn't the nerve to sink himself into the ranks of ordinary men. You understand why? It would have meant the realisation of what was the inmost fear of his heart. He had to keep up the delusion that he was some sort of a swell – had to have authority to buttress his tottering vanity.

'So he had a selection of footling staff jobs – *liaison* with this and that, deputy-assistant to Tom, Dick and Harry, quite futile, but able to command special passes and staff cars. He ranked, I think, as a full colonel, but an Army Service Corps private was more useful than ten of him. And he was as miserable as a man could be. He liked people to think that his trouble was the strain of the war, but the real strain was that there was no strain. He knew that he simply didn't matter. At least he was candid with himself, and he was sometimes candid with me. He rather hoped, I think, that I would inspan him into something worth doing, but in common honesty I couldn't, for you see I too had come to disbelieve in him utterly.

'Well, that went on till March 1918, when his brother Reggie was killed in the German push. Ninth Division, wasn't it?'

Palliser-Yeates nodded. 'Ninth. South African Brigade. He went down at Marrières Wood, but he and his lot stuck up the enemy for the best part of a Sunday, and I solemnly believe, saved our whole front. They were at the critical point, you see, the junction of Gough and Byng. His body was never found.'

'I know,' said Sir Arthur, 'and that is just the point of my story.'

He stopped. 'I suppose I'm right to tell you this. He left

instructions that if anything happened to him I was to have his diary. He can't have meant me to keep it secret . . . No, I think he would have liked one or two people to know.'

He looked towards Palliser-Yeates. 'You knew Reggie Souldern? How would you describe him?'

'The very best stamp of British regimental officer,' was the emphatic reply.

'Clever?'

'Not a bit. Only average brains, but every ounce of them useful. Always cheery and competent, and a born leader of men. He was due for a brigade when he fell, and if the war had lasted another couple of years he might have had a corps. I never met the other Souldern, but from what you say he must have been the plumb opposite of Reggie.'

'Just so. George had a great opinion of his brother – in addition to the ordinary brotherly love, for there were only the two of them. I thought the news of his death would break him altogether. But it didn't. He took it with extra-ordinary calm, and presently it looked as if he were actually more cheerful . . . You see, they never found the body. He never saw him lying dead, or even the grave where he was buried, and he never met anybody who had. Reggie had been translated mysteriously out of the world, but the melancholy indisputable signs of death were lacking.'

'You mean he thought he was only missing and might turn up some day?'

'No. He *knew* he was dead – the proof was too strong, the presumption was too heavy . . . But while there was enough to convince his reason, there was too little for his imagination – no white face and stiff body, no wooden cross in the cemetery. He could *picture* him as still alive, and George had a queer sensitive imagination about which most people knew nothing.'

Sir Arthur looked round the table and saw that we were puzzled.

'It is a little difficult to explain . . . Do you remember a story of the French at Verdun making an attack over ground they had been fighting on for months? They shouted "*En avant, les morts*", and they believed that the spirits of the dead responded and redressed the balance. I think it was the last action at Vaux . . . I don't suppose the *poilu* thought the dead came back to help him, but he pretended they were still combatants, and got a moral support from the fancy . . . That was something like George Souldern's case. If you had asked him, you would have found that he had no doubt that what was left of Reggie was somewhere in the churned-up wilderness north of Péronne. And there was never any nonsense about visitations or messages from the dead . . . But the lack of *visible* proofs enabled his imagination to picture Reggie as still alive, and going from strength to strength. He nursed the fancy till it became as real to him as anything in his ordinary life . . . Reggie was becoming a great man and would soon be the most famous man in the world, and something of Reggie went into him and he shared in Reggie's glory. In March '18 a partnership began for George Souldern with his dead brother, and the dead, who in his imagination was alive and triumphant, lifted him out of the sticky furrow which he had been ploughing since he left Oxford.'

We were all silent except Pugh, who said that he had come across the same thing in the East – some Rajput prince, I think.

'How did you know this?' Lamancha asked.

'From the diary. George set down very fully every stage of his new career. But I very nearly guessed the truth for myself. You see, knowing him as I did, I had to admit a sudden and staggering change.'

'How soon?'

'The week after the news came. I had been in Paris, and on my return ran across George in the Travellers' and said the ordinary banal words of sympathy. He looked at me queerly, as he thanked me, and if I had not known how deeply attached the brothers were, I would have said that he was exhilarated by his loss. It was almost as if he had been given a drug to strengthen his arteries. He seemed to me suddenly a more substantial fellow, calmer, more at peace with himself. He said an odd thing too. "Old Reggie has got his chance," he said, and then, as if pulling himself up, "I mean, he had the chance he wanted."

'In June it was clear that something had happened to George Souldern. Do you remember how about that time a wave of dejection passed over all the Allied countries? It was partly the mess in Russia, partly in this country a slight loss of confidence in the Government, which seemed to have got to loggerheads with the soldiers, but mainly the "drag" that comes in all wars. It was the same in the American Civil War before Gettysburg. Foch was marking time, but he was doing it by retreating pretty fast on the Aisne. Well, our people needed a little cheering up, and our politicians tried their hand at it. There was a debate in Parliament, and far the best speech was George's. The rest was mere platitude and rhetoric, but he came down on the point like a steam-hammer.'

'I know,' said Lamancha. 'I read it in *The Times* in a field hospital in Palestine.'

275

'In his old days nobody would have paid much attention. He would have been clever and epigrammatic – sound enough, but "precious". His speech would have read well, if it had been reported, but it wouldn't have mattered a penn'orth to anybody . . . Instead he said just the wise, simple, stalwart thing that every honest man had at the back of his head, and he said it with an air which made everybody sit up. For the first time in his life he spoke as one having authority. The press reported him nearly verbatim, for the journalists in the Gallery have a very acute sense of popular values.

'The speech put George, as the phrase goes, on the political map. The Prime Minister spoke to me about him, and there was some talk of employing him on a mission which never materialised. I met him one day in the street and congratulated him, and I remember that I was struck by the new vigour in his personality. He made me come home with him to tea, and to talk to him was like breathing ozone. He asked me one or two questions about numbers, and then he gave me his views on the war. At the time it was fashionable to think that no decision would be reached till the next summer, but George maintained that, if we played our cards right, victory was a mathematical certainty before Christmas. He showed a knowledge of the military situation which would have done credit to any soldier, and he could express himself, which few soldiers can do. His arguments stuck in my head, and I believe I used them in the War Cabinet. I left with a very real respect for one whom I had written off as a failure.

'Well, then came the last battle of the Marne, and Haig's great advance, and all the drama and confusion of the autumn months. I lost sight of George, for I was busy with the peace overtures, and I don't think I even heard of him again till the new year . . . But the diary tells all about those months. I am giving you the bones of the story, but I am going to burn the diary, for it is too intimate for other eyes . . . According to it Reggie finished the war as a blazing hero. It was all worked out in detail with maps and diagrams. He had become a corps commander by August, and in October he was the chief fighting figure on the British front, the conduit pipe of Foch's ideas, for he could work out in practice what the great man saw as a vision. It sounds crazy, but it was so convincingly done that I had to rub my eyes and make myself remember that Reggie was lying in a nameless grave on the Somme and not a household word in two hemispheres . . . George, too, shared in his glory, but just how was not very clear. Anyway, the brothers were in the front of the stage, Reggie the bigger man and George his civilian adviser and opposite number. I can see now how he got his confidence. He was no longer a struggler, but a made man; he had arrived, he was proved, the world required him. Whatever he said or did must be attended to, and, because he believed this, it was.'

Lamancha whistled long and low. 'But how could his mind work, if he lived among fairy tales?' he asked.

'He didn't,' said Sir Arthur. 'He lived very much in the real world. But he had all the time his private imaginative preserve, into which his normal mind did not penetrate. He drew his confidence from this preserve, and, having once got it, could carry it also into the real world.'

'Wasn't he intolerably conceited?' someone asked.

'No, for the great man was Reggie and he was only a satellite. He was Reggie's prophet, and assured enough on that side, but there was no personal arrogance. His dead brother had become, so to speak, his familiar spirit, his *demon*. The fact is that George was less of an egotist than he had ever been before. His vanity was burned up in a passion of service.

'I saw him frequently during the first half of '19, and had many talks with him. He had been returned to Parliament by a big majority, but he wasn't much in the public eye. He didn't like the way things were going, but at the same time as a good citizen he declined to make things more difficult for the Government. The diary gives his thoughts at that time. He considered that the soldiers should have had the chief share in the settlement of the world – Foch and Haig and Hindenburg – and Reggie. He held that they would have made a cleaner and fairer job of it than the kind of circus that appeared at Versailles. Perhaps he was right – I can't be dogmatic, for I was a performer in the circus.

'That, of course, I didn't know till the other day. But the change in George Souldern was soon manifest to the whole world. There was the Irish business, when he went down to the worst parts of the South and West, and seemed to be simply asking for a bullet in his head. He was half Irish, you know. He wrote and said quite frankly that he didn't care a straw whether Ireland was inside or outside the British Empire, that the only thing which mattered was that she should find a soul, and that she had a long road to travel before she got one. He told her that at present she was one vast perambulating humbug, and that till she got a little discipline and sense of realities she would remain on the level of Haiti. Why some gunman didn't have a shot at him I can't imagine, except that such naked candour and courage was a new thing and had to be respected . . . Then there was the Unemployment Commission. You remember the majority report – pious generalities and futile compromises; George's dissenting report made him for a month the best abused man in Britain, for he was impartially contemptuous of all sides. Today – well, I fancy most of us would agree with George, and I observe that he is frequently quoted by the Labour people.

'What struck me about his line of country was that it was like that of a good soldier's. He had the same power of seeing simple facts and of making simple syllogisms, which the clever intellectual – such as George used to be – invariably misses. And there was the soldier's fidelity and sense of service. George plainly had no axe to grind. He had intellectual courage and would back his views as a general backs his strategy, but he kept always a curious personal modesty. I tell you it seemed nothing short of a miracle to one who had known him in the old days.

'I accepted it as the act of God and didn't look for any further explanation. I think that what first set me questioning was his behaviour about Reggie's memorial. The family wanted a stone put up in the churchyard of the family place in Gloucestershire. George absolutely declined. He stuck his toes into the ground and gave nothing but a flat refusal. One might have thought that the brothers had been estranged, but it was common knowledge that they had been like twins and had written to each other every day.

'Then there was the business about a memoir of Reggie. The regiment wanted one, and his Staff College contemporaries. Tollett – you remember him, the man on the Third Army Staff – volunteered to write it, of course with George's assistance. George refused bluntly and said that he felt the strongest distaste for the proposal. Tollett came to me about it, and I had George to luncheon and thrashed it out with him. I found his reasons very difficult to follow, for he objected even to a regimental history being compiled. He admitted that Tollett was as good a man as could be found for the job, but he said he hated the idea. Nobody understood Reggie but himself. Some day, he suggested, he might try to do justice to him in print – but not yet. I put forward all the arguments I could think of, but George was adamant.

'Walking home, I puzzled a good deal about the affair. It couldn't be merely the jealousy of a writer who wanted to reserve a good subject for himself – that wasn't George's character, and he had no literary vanity. Besides, that wouldn't explain his aversion to a prosaic regimental chronicle, and still less his objection to the cenotaph in the Gloucestershire churchyard. I wondered if there was not some quirk in George, some odd obsession about his brother. For a moment I thought that he might have been dabbling in spiritualism and have got some message from Reggie, till I remembered that I had heard him a week before declare his unbridled contempt for such mumbo-jumbo.

'I thought a good deal about it, and the guess I made was that George was living a double life – that in his sub-consciousness Reggie was still alive for him. It was only a guess, but it was fairly near the truth, and last year I had it from his own lips.

'We were duck-shooting together on Croftsmoor, the big marsh near his home. That had been Reggie's pet game; he used to be out at all hours in the winter dawns and dusks stalking wildfowl. George never cared for it, or indeed for any field sport. He would take his place at a

covert shoot or a grouse drive and was useful enough with a gun, but he would have been the first to disclaim the title of sportsman. But now he was as keen and tireless as Reggie. He kept me out for eight hours in a filthy day of rain wading in trench boots in Gloucestershire mud.

'We did fairly well, and just before sunset the weather improved. The wind had gone into the north, and promised frost, and as we sat on an old broken-backed stone bridge over one of the dykes, waiting for the birds to be collected from the different stands, the western sky was one broad band of palest gold. We were both tired, and the sudden change from blustering rain to a cold stillness, and from grey mist to colour and light, had a strange effect upon my spirits. I felt peaceful and solemnised. I lit a pipe, but let it go out, for my attention was held by the shoreless ocean in the west, against which the scarp of the Welsh hills showed in a dim silhouette. The sharp air, the wild marsh scents, the faint odour of tobacco awoke in me a thousand half-sad and half-sweet recollections.

'I couldn't help it. I said something about Reggie.

'George was sitting on the bridge with his eyes fixed on the sky. I thought he hadn't heard me, till suddenly he repeated "Reggie. Yes, old Reggie."

' "This was what he loved," I said.

' "He still loves it," was the answer, spoken very low. And then he repeated – to himself as it were:

> " 'Fight on, fight on,' said Sir Andrew Barton.
> 'Though I be wounded I am not slain.
> I'll lay me down and bleed awhile
> And then I'll rise and fight again.' "

He turned his fine-drawn face to me.

' "You think Reggie is dead?"

'I didn't know what to say. "Yes," I stammered, "I suppose—"

' "What do you mean by death?" His voice was almost shrill. "We know nothing about it. What does it matter if the body is buried in a shell-hole—?"

'He stopped suddenly, as a lamp goes out when you press the switch. I had the impression that those queer shrill words came not from George but from some other who had joined us.

' "I believe that the spirit is immortal," I began.

' "The spirit—" again the shrill impersonal voice – "I tell you the whole man lives . . . He is nearer to me than he ever was . . . we are never parted . . ."

'Again the light went out. He seemed to gulp, and when he spoke it was in his natural tones.

' "I apologise," he said, "I must seem to you to be talking nonsense . . . You don't understand. *You* would understand, if anyone could, but I can't explain – yet – some day . . ."

'The head-keeper, the beaters and the dogs came out of the reed beds, and at the same time the uncanny glow in the west was shrouded with the film of the coming night. It was almost dark when we turned to walk home, and I was glad of it, for neither of us wished to look at the other's face.

'I felt at once embarrassed and enlightened. I had been given a glimpse into the cloudy places of a man's soul, and had surprised his secret. My guess had been right. In George's subconscious mind Reggie was still alive – nay more, was progressing in achievement as if he had never disappeared in the March battle. It was no question of a disembodied spirit establishing communication with the living – that was a business I knew nothing about, nor George either. It was a question of life, complete life, in a peculiar world, companionship in some spiritual fourth dimension, and from that companionship he was drawing sustenance. He had learned Reggie's forthrightness and his happy simplicity . . . I wondered and I trembled. There is a story of an early Victorian statesman who in his leisure moments played at being Emperor of Byzantium. The old Whig kept the two things strictly separate – he was a pious humanitarian in his English life, though he was a ruthless conqueror in the other. But in George's case the two were mingling. He was going about his daily duties with the power acquired from his secret world; that secret world, in which, with Reggie, he had become a master, was giving him a mastery over our common life . . . I did not believe it would last. It was against nature that a man could continue to live as a parasite on the dead.

'I am almost at the end of my story. Two months later, George became a figure of national importance. It was he who chiefly broke up the Coalition at the Grafton House meeting, and thereby, I suppose, saved his party. His speech, you remember, clove through subtleties and irrelevances with the simple declaration that he could not work with what he could not trust, and unless things changed, must go out of public life. That was Reggie's manner, you know – pure Reggie. Then came the general election and the new Government, and George, very much to people's surprise, refused Cabinet office. The reason he gave was that on grounds of principle he had taken a chief part in wrecking the late Ministry, and he felt he could not allow himself to benefit personally by his action. We all thought him high-minded, if finical and quixotic, but the ordinary man liked it – it was a welcome change from the old gang of *arrivistes*. But it was not the real reason. I found that in the diary.'

Sir Arthur stopped, and there was a silence while he seemed to be fumbling for words.

'Here we are walking on the edge of great mysteries,' he continued. 'The reason why he refused the Prime Minister's offer was Reggie . . . Somehow the vital force in that subconscious world of his was ebbing . . . I cannot explain how, but Reggie was moving away from what we call realities and was beckoning him to follow . . . The Grafton House speech was George's last public utterance. Few people saw him after that, for he rarely attended the House. I saw him several times in Gloucestershire . . . Was he happy? Yes, I should say utterly happy, but too detached, too peaceful, as if he had done with the cares of his world . . . I think I guessed what was happening, when he told me that he had consented to the cenotaph in the churchyard. He took a good deal of pains about it, too, and chose an inscription, which his maiden aunts thought irreligious. It was Virgil's "*Tendebant manus ripae ulterioris amore*" . . . He withdrew his objection to the memoir, too, and Tollett got to work, but he gave him no help – it was as if he had lost interest . . . It is an odd thing to say, but I have been waiting for the news which was in last week's paper.'

'You don't mean that he engineered the motor smash?' Lamancha asked.

'Oh no,' said Sir Arthur gently. 'As I said, we are treading on the brink of great mysteries. Say that it was predestined, fore-ordained, decreed by the Master of Assembly . . . I know that it had to be. If you join hands with the dead they will pull you over the stream.'

The Last Crusade

It is often impossible, in these political inquiries, to find any proportion between the apparent force of any moral causes we may assign, and their known operation. We are therefore obliged to deliver up that operation to mere chance; or, more piously (perhaps more rationally), to the occasional interposition and the irresistible hand of the Great Disposer.

BURKE

One evening the talk at dinner turned on the Press. Lamancha was of opinion that the performances of certain popular newspapers in recent years had killed the old power of the anonymous printed word. 'They bluffed too high,' he said, 'and they had their bluff called. All the delphic oracle business has gone from them. You haven't today what you used to have – papers from which the ordinary man docilely imbibes all his views. There may be one or two still, but not more.'

Sandy Arbuthnot, who disliked journalism as much as he liked journalists, agreed, but there was a good deal of difference of opinion among the others. Palliser-Yeates thought that the Press had more influence than ever, though it might not be much liked; a man, he said, no longer felt the kind of loyalty towards his newspaper that he felt towards his club and his special brand of cigar, but he was mightily influenced by it all the same. He might read it only for its news, but in the selection of news a paper could wield an uncanny power.

Francis Martendale was the only journalist among us, and he listened with half-closed sleepy eyes. He had been a war correspondent as far back as the days of the South African War, and since then had seen every serious row on the face of the globe. In France he had risen to command a territorial battalion, and that seemed to have satisfied his military interest, for since 1919 he had turned his mind to business. He was part-owner of several provincial papers, and was connected in some way with the great Ladas news agency. He had several characters which he kept rigidly separate. One was a philosopher, for he had translated Henri Poincaré, and published an acute little study of Bergson; another was a yachtsman, and he used to race regularly in the twelve-metre class at Cowes. But these were his relaxations, and five days in the week he spent in an office in the Fleet Street neighbourhood. He was an enthusiast about his hobbies and a cynic about his profession, a not uncommon mixture; so we were surprised when he differed from Lamancha and Sandy and agreed with Palliser-Yeates.

'No doubt the power of the leader-writer has waned,' he said. 'A paper cannot set a Cabinet trembling because it doesn't like its policy. But it can colour the public mind most damnably by a steady drip of tendentious news.'

'Lies?' Sandy asked.

'Not lies – truths judiciously selected – half-truths with no context. Facts – facts all the time. In these days the Press is obliged to stick to facts. But it can make facts into *news*, which is a very different class of goods. And it can interpret facts – don't forget that. It can report that Burminster fell asleep at a public dinner – which he did – in such a way as to make everybody think that he was drunk – which he wasn't.'

286

'Rather a dirty game?' someone put in.

'Sometimes – often perhaps. But now and then it works out on the side of the angels. Do any of you know Roper Willinck?'

There was a general confession of ignorance.

'Pity. He would scarcely fit in here, but he is rather a great man and superbly good company. There was a little thing that Willinck once did – or rather helped to do, with about a million other people who hadn't a notion what was happening. That's the fun of journalism. You light a match and fling it away, and the fire goes smouldering round the globe, and ten thousand miles off burns down a city. I'll tell you about it if you like, for it rather proves my point.'

It all began – said Martendale – with an old Wesleyan parson of the name of Tubb, who lived at a place called Rhenosterspruit on the east side of Karroo. He had been a missionary, but the place had grown from a small native reserve to an ordinary up-country dorp; the natives were all Christians now, and he had a congregation of store-keepers, and one or two English farmers, and the landlady of the hotel, and the workmen from an adjacent irrigation dam. Mr Tubb was a man of over seventy, a devoted pastor with a gift of revivalist eloquence, but not generally con-sidered very strong in the head. He was also a bachelor. He had caught a chill and had been a week in bed, but he rose on the Sunday morning to conduct service as usual.

Now about that time the Russian Government had been rather distinguishing themselves. They had had a great function at Easter, run by what they called the Living Church, which had taken the shape of a blasphemous par-ody of the Christian rites and a procession of howling dervishes who proclaimed that God was dead and Heaven and Hell wound up. Also they had got hold of a Patriarch, a most respected Patriarch, put him on trial for high treason, and condemned him to death. They had postponed the execution, partly by way of a refinement of cruelty, and partly, I suppose, to see just how the world would react; but there seemed not the slightest reason to doubt that they meant to have the old man's blood. There was a great outcry, and the Archbishop of Canterbury and the Pope had something to say, and various Governments made official representations, but the Bolshies didn't give a hoot. They felt that they needed to indulge in some little bit of extra blackguardism just to show what stout fellows they were.

Well, all this was in the cables from Riga and Warsaw and Helsingfors, and it got into the weekly edition of the *Cape Times*. There Mr Tubb read it, as he lay sick in bed, and, having nothing else to worry about, it fretted him terribly. He could not bear to think of those obscene orgies in Moscow, and the story of the Patriarch made him frantic. This, it seemed to him, was a worse persecution than Nero's or Diocletian's, and the Patriarch was a nobler figure than any martyr of the Roman amphitheatre; and all the while the Christian peoples of the world were doing nothing. So Mr Tubb got out of bed on that Sunday morning, and, having had no time to prepare a sermon, delivered his soul from the pulpit about the Bolshies and their doings. He said that what was needed was a new crusade, and he called on every Christian man and woman to devote their prayers, their money and, if necessary, their blood to this supreme cause. Old as he was, he said, he would gladly set off for Moscow that instant and die beside the Patriarch, and count his life well lost in such a testimony of his faith.

I am sure that Mr Tubb meant every word he said, but he had an unsympathetic audience, who were not interested in Patriarchs; and the hotel-lady slumbered, and the store-keepers fidgeted and the girls giggled and whispered just as usual. There the matter would have dropped, had not a young journalist from Cape Town been spending his holidays at Rhenosterspruit and out of some caprice been present at the service. He was an ambitious lad, and next morning despatched to his paper a brightly written account of Mr Tubb's challenge. He wrote it with his tongue in his cheek, and headed it, 'Peter the Hermit at Rhenosterspruit' with, as a sub-title, 'The Last Crusade'. His editor cut it savagely, and left out all his satirical touches, so that it read rather bald and crude. Still, it got about a quarter of a column.

That week the Ladas representative at Cape Town was rather short of material, and just to fill up his budget of out-going news put in a short message about Rhenosterspruit. It ran: 'On Sunday Tubb Wesleyan Minister Rhenoster-spruit summoned congregation in name Christianity release Patriarch and announced intention personally lead crusade Moscow.' That was the result of the cutting of the bright young correspondent's article. What he had meant as fantasy and farce was so summarised as to appear naked facts. Ladas in London were none too well pleased with the message. They did not issue it to the British Press, and they cabled to the Cape Town people that, while they welcomed 'human interest' stories, they drew the line at that sort of thing. What could it matter to the world what a Wesleyan parson in the Karroo thought about Zinovieff? They wanted news, not nonsense.

Now behold the mysterious workings of the Comic Spirit. Ladas, besides their general service to the Canadian

Press, made special services to several Canadian papers. One of these was called, shall we say? the *Toronto Watchman*. The member of the Ladas staff who had the compiling of the *Watchman* budget was often hard-pressed, for he had to send news which was not included in the general service. That week he was peculiarly up against it, so he went through the files of the messages that had come in lately and had not already been transmitted to Canada, and in the Cape Town section he found the Rhenosterspruit yarn. He seized on it joyfully, for he did not know of the disfavour with which his chief had regarded it, and he dressed it up nicely for Toronto. The *Watchman* he knew was a family paper, with a strong religious connection, and this would be meat and drink to it. So he made the story still more matter-of-fact. Mr Tubb had sounded a call to the Christian Church, and was himself on the eve of setting out against Trotsky like David against Goliath. He left the captions to the Toronto sub-editors, but of his own initiative he mentioned John Knox. That, he reflected comfortably, as he closed up and went off to play golf, would fetch the Presbyterian-minded *Watchman*.

It did. The Editor of the *Watchman*, who was an elder of the Kirk and Liberal Member of Parliament, had been getting very anxious about the ongoings in Russia. He was not very clear what a Patriarch was, but he remembered that various Anglican ecclesiastics had wanted to affiliate the English and Greek Churches, so he concluded that he was some kind of Protestant. He had, like most people, an intense dislike of Moscow and its ways, and he had been deeply shocked by the Easter sacrilege. So he went large on the Ladas message. It was displayed on his chief page, side by side with all the news he could collect about the

Patriarch, and he had no less than two leaders on the subject. The first, which he wrote himself, was headed 'The Weak Things of the World and the Strong'. He said that Mr Tubb's clarion-call, 'the voice of a simple man of God echoing from the lonely veld', might yet prove a turning-point in history, and he quoted Burke about a child and a girl at an inn changing the fate of nations. It might – it should – arouse the conscience of the Christian world, and inaugurate a new crusade, which would lift mankind out of the rut of materialism and open its eyes to the eternal verities. Christianity had been challenged by the miscreants in Russia, and the challenge must be met. I don't think he had any very clear idea what he meant, for he was strongly opposed to anything that suggested war, but it was a fine chance for 'uplift' writing. The second leader was called 'The Deeper Obligations of Empire', and, with a side glance at Mr Tubb, declared that unless the British Empire was a spiritual and moral unity it was not worth talking about.

The rest of the Canadian Press did not touch the subject. They had not had the Rhenosterspruit message, and were not going to lift it. But the *Watchman* had a big circulation, and Mr Tubb began to have a high, if strictly local, repute. Several prominent clergymen preached sermons on him, and a weekly paper printed a poem in which he was compared to St Theresa and Joan of Arc.

The thing would have been forgotten in a fortnight, if McGurks had not chosen to take a hand. McGurks, as you probably know, is the biggest newspaper property in the world directed by a single hand. It owns outright well over a hundred papers, and has a controlling interest in perhaps a thousand. Its tone is strictly national, not to say chauvinistic; its young men in Europe at that time were all hundred-per-cent Americans, and returned to the States a hundred and twenty per cent, to allow for the difference in the exchange. McGurks does not love England, for it began with strong Irish connections, and it has done good work in pointing out to its immense public the predatory character of British Imperialism and the atrocities that fill the shining hours in India and Egypt. As a matter of fact, however, its politics are not very serious. What it likes is a story that can be told in thick black headlines, so that the stupidest of its free-born readers, glancing in his shirt-sleeves at the first page of his Sunday paper, can extract nourishment. Murders, rapes, fires and drownings are its daily bread, and it fairly revels in details – measurements and plans, names and addresses of witnesses, and appalling half-tone blocks. Most unfairly it is called sensational, for the stuff is as dull as a directory.

With regard to Russia, McGurks had steered a wavy course. It had begun in 1917 by flaunting the banner of freedom, for it disliked monarchies on principle. In 1919 it wanted America to recognise the Russian Government, and take hold of Russian trade. But a series of rebuffs to its special correspondents changed its view, and by 1922 it had made a speciality of Bolshevik horrors. The year 1923 saw it again on the fence, from which in six months it had tumbled off in a state of anti-Bolshevik hysteria. It was out now to save God's country from foreign microbes, and it ran a good special line of experts who proved that what America needed was a *cordon sanitaire* to protect her purity from a diseased world. At the time of which I speak it had worked itself up into a fine religious enthusiasm, and had pretty well captured the 'hick' public. McGurks was first and foremost a business proposition, and it had decided that crime and piety were the horses to back. I should add that, besides its papers, it ran a news agency, the PU, which stood for Press Union, but which was commonly and affectionately known as Punk.

McGurks seized upon the story in the *Toronto Watchman* as a gift from the gods, and its headlines were a joy for ever. All over the States men read 'Aged Saint Defies Demoniacs – Says That In God's Name He Will Move Mountains' – 'Vengeance From The Veld' – 'The First Trumpet Blast' – 'Who Is On The Lord's Side – WHO?' I daresay that in the East and beyond the Rockies people were only mildly interested, but in the Middle West and in the South the thing caught like measles. McGurks did not leave its stunts to perish of inanition. As soon as it saw that the public was intrigued it started out to organise that interest. It circularised every parson over big areas, it arranged meetings of protest and sympathy, it opened subscription lists, and, though it refrained from suggesting Government action, it made it clear that it wanted to create such a popular feeling that the Government would be bound to bestir itself. The home towns caught fire, the Bible Belt was moved to its foundations, every Methodist minister rallied to his co-religionist of Rhenosterspruit, the Sunday Schools uplifted their voice, and even the red-blooded he-men of the Rotary Clubs got going. The Holiness Tabernacle of Sarcophagus, Neb., produced twenty volunteers who were ready to join Mr Tubb in Moscow, and the women started knitting socks for them, just as they did in the war. The First Consecration Church of Jumpersville, Tenn., followed suit, and McGurks made the most of the doings of every chapel in every one-horse township. Punk, too, was busy, and cabled wonderful stories of the new crusade up and down the earth. Old-established papers did not as a rule take the Punk service, so only a part of it was printed, but it all helped to create an atmosphere.

Presently Concord had to take notice. This, as you know, is the foremost American press agency – we call it the CC – and it had no more dealings with Punk than the Jews with the Samaritans. It was in close alliance with Ladas, so it cabled testily wanting to know why it had not received the Rhenosterspruit message. Ladas replied that they had considered the story too absurd to waste tolls on, but, since the CC was now carrying a lot of stuff about the new crusade, they felt obliged to cable to Cape Town to clear things up. Punk had already got on to that job, and was asking its correspondents for pictures of Rhenosterspruit, interviews with the Reverend Tubb, details about what he wore and ate and drank, news of his mother and his childhood, and his premonitions of future greatness. Half a dozen anxious journalists converged upon Rhenosterspruit.

But they were too late. For Mr Tubb was dead – choked on a chicken-bone at his last Sunday dinner. They were only in time to attend the funeral in the little, dusty, sun-baked cemetery. Very little was to be had from his congregation, which, as I have said, had been mostly asleep during the famous sermon; but a store-keeper remembered that the minister had not been quite like himself on that occasion and that he had judged from his eyes that he had still a bad cold. McGurks made a great fuss with this scrap of news. The death of Mr Tubb was featured like the demise of a President or a film star, and there was a moving picture of the old man, conscious that he was near his end (the chicken-bone was never mentioned), summoning his failing strength to one supreme appeal – 'his eyes', said McGurks, 'now wet with tears for the world's sins, now shining with the reflected radiance of the Better Country'.

I fancy that the thing would have suddenly died away, for there was a big prize-fight coming on, and there seemed to be the risk of the acquittal of a nigger who had knifed a bootlegger in Chicago, and an Anti-Kink Queen was on the point of engaging herself to a Dentifrice King, and similar stirring public events were in the offing. But the death of Mr Tubb kept up the excitement, for it brought in the big guns of the Fundamentalists. It seemed to them that the old man had not died but had been miraculously translated, just like Elijah or William Jennings Bryan after the Dayton trial. It was a Sign, and they were bound to consider what it signified.

This was much heavier metal than the faithful of Sarcophagus and Jumpersville. The agitation was now of national importance; it had attained 'normalcy', as you might say, the 'normalcy' of the periodic American movement. Conventions were summoned and addressed by divines whose names were known even in New York. Senators and congressmen took a hand, and J. Constantine Buttrick, the silver trumpet of Wisconsin, gave tongue, and was heard by several million wireless outfits. Articles even appeared about it in the intellectual weeklies. Congress wasn't in session, which was fortunate, but Washington began to be uneasy, for volunteers for the crusade were enrolling fast. The CC was compelled to carry long despatches, and Ladas had to issue them to the English Press, which usually printed them in obscure corners with the names misspelt. England is always apathetic about

American news, and, besides, she had a big strike on her hands at the time. Those of us who get American press-clippings realised that quite a drive was starting to do something to make Moscow respectful to religion, but we believed that it would be dropped before any serious action could be taken. Meanwhile Zinovieff and Trotsky carried on as usual, and we expected any day to hear that the Patriarch had been shot and buried in the prison yard.

Suddenly Fate sent Roper Willinck mooning round to my office. I suppose Willinck is the least known of our great men, for you fellows have never even heard his name. But he *is* a great man in his queer way, and I believe his voice carries farther than any living journalist's, though most people do not know who is speaking. He doesn't write much in the Press here, only now and then a paper in the heavy monthlies, but he is the prince of special correspondents, and his 'London Letters' in every known tongue are printed from Auckland to Seattle. He seems to have found the common denominator of style which is calculated to interest the whole human family. On the Continent he is the only English journalist whose name is known to the ordinary reader – rather like Maximilian Harden before the war. In America they reckon him a sort of Pope, and his stuff is syndicated in all the country papers. His enthusiasms make a funny hotch-potch – the League of Nations and the British Empire, racial purism and a sentimental socialism; but he is a devout Catholic, and Russia had become altogether too much for him. That was why I thought he would be interested in McGurks' stunt, of which he had scarcely heard; so he sat down in an armchair and, during the consumption of five caporal cigarettes, studied my clippings.

I have never seen a man so roused. 'I see light,' he cried, pushing his double glasses up on his forehead. 'Martendale, this is a revelation. Out of the mouths of babes and sucklings . . . Master Ridley, Master Ridley, we shall this day kindle a fire which will never be extinguished . . .'

'Nonsense,' I said. 'The thing will fizzle out in a solemn protest from Washington to Moscow with which old Trotsky will light his pipe. It has got into the hands of highbrows, and in a week will be clothed in the jargon of the State Department, and the home towns will wonder what has been biting them.'

'We must retrieve it,' he said softly. 'Get it back to the village green and the prayer-meeting. It was the prayer-meeting, remember, which brought America into the war.'

'But how? McGurks has worked that beat to death.'

'McGurks!' he cried contemptuously. 'The time is past for slobber, my son. What they want is the prophetic, the apocalyptic, and by the bones of Habbakuk they shall have it. I am going to solemnise the remotest parts of the great Republic, and then', he smiled serenely, 'I shall interpret that solemnity to the world. First the fact and then the moral – that's the lay-out.'

He stuffed my clippings into his pocket and took himself off, and there was that in his eye which foreboded trouble. Someone was going to have to sit up when Willinck looked like that. My hope was that it would be Moscow, but the time was getting terribly short. Any day might bring the news that the Patriarch had gone to his reward.

I heard nothing for several weeks, and then Punk suddenly became active, and carried some extraordinary stuff. It was mostly extracts from respectable papers in the Middle West and the South, reports of meetings which seemed to have worked themselves into hysteria, and rumours of secret gatherings of young men which suggested the Ku-Klux-Klan. Moscow had a Press agency of its own in London, and it began to worry Ladas for more American news. Ladas in turn worried the CC, but the CC was reticent. There was a Movement, we were told, but the Government had it well in hand, and we might disregard the scare-stuff Punk was sending; everything that was important and reliable would be in its own service. I thought I detected Willinck somewhere behind the scenes, and tried to get hold of him, but learned that he was out of town.

One afternoon, however, he dropped in, and I noticed that his high-boned face was leaner than ever, but that his cavernous eyes were happy. ' "The good work goes cannily on," ' he said – he was always quoting – and he flung at me a bundle of green clippings.

They were articles of his own in the American Press, chiefly the Sunday editions, and I noticed that he had selected the really influential country papers – one in Tennessee, one in Kentucky, and a batch from the Corn States.

I was staggered by the power of his stuff – Willinck had never to my knowledge written like this before. He didn't rave about Bolshevik crimes – people were sick of that – and he didn't bang the religious drum or thump the harmonium. McGurks had already done that to satiety. He quietly took it for granted that the crusade had begun and that plain men all over the earth, who weren't looking for trouble, felt obliged to start out and abolish an infamy or never sleep peacefully in their beds again. He assumed that presently from all corners of the Christian world there would be an invading army moving towards Moscow, a thing that Governments could not check, a people's rising as irresistible as the change of the seasons. Assuming this, he told them just exactly what they would see.

I can't do justice to Willinck by merely describing these articles; I ought to have them here to read to you. Noble English they were, and as simple as the Psalms . . . He pictured the constitution of the army, every kind of tongue and dialect and class, with the same kind of discipline as Cromwell's New Model – Ironsides every one of them, rational, moderate-minded fanatics, the most dangerous kind. It was like *Paradise Lost* – Michael going out against Belial . . . And then the description of Russia – a wide grey world, all pale colours and watery lights, broken villages, tattered little towns ruled by a few miscreants with rifles, railway tracks red with rust, ruinous great palaces plastered over with obscene posters, starving hopeless people, children with old vicious faces . . . God knows where he got the stuff from – mainly his *macabre* imagination, but I daresay there was a lot of truth in the details, for he had his own ways of acquiring knowledge.

But the end was the masterpiece. He said that the true rulers were not those whose names appeared in the papers, but one or two secret madmen who sat behind the screen and spun their bloody webs. He described the crusaders breaking through shell after shell, like one of those Chinese boxes which you open only to find another inside till you end with a thing like a pea. There were layers of Jew officials and Lett mercenaries and camouflaging journalists, and always as you went deeper the thing became more inhuman and the air more fetid. At the end you had the demented Mongol – that was a good touch for the Middle West – the incarnation of the backworld of the Orient. Willinck only hinted at this ultimate camarilla, but his hints were gruesome. To one of them he gave the name of Uriel – a kind of worm-eaten archangel of the Pit, but the worst he called Glubet. He must have got the word out of a passage in Catullus which is not read in schools, and he made a shuddering thing of it – the rancid toad-man, living among the half-lights and blood, adroit and sleepless as sin, but cracking now and then into idiot laughter.

You may imagine how this took hold of the Bible Belt. I never made out what exactly happened, but I have no doubt that there were the rudiments of one of those mass movements, before which Governments and newspapers, combines and Press agencies, Wall Street and Lombard Street and common prudence are helpless. You could see it in the messages CC sent and its agitated service cables to its people. The Moscow Agency sat on our doorstep and bleated for more news, and all the while Punk was ladling out fire-water to every paper that would take it.

'So much for the facts,' Willinck said calmly. 'Now I proceed to point the moral in the proper quarters!'

If he was good at kindling a fire he was better at explaining just how hot it was and how fast it would spread. I have told you that he was about the only English journalist with a Continental reputation. Well, he proceeded to exploit that reputation in selected papers which he knew would cross the Russian frontier. He was busy in the Finnish and Latvian and Lithuanian Press, he appeared in the chief Polish daily, and in Germany his stuff was printed in the one big Berlin paper and – curiously enough – in the whole financial chain. Willinck knew just how and where to strike. The line he took was very simple. He quietly explained what was happening in America and the British Dominions – that the outraged conscience of Christiandom had awakened among simple folk, and that nothing on earth could hold it. It was a Puritan crusade, the most deadly kind. From every corner of the globe believers were about to assemble, ready to sacrifice themselves to root out an infamy. This was none of your Denikins and Koltchaks and Czarist *émigré* affairs; it was the world's Christian democracy, and a business democracy. No flag-waving or shouting, just a cold steady determination to get the job done, with ample money and men and an utter carelessness of what they spent on both. Cautious Governments might try to obstruct, but the people would compel them to toe the line. It was a militant League of Nations, with the Bible in one hand and the latest brand of munition in the other.

We had a feverish time at Ladas in those days. The British Press was too much occupied with the strike to pay full attention, but the Press of every other country was on its hind legs. Presently things began to happen. The extracts from *Pravda* and *Izvestia*, which we got from Riga and Warsaw, became every day more like the howling of epileptic wolves; then came the news that Moscow had ordered a very substantial addition to the Red Army. I telephoned this item to Willinck, and he came round to see me.

'The wind is rising,' he said. 'The fear of the Lord is descending on the tribes, and that we know is the beginning of wisdom.'

I observed that Moscow had certainly got the wind up, but that I didn't see why. 'You don't mean to say that you have got them to believe in your precious crusade.'

He nodded cheerfully. 'Why not? My dear Martendale, you haven't studied the mentality of these gentry as I have. Do you realise that the favourite reading of the Russian peasant used to be Milton? Before the war you could buy a translation of *Paradise Lost* at every book kiosk in every country fair. These rootless intellectuals have cast off all they could, but at the back of their heads the peasant superstition remains. They are afraid in their bones of a spirit that they think is in Puritanism. That's why this American business worries them so. They think they are a match for Rome, and they wouldn't have minded if the racket had been started by the Knights of Columbus or that kind of show. But they think it comes from the meeting-house, and that scares them cold.'

'Hang it all,' I said, 'they must know the soft thing modern Puritanism is – all slushy hymns and inspirational advertising.'

'Happily they don't. And I'm not sure that their ignorance is not wiser than your knowledge, my emancipated friend. I'm inclined to think that something may yet come out of the Bible Christian that will surprise the world . . . But not this time. I fancy the trick has been done. You might let me know as soon as you hear anything.' And he moved off, whistling contentedly through his teeth.

He was right. Three days later we got the news from Warsaw, and the Moscow Agency confirmed it. The Patriarch had been released and sent across the frontier, and was now being coddled and fêted in Poland. I rang up Willinck, and listened to his modest *Nunc dimittis* over the telephone.

He said he was going to take a holiday and go into the country to sleep. He pointed out for my edification that the weak things of the world – meaning himself – could still confound the strong, and he advised me to reconsider the foundations of my creed in the light of this surprising miracle.

*

Well, that is my story. We heard no more of the crusade in America, except that the Fundamentalists seemed to have got a second wind from it and started a large-scale heresy hunt. Several English bishops said that the release of the Patriarch was an answer to prayer; our Press pointed out how civilisation, if it spoke with one voice, would be listened to even in Russia; and Labour papers took occasion to enlarge on the fundamental reasonableness and urbanity of the Moscow Government.

Personally I think that Willinck drew the right moral. But the main credit really belonged to something a great deal weaker than he – the aged Tubb, now sleeping under a painted cast-iron gravestone among the dust-devils and meerkats of Rhenosterspruit.

Sing a Song of Sixpence

The effect of night, of any flowing water, of lighted cities, of the peep of day, of ships, of the open ocean, calls up in the mind an army of anonymous desires and pleasures. Something, we feel, should happen; we know not what, yet we proceed in quest of it.

R. L. STEVENSON

Leithen's face had that sharp chiselling of the jaw and that compression of the lips which seem to follow upon high legal success. Also an overdose of German gas in 1918 had given his skin a habitual pallor, so that he looked not unhealthy, but notably urban. As a matter of fact he was one of the hardest men I have ever known, but a chance observer might have guessed from his complexion that he rarely left the pavements.

Burminster, who had come back from a month in the grass countries with a face like a deep-sea mariner's, commented on this one evening.

'How do you manage always to look the complete Cit, Ned?' he asked. 'You're as much a Londoner as a Parisian is a Parisian, if you know what I mean.'

Leithen said that he was not ashamed of it, and he embarked on a eulogy of the metropolis. In London you met sooner or later everybody you had ever known; you could lay your hand on any knowledge you wanted; you could pull strings that controlled the innermost Sahara and the topmost Pamirs. Romance lay in wait for you at every street corner. It was the true City of the Caliphs.

'That is what they say,' said Sandy Arbuthnot sadly, 'but I never found it so. I yawn my head off in London. Nothing amusing ever finds me out – I have to go and search for it, and it usually costs the deuce of a lot.'

'I once stumbled upon a pretty generous allowance of romance,' said Leithen, 'and it cost me precisely sixpence.'

Then he told us this story.

It happened a good many years ago, just when I was beginning to get on at the Bar. I spent busy days in court and chambers, but I was young and had a young man's appetite for society, so I used to dine out most nights and go to more balls than were good for me. It was pleasant after a heavy day to dive into a different kind of life. My rooms at the time were in Down Street, the same house as my present one, only two floors higher up.

On a certain night in February I was dining in Bryanston Square with the Nantleys. Mollie Nantley was an old friend, and used to fit me as an unattached bachelor into her big dinners. She was a young hostess and full of ambition, and one met an odd assortment of people at her house. Mostly political, of course, but a sprinkling of art and letters, and any visiting lion that happened to be passing through. Mollie was a very innocent lion-hunter, but she had a partiality for the breed.

I don't remember much about the dinner, except that the principal guest had failed her. Mollie was loud in her lamentations. He was a South American President who had engineered a very pretty *coup d'état* the year before, and was now in England on some business concerning the finances of his State. You may remember his name – Ramón Pelem – he made rather a stir in the world for a year or two. I had read about him in the papers, and had looked forward to meeting him, for he had won his way to power by extraordinary boldness and courage, and he was quite young. There was a story that he was partly English and that his grandfather's name had been Pelham. I don't know what truth there was in that, but he knew England well and Englishmen liked him.

Well, he had cried off on the telephone an hour before, and Mollie was grievously disappointed. Her other guests bore the loss with more fortitude, for I expect they thought he was a brand of cigar.

In those days dinners began earlier and dances later than they do today. I meant to leave soon, go back to my rooms and read briefs, and then look in at Lady Samplar's dance between eleven and twelve. So at nine-thirty I took my leave.

Jervis, the old butler, who had been my ally from boyhood, was standing on the threshold, and in the square there was a considerable crowd now thinning away. I asked what the trouble was.

'There's been an arrest, Mr Edward,' he said in an awestruck voice. 'It 'appened when I was serving coffee in the dining-room, but our Albert saw it all. Two foreigners, he said – proper rascals by their look – were took away by the police just outside this very door. The constables was very nippy and collared them before they could use their pistols – but they 'ad pistols on them and no mistake. Albert says he saw the weapons.'

'Did they propose to burgle you?' I asked.

'I cannot say, Mr Edward. But I shall give instructions for a very careful lock-up tonight.'

There were no cabs about, so I decided to walk on and

pick one up. When I got into Great Cumberland Place it began to rain sharply, and I was just about to call a prowling hansom, when I put my hand into my pocket. I found that I had no more than one solitary sixpence.

I could of course have paid when I got to my flat. But as the rain seemed to be slacking off, I preferred to walk. Mollie's dining-room had been stuffy, I had been in court all day, and I wanted some fresh air.

You know how in little things, when you have decided on a course, you are curiously reluctant to change it. Before I got to the Marble Arch it had begun to pour in downright earnest. But I still stumped on. Only I entered the Park, for even in February there is a certain amount of cover from the trees.

I passed one or two hurried pedestrians, but the place was almost empty. The occasional lamps made only spots of light in a dripping darkness, and it struck me that this was a curious patch of gloom and loneliness to be so near to crowded streets, for with the rain had come a fine mist. I pitied the poor devils to whom it was the only home. There was one of them on a seat which I passed. The collar of his thin shabby overcoat was turned up, and his shameful old felt hat was turned down, so that only a few square inches of pale face were visible. His toes stuck out of his boots, and he seemed sunk in a sodden misery.

I passed him and then turned back. Casual charity is an easy dope for the conscience, and I indulge in it too often. When I approached him he seemed to stiffen, and his hands moved in his pockets.

'A rotten night,' I said. 'Is sixpence any good to you?' And I held out my solitary coin.

He lifted his face, and I started. For the eyes that looked

307

at me were not those of a waster. They were bright, penetrating, authoritative – and they were young. I was conscious that they took in more of me than mine did of him.

'Thank you very much,' he said, as he took the coin, and the voice was that of a cultivated man. 'But I'm afraid I need rather more than sixpence.'

'How much?' I asked. This was clearly an original.

'To be accurate, five million pounds.'

He was certainly mad, but I was fascinated by this wisp of humanity. I wished that he would show more of his face.

'Till your ship comes home,' I said, 'you want a bed, and you'd be the better of a change. Sixpence is all I have on me. But if you come to my rooms I'll give you the price of a night's lodging, and I think I might find you some old clothes.'

'Where do you live?' he asked.

'Close by – in Down Street.' I gave the number.

He seemed to reflect, and then he shot a glance on either side into the gloom behind the road. It may have been fancy, but I thought that I saw something stir in the darkness.

'What are you?' he asked.

I was getting abominably wet, and yet I submitted to be cross-examined by this waif.

'I am a lawyer,' I said.

He looked at me again, very intently.

'Have you a telephone?' he asked.

I nodded.

'Right,' he said. 'You seem a good fellow, and I'll take you at your word. I'll follow you ... Don't look back, please. It's important ... I'll be in Down Street as soon as you ... *Marchons.*'

It sounds preposterous, but I did exactly as I was bid. I never looked back, but I kept my ears open for the sound of following footsteps. I thought I heard them, and then they seemed to die away. I turned out of the Park at Grosvenor Gate and went down Park Lane. When I reached the house which contained my flat, I looked up and down the street, but it was empty except for a waiting four-wheeler. But just as I turned in I caught a glimpse of someone running at the Hertford Street end. The runner came to a sudden halt, and I saw that it was not the man I had left.

To my surprise I found the waif on the landing outside my flat. I was about to tell him to stop outside, but as soon as I unlocked the door he brushed past me and entered. My man, who did not sleep on the premises, had left the light burning in the little hall.

'Lock the door,' he said in a tone of authority. 'Forgive me taking charge, but I assure you it is important.'

Then to my amazement he peeled off the sopping over-coat, and kicked off his disreputable shoes. They were odd shoes, for what looked like his toes sticking out was really part of the make-up. He stood up before me in underclothes and socks, and I noticed that his underclothing seemed to be of the finest material.

'Now for your telephone,' he said.

I was getting angry at these liberties.

'Who the devil are you?' I demanded.

'I am President Pelem,' he said, with all the dignity in the world. 'And you?'

'I? – oh, I am the German Emperor.'

He laughed. 'You know you invited me here,' he said. 'You've brought this on yourself.' Then he stared at me. 'Hullo, I've seen you before. You're Leithen. I saw you play at Lord's. I was twelfth man for Harrow that year . . . Now for the telephone.'

There was something about the fellow, something defiant and debonair and young, that stopped all further protest on my part. He might or might not be President Pelem, but he was certainly not a wastrel. Besides, he seemed curiously keyed up, as if the occasion were desperately important, and he infected me with the same feeling. I said no more, but led the way into my sitting-room. He flung himself on the telephone, gave a number, was instantly connected, and began a conversation in monosyllables.

It was a queer jumble that I overheard. Bryanston Square was mentioned, and the Park, and the number of my house was given – to somebody. There was a string of foreign names – Pedro and Alejandro and Manuel and Alcaza – and short breathless enquiries. Then I heard – 'a good fellow – looks as if he might be useful in a row', and I wondered if he was referring to me. Some rapid Spanish followed, and then, 'Come round at once – they will be here before you. Have policemen below, but don't let them come up. We should be able to manage alone. Oh, and tell Burton to ring up here as soon as he has news.' And he gave my telephone number.

I put some coals on the fire, changed into a tweed jacket, and lit a pipe. I fetched a dressing-gown from my bedroom and flung it on the sofa. 'You'd better put that on,' I said when he had finished.

He shook his head.

'I would rather be unencumbered,' he said. 'But I should dearly love a cigarette . . . and a liqueur brandy, if you have such a thing. That Park of yours is infernally chilly.'

I supplied his needs, and he stretched himself in an armchair, with his stockinged feet to the fire.

'You have been very good-humoured, Leithen,' he said. 'Váldez – that's my aide-de-camp – will be here presently, and he will probably be preceded by other guests. But I think I have time for the short explanation which is your due. You believe what I told you?'

I nodded.

'Good. Well, I came to London three weeks ago to raise a loan. That was a matter of life or death for my big stupid country. I have succeeded. This afternoon the agreement was signed. I think I mentioned the amount to you – five million sterling.'

He smiled happily and blew a smoke-ring into the air.

'I must tell you that I have enemies. Among my happy people there are many rascals, and I had to deal harshly with them. "So foul a sky clears not without a storm" – that's Shakespeare, isn't it? I learned it at school. You see, I had Holy Church behind me, and therefore I had against me all the gentry who call themselves liberators. Red Masons, anarchists, communists, that sort of crew. A good many are now reposing beneath the sod, but some of the worst remain. In particular, six followed me to England with instructions that I must not return.

'I don't mind telling you, Leithen, that I have had a peculiarly rotten time the last three weeks. It was most important that nothing should happen to me till the loan was settled, so I had to lead the sheltered life. It went against the grain, I assure you, for I prefer the offensive to the defensive. The English police were very amiable, and I never stirred without a cordon, your people and my own. The Six wanted to kill me, and as it is pretty easy to kill anybody if you don't mind being killed yourself, we had to take rather elaborate precautions. As it was, I was twice nearly done in. Once my carriage broke down mysteriously, and a crowd collected, and if I hadn't had the luck to board a passing cab, I should have had a knife in my ribs. The second was at a public dinner – something not quite right about the cayenne pepper served with the oysters. One of my staff is still seriously ill.'

He stretched his arms.

'Well, that first stage is over. They can't wreck the loan, whatever happens to me. Now I am free to adopt different tactics and take the offensive. I have no fear of the Six in my own country. There I can take precautions, and they will find it difficult to cross the frontier or to live for six hours thereafter if they succeed. But here you are a free people, and protection is not so easy. I do not wish to leave England just yet – I have done my work and have earned a little play. I know your land and love it, and I look forward to seeing something of my friends. Also I want to attend the Grand National. Therefore, it is necessary that my enemies should be confined for a little, while I take my holiday. So for this evening I made a plan. I took the offensive. I deliberately put myself in their danger.'

He turned his dancing eyes towards me, and I have rarely had such an impression of wild and mirthful audacity.

'We have an excellent intelligence system,' he went on, 'and the Six have been assiduously shadowed. But as I have told you, no precautions avail against the fanatic, and I do not wish to be killed on my little holiday. So I resolved to draw their fire – to expose myself as ground bait, so to speak, that I might have the chance of netting them. The Six usually hunt in couples, so it was necessary to have three separate acts in the play, if all were to be gathered in. The first—'

'Was in Bryanston Square,' I put in, 'outside Lady Nantley's house?'

'True. How did you know?'

'I have just been dining there, and heard that you were expected. I saw the crowd in the square as I came away.'

'It seems to have gone off quite nicely. We took pains to let it be known where I was dining. The Six, who mistrust me, delegated only two of their number for the job. They never put all their eggs in one basket. The two gentlemen were induced to make a scene, and, since they proved to be heavily armed, were taken into custody and may get a six months' sentence. Very prettily managed, but unfortunately it was the two that matter least – the ones we call Little Pedro and Alejandro the Scholar. Impatient, blundering children, both of them. That leaves four.'

The telephone bell rang, and he made a long arm for the receiver. The news he got seemed to be good, for he turned a smiling face to me.

'I should have said two. My little enterprise in the Park has proved a brilliant success . . . But I must explain. I was to be the bait for my enemies, so I showed myself to the remaining four. That was really rather a clever piece of business. They lost me at the Marble Arch and they did not recognise me as the scarecrow sitting on the seat in the rain. But they knew I had gone to earth there, and they stuck to the scent like terriers. Presently they would have found me, and there would have been shooting. Some of my own people were in the shadow between the road and the railings.'

'When I saw you, were your enemies near?' I asked.

'Two were on the opposite side of the road. One was standing under the lamp-post at the gate. I don't know where the fourth was at that moment. But all had passed me more than once . . . By the way, you very nearly got yourself shot, you know. When you asked me if sixpence was any good to me . . . That happens to be their password. I take great credit to myself for seeing instantly that you were harmless.'

'Why did you leave the Park if you had your trap so well laid?' I asked.

'Because it meant dealing with all four together at once, and I do them the honour of being rather nervous about them. They are very quick with their guns. I wanted a chance to break up the covey, and your arrival gave it me. When I went off two followed, as I thought they would. My car was in Park Lane, and gave me a lift; and one of them saw me in it. I puzzled them a little, but by now they must be certain. You see, my car has been waiting for some minutes outside this house.'

'What about the other two?' I asked.

'Burton has just telephoned that they have been gathered in. Quite an exciting little scrap. To your police it must have seemed a bad case of highway robbery – two ruffianly looking fellows hold up a peaceful elderly gentleman returning from dinner. The odds were not quite like that, but the men I had on the job are old soldiers of the Indian wars and can move softly . . . I only wish I knew which two they have got. Burton was not sure. Alcaza is one, but I can't be certain about the other. I hope it is not the Irishman.'

My bell rang very loud and steadily.

'In a few seconds I shall have solved that problem,' he

said gaily. 'I am afraid I must trouble you to open the door, Leithen.'

'Is it your aide-de-camp?'

'No. I instructed Váldez to knock. It is the residuum of the Six. Now listen to me, my friend. These two, whoever they are, have come here to kill me, and I don't mean to be killed . . . My first plan was to have Váldez here – and others – so that my two enemies should walk into a trap. But I changed my mind before I telephoned. They are very clever men, and by this time they will be very wary. So I have thought of something else.'

The bell rang again, and a third time insistently.

'Take these,' and he held out a pair of cruel little bluish revolvers. 'When you open the door, you will say that the President is at home and, in token of his confidence, offers them these. "*Une espèce d'Irlandais, Messieurs. Vous commencez trop tard, et vous finissez trop tôt.*" Then bring them here. Quick now. I hope Corbally is one of them.'

I did exactly as I was told. I cannot say that I had any liking for the task, but I was a good deal under the spell of that calm young man, and I was resigned to my flat being made a rendezvous for desperadoes. I had locked and chained and bolted the door, so it took me a few moments to open it.

I found myself looking at emptiness.

'Who is it?' I called. 'Who rang?'

I was answered from behind me. It was the quickest thing I have ever seen, for they must have slipped through in the moment when my eyes were dazzled by the change from the dim light of the hall to the glare of the landing. That gave me some notion of the men we had to deal with.

'Here,' said the voice. I turned and saw two men in waterproofs and felt hats, who kept their hands in their pockets and had a fraction of an eye on the two pistols I swung by the muzzles.

'M. le Président will be glad to see you, gentlemen,' I said. I held out the revolvers, which they seemed to grasp and flick into their pockets with a single movement. Then I repeated slowly the piece of rudeness in French.

One of the men laughed. 'Ramón does not forget,' he said. He was a young man with sandy hair and hot blue eyes and an odd break in his long drooping nose. The other was a wiry little fellow, with a grizzled beard and what looked like a stiff leg.

I had no guess at my friend's plan, and was concerned to do precisely as I was told. I opened the door of my sitting-room, and noticed that the President was stretched on my sofa facing the door. He was smoking and was still in his underclothes. When the two men behind me saw that he was patently unarmed they slipped into the room with a quick cat-like movement, and took their stand with their backs against the door.

'Hullo, Corbally,' said the President pleasantly. 'And you, Manuel. You're looking younger than when I saw you last. Have a cigarette?' and he nodded towards my box on the table behind him. Both shook their heads.

'I'm glad you have come. You have probably seen the news of the loan in the evening papers. That should give you a holiday, as it gives me one. No further need for the hectic oversight of each other, which is so wearing and takes up so much time.'

'No,' said the man called Manuel, and there was something very grim about his quiet tones. 'We shall take steps to prevent any need for that in the future.'

'Tut, tut – that is your old self, Manuel. You are too

fond of melodrama to be an artist. You are a priest at heart.'

The man snarled. 'There will be no priest at your deathbed.' Then to his companion. 'Let us get this farce over.'

The President paid not the slightest attention but looked steadily at the Irishman. 'You used to be a sportsman, Mike. Have you come to share Manuel's taste for potting the sitting rabbit?'

'We are not sportsmen, we are executioners of justice,' said Manuel.

The President laughed merrily. 'Superb! The best Roman manner.' He still kept his eyes on Corbally.

'Damn you, what's your game, Ramón?' the Irishman asked. His freckled face had become very red.

'Simply to propose a short armistice. I want a holiday. If you must know, I want to go to the National.'

'So do I.'

'Well, let's call a truce. Say for two months or till I leave England – whichever period shall be the shorter. After that you can get busy again.'

The one he had named Manuel broke into a spluttering torrent of Spanish, and for a little they all talked that language. It sounded like a commination service on the President, to which he good-humouredly replied. I had never seen this class of ruffian before, to whom murder was as simple as shooting a partridge, and I noted curiously the lean hands, the restless wary eyes and the ugly lips of the type. So far as I could make out, the President seemed to be getting on well with the Irishman but to be having trouble with Manuel.

'Have ye really and truly nothing on ye?' Corbally asked.

The President stretched his arms and revealed his slim figure in its close-fitting pants and vest.

'Nor him there?' and he nodded towards me.

'He is a lawyer; he doesn't use guns.'

'Then I'm damned if I touch ye. Two months it is. What's your fancy for Liverpool?'

This was too much for Manuel. I saw in what seemed to be one movement his hand slip from his pocket, Corbally's arm swing in a circle, and a plaster bust of Julius Caesar tumble off the top of my bookcase. Then I heard the report.

'Ye nasty little man,' said Corbally, as he pressed him to his bosom in a bear's hug.

'You are a traitor,' Manuel shouted. 'How will we face the others? What will Alejandro say and Alcaza—'

'I think I can explain,' said the President pleasantly. 'They won't know for quite a time, and then only if you tell them. You two gentlemen are all that remain for the moment of your patriotic company. The other four have been the victims of the English police – two in Bryanston Square, and two in the Park close to the Marble Arch.'

'Ye don't say!' said Corbally with admiration in his voice. 'Faith, that's smart work!'

'They too will have a little holiday. A few months to meditate on politics, while you and I go to the Grand National.'

Suddenly there was a sharp rat-tat at my door. It was like the knocking in *Macbeth* for dramatic effect. Corbally had one pistol at my ear in an instant, while a second covered the President.

'It's all right,' said the latter, never moving a muscle. 'It's General Váldez, whom I think you know. That was another argument which I was coming to if I hadn't had the good fortune to appeal to Mr Corbally's higher nature. I know you have sworn to kill me, but I take it that the killer wants to have a sporting chance of escape. Well, there wouldn't have been the faintest shadow of a chance here. Váldez is at the door, and the English police are below. You are brave men, I know, but even brave men dislike the cold gallows.'

The knocker fell again. 'Let him in, Leithen,' I was told, 'or he will be damaging your valuable door. He has not the northern phlegm of you and me and Mr Corbally.'

A tall man in an ulster, which looked as if it covered a uniform, stood on the threshold. Someone had obscured the lights on the landing so that the staircase was dark, but I could see in the gloom other figures. 'President Pelem . . .' he began.

'The President is here,' I said. 'Quite well and in great form. He is entertaining two other guests.'

The General marched to my sitting-room. I was behind him and did not see his face, but I can believe that it showed surprise when he recognised the guests. Manuel stood sulkily defiant, his hands in his waterproof pockets, but Corbally's light eyes were laughing.

'I think you know each other,' said the President graciously.

'My God!' Váldez seemed to choke at the sight. 'These swine! . . . Excellency, I have . . .'

'You have nothing of the kind. These are friends of mine for the next two months, and Mr Corbally and I are going to the Grand National together. Will you have the goodness to conduct them downstairs and explain to the inspector of police below that all has gone well and that I am perfectly satisfied, and that he will hear from me in the morning? . . . One moment. What about a stirrup-cup? Leithen, does your establishment run to a whisky and soda all round?'

It did. We all had a drink, and I believe I clinked glasses with Manuel.

I looked in at Lady Samplar's dance as I had meant to. Presently I saw a resplendent figure arrive – the President, with the ribbon of the Gold Star of Bolívar across his chest. He was no more the larky undergraduate, but the responsible statesman, the father of his country. There was a considerable crowd in his vicinity when I got near him, and he was making his apologies to Mollie Nantley. She saw me and insisted on introducing me. 'I so much wanted you two to meet. I had hoped it would be at my dinner – but anyhow I have managed it.' I think she was a little surprised when the President took my hand in both of his. 'I saw Mr Leithen play at Lord's in '97,' he said. 'I was twelfth man for Harrow that year. It is delightful to make his acquaintance; I shall never forget this meeting.'

'How English he is!' Mollie whispered to me as we made our way out of the crowd.

They got him next year. They were bound to, for in that kind of business you can have no real protection. But he managed to set his country on its feet before he went down . . . No, it was neither Manuel nor Corbally. I think it was Alejandro the Scholar.

The Wind in the Portico

A dry wind of the high places . . . not to fan nor to cleanse, even a full wind from those places shall come unto me.

Jeremiah IV. xi–xii

Nightingale was a hard man to draw. His doings with the Bedawin had become a legend, but he would as soon have talked about them as claimed to have won the war. He was a slim dark fellow about thirty-five years of age, very short-sighted, and wearing such high-powered double glasses that it was impossible to tell the colour of his eyes. This weakness made him stoop a little and peer, so that he was the strangest figure to picture in a burnous leading an army of desert tribesmen. I fancy his power came partly from his oddness, for his followers thought that the hand of Allah had been laid on him, and partly from his quick imagination and his flawless courage. After the war he had gone back to his Cambridge fellowship, declaring that, thank God, that chapter in his life was over.

As I say, he never mentioned the deeds which had made him famous. He knew his own business, and probably realised that to keep his mental balance he had to drop the curtain on what must have been the most nerve-racking four years ever spent by man. We respected his decision and kept off Arabia. It was a remark of Hannay's that drew from him the following story. Hannay was talking about his Cotswold house, which was on the Fosse Way, and saying that it always puzzled him how so elaborate a civilisation as Roman Britain could have been destroyed utterly and left no mark on the national history beyond a few roads and ruins and place-names. Peckwether, the historian, demurred, and had a good deal to say about how much the Roman tradition was woven into the Saxon culture. 'Rome only sleeps,' he said; 'she never dies.'

Nightingale nodded. 'Sometimes she dreams in her sleep and talks. Once she scared me out of my senses.'

After a good deal of pressing he produced this story. He was not much of a talker, so he wrote it out and read it to us.

There is a place in Shropshire which I do not propose to visit again. It lies between Ludlow and the hills, in a shallow valley full of woods. Its name is St Sant, a village with a big house and park adjoining, on a stream called the Vaun, about five miles from the little town of Faxeter. They have queer names in those parts, and other things queerer than the names.

I was motoring from Wales to Cambridge at the close of the long vacation. All this happened before the war, when I had just got my fellowship and was settling down to academic work. It was a fine night in early October, with a full moon, and I intended to push on to Ludlow for supper and bed. The time was about half-past eight, the road was empty and good going, and I was trundling pleasantly along when something went wrong with my headlights. It was a small thing, and I stopped to remedy it beyond a village and just at the lodge-gates of a house.

On the opposite side of the road a carrier's cart had drawn up, and two men, who looked like indoor servants, were lifting some packages from it on to a big barrow. The moon was up, so I didn't need the feeble light of the carrier's lamp to see what they were doing. I suppose I wanted to stretch my legs for a moment, for when I had finished my job I strolled over to them. They did not hear me coming, and the carrier on his perch seemed to be asleep.

The packages were the ordinary consignments from some big shop in town. But I noticed that the two men handled them very gingerly, and that, as each was laid in the barrow, they clipped off the shop label and affixed one of their own. The new labels were odd things, large and square, with some address written on them in very black capital letters. There was nothing in that, but the men's faces puzzled me. For they seemed to do their job in a fever, longing to get it over and yet in a sweat lest they should make some mistake. Their commonplace task seemed to be for them a matter of tremendous importance. I moved so as to get a view of their faces, and I saw that they were white and strained. The two were of the butler or valet class, both elderly, and I could have sworn that they were labouring under something like fear.

I shuffled my feet to let them know of my presence and remarked that it was a fine night. They started as if they had been robbing a corpse. One of them mumbled something in reply, but the other caught a package which was slipping, and in a tone of violent alarm growled to his mate to be careful. I had a notion that they were handling explosives.

I had no time to waste, so I pushed on. That night, in my room at Ludlow, I had the curiosity to look up my map and identify the place where I had seen the men. The village was St Sant, and it appeared that the gate I had stopped at belonged to a considerable demesne called Vauncastle. That was my first visit.

At that time I was busy on a critical edition of Theocritus, for which I was making a new collation of the manuscripts. There was a variant of the Medicean Codex in England, which nobody had seen since Gaisford, and after a good deal of trouble I found that it was in the library of a man called Dubellay. I wrote to him at his London club, and got a reply to my surprise from Vauncastle Hall, Faxeter. It was an odd letter, for you could see that he longed to tell me to go to the devil, but couldn't quite reconcile it with his conscience. We exchanged several letters, and the upshot was that he gave me permission to examine his manuscript. He did not ask me to stay, but mentioned that there was a comfortable little inn in St Sant.

My second visit began on the 27th of December, after I had been home for Christmas. We had had a week of severe frost, and then it had thawed a little; but it remained bitterly cold, with leaden skies that threatened snow. I drove from Faxeter, and as we ascended the valley I remember thinking that it was a curiously sad country. The hills were too low to be impressive, and their outlines were mostly blurred with woods; but the tops showed clear, funny little knolls of grey bent that suggested a volcanic origin. It might have been one of those backgrounds you find in Italian primitives, with all the light and colour left out. When I got a glimpse of the Vaun in the bleached meadows it looked like the 'wan water' of the Border ballads. The woods, too, had not the friendly bareness of English copses in winter-time. They remained dark and cloudy, as if they were hiding secrets. Before I reached St Sant, I decided that the landscape was not only sad, but ominous.

I was fortunate in my inn. In the single street of one-storeyed cottages it rose like a lighthouse, with a cheery glow from behind the red curtains of the bar parlour. The inside proved as good as the outside. I found a bedroom with a bright fire, and I dined in a wainscoted room full of preposterous old pictures of lanky hounds and hollow-backed horses. I had been rather depressed on my journey, but my spirits were raised by this comfort, and when the house produced a most respectable bottle of port I had the landlord in to drink a glass. He was an ancient man who had been a gamekeeper, with a much younger wife, who was responsible for the management. I was curious to hear something about the owner of my manuscript, but I got little from the landlord. He had been with the old squire, and had never served the present one. I heard of Dubellays in plenty – the landlord's master, who had hunted his own hounds for forty years, the Major his brother, who had fallen at Abu Klea; Parson Jack, who had had the living till he died, and of all kinds of collaterals. The 'Deblays' had been a high-spirited, open-handed stock, and much liked in the place. But of the present master of the Hall he could or would tell me nothing. The Squire was a 'great scholard', but I gathered that he followed no sport and was not a convivial soul like his predecessors. He had spent a mint of money on the house, but not many people went there. He, the landlord, had never been inside the grounds in the new master's time, though in the old days there had been hunt breakfasts on the lawn for the whole country-side, and mighty tenantry dinners. I went to bed with a clear picture in my mind of the man I was to interview on the morrow. A scholarly and autocratic recluse, who collected treasures and beautified his dwelling and probably lived in his library. I rather looked forward to meeting him, for the bonhomous sporting squire was not much in my line.

After breakfast next morning I made my way to the Hall. It was the same leaden weather, and when I entered the gates the air seemed to grow bitterer and the skies darker. The place was muffled in great trees which even in their winter bareness made a pall about it. There was a long avenue of ancient sycamores, through which one caught only rare glimpses of the frozen park. I took my bearings, and realised that I was walking nearly due south, and was gradually descending. The house must be in a hollow. Presently the trees thinned, I passed through an iron gate, came out on a big untended lawn, untidily studded with laurels and rhododendrons, and there before me was the house front.

I had expected something beautiful – an old Tudor or Queen Anne façade or a dignified Georgian portico. I was disappointed, for the front was simply mean. It was low and irregular, more like the back parts of a house, and I guessed that at some time or another the building had been turned round, and the old kitchen door made the chief entrance. I was confirmed in my conclusion by observing that the roofs rose in tiers, like one of those recessed New York skyscrapers, so that the present back parts of the building were of an impressive height.

The oddity of the place interested me, and still more its dilapidation. What on earth could the owner have spent his money on? Everything – lawn, flower-beds, paths – was neglected. There was a new stone doorway, but the walls badly needed pointing, the window woodwork had not been painted for ages, and there were several broken panes.

The bell did not ring, so I was reduced to hammering on the knocker, and it must have been ten minutes before the door opened. A pale butler, one of the men I had seen at the carrier's cart the October before, stood blinking in the entrance.

He led me in without question, when I gave my name, so I was evidently expected. The hall was my second surprise. What had become of my picture of the collector? The place was small and poky, and furnished as barely as the lobby of a farmhouse. The only thing I approved was its warmth. Unlike most English country houses there seemed to be excellent heating arrangements.

I was taken into a little dark room with one window that looked out on a shrubbery, while the man went to fetch his master. My chief feeling was of gratitude that I had not been asked to stay, for the inn was paradise compared with this sepulchre. I was examining the prints on the wall, when I heard my name spoken and turned round to greet Mr Dubellay.

He was my third surprise. I had made a portrait in my mind of a fastidious old scholar, with eye-glasses on a black cord, and a finical *Weltkind*-ish manner. Instead I found a man still in early middle age, a heavy fellow dressed in the roughest country tweeds. He was as untidy as his demesne, for he had not shaved that morning, his flannel collar was badly frayed, and his fingernails would have been the better for a scrubbing brush. His face was hard to describe. It was high-coloured, but the colour was not healthy; it was friendly, but it was also wary; above all, it was *unquiet*. He gave me the impression of a man whose nerves were all wrong, and who was perpetually on his guard.

He said a few civil words, and thrust a badly tied brown paper parcel at me.

'That's your manuscript,' he said jauntily.

I was staggered. I had expected to be permitted to collate the codex in his library, and in the last few minutes had realised that the prospect was distasteful. But here was this casual owner offering me the priceless thing to take away.

I stammered my thanks, and added that it was very good of him to trust a stranger with such a treasure.

'Only as far as the inn,' he said. 'I wouldn't like to send it by post. But there's no harm in your working at it at the inn. There should be confidence among scholars.' And he gave an odd cackle of a laugh.

'I greatly prefer your plan,' I said. 'But I thought you would insist on my working at it here.'

'No, indeed,' he said earnestly. 'I shouldn't think of such a thing . . . Wouldn't do at all . . . An insult to our freemasonry . . . That's how I should regard it.'

We had a few minutes' further talk. I learned that he had inherited under the entail from a cousin, and had been just over ten years at Vauncastle. Before that he had been a London solicitor. He asked me a question or two about Cambridge – wished he had been at the University – much hampered in his work by a defective education. I was a Greek scholar? – Latin, too, he presumed. Wonderful people the Romans . . . He spoke quite freely, but all the time his queer restless eyes were darting about, and I had a strong impression that he would have liked to say something to me very different from these commonplaces – that he was longing to broach some subject but was held back by shyness or fear. He had such an odd appraising way of looking at me.

328

I left without his having asked me to a meal, for which I was not sorry, for I did not like the atmosphere of the place. I took a short cut over the ragged lawn, and turned at the top of the slope to look back. The house was in reality a huge pile, and I saw that I had been right and that the main building was all at the back. Was it, I wondered, like the Alhambra, which behind a front like a factory concealed a treasure-house? I saw, too, that the woodland hollow was more spacious than I had fancied. The house, as at present arranged, faced due north, and behind the south front was an open space in which I guessed that a lake might lie. Far beyond I could see in the December dimness the lift of high dark hills.

That evening the snow came in earnest, and fell continuously for the better part of two days. I banked up the fire in my bedroom and spent a happy time with the codex. I had brought only my working boots with me and the inn boasted no library, so when I wanted to relax I went down to the tap-room, or gossiped with the landlady in the bar parlour. The yokels who congregated in the former were pleasant fellows, but, like all the folk on the Marches, they did not talk readily to a stranger and I heard little from them of the Hall. The old squire had reared every year three thousand pheasants, but the present squire would not allow a gun to be fired on his land and there were only a few wild birds left. For the same reason the woods were thick with vermin. This they told me when I professed an interest in shooting. But of Mr Dubellay they would not speak, declaring that they never saw him. I daresay they gossiped wildly about him, and their public reticence struck me as having in it a touch of fear.

The landlady, who came from a different part of the

shire, was more communicative. She had not known the former Dubellays and so had no standard of comparison, but she was inclined to regard the present squire as not quite right in the head. 'They do say,' she would begin, but she, too, suffered from some inhibition, and what promised to be sensational would tail off into the commonplace. One thing apparently puzzled the neighbourhood above others, and that was his rearrangement of the house. 'They do say', she said in an awed voice, 'that he have built a great church.' She had never visited it – no one in the parish had, for Squire Dubellay did not allow intruders – but from Lyne Hill you could see it through a gap in the woods. 'He's no good Christian,' she told me, 'and him and Vicar has quarrelled this many a day. But they do say as he worships summat there.' I learned that there were no women servants in the house, only the men he had brought from London. 'Poor benighted souls, they must live in a sad hobble,' and the buxom lady shrugged her shoulders and giggled.

On the last day of December I decided that I needed exercise and must go for a long stride. The snow had ceased that morning, and the dull skies had changed to a clear blue. It was still very cold, but the sun was shining, the snow was firm and crisp underfoot, and I proposed to survey the country. So after luncheon I put on thick boots and gaiters, and made for Lyne Hill. This meant a considerable circuit, for the place lay south of the Vauncastle park. From it I hoped to get a view of the other side of the house.

I was not disappointed. There was a rift in the thick woodlands, and below me, two miles off, I suddenly saw a strange building, like a classical temple. Only the entablature and the tops of the pillars showed above the trees, but they stood out vivid and dark against the background of snow. The spectacle in that lonely place was so startling that for a little I could only stare. I remember that I glanced behind me to the snowy line of the Welsh mountains, and felt that I might have been looking at a winter view of the Apennines two thousand years ago.

My curiosity was now alert, and I determined to get a nearer view of this marvel. I left the track and ploughed through the snowy fields down to the skirts of the woods. After that my troubles began. I found myself in a very good imitation of a primeval forest, where the undergrowth had been unchecked and the rides uncut for years. I sank into deep pits, I was savagely torn by briars and brambles, but I struggled on, keeping a line as best I could. At last the trees stopped. Before me was a flat expanse which I knew must be a lake, and beyond rose the temple.

It ran the whole length of the house, and from where I stood it was hard to believe that there were buildings at its back where men dwelt. It was a fine piece of work – the first glance told me that – admirably proportioned, classical, yet not following exactly any of the classical models. One could imagine a great echoing interior dim with the smoke of sacrifice, and it was only by reflecting that I realised that the peristyle could not be continued down the two sides, that there was no interior, and that what I was looking at was only a portico.

The thing was at once impressive and preposterous. What madness had been in Dubellay when he embellished his house with such a grandiose garden front? The sun was setting and the shadow of the wooded hills darkened the interior, so I could not even make out the back wall of the porch. I wanted a nearer view, so I embarked on the frozen lake.

Then I had an odd experience. I was not tired, the snow lay level and firm, but I was conscious of extreme weariness. The biting air had become warm and oppressive. I had to drag boots that seemed to weigh tons across that lake. The place was utterly silent in the stricture of the frost, and from the pile in front no sign of life came.

I reached the other side at last and found myself in a frozen shallow of bulrushes and skeleton willow-herbs. They were taller than my head, and to see the house I had to look upward through their snowy traceries. It was perhaps eighty feet above me and a hundred yards distant, and, since I was below it, the delicate pillars seemed to spring to a great height. But it was still dusky, and the only detail I could see was on the ceiling, which seemed either to be carved or painted with deeply-shaded monochrome figures.

Suddenly the dying sun came slanting through the gap in the hills, and for an instant the whole portico to its farthest recesses was washed in clear gold and scarlet. That was wonderful enough, but there was something more. The air was utterly still with not the faintest breath of wind – so still that when I had lit a cigarette half an hour before the flame of the match had burned steadily upward like a candle in a room. As I stood among the sedges not a single frost crystal stirred . . . But there was a wind blowing in the portico.

I could see it lifting feathers of snow from the base of the pillars and fluffing the cornices. The floor had already been swept clean, but tiny flakes drifted on to it from the exposed edges. The interior was filled with a furious movement, though a yard from it was frozen peace. I felt nothing of the action of the wind, but I knew that it was hot, hot as the breath of a furnace.

I had only one thought, dread of being overtaken by night near that place. I turned and ran. Ran with labouring steps across the lake, panting and stifling with a deadly hot oppression, ran blindly by a sort of instinct in the direction of the village. I did not stop till I had wrestled through the big wood, and come out on some rough pasture above the highway. Then I dropped on the ground, and felt again the comforting chill of the December air.

The adventure left me in an uncomfortable mood. I was ashamed of myself for playing the fool, and at the same time hopelessly puzzled, for the oftener I went over in my mind the incidents of that afternoon the more I was at a loss for an explanation. One feeling was uppermost, that I did not like this place and wanted to be out of it. I had already broken the back of my task, and by shutting myself up for two days I completed it; that is to say, I made my collation as far as I had advanced myself in my commentary on the text. I did not want to go back to the Hall, so I wrote a civil note to Dubellay, expressing my gratitude and saying that I was sending up the manuscript by the landlord's son, as I scrupled to trouble him with another visit.

I got a reply at once, saying that Mr Dubellay would like to give himself the pleasure of dining with me at the inn before I went, and would receive the manuscript in person.

It was the last night of my stay in St Sant, so I ordered the best dinner the place could provide, and a magnum of claret, of which I discovered a bin in the cellar. Dubellay appeared promptly at eight o'clock, arriving to my surprise in a car. He had tidied himself up and put on a dinner jacket, and he looked exactly like the city solicitors you see dining in the Junior Carlton.

He was in excellent spirits, and his eyes had lost their air of being on guard. He seemed to have reached some conclusion about me, or decided that I was harmless. More, he seemed to be burning to talk to me. After my adventure I was prepared to find fear in him, the fear I had seen in the faces of the men-servants. But there was none; instead there was excitement, overpowering excitement.

He neglected the courses in his verbosity. His coming to dinner had considerably startled the inn, and instead of a maid the landlady herself waited on us. She seemed to want to get the meal over, and hustled the biscuits and the port on to the table as soon as she decently could. Then Dubellay became confidential.

He was an enthusiast, it appeared, an enthusiast with a single hobby. All his life he had pottered among antiquities, and when he succeeded to Vauncastle he had the leisure and money to indulge himself. The place, it seemed, had been famous in Roman Britain – Vauni Castra – and Faxeter was a corruption of the same. 'Who was Vaunus?' I asked. He grinned, and told me to wait.

There had been an old temple up in the high woods. There had always been a local legend about it, and the place was supposed to be haunted. Well, he had had the site excavated and he had found – Here he became the cautious solicitor, and explained to me the law of treasure trove. As long as the objects found were not intrinsically valuable, not gold or jewels, the finder was entitled to keep them. He had done so – had not published the results of his excavations in the proceedings of any learned society – did not want to be bothered by tourists. I was different, for I was a scholar.

What had he found? It was really rather hard to follow

his babbling talk, but I gathered that he had found certain carvings and sacrificial implements. And – he sank his voice – most important of all, an altar, an altar of Vaunus, the tutelary deity of the vale.

When he mentioned this word his face took on a new look – not of fear but of secrecy, a kind of secret excitement. I have seen the same look on the face of a street-preaching Salvationist.

Vaunus had been a British god of the hills, whom the Romans in their liberal way appear to have identified with Apollo. He gave me a long confused account of him, from which it appeared that Mr Dubellay was not an exact scholar. Some of his derivations of place-names were absurd – like St Sant from Sancta Sanctorum – and in quoting a line of Ausonius he made two false quantities. He seemed to hope that I could tell him something more about Vaunus, but I said that my subject was Greek, and that I was deeply ignorant about Roman Britain. I mentioned several books, and found that he had never heard of Haverfield.

One word he used, 'hypocaust', which suddenly gave me a clue. He must have heated the temple, as he heated his house, by some very efficient system of hot air. I know little about science, but I imagined that the artificial heat of the portico, as contrasted with the cold outside, might create an air current. At any rate that explanation satisfied me, and my afternoon's adventure lost its uncanniness. The reaction made me feel friendly towards him, and I listened to his talk with sympathy, but I decided not to mention that I had visited his temple.

He told me about it himself in the most open way. 'I couldn't leave the altar on the hillside,' he said, 'I had to make a place for it, so I turned the old front of the house into a sort of temple. I got the best advice, but architects are ignorant people, and I often wished I had been a better scholar. Still the place satisfies me.'

'I hope it satisfies Vaunus,' I said jocularly.

'I think so,' he replied quite seriously, and then his thoughts seemed to go wandering, and for a minute or so he looked through me with a queer abstraction in his eyes.

'What do you do with it now you've got it?' I asked.

He didn't reply, but smiled to himself.

'I don't know if you remember a passage in Sidonius Apollinaris,' I said, 'a formula for consecrating pagan altars to Christian uses. You begin by sacrificing a white cock or something suitable, and tell Apollo with all friendliness that the old dedication is off for the present. Then you have a Christian invocation—'

He nearly jumped out of his chair.

'That wouldn't do – wouldn't do at all! . . . Oh Lord, no! . . . Couldn't think of it for one moment!'

It was as if I had offended his ears by some horrid blasphemy, and the odd thing was that he never recovered his composure. He tried, for he had good manners, but his ease and friendliness had gone. We talked stiffly for another half-hour about trifles, and then he rose to leave. I returned him his manuscript neatly parcelled up, and expanded in thanks, but he scarcely seemed to heed me. He stuck the thing in his pocket, and departed with the same air of shocked absorption.

After he had gone I sat before the fire and reviewed the situation. I was satisfied with my hypocaust theory, and had no more perturbation in my memory about my afternoon's adventure. Yet a slight flavour of unpleasantness hung about it, and I felt that I did not quite like Dubellay. I set him down as a crank who had tangled himself up with a half-witted hobby, like an old maid with her cats, and I was not sorry to be leaving the place.

My third and last visit to St Sant was in the following June – the midsummer of 1914. I had all but finished my Theocritus, but I needed another day or two with the Vauncastle manuscript, and, as I wanted to clear the whole thing off before I went to Italy in July, I wrote to Dubellay and asked if I might have another sight of it. The thing was a bore, but it had to be faced, and I fancied that the valley would be a pleasant place in that hot summer.

I got a reply at once, inviting, almost begging me to come, and insisting that I should stay at the Hall. I couldn't very well refuse, though I would have preferred the inn. He wired about my train, and wired again saying he would meet me. This time I seemed to be a particularly welcome guest.

I reached Faxeter in the evening, and was met by a car from a Faxeter garage. The driver was a talkative young man, and, as the car was a closed one, I sat beside him for the sake of fresh air. The term had tired me, and I was glad to get out of stuffy Cambridge, but I cannot say that I found it much cooler as we ascended the Vaun valley. The woods were in their summer magnificence but a little dulled and tarnished by the heat, the river was shrunk to a trickle, and the curious hill-tops were so scorched by the sun that they seemed almost yellow above the green of the trees. Once again I had the feeling of a landscape fantastically un-English.

'Squire Dubellay's been in a great way about your coming, sir,' the driver informed me. 'Sent down three times to the boss to make sure it was all right. He's got a car of his own, too, a nice little Daimler, but he don't seem to use it much. Haven't seen him about in it for a month of Sundays.'

As we turned in at the Hall gates he looked curiously about him. 'Never been here before, though I've been in most gentlemen's parks for fifty miles round. Rum old-fashioned spot, isn't it, sir?'

If it had seemed a shuttered sanctuary in midwinter, in that June twilight it was more than ever a place enclosed and guarded. There was almost an autumn smell of decay, a dry decay like touchwood. We seemed to be descending through layers of ever-thickening woods. When at last we turned through the iron gate I saw that the lawns had reached a further stage of neglect, for they were as shaggy as a hay-field.

The white-faced butler let me in, and there, waiting at his back, was Dubellay. But he was not the man whom I had seen in December. He was dressed in an old baggy suit of flannels, and his unwholesome red face was painfully drawn and sunken. There were dark pouches under his eyes, and these eyes were no longer excited, but dull and pained. Yes, and there was more than pain in them – there was fear. I wondered if his hobby were becoming too much for him.

He greeted me like a long-lost brother. Considering that I scarcely knew him, I was a little embarrassed by his warmth. 'Bless you for coming, my dear fellow,' he cried. 'You want a wash and then we'll have dinner. Don't bother to change, unless you want to. I never do.' He led me to my bedroom, which was clean enough but small and shabby like a servant's room. I guessed that he had gutted the house to build his absurd temple.

We dined in a fair-sized room which was a kind of library. It was lined with old books, but they did not look as if they had been there long; rather it seemed like a lumber room in which a fine collection had been stored. Once no doubt they had lived in a dignified Georgian chamber. There was nothing else, none of the antiques which I had expected.

'You have come just in time,' he told me. 'I fairly jumped when I got your letter, for I had been thinking of running up to Cambridge to insist on your coming down here. I hope you're in no hurry to leave.'

'As it happens,' I said, 'I *am* rather pressed for time, for I hope to go abroad next week. I ought to finish my work here in a couple of days. I can't tell you how much I'm in your debt for your kindness.'

'Two days,' he said. 'That will get us over midsummer. That should be enough.' I hadn't a notion what he meant.

I told him that I was looking forward to examining his collection. He opened his eyes. 'Your discoveries, I mean,' I said, 'the altar of Vaunus . . .'

As I spoke the words his face suddenly contorted in a spasm of what looked like terror. He choked and then recovered himself. 'Yes, yes,' he said rapidly. 'You shall see it – you shall see everything – but not now – not tonight. Tomorrow – in broad daylight – that's the time.'

After that the evening became a bad dream. Small talk deserted him, and he could only reply with an effort to my commonplaces. I caught him often looking at me furtively, as if he were sizing me up and wondering how far he could go with me. The thing fairly got on my nerves, and to crown all it was abominably stuffy. The windows of the room gave on a little paved court with a background of laurels, and I might have been in Seven Dials for all the air there was.

When coffee was served I could stand it no longer. 'What about smoking in the temple?' I said. 'It should be cool there with the air from the lake.'

I might have been proposing the assassination of his mother. He simply gibbered at me. 'No, no,' he stammered. 'My God, no!' It was half an hour before he could properly collect himself. A servant lit two oil lamps, and we sat on in the frowsty room.

'You said something when we last met,' he ventured at last, after many a sidelong glance at me. 'Something about a ritual for re-dedicating an altar.'

I remembered my remark about Sidonius Apollinaris.

'Could you show me the passage? There is a good classical library here, collected by my great-grandfather. Unfortunately my scholarship is not equal to using it properly.'

I got up and hunted along the shelves, and presently found a copy of Sidonius, the Plantin edition of 1609. I turned up the passage, and roughly translated it for him. He listened hungrily and made me repeat it twice.

'He says a cock,' he hesitated. 'Is that essential?'

'I don't think so. I fancy any of the recognised ritual stuff would do.'

'I am glad,' he said simply. 'I am afraid of blood.'

'Good God, man,' I cried out, 'are you taking my nonsense seriously? I was only chaffing. Let old Vaunus stick to his altar!'

He looked at me like a puzzled and rather offended dog. 'Sidonius was in earnest . . .'

'Well, I'm not,' I said rudely. 'We're in the twentieth century and not in the third. Isn't it about time we went to bed?'

He made no objection, and found me a candle in the hall. As I undressed I wondered into what kind of lunatic asylum I had strayed. I felt the strongest distaste for the place, and longed to go straight off to the inn; only I couldn't make use of a man's manuscripts and insult his hospitality. It was fairly clear to me that Dubellay was mad. He had ridden his hobby to the death of his wits and was now in its bondage. Good Lord! he had talked of his precious Vaunus as a votary talks of a god. I believed he had come to worship some figment of his half-educated fancy.

I think I must have slept for a couple of hours. Then I woke dripping with perspiration, for the place was simply an oven. My window was as wide open as it would go, and, though it was a warm night, when I stuck my head out the air was fresh. The heat came from indoors. The room was on the first floor near the entrance and I was looking on to the overgrown lawns. The night was very dark and utterly still, but I could have sworn that I heard wind. The trees were as motionless as marble, but somewhere close at hand I heard a strong gust blowing. Also, though there was no moon, there was somewhere near me a steady glow of light; I could see the reflection of it round the end of the house. That meant that it came from the temple. What kind of saturnalia was Dubellay conducting at such an hour?

When I drew in my head I felt that if I was to get any sleep something must be done. There could be no question about it; some fool had turned on the steam heat, for the room was a furnace. My temper was rising. There was no bell to be found, so I lit my candle and set out to find a servant.

I tried a cast downstairs and discovered the room where we had dined. Then I explored a passage at right angles, which brought me up against a great oak door. The light showed me that it was a new door, and that there was no apparent way of opening it. I guessed that it led into the temple, and, though it fitted close and there seemed to be no keyhole, I could hear through it a sound like a rushing wind . . . Next I opened a door on my right and found myself in a big store cupboard. It had a funny, exotic, spicy smell, and, arranged very neatly on the floor and shelves, was a number of small sacks and coffers. Each bore a label, a square of stout paper with very black lettering. I read '*Pro servitio Vauni*'.

I had seen them before, for my memory betrayed me if they were not the very labels that Dubellay's servants had been attaching to the packages from the carrier's cart that evening in the past autumn. The discovery made my suspicions an unpleasant certainty. Dubellay evidently meant the labels to read 'For the service of Vaunus'. He was no scholar, for it was an impossible use of the word '*servitium*', but he was very patently a madman.

However, it was my immediate business to find some way to sleep, so I continued my quest for a servant. I followed another corridor, and discovered a second staircase. At the top of it I saw an open door and looked in. It must have been Dubellay's, for his flannels were tumbled untidily on a chair, but Dubellay himself was not there and the bed had not been slept in.

I suppose my irritation was greater than my alarm – though I must say I was getting a little scared – for I still pursued the evasive servant. There was another stair which apparently led to attics, and in going up it I slipped and made a great clatter. When I looked up the butler in his nightgown was staring down at me, and if ever a mortal face held fear it was his. When he saw who it was he seemed to recover a little.

'Look here,' I said, 'for God's sake turn off that infernal hot air. I can't get a wink of sleep. What idiot set it going?'

He looked at me owlishly, but he managed to find his tongue.

'I beg your pardon, sir,' he said, 'but there is no heating apparatus in this house.'

There was nothing more to be said. I returned to my bedroom and it seemed to me that it had grown cooler. As I leaned out of the window, too, the mysterious wind seemed to have died away, and the glow no longer showed from beyond the corner of the house. I got into bed and slept heavily till I was roused by the appearance of my shaving water about half-past nine. There was no bathroom, so I bathed in a tin pannikin.

It was a hazy morning which promised a day of blistering heat. When I went down to breakfast I found Dubellay in the dining-room. In the daylight he looked a very sick man, but he seemed to have taken a pull on himself, for his manner was considerably less nervy than the night before. Indeed, he appeared almost normal, and I might have reconsidered my view but for the look in his eyes.

I told him that I proposed to sit tight all day over the manuscript, and get the thing finished. He nodded. 'That's all right. I've a lot to do myself, and I won't disturb you.'

'But first', I said, 'you promised to show me your discoveries.'

He looked at the window where the sun was shining on the laurels and on a segment of the paved court.

'The light is good,' he said – an odd remark. 'Let us go there now. There are times and seasons for the temple.'

He led me down the passage I had explored the previous night. The door opened not by a key but by some lever in the wall. I found myself looking suddenly at a bath of sunshine with the lake below as blue as a turquoise.

It is not easy to describe my impressions of that place. It was unbelievably light and airy, as brilliant as an Indian colonnade in midsummer. The proportions must have been good, for the columns soared and swam, and the roof (which looked like cedar) floated as delicately as a flower on its stalk. The stone was some local limestone, which on the floor took a polish like marble. All around was a vista of sparkling water and summer woods and far blue mountains. It should have been as wholesome as the top of a hill.

And yet I had scarcely entered before I knew that it was a prison. I am not an imaginative man, and I believe my nerves are fairly good, but I could scarcely put one foot before the other, so strong was my distaste. I felt shut off from the world, as if I were in a dungeon or on an ice-floe. And I felt, too, that though far enough from humanity, we were not alone.

On the inner wall there were three carvings. Two were imperfect friezes sculptured in low-relief, dealing apparently with the same subject. It was a ritual procession, priests bearing branches, the ordinary *dendrophori* business. The faces were only half-human, and that was from no lack of skill, for the artist had been a master. The striking thing was that the branches and the hair of the hierophants were being tossed by a violent wind, and the expression of each was of a being in the last stage of endurance, shaken to the core by terror and pain.

Between the friezes was a great roundel of a Gorgon's head. It was not a female head, such as you commonly find,

344

but a male head, with the viperous hair sprouting from chin and lip. It had once been coloured, and fragments of a green pigment remained in the locks. It was an awful thing, the ultimate horror of fear, the last dementia of cruelty made manifest in stone. I hurriedly averted my eyes and looked at the altar.

That stood at the west end on a pediment with three steps. It was a beautiful piece of work, scarcely harmed by the centuries, with two words inscribed on its face – APOLL. VAUN. It was made of some foreign marble, and the hollow top was dark with ancient sacrifices. Not so ancient either, for I could have sworn that I saw there the mark of recent flame.

I do not suppose I was more than five minutes in the place. I wanted to get out, and Dubellay wanted to get me out. We did not speak a word till we were back in the library.

'For God's sake give it up!' I said. 'You're playing with fire, Mr Dubellay. You're driving yourself into Bedlam. Send these damned things to a museum and leave this place. Now, now, I tell you. You have no time to lose. Come down with me to the inn straight off and shut up this house.'

He looked at me with his lip quivering like a child about to cry.

'I will. I promise you I will . . . But not yet . . . After tonight . . . Tomorrow I'll do whatever you tell me . . . You won't leave me?'

'I won't leave you, but what earthly good am I to you if you won't take my advice?'

'Sidonius . . .' he began.

'Oh, damn Sidonius! I wish I had never mentioned him. The whole thing is arrant nonsense, but it's killing you.

345

You've got it on the brain. Don't you know you're a sick man?'

'I'm not feeling very grand. It's so warm today. I think I'll lie down.'

It was no good arguing with him, for he had the appalling obstinacy of very weak things. I went off to my work in a shocking bad temper.

The day was what it had promised to be, blisteringly hot. Before midday the sun was hidden by a coppery haze, and there was not the faintest stirring of wind. Dubellay did not appear at luncheon – it was not a meal he ever ate, the butler told me. I slogged away all the afternoon, and had pretty well finished my job by six o'clock. That would enable me to leave next morning, and I hoped to be able to persuade my host to come with me.

The conclusion of my task put me into a better humour, and I went for a walk before dinner. It was a very close evening, for the heat haze had not lifted; the woods were as silent as a grave, not a bird spoke, and when I came out of the cover to the burnt pastures the sheep seemed too languid to graze. During my walk I prospected the environs of the house, and saw that it would be very hard to get access to the temple except by a long circuit. On one side was a mass of outbuildings, and then a high wall, and on the other the very closest and highest quickset hedge I have ever seen, which ended in a wood with savage spikes on its containing wall. I returned to my room, had a cold bath in the exiguous tub, and changed.

Dubellay was not at dinner. The butler said that his master was feeling unwell and had gone to bed. The news pleased me, for bed was the best place for him. After that I settled myself down to a lonely evening in the library. I browsed among the shelves and found a number of rare editions which served to pass the time. I noticed that the copy of Sidonius was absent from its place.

I think it was about ten o'clock when I went to bed, for I was unaccountably tired. I remember wondering whether I oughtn't to go and visit Dubellay, but decided that it was better to leave him alone. I still reproach myself for that decision. I know now I ought to have taken him by force and haled him to the inn.

Suddenly I came out of heavy sleep with a start. A human cry seemed to be ringing in the corridors of my brain. I held my breath and listened. It came again, a horrid scream of panic and torture.

I was out of bed in a second, and only stopped to get my feet into slippers. The cry must have come from the temple. I tore downstairs expecting to hear the noise of an alarmed household. But there was no sound, and the awful cry was not repeated.

The door in the corridor was shut, as I expected. Behind it pandemonium seemed to be loose, for there was a howling like a tempest – and something more, a crackling like fire. I made for the front door, slipped off the chain, and found myself in the still, moonless night. Still, except for the rending gale that seemed to be raging in the house I had left.

From what I had seen on my evening's walk I knew that my one chance to get to the temple was by way of the quickset hedge. I thought I might manage to force a way between the end of it and the wall. I did it, at the cost of much of my raiment and my skin. Beyond was another rough lawn set with tangled shrubberies, and then a precipitous slope to the level of the lake. I scrambled along the sedgy margin, not daring to lift my eyes till I was on the temple steps.

The place was brighter than day with a roaring blast of fire. The very air seemed to be incandescent and to have become a flaming ether. And yet there were no flames – only a burning brightness. I could not enter, for the waft from it struck my face like a scorching hand and I felt my hair singe . . .

I am short-sighted, as you know, and I may have been mistaken, but this is what I think I saw. From the altar a great tongue of flame seemed to shoot upwards and lick the roof, and from its pediment ran flaming streams. In front of it lay a body – Dubellay's – a naked body, already charred and black. There was nothing else, except that the Gorgon's head in the wall seemed to glow like a sun in hell.

I suppose I must have tried to enter. All I know is that I found myself staggering back, rather badly burned. I covered my eyes, and as I looked through my fingers I seemed to see the flames flowing under the wall, where there may have been lockers, or possibly another entrance. Then the great oak door suddenly shrivelled like gauze, and with a roar the fiery river poured into the house.

I ducked myself in the lake to ease the pain, and then ran back as hard as I could by the way I had come. Dubellay, poor devil, was beyond my aid. After that I am not very clear what happened. I know that the house burned like a haystack. I found one of the men-servants on the lawn, and I think I helped to get the other down from his room by one of the rainpipes. By the time the neighbours arrived the house was ashes, and I was pretty well mother-naked. They took me to the inn and put me to bed, and I remained there till after the inquest. The coroner's jury were puzzled, but they found it simply death by misadventure; a lot of country houses were burned that summer. There was nothing found of Dubellay; nothing remained of the house except a few blackened pillars; the altar and the sculptures were so cracked and scarred that no museum wanted them. The place has not been rebuilt, and for all I know they are there today. I am not going back to look for them.

Nightingale finished his story and looked round his audience.

'Don't ask me for an explanation,' he said, 'for I haven't any. You may believe if you like that the god Vaunus inhabited the temple which Dubellay built for him, and, when his votary grew scared and tried Sidonius's receipt for shifting the dedication, became angry and slew him with his flaming wind. That wind seems to have been a perquisite of Vaunus. We know more about him now, for last year they dug up a temple of his in Wales.'

'Lightning,' someone suggested.

'It was a quiet night, with no thunderstorm,' said Nightingale.

'Isn't the countryside volcanic?' Peckwether asked. 'What about pockets of natural gas or something of the kind?'

'Possibly. You may please yourself in your explanation. I'm afraid I can't help you. All I know is that I don't propose to visit that valley again!'

'What became of your Theocritus?'

'Burned, like everything else. However, that didn't worry me much. Six weeks later came the war, and I had other things to think about.'

The Strange Adventures of Mr Andrew Hawthorn

Any disappearance is a romantic thing, especially if it be unexpected and inexplicable. To vanish from the common world and leave no trace, and to return with the same suddenness and mystery, satisfies the eternal human sense of wonder. That is why the old stories make so much of it. Tamlane and Kilmeny and Ogier the Dane retired to Fairyland, and Oisin to the Land of the Ever Living, and no man knows the manner of their going or their return. The common world goes on, but they are far away in a magic universe of their own.

But even ordinary folk can disappear. Sometimes they never come back and leave only blank mystery behind them. But sometimes they return and can explain what happened. Here is a true tale of what befell a most prosaic Scots gentleman rather less than two centuries ago.

Let us call him Andrew Hawthorn. He was thirty-two years of age and had no wife, but lived with his sister, Barbara, in a steep-roofed, stone house a dozen miles from Edinburgh. The house stood above a narrow wooded glen, what is called in Scotland a 'dean', at the bottom of which ran a brawling stream.

Mr Hawthorn was a stiff gentleman, very set in his ways. His wig was always carefully powdered, his clothes were trim, and his buckles bright. He enjoyed a modest competence, which enabled him to devote his life to his hobbies.

These were principally antiquities, and he had been busy for some years on a great work on the Antonines.

He was in the habit of breakfasting at seven with his sister, and being particular in his habits, he liked to have his meal served punctually at that hour. He was always in the little dining-room as the clock struck, while his sister was usually a few minutes late. His custom was to take a walk after breakfast and be at his books at eight o'clock. Therefore he liked to finish his meal by a quarter after seven, and this meant punctilious service. In especial he disliked having his porridge so hot that he had to delay some minutes before he could begin on it.

On a fine May morning Mr Hawthorn appeared in the breakfast room at the exact hour. His sister was not down, but two steaming bowls of porridge stood on the table. Mr Hawthorn was annoyed. He strode into the little hall and shouted upstairs.

'Babbie,' he cried, 'how often have I told you the porridge should be dished up earlier? They are scalding hot again. I am going out of doors until they cool.'

He walked out into the garden. He also walked out of the world for five years and seven months.

There was a great hue and cry in the countryside. The Procurator Fiscal made his precognitions, and even the capital city was stirred by the mystery, but no trace could be found of Mr Andrew Hawthorn. His footsteps were followed on the coarse dewy turf which ran along the edge of the dean, and there they disappeared. In the dean itself there were signs of an old fire on a little shelf of ground, and a good deal of trampled grass and broken underwood; but the latter might have been due to the cattle-beasts that were always straying in from the neighbouring hillside.

Mr Hawthorn had no near kin besides his sister, but his lawyers offered a considerable reward for news of him. None came, and most people assumed that he was dead. His sister, who was his heir-at-law, would have succeeded to his estate had his death been presumed, but she resolutely refused to admit the presumption. Andrew, she said, would come back, though she would give no grounds for her belief. She conducted the household as usual, and every morning she had a plate of porridge set for him at breakfast, as if at any moment he might appear from the garden. She even remembered his wishes and saw to it that the porridge was dished up a little earlier.

Mr Hawthorn went out into the bright sunshine and impatiently sniffed the morning freshness. He walked to the edge of the dean, and there, on the well-trodden path among the fir trees, he saw one Bauldy Grieve, a packman, whose rounds took him up and down the Lowlands. Bauldy was an old friend who had often provided him with minor antiquities. It appeared that he had something important to communicate, for he was sitting there to intercept the laird on his morning walk.

'I've some michty wonders to show your honour,' he announced. 'The pleughman at the Back o' the Buss turned up an auld kist in the field. He didna let on to his master, but he telled me. I bocht what was in it, a wheen auld siller coins and some muckle flaigons. The pleughman – Tam Dod is his name – thocht the flaigons were brass, so I got them cheap, though he haggled sair over the siller. But they are no brass, your honour – they're gowd, as sure as I'm a living man. Nae doot they were buried by the ancient Romans. So I cam off post haste to see ye, and have gotten them in my pack. Will your honour step doun wi' me and hae a look at them?'

352

Mr Hawthorn was excited and forgot all about breakfast. He followed the packman down through the bracken to a shelf above the burn, where Bauldy had spent the night. At the first sight of the flagons his eyes opened wide. They were amphorae of exquisite design, probably vessels used for some ceremonial rite. He scraped off a little of the encrusted dirt, and saw the gleam of bright metal.

Now, as ill-luck would have it, news of the find had got abroad, perhaps because Bauldy had gossiped in his cups. Anyhow, three tinkler ruffians of the Baillie clan were on the trail, and had followed Bauldy to his camp for the night. They had seen him speak to the laird and were now lurking in the undergrowth.

'Guid save us, Bauldy,' said Mr Hawthorn. 'This is a most remarkable discovery. The like has not been seen in Scotland.'

'Are they gowd, your honour?' the packman asked.

'I have little doubt of it,' said Mr Hawthorn. 'Things so beautiful could be made of no baser metal.'

This was enough for the tinklers. They leaped out upon the two, and one, with his big staff, or 'kent', struck the packman a savage blow on the back of his head. Mr Hawthorn, though taken by surprise, put up a stout fight, for the passion of the antiquarian put fire into his manhood. But he was soon overpowered and knocked senseless by a blow from behind.

After that Mr Hawthorn's memory became confused. The tinklers were men of caution and foresight. It was not enough to annex the contents of the pedlar's pack, they must get rid of compromising evidence. The pedlar looked pretty bad, and the gentleman not much better. It would never do to leave them on the scene of the assault, for they had seen too much of their assailants.

Now, on the highway on the other side of the dean, the tinklers had a covered cart, which they were accustomed to use for nefarious business. They swung their two victims on their shoulders and cautiously made their way to the cart, and some time that evening were safe in a hovel near the water-front in Leith.

The pedlar never recovered, for his neck had been broken. Mr Hawthorn came back to consciousness with an intolerable headache and a raging thirst; he was given a drink, which must have been hocussed, for he lost his senses again. The body of the pedlar was secretly buried, a ceremony for which the tinklers had their own contrivances, and it was not likely that a wandering packman would be missed.

But Mr Hawthorn was a different matter. The hue and cry over his loss alarmed them, and they saw no other course but to get rid of him too. Murder was their first idea, but presently a better presented itself. They had already done some traffic in kidnapping and exporting the ablebodied to the American plantations, and they had a shipmaster who was in their secret. One dark night Mr Hawthorn, still hocussed, was smuggled aboard a vessel, and when his wits fully returned to him he was a prisoner on the broad Atlantic.

It would take a long time to tell the full story of Mr Hawthorn's life in the Carolinas. He was sold under an indenture to a tobacco planter, which meant that till the period of his indenture expired he was virtually a slave. His ill-treatment at the hands of the tinklers had affected both his memory and his wits, and it was a long time before his head cleared. Bit by bit, however, recollection came back to him, but the last scene he remembered clearly was leaving his steaming porridge in the little dining-room of his house. All that had happened in the dean remained in a misty confusion.

He was strong in body and of careful habits, and this stood him well in the hard toil of the plantation. Also he was a prudent soul, and, having decided that there was nothing for it but to submit, he did his work and kept his thoughts to himself. His companions were mostly the scum of British prisons, and he might have endured a good deal of rough usage at their hands. But Mr Hawthorn had a stiff temper of his own, and his fellows realised that there was a point when he would show fight and defend himself. So slowly he won a position of some respect among the others, while his industry and docility secured him reasonable treatment from the overseer.

His master was a man of pleasure who spent his days chiefly in horse-racing and card-playing. Several times Mr Hawthorn, after his memory returned to him, tried to approach him to state his case, but it was long before he got an opportunity. When it came he found that he was not believed. Such yarns had often been heard before from redemptioners. But the superior breeding of Mr Hawthorn impressed his master. Here was one who in deportment and speech appeared to be a gentleman, though he looked a dull dog and spoke with a strong Scots accent. The upshot was that when the butler broke his neck one dark night Mr Hawthorn was promoted to fill his place. Among his other gifts it appeared that he had a very fair knowledge of wine.

Now it happened some months later, when the household under Mr Hawthorn's sway had acquired a new precision, that a neighbouring squire came to dinner. The guest was of a very different type from the master of the house, for he was something of a politician and something of a scholar. During the meal he quoted a tag from Horace, but could not remember its conclusion. His host could not help him out, but, to his surprise, the butler volunteered the missing line.

The result was that the guest had some speech with Mr Hawthorn before he left, heard his story, and believed it. He was a man of a philanthropic spirit, and his first aim was to remove this unhappy scholar to more congenial surroundings. So after various negotiations, which had something to do with a young thoroughbred filly, Mr Hawthorn was transferred to the establishment of his new-found friend.

There he dwelt not unhappily for a considerable time. At his request his new master wrote to a Scottish correspondent, and, without revealing Mr Hawthorn's existence, secured the full details of the events which had mystified all Lothian. He learned that Miss Barbara was living in the house, confident that her brother would some day return. Mr Hawthorn would not let him proceed further. Somewhere in his sober bosom was a spark of romance; as he had departed mysteriously, so he would return. His new life interested him, he had formed an attachment to his new master, and he had almost forgotten about his great work on the Antonines. Also, Mr Hawthorn was proud. He was determined to be beholden to no man for the cost of his return, and he was waiting until he had saved sufficient money from his wages.

At last the day arrived when he was ready and willing to leave. But in those days of continuous war with France it was no slight business to cross the Atlantic, and there were many adventures in store for him before he reached his native land.

He embarked on a ship which was taken off Land's End by a French privateer. He was carried to Havre and found himself a prisoner in the enemy's hands. This misfortune achieved what none of his sufferings in Carolina had achieved – it broke Mr Hawthorn's temper. He managed to escape, and for several months was a fugitive on the French roads. Having some command of the French tongue, and dwelling much upon his Scottish nationality and the old friendship between Scotland and France, he managed to secure the good offices of a priest, who facilitated his journey to the capital.

In Paris Mr Hawthorn had a friend, a fellow antiquarian, to whom he appealed for help. This was willingly given, but it was not easy at the moment to leave France, and Mr Hawthorn had to spend several months in Paris, where, after his proud fashion, he insisted on supporting himself by teaching. He had to pass as a Scottish Jacobite, a disguise which gave him intense annoyance, for he was a zealous supporter of the Hanoverian Government.

It was April when he found it possible to depart from French soil. A smuggler's sloop landed him by night on the Sussex coast, and he was free once more to assume the character of a law-abiding Scotsman. He had enough money for the journey to the North, but, having acquired frugal habits during his wanderings, he insisted on making that journey in the most inexpensive fashion. Late on the evening of a day in early May, a timber barque from Hull deposited him at the pier at Leith.

He slept the night in a waterside inn, and before dawn next morning he was well on the road for his home. It was a fresh, bright day, very much the same weather as when he had left. He ascended the dean and crossed the strip of rough lawn. As he entered the dining-room the clock was striking seven.

There were two plates of smoking porridge on the table, much too hot to eat.

He strode into the hall. 'Babbie!' he cried, 'how often have I told you that the porridge should be dished up earlier?'

But he did not go out into the garden again to wait until it cooled.